Inflation, Development and Integration

ESSAYS IN HONOUR OF A. J. BROWN

ARTHUR JOSEPH BROWN

Inflation, Development and Integration

ESSAYS IN HONOUR OF A. J. BROWN

Edited by J. K. Bowers

LEEDS UNIVERSITY PRESS

ISBN 0 85316 122 4

Printed in Great Britain by Leeds University Press

CONTENTS

Trade and Integration

NA.

PREFACE

This volume of essays is presented to Arthur Brown on the occasion of his retirement after thirty-two years in the Chair of Economics at the University of Leeds. The editing and preparation of the volume has been conducted from the School of Economic Studies and has involved many more people than those whose names appear in the list of contents. The task of typing and re-typing sections of the manuscript was performed by Margaret Mann, Elsie Merrick, Maureen Gorman, and Teresa Brier. Teresa also drew the charts and diagrams. I am very grateful to them all for the patience and care with which the work was accomplished. Michael Hudson undertook the work of sub-editing the contributions and helped with proofreading. Without his willing assistance I should not have met the various deadlines. I received active help and advice from Ruth Newland and George Rainnie. I am also deeply indebted to the Vice-Chancellor, Lord Boyle, whose contribution to the enterprise has far exceeded what he has written.

Finally, in case it is not implicit in what has already been said, I have received support and encouragement from the School as a whole. The dedication of this book is *inter alia* from the School to its Professor.

J. K. Bowers
October 1979

1

The economist in government

EDWARD BOYLE

'Economics tends to become polarised between the limits of fruitless science and very debatable art, although a useful but under-cultivated middle ground certainly exists.'[1]

I

When I was Financial Secretary to the Treasury between 1959 and 1962 there were twelve professional economists in the Economic Section, most of whom I got to know personally, and practically none in the rest of Whitehall. True, there were specialized agricultural economists servicing the Agricultural Departments, but Sir Alec Cairncross has doubted whether, when he entered the Treasury in 1961 as Chief Economic Adviser, 'there was a single economist anywhere in Whitehall who was engaged on a full-time basis in analysing the problems posed by the need to manage the public sector'.[2] Today the Government Economic Service (which was formed in 1965) comprises 400 economists, including over 60 employed within the Treasury, though a still larger contingent of 75 are shared between the two closely-related Departments of Transport and the Environment. These economists 'operate under the direction of the Departments to which they belong', and they are most frequently 'organised in central divisions'; there is a small central management unit located within the Treasury.[3]

This increase in the numbers of professional economists within government has been accompanied by other marked changes. Economics as a subject has become much more econometric, and an entrant to the GES needs not only to have mastered mathematical and statistical techniques, but also to have acquired some grasp of the particular difficulties encountered in applying statistical methods both to economic hypotheses and to quantitative predictions. Treasury administrators have themselves become far more economically literate. (Professor) Ian Little, writing about his experiences as deputy-director of the Economic Section, between 1953 and 1955, returned to Nuffield College feeling that non-economist administrators 'abstract too much from the real world', and that he had been sometimes 'shocked by the naïve sureness with which very questionable bits of economic analysis were advanced in

Whitehall'.[4] It is this 'naïve sureness' which, one suspects, has now largely disappeared, partly through hard experience, but partly also through the example set by a number of those who now hold the most senior positions within the Civil Service. The present Permanent Secretary to the Treasury, Sir Douglas Wass, has described himself as a 'pragmatic scientist' (his own discipline was Applied Mathematics) who would endorse the remark 'that in macro-economics one can always find a simple rule which seems to have been valid for the last ten years; but that the chances of it surviving the next two years are usually very slim'.[5]

The Chief Economic Adviser doesn't have the same position today that he used to have, and his job must seem less agreeable. This must be particularly so since December 1976 when there was what amounted to an international vote of no confidence in Britain's handling of her economic affairs. That occasion prompted the comment, in Britain's leading weekly journal, that '[The] period of rule by IMF inspectorate-general should give the country better government than successive teams of British politicians have done'.[6] It is fair to remember that the same journal, in the spring of 1973 had thought that Britain was 'right in the middle' of an economic miracle, had commended Mr Heath for bringing the rate of inflation down to one of the lowest in the industrial world, and had urged that there was 'less reason to be worried' about the 20 per cent a year growth in the money supply than monetarists were claiming.[7] To put it mildly, it is very much easier to be a lively and informed economic journalist than to give consistently wise and far-seeing economic advice within the constraints of party government. Every economic adviser must have reflected at some time or other on what one academic has described as 'the basic distinction that exists in British politics between the Government and "the rest", with "the rest" embracing Opposition leaders, back-bench MPs of all parties, pressure groups, the press, and the many groups and individuals who comment upon Government activities. The Government alone is responsible for taking action in defence of the national interest'.[8]

The growth of the Government Economic Service has been so rapid, and the relative decline in Britain's economic performance has been so conspicuous, that it is easy to overlook those aspects of 'economic government' that have hardly changed at all. Thus I do not believe that the basic character of the Treasury has altered significantly from the days when I knew it. It remains hard and critical and disinterested, and deeply concerned with economic questions. This is one of several reasons why the 1964 model of a separate Treasury and Department of Economic Affairs could not have worked for long. There was, in fact, as Sir Donald Macdougall has convincingly shown,[9] a plausible argument at that particular moment for setting up a new department to initiate and co-ordinate economic policies on the 'supply' side. But quite apart from the virtual impossibility of divided responsibility for short-term and long-term policies, I think many critics at the time underrated the sheer force of commitment within the Treasury where economic management was concerned. Treasury economists have never been 'under the thumb' of administrators, in sharp contrast to what has happened in some other departments. The danger has been rather that, as Sir Donald goes on to say, the Treasury has appeared at times to have 'too much monopoly of information and power on the major economic decisions'. It certainly isn't easy to reconcile the theory of collective decision-taking by the Cabinet with the claim, by one of the most influential civil servants of his generation, that the Treasury must not only 'formulate the general objectives of economic policy in its totality' but also 'act as the co-ordinator of the policies of individual departments towards the achievement of these objectives'.[10] One would have thought that this was precisely the function of Cabinet and its main Committees.

I have been writing of 'economists' and 'administrators' as though these were by definition different people, but of course this is not necessarily true. There have always been a number of trained economists among administrative civil servants, and it may well be that economists by training who have also spent the whole of their working lives within Whitehall as administrators may prove among the best assessors of recent British economic history and the best judges of 'what went wrong'. Sir Douglas Allen (Lord Croham), who retired as head of the Civil Service at the end of 1977, was secretary (1947–49) to Sir Edwin (Lord) Plowden when he was head of the Central Economic Planning Staff, and his next post was that of Assistant-Secretary in the Overseas Finance division of the Treasury. In a press interview shortly after his retirement, Lord Croham gave it as his view that British industry had never made up for the jolt in post-war industrial recovery caused by the scale of the rearmament programme undertaken at the time of the Korean War. There was, he pointed out, already a shortage of steel, and on top of that 'heavy industry was obliged to turn its attention to the manufacture of weapons rather than to the re-equipment of the industrial base'.[11]

There have been several recent indications that future researchers, enquiring into the course of Britain's industrial decline, will feel that here is one factor that merits close examination. The share of military expenditure in our Gross National Product did rise dramatically, from 7.4 per cent in 1950 to nearly 12 per cent in 1952; it was still running at 10.6 per cent in 1954,[12] by which time total factor productivity in West Germany was already growing significantly

3

faster than in Britain. It seems likely that the size of the rearmament programme also helped to distort the pattern of industrial research and development. As a Junior Minister at Supply (1954–55), and an MP for a large industrial city, I remember making the point on many occasions about the industrial 'spin-off' from defence expenditure; but this applied principally to those industries where we were bound sooner or later to lose out to the superior resources of the US.[13]

This is not a condemnation of those who decided to embark on the rearmament programme, and it is easy at this point of time to exercise the pleasures of hindsight. Direct personal memories of the 1930s were still very much alive in 1950, and Attlee, in his parliamentary speech announcing the programme, would have been voicing the thoughts of many people when he reminded his audience of 'how failure to meet aggression ultimately destroyed the League of Nations'. No one could confidently have forecast at that time that Communism ('a militant and imperialist creed' as Attlee called it) would prove so cautious; and it seemed, as Andrew Shonfield wrote a few years later,[14] 'profoundly right' that Britain, still by far the strongest West European country, should give a clear military lead. Gaitskell, speaking the day after Attlee, stressed the essential contribution of United States financial assistance; I have heard it said that the US ambassador, Lewis Douglas, a strong supporter of Britain (he particularly admired the evolution of Empire into Commonwealth) used the phrase 'we'll pick up the cheque'. But somehow this assistance never materialized, and it is not fully clear how much the British pressed for it. Many people tended at the time to view the 'sacrifices' entailed by the rearmament programme too exclusively in terms of *personal* austerity; as Shonfield shrewdly points out, the main political dispute should have been, not about health charges, but about the decision in the 1951 Budget to suspend the initial depreciation allowances for productive industry. Relatively few people seem to have realized the urgency of the situation if British industry was to be reequipped in time, though Professor Sir Hubert Henderson had stressed as far back as 1947 that there were '*not* good reasons for slowing down the work of renewing and modernising industrial plant'.[15]

My reasons for taking up Lord Croham's point are first that he may well have been right; and secondly, that when we enquire into the reasons for Britain's disappointing economic performance, it isn't enough simply to examine the policies of successive Chancellors and to attempt to trace the influence of their leading economic advisers. It is easy to overlook the unintended effects of major decisions which were widely endorsed at the time; and it is also useful to be reminded that not all government actions, affecting

4

the economy, can be neatly categorized either as 'general stimuli' or 'detailed controls'.

It is important to remember that economists in government are involved nearly all the time not so much with economics as with political economy. In so far as British governments still have freedom of action, economic choices and fiscal priorities involve value judgements, and they constitute political decisions which Ministers must defend in Parliament. Granted that Government and Opposition front-benchers may be less far apart than their respective followers, it still does not often happen that Senior Ministers and their 'shadows' are essentially agreed over policy-areas that have affected large numbers of votes. The word 'Butskellite' has now passed into common use, but no one active in politics at the time thought that Butler and Gaitskell held near-identical views, and the slightly confused article that started it all, 'Mr. Butskell's Dilemma'[16] shows that in fact they didn't. (All the article really proved was that both men shared the common task of trying to moderate their less responsible followers.) There is a great deal of difference between the feeling that we have too much 'adversary government' (which may sometimes be true) and the attempt to deny to an incoming government, within the limits of restraints which it soon discovers, the right to choose afresh. In addition to party differences, every government is subject to certain political sensitivities which goad it into neglecting the teaching of even the most rudimentary economic textbooks. One obvious example is mortgage rates, and Terence Higgins, writing about the period of the Heath Government, is probably right in suggesting that it would have been preferable to have continued with a fiscal subsidy for house-owners for some while longer, if such a decision had removed the inhibitions against allowing monetary policy to operate more effectively.[17]

One can give a yet wider meaning to the concept of political economy in a country where there is a constitutional fusion of politics and the state machine.[18] A Budget is a major political event, and as such will normally be handled in the Press by a member of the parliamentary lobby. But a financial journalist may well want to understand the rationale of government policy in greater depth, and to be briefed by an economist within the Treasury whom he has learnt to trust for his accuracy and reliability. All economic decisions exist within the matrix of politics, but it must be the aim of Ministers and their advisers to command a measure of respect and understanding beyond the world of politics, first among those on whom they depend for co-operation, and secondly among all those who help to form opinion.

Governments and their supporters, when they take office, want to be able to feel that the policies on which they have campaigned are not only viable in terms of administrative action, but also that they can be defined and defended in terms that carry conviction; and it is here that precision in drafting, not just by an all-round administrator, but by a mind attuned to a specific discipline can make all the difference. Let me give an example. During the years of Labour Government after 1945, it was a regular Opposition theme that Labour Chancellors thought too little about the relationship between the balance of the domestic economy and the external balance of payments. The Cabinet material which has recently been released suggests that, at any rate in the earlier years of Labour Government, this was not simply tilting at windmills; for instance one comes across this surely classic example of the fallacy of assuming a closed economy, from a report by the Economic Survey Working Party (January 1947).

> By one means or another total resources and demands will be brought into balance in 1947. If the process is left to work itself without any conscious intervention, there would be a danger that the less essential needs would be met rather than the more essential, and that a serious inflationary movement might start.[19]

Interestingly, when the balance of payments crisis followed in the summer of that year, Aneurin Bevan showed himself readier than his colleagues to accept some reductions in the domestic capital investment programme 'as a redeployment of the nation's productive effort rendered necessary by the current economic situation'.[20]

Two years later, after the 1949 devaluation, Stafford Cripps as Chancellor recognized that 'to recreate the circumstances favourable to our export drive, we must take fresh measures to reduce the domestic pressure of demand in all three spheres of expenditure I have mentioned',[21] but it took a keen ear and even a keen eye to register the point (going back three columns of *Hansard*) that these 'spheres' included government expenditure as well as personal consumption and capital goods. It was not until Lord Butler's economic statement of January 1952 that battle was finally and decisively joined on this issue.

> It may be urged, and is urged by some economists of various schools, that there is little connection between Government expenditure, for example, on social services and the balance of payments. This is a complete misunderstanding of the true position. Every pound spent by the Government means either a direct call on man-power and materials or a transfer of income to someone else, who is thus enabled to make such a direct call. Our fundamental task is to increase the resources available for export, and this cannot be done unless we are willing to release them from the other calls made upon them.[22]

6

It may be thought in retrospect that this was all pretty obvious. But that is not how it appeared at the time, neither to Gaitskell speaking on the following afternoon, nor — most strikingly — to Attlee when challenged ten months later in a debate on the Address. Asked by Alec Spearman, the MP for Scarborough, whether he still believed that cuts in Government expenditure had no bearing on the balance of payments, Attlee replied: 'That depends entirely on exactly what the question involves — whether it is purely a matter of finance or whether it is something to do with importation from abroad.'[23] After all the years of controversy, to hear Lord Butler's statement uttered from the despatch-box, and to learn that it carried the imprimatur of the Government's Economic Adviser (then still located within the Cabinet Office), did a great deal for party morale at a time when the narrowness of the majority, and the incompetent handling of parliamentary business by a distinctly rusty Front Bench, combined to make the prospect of any long stay in office seem improbable.

Both Lord Butler and Mr Macmillan, in their respective memoirs, have paid tributes to the influence and judgement of Sir Robert Hall (Lord Roberthall) as Economic Adviser, and I share the view of Sam Brittan that Hall and Sir Edwin (Lord) Plowden, as head of the Central Economic Planning Staff must have made an extremely strong pair. To illustrate the range of what this influence could mean, I will mention three contributions of the Economic Adviser during the 1950s: the first concerned a specific policy decision, the second a constructive instalment of tax reform, and the third an innovation which has had a lasting effect on the way we discuss, nationally, current issues of political economy.

The specific policy decision was the 'Robot' controversy in 1952 — the proposal to float the rate of exchange, to make sterling held by all non-residents of the sterling area convertible into dollars, but to block 90 per cent of the existing sterling balances held by non-residents of the sterling area other than the dollar countries. The story of this proposal, and of the ultimately successful opposition to it, has been told fully both in Lord Birkenhead's life of Lord Cherwell, *The Prof in Two Worlds*, and in Lord Salter's *Slave of the Lamp*. It may well be that the opening of the archives in the 1980s will not reveal very much more, but two points deserve emphasis. First, it was never clear who, outside a fairly narrow circle within the Treasury and the Bank of England, was going to support Robot; certainly not 'liberal' economists like Lionel (Lord) Robbins, disposed to be friendly to the government, who would have been outraged by the blocking of the sterling balances, and by the fact that the decision to transfer the strain to the rate of exchange was not to be accompanied by any let-up on quota restrictions. Secondly, the remarkable thing is how nearly this controversial proposal slipped through. It was probably fortunate that Eden, whose acquiescence as the unquestioned second-in-command within the Churchill Government was regarded as vital, happened to be away in Lisbon for a NATO meeting in February 1952 when the plan had been provisionally approved. There is good reason to think that Robert Hall's views, forwarded, on paper, to Lisbon, were highly influential in pressing for the postponement of a final decision until after Eden's return, and that this provided a vital margin of time for the opponents to regroup. Interestingly Eden was also abroad, flying via the Middle East to the SEATO Conference in Bangkok, when the decision was taken to support the transferable rate for sterling in February 1955; a step which amounted very nearly to *de facto* convertibility.[24] Once again he would have wished to urge caution, this time on his own initiative, but landing difficulties denied him access to a telephone.[25]

Next, I think one can take it as certain that Robert Hall, no doubt backed by the views of others in the Economic Section, and also by Reginald Maudling as Economic Secretary, played a notable part in ensuring Lord Butler's decision to introduce an Investment Allowance in the Budget of 1954. The Inland Revenue resisted this proposal almost to the end, and from their point of view understandably, since, as Professor Alan Day has pointed out,[26] our present arrangements for company taxation, which still bear the impress of the 1954 innovation, logically lead in the direction of the radical revision of personal taxation put forward in the recent Meade Report. I believe the investment-led boom of 1954–55 may have been the last occasion when we came close to achieving, if not a British economic miracle, at least a decisive breakthrough. Unfortunately the belief took hold, and was shared surprisingly by Lord Butler himself, that the 1954 Budget, despite its strong stimulus to investment, had been 'cautious', and subsequent decisions allowed the economy to overheat. Building controls were finally abolished that autumn, without any prior consultation with the Economic Section. This is a good example of how the practice of using government economists was still in its infancy, because officials asked themselves the administrative question 'will the building industry be able to cope?' instead of the economic question 'should we encourage the building industry to suck in a lot more labour at a time when the economy is already fully stretched?' In any case there was a strong argument, as Robert Hall would certainly have wished to urge, for retaining 'fall-back' permanent powers. In the following April there was the controversial decision to give away half the prospective budget surplus in tax reliefs. I would amend

Sam Brittan's account of what he calls 'the 1955 error' in one respect. The senior Civil Servants to whom he alludes[27] were not, I think, so much preoccupied with Lord Butler's political difficulties as with their own desire to see some further reduction in tax-rates (which were still historically high) before the impending General Election. However, in the following year Robert Hall was not alone on the official side of the Treasury in sympathizing with Mr Macmillan's interest in a capital gains tax, though it was he who set out the arguments most clearly, including the advantages of a tax which would bring in most revenue when the pressure on resources was greatest.

Thirdly, and no less important, lasting credit is due to Robert Hall for his initiative in the later 1950s in launching the regular *Economic Review* prepared by the National Institute of Economic and Social Research. At that time there was no regular publication of national income forecasts in Britain, except that occasional articles in the *Bulletin of the London and Cambridge Economic Service* used to comment on various aspects of the economic outlook. In preparing his Budget, the Chancellor and his closest advisers relied on a Treasury forecast which was, of course, not published, and could never be tested by those who prepared it against other trained and systematic forecasts made by outside experts. It was this situation that the *Economic Review* was designed to correct. Apart from the advantages of encouraging free discussion, and a more educated view of the economic outlook, there was the further advantage to the government of enlarging the field of potential recruitment to the Economic Section, and of permitting an interchange of staff with at least one other institution similarly engaged on studying how the economy really worked. The very first issue of the *Economic Review* early in 1959 was widely discussed outside and inside government, and the published estimate of spare capacity within the economy certainly added to the pressures on the Chancellor to introduce a far less cautious Budget in 1959 than in 1958.

It is important to remember that at this period there were still virtually no economists employed in government departments outside the Treasury. This state of affairs was already provoking criticism, and I recall the point being raised at a meeting of the Oxford Economic Society that no professional economist had been consulted before confident pronouncements had been made about the economic benefits to be gained by Central African Federation. An important article in the *Oxford Bulletin* by (Professor) P. D. Henderson and Arthur Hazlewood went unacknowledged in the 1960 Monckton Report, and a subsequent critical broadcast by Hazlewood[28] drew a measure of agreement within the Economic Section of the Treasury (whom I asked to comment) certainly as regards Hazlewood's contention that 'Nyasaland could have been better off financially if the link had been with Northern Rhodesia alone'. Whitehall in the 1950s was very patchy in its attitude to social science generally, and one recalls the Morton Commission on Divorce which did not think it worthwhile to enquire into how far our arrangements, for marriages that had broken down, amounted to divorce for the better-off and maintenance orders for the rest. But the situation changed rapidly in the 1960s, and I believe that, even without a change of government in 1964, an expansion of the employment of economists in government service would have taken place. The first reason was the growing concern over the management of the public sector of the economy, as shown by the 1961 Plowden Report on the Control of Public Expenditure (Cmd 1432) and also the White Paper on the Nationalized Industries (Cmd 1337). Secondly there was a wave of social optimism, like the belief that the 'pool of ability' was both wider and deeper than had been supposed, and a major enquiry such as Robbins was bound to raise economic concepts like 'opportunity cost'. Thirdly, the urge in the early 1960s to 'get Britain moving again' became closely associated with the demand for greater professionalism within government; there was the specific need for larger numbers of specialist engineers and scientists and economists, as well as a more general need within all departments for greater expertise. Even though the optimism of those days has become muted, some of the changes associated with that period, like the growth of specialists within the civil service, have proved irreversible.

II

Now I should like to turn to what economic advisers actually do, and my list of their functions will overlap considerably with that set out in the article by Sir Alec Cairncross on *The Work of an Economic Adviser* which I have already quoted.[29] First, there is their work as specialists in economic intelligence: 'experts on the available information of interest to their colleagues' who can 'assess the current situation in the light of the latest statistics as they come to hand'. This may sound like a routine function, but in fact nothing is trickier than assessing the current situation correctly, and 'knowing where you are' with regard to the key economic indicators. When the Heath Government took office in June 1970, it was clearly given very cautious advice over reflation, so that Mr Heath found himself unable to redeem his personal pledge to cut prices 'at a stroke' by reducing indirect taxation. Now it is arguable that this advice was in fact over-cautious, and that it was itself partly responsible for the Heath Government over-correcting in 1972 as unemployment reached the unprecedented post-war figure of a million. And yet the last months of the

Crossman Diaries, which record Treasury advice in the period immediately before the change of government, make it easy to understand how this cautious attitude in the summer of 1970 came into being. No one could feel confident that the 1969 inflow of private capital would go on sustaining the balance of payments; consumer spending might well have risen faster than it did after incomes policy had been virtually abandoned; and it seemed wise to take a cautious view of export prospects when the American stock-exchange in May 1970 reached its lowest point for eight years.[30] But, as Cairncross says, every economic adviser 'has to acquire the ability to judge a situation from limited and uncertain evidence' as best he can; indeed 'a new adviser usually finds that he has to begin by gorging himself with statistics. He has to learn how to handle data . . . by steeping himself in the figures so as to learn when and how far to trust them.'

The second function of an economic adviser is economic forecasting, and this, in its modern and most sophisticated form, must surely be regarded as the aspect of an adviser's work which approximates most closely to a science. As far back as the 1950s, and even earlier, it was a major task of the Economic Section to play the leading role in the preparation of forecasts of the main economic aggregates, including the Gross Domestic Product and the Balance of Payments. The present far more elaborate procedure for short-term forecasting, exploiting modern economic techniques to the full, is described in the recent report of the Ball Committee on Policy Optimization (Cmnd 7148), and Sir Douglas Wass also gave a briefer but valuable account in the Cambridge lecture from which I have already quoted. The Treasury nowadays maintains a 'macro-economic model' — a national income forecasting model that 'consists of a set of some 650 mathematical equations which assert relationships between two or more economic variables and their movement over time'.[31] We are reminded that some of these equations 'inevitably have a limited empirical foundation and rest heavily on *a priori* supposition', but such suppositions which are disproved are immediately discarded. In addition to the national income model, there is now also available 'a structural model of domestic capital flows together with a similar model of external capital flows'. These two models, together with the national income model, 'provide a complete integrated model of the economy', and they enable forecasts to be made and the results analysed based on a wide range of initial assumptions. The actual computation is rapid, but a great deal of judgement is needed in adjusting the predictions to take account of past experience of divergencies between what the calculations showed and what actually happened. As Douglas Wass points out, certain key judgements in a forecast may have to rest on a slender empirical base. No one should attempt to

11

claim too much for forecasting. But each error rigourously analysed may provide some fresh clue to the better understanding of how the economy actually works.

Thirdly, there is the function of government economist as policy adviser. Cairncross, with his long and varied experience, has pointed out that few economic advisers can count on seeing their ministers frequently. 'An economic adviser to be effective, has to work within the administrative machine, not as a kind of hanger-on of the minister or eminence grise who can get his way single-handed. He is advising the administrators far more than he is advising the minister.'[32] This means, of course, that a government economist needs, next only to his professional skills, the ability to communicate. His advice must be clear, begging no questions, and capable of withstanding a process of filtering. Otherwise administrators will turn his advice into a part of what they themselves want to say.

Even when an economic adviser is closest to his minister, his advice will still be more effective if the views of the Permanent Secretary have been moving in the same direction. The excellent account of Incomes Policy by F. T. Blackaby,[33] rightly judges that Sir Robert Hall's advice had contributed to the Selwyn Lloyd 'pay pause' of July 1961. Indeed when I became Economic Secretary in 1955 Robert Hall told me that he regarded the annual wage round as one of the most worrying features of the British economy, and the author of the most authoritative survey of economic management in the earlier post-war years has commented that 'By 1953 it was clear that wage inflation was to be a continuing problem, not just a problem of the immediate transition from the war.'[34] The Treasury Economic Section had played a big part in drafting the 1956 White Paper on *The Economic Implications of Full Employment* (Cmnd 9725). Mr Blackaby is also right on two other points: the effect of hourly wage rates rising by 7 per cent in 1961, and prices rising by 4 per cent came as all the greater shock after the interval of wage and price stability only two years before; and the OEEC Report of 1961,[35] which spoke of the 'Wage-Wage Spiral' and rejected the view that 'the problem will be solved solely by a firm control of total demand', and concluded that in Britain 'excessive wage increases constituted both an important and independent inflationary force', proved to be a powerful reinforcement to the 'cost-push' school of thought. One of the principal authors of the Report was Professor R. F. (Lord) Kahn, and his closely-argued, compelling speeches on this theme have been a notable feature of some recent economic debates in the House of Lords.

What may not be so widely known is that this Report finally convinced Sir Frank Lee, then Permanent Secretary to the Treasury, that incomes policy (it was still then usually referred to as 'wages policy') had an essential role to play as part of a co-ordinated set of policies to contain inflation. Frank Lee was by instinct a believer in the 'market economy', but he was also one of the ablest and most open-minded men I have ever had the privilege of knowing. And having become convinced of the need to embark on a new policy, he brought into play all his skills as an administrator. He realized clearly the need for a policy which would develop in stages. He saw the importance of always being briefed in advance for the specific wage demands that were going to follow next, and he worked closely alongside other departments in the attempt to devise institutional machinery that could cure anomalies and undertake 'revaluations'.

Treasury Ministers, administrators and economists worked closely together in 1961/62, and those who criticized Selwyn Lloyd for not making faster progress ought to have realized the extraordinary difficulty of his position. An 'Incomes Policy' was such a new and far-reaching concept for government, affecting so many departments (nearly twenty were represented at those 'fruitless' meetings of the Economic Policy Committee of which Harold Macmillan complains in his memoirs) that I think it had to be the Prime Minister himself who took the lead in steering the policy through Cabinet. But Mr Macmillan is entitled to claim credit for his unqualified declaration in the debate that followed Selwyn Lloyd's dismissal, when he said that 'an incomes policy is necessary as a permanent feature of our national life'. Mr Macmillan wrote in 1973 that he still adhered to those words,[36] and it was a great pity that they were not heeded before the unwise decision by the next Conservative Government to abolish the Prices and Incomes Board.

Of course policy advice from government economists is not confined to major decisions of economic management. I much enjoyed consulting members of the Economic Section on a whole range of matters, often informally, and I remember the occasion when such a discussion finally convinced me that there were no valid arguments for the general retention of Resale Price Maintenance.

People sometimes ask whether it makes sense for economists with Labour sympathies to advise Conservative governments and vice versa. I do not believe that there is a real difficulty here. As a former political adviser, Jack Straw said, in his Leeds Convocation Lecture last year, 'What is sought is technical or expert advice that is intellectually rigorous; advice that does not duck inconvenient questions which may well have been ignored when the policy idea was prepared by party, trade union or pressure group.'[37] Of course these words apply even more to specialists in government departments than to the administrative civil servants with whom Jack Straw was chiefly concerned.

13

Government economists, for their part, are usually more concerned with the coherence of policy, and its relevance to the most urgent economic objectives, than with their own personal priorities and preoccupations; they also soon discover whether the Minister for whom they work commands their personal respect. What does matter enormously is that government economists should be scrupulous in telling the truth and in presenting the news as they see it, and that Ministers should accept this. Our modern democracy doesn't always wish to know the truth, and even good administrators will sometimes be tempted to say 'I can't tell the Minister this'. But specialists owe it to their training always to put rigour and honesty first, and not to shirk those difficult words 'We were wrong . . .'.

The fourth function of the economic adviser is briefing — something that gets underrated in most writing on this subject. Crossman hasn't helped with his frequent complaints in his Diaries of briefs and counter-briefs being read out (as Harold Macmillan would say, 'illegibly') at Ministers' meetings, which suggests that Harold Wilson was much less severe than Mr Attlee in insisting that 'briefs are for study'. But good briefing, well mastered, can play an important role in the work of government. I still remember the quality of the briefing I received from Ian Little on coal pricing, and, frankly, universities might well have been still shorter of essential accommodation to meet the peak of the post-Robbins bulge had I not myself in the spring of 1964 learnt thoroughly a good but quite difficult brief from a future officer of the UGC, just at the time when Treasury counter-arguments were beginning to over-reach themselves. It is also worth remembering the extent to which politics is an oral culture. It was no good in my day sending long memoranda to one or two older Ministers, especially those without departmental responsibilities. You were far more likely to win their support by going to see them, well-briefed and accompanied by a congenial colleague.

Good briefing for parliamentary debates is also essential. The House of Commons rightly loathes block phrases that smell of official drafting, like 'mention has been made of . . .'. As for what the House does like, this has never been better put than by Dr Eric Taylor, a senior Clerk who once wrote: 'Don't argue, explain. And have your facts right.'[38] Mr Macmillan was complimentary in his memoirs about a speech I made in an economic debate at the end of July 1961, and this one certainly did go well; it followed the Taylor principles, and it caught the mood of the House. Looking at it again, I realize that at least a third of it was a straight exposition, suitably adapted, of the brief which I had received from the Economic Section. Economists could also be very valuable as tactical advisers during a debate, especially when they urged one not to be too definite, or too dogmatic. From my talks with economists at the Treasury, I learned greatly to value their hard-headed combination of reason, knowledge, experience, scepticism, and good sense — and this is an attitude of mind which the House of Commons will also respect from a Minister provided he has taken sufficient trouble over preparation.

Any Cabinet Minister who has previously done a spell at the Treasury must sometimes wish that he could be better briefed on important economic questions after he has left. The broadcasts by Professor David Henderson in the late autumn of 1977 on 'The Unimportance of Being Right',[39] and the relevant chapter of *The Power Game* by Jock Bruce-Gardyne and Nigel Lawson,[40] both sent my mind back to the crucial ministerial debate on the Concorde proposal in November 1962. Professor Henderson asks how a group of people, of whom I was one, came to take what he regards as one of the 'three worst civil investment decisions in the history of mankind'. I can, from memory, add just two more reasons to those which he mentions in the second of his five talks. First, I think the desire to demonstrate the interdependence of Britain and France was not only due to the belief that Concorde might prove an entry-card for Europe; at this stage there was just as much concern among Ministers to 'sell' membership of the EEC to public opinion at home, and to accustom home opinion to the idea of Britain and France engaging in major projects together. Secondly, I distinctly remember the argument being advanced that the Anglo-French project should be able to exploit its clear lead in time, and that in any case none of us in 1962 could hope to form a commercial judgement about a service that wouldn't be coming into operation until the 1970s. I have always felt that this episode shows the importance of senior ministers not directly involved in a policy decision having access to an informed source of briefing outside their departments, when large sums of public money are at stake.

There are two other functions of economic advisers which I should mention more briefly. They ought to be able to spend a part of their time not just clearing the in-tray, or advising on day-to-day issues, but researching into specific topics that may well prove to have relevance for policy. Not all the results of these researches will bear fruit, but some may attract notice at a high level, and economic advisers must learn the art of cultivating the market for their products. Lastly, advisers have occasionally been important witnesses when the government is presenting oral evidence to an outside Committee. The Minutes of Evidence presented to the Radcliffe Committee on the Working of the Monetary System (1960) is likely to prove an almost inexhaustible quarry for future economic historians, and it may well be that in future government economists will need to appear more often, side by side with administrators, when departments are presenting evidence to Select Committees of the House of Commons. This will certainly be the case if Select Committees heed the wise advice of the former Secretary of State for Trade, and remember that their prime function is to act as a check on what government has been doing rather than as advocates of their own independent policy recommendations.[42]

III

Lastly, I should like to make some more general comments about the Government Economic Service as it operates at the present time. One notices, first of all, that 'the majority of GES economists are employed on work of a micro- rather than a macro-economic nature. Within the Treasury, the bulk of the economic work on the public expenditure side is of a micro nature'.[41] In other words it would be wrong, today, to suppose that the average economist in government spends his time thinking about incomes policy, or whether it still makes sense to believe in demand management. He is much more likely to be involved in such questions as how a specific part of the public sector could be managed more efficiently, what kind of guide-lines should be laid down for the nationalized industries, how the benefits of social programmes might be better evaluated, or how the flow of funds to building societies (a key aspect of the private sector for any government) actually circulates. It is significant that the new deputy chief economic adviser to the Treasury, Ian Byatt, considers that his most valuable achievement as head of the public sector economic group has been 'a new emphasis on the practical rather than the theoretical difficulties of running [nationalized] concerns'.[43]

Despite the growth of the Economic Service, the distribution of economists among government departments is still surprisingly unequal. The Departments of the Environment and Transport are, as I have already shown, well served. The use of economists by Transport goes back to the 1960s, and I suspect owes much to the enthusiasm and determination of (Professor) C. D. Foster. Of course this is a marketed service, unlike for example very nearly the whole of Education. It seems wrong that there should only be one single economist working in the Home Office, though admittedly there is also a research unit. But prima facie one would have thought that economists could contribute some expertise in areas like the relationship between crime and unemployment, the deployment of the police, or fire insurance and the manning of the fire service. Within the Department of Health and Social Security, it is obviously desirable that economists as well as statisticians should contribute towards our knowledge of the effects of supplementary benefit on the incentive to work; in fact there is probably also a need for social scientists who can make due

16

allowance for the fact that those actually administering social security benefits at the 'coal-face' have tended to be men and women imbued with the 'Protestant ethic' who are by no means conspicuously well-paid themselves. It is good to see that the Department of Employment uses a fair number of economists (over twenty), since the understanding of the labour market — and whether, indeed, it makes sense to think in terms of a single labour market — is certainly going to grow in importance during the years ahead. From my experience as a member of the Pearson Commission on International Development I should judge that the ODM has always used economists well, especially at the lower levels, and that this tradition dates back to the period when Sir Andrew Cohen was Permanent Secretary, originally at the old Department of Technical Co-operation. But one has a rather less cheerful impression of the morale of the economists employed within the Foreign and Commonwealth Office, and it might be a good thing if there could be rather more diplomats with economic degrees.

The expansion of the Economic Service has also thrown up one more general difficulty in that a number of senior economic advisers find themselves starting to become not so much economists as managers, possessed sometimes of more modest technical skills, or expertise less-recently acquired, than those beneath them. Of course this is not a unique problem, and it was pointed out to me not long ago that a high proportion of graduate social workers in our society are employed in administering other social workers. But it is important that economic advisers, quite apart from their need to keep in touch with current ideas, should also have the opportunity to refurbish their techniques.

The Treasury, of course, remains a special case. It recruits extremely able people into the lower ranks, particularly applied economists from the best graduate schools. Higher up in the Treasury hierarchy, at the level of Under-Secretary and above, there are relatively few specialist economists; indeed economists have actually been losing posts at these levels, though a certain number will have become ordinary civil servants in the standard administrative grades. There is still the problem of whether, in Sir Donald Macdougall's words, the Treasury has 'too much monopoly of information and power', quite apart from the authority wielded by individual Chancellors. Ministers, in a telling phrase I have heard used, do get 'locked into' Treasury thinking. When Mr Heath, in his broadcast conversations with Anthony Barker,[44] described the six-monthly Chequers meetings of his Cabinet with the Central Policy Review Staff, I noticed he did *not* say that the CPRS provided Ministers with its own assessment, independent of the Treasury, of where the economy stood. While the present head of the CPRS is sometimes asked to give his views on economic

17

questions and the CPRS is still involved alongside the Treasury in such matters as the preparation of the annual White Paper on Public Expenditure,[45] much of its work seems to have moved away in the direction of becoming 'just one more [independent] advisory unit',[46] concentrating on issues like the social aspects of housing or micro-electronic chips.

There is also the danger that the ablest minds within the Treasury get too shut off from thinking that is going on outside. This point should not be exaggerated. Relations have been close between the Treasury and the National Institute ever since it was established, and there have always been individual economists like Wynne Godley (himself a former member of the Economic Section) who have commanded special respect; indeed I understand that contact with the 'New Cambridge' school bore fruit a few years back in a big double-seminar at the Treasury, with two meetings held a fortnight apart. There is also the Academic Panel of some half-dozen outstanding younger economists, which was set up in 1976 to offer advice on how the Treasury's macroeconomic model should develop, and to act as an intermediary between Treasury economists and relevant academic research. It has been university groups of economists further away from London who have sometimes felt that they were not sufficiently listened to, and it is good to know that Mr Byatt regards it as one of his main functions, taking over as deputy chief adviser at the Treasury, 'to keep abreast of new thinking about economics in the universities and elsewhere'.

This leads me to the 'supply' side of the equation — whether the universities are producing the right kind of economist, in sufficient numbers. So far as numbers are concerned, the output of university undergraduates with first degrees in economics did not change very greatly between 1968 (1409) and 1976 (1557), the last year for which figures are available; the numbers with higher degrees rose much faster (297 to 650). The numbers of full-time teaching and research staff engaged in Social, Administrative and Business Studies, in posts wholly financed from university income, rose from 4430 in 1970 to 5978 in 1976.[47] I think on the whole the government has been able to recruit the right kind of economist during the rapid growth of the Economic Service, but there has been something of a problem caused, during the years of university expansion, by the tendency of the universities themselves to retain such a high proportion of their own ablest students.

One sometimes hears complaints about the ignorance of the real world shown by people who have spent four or five years (or even longer) largely on economics, but unfortunately almost wholly on theoretical, mathematical and econometric studies. This is not an easy issue to resolve. A first degree course in economics ought to be rigorous, and even an arid approach has its point; unless curves and econometric techniques are mastered while still at university, it is unlikely that they ever will be. The fact that in some universities a high proportion of a macroeconomics paper, even up to 90 per cent, consists of examination in economic theory is not altogether to those universities' discredit. But two reservations may, perhaps, be made. First, an interested layman can't help noticing how long it seems to take for important articles to become reflected in what is taught in the economic textbooks. This was indeed one of the reasons why Penguin Books launched, back in the late 1960s, their series of Modern Economic Readings, so that (for example) the student of monetary theory could have easy and inexpensive access to influential articles on the significance of Keynes by Clower and Leijonhufvud. Secondly, I wonder whether economics as taught in some universities has not become really too little concerned with economic policy, especially when the subject is taught by members of departments who have never themselves had experience of government service, nor worked in an organization which has had to concern itself with applications of the subject.

I remember that Sir Hubert Henderson, as Drummond Professor at Oxford, gave a lecture-course in the year after the end of the war on 'The Economics of the Modern World', and he repeated this course in 1950–51. He used to poke some not altogether gentle fun at Nicholas (Lord) Kaldor's model calculation of the National Income in 1948 in the appendix to Lord Beveridge's book on *Full Employment*, though he was no less astringent when dealing with the illusion that 'our present austerities . . . would vanish like the snow if the sun of the price system were allowed to shine'.[48] Henderson had extraordinary abilities as an economic debator and controversialist and I don't say that many other academics could have presented a similar course so convincingly. But I think also that the spread of subjects in the Oxford PPE school did have great value for many undergraduates. The relevance for economics of contemporary Oxford philosophy was never clearer than when one of the keenest intellectual products of this school reminded economists that 'making one's value premises explicit' was much more reputable than 'moralising', and that each person had to answer for himself the question 'Would this change [in policy] affect real income favourably or unfavourably?'[49] I think it can be argued that the philosophy of this period with its strong emphasis on 'ethics as prescription', sometimes led economists into excessive optimism over what could actually be done.[50] But the impetus it gave to clear thought, to the elimination of moralism and self-deception, and above all to the readiness to seek the truth, was wholly beneficial.

A government economist needs to have been rigorously trained, and to have acquired not only the technique but also the commitment and self-discipline of the true professional. But this must not be at the expense of other qualities like the vital spark of creative imagination and the impetus of genuine interest in what is going on. He also needs to be, in some measure, a man of affairs, and this means more than simply understanding how doors open and shut in a particular department. 'Men of common kinship know they can continually bargain and fight for what they want from each other in the market place of an agreed culture [where] the medium of exchange is repute . . . The kinsmen must speak in common idioms or they will have difficulty in communicating. They must refine the technical apparatus, or they will not be able to distinguish their own messages from the confusion of a world filled with static.'[51] The language is ornate but the underlying thought is correct.

Of course if the government wants to recruit first-class economists to its Economic Service it cannot neglect pay, and it must also afford reasonable opportunities for publication. With regard to the latter point, I do not think much is wrong, especially now that the series of Government Economic Papers, published by HMSO, has been supplemented by a new series of Treasury Working Papers on key topical issues like the impact of devaluation on competitiveness. The one difficulty is that the pressure of work makes it difficult to achieve the degree of polish, and precise documentation, expected of 'refereed' publications in academic journals. This difference can affect career expectations, as any Vice-Chancellor concerned with academic promotions will know well. One can only urge that the management of the Economic Service should bear in mind the importance of enabling a high-flyer to achieve and retain a reputation, not only in Whitehall, but also in the wider economic profession.

The Government Economic Service has now become so large that one sometimes hears it suggested that it should soon be transformed. Civil servants, it is said, should be appointed to specific posts because they received their university training in economics; and there should be a return to a much smaller cadre of professional economists, mostly very high-powered, and recruited for fixed periods of government service. Such a case can undoubtably be made, but it seems to me that there are also strong arguments on the other side. Economists who become administrative civil servants, however much they try to keep up their interest in economics, tend to develop a quite distinct specialism, that of public administration. The economist has the specific role of identifying and analysing the economic factors in any policy decision, and of making explicit (indeed, where possible quantifying) the costs and benefits of alternative policies and approaches. The economist may also be needed, and the precision of his trained mind be most valuable when it is a matter of inculcating the most elementary lessons; as when he reminds interventionists that laws of supply and demand cannot simply be disregarded, or that in most societies the invention of money was regarded as a step forward. It may be no less desirable for him to remind Ministers of the 'social market' school of thought that economics is about the behaviour of actual human beings, and that 'stocks and flows do not move of themselves'.[52]

It may be that a growing number of serious and challenging problems facing government will need to be studied by specialist advisers drawn from more than one social science discipline. This applies, for instance, to the evaluation of social programmes, and to the criteria for operating a policy of positive discrimination. Again, labour economics is a subject to which economists, sociologists and also economic historians will all have contributions to make. Of all the many letters which appeared in *The Times* last year on the subject of trade union power and economic performance, the most significant, I thought, was one from Sir Henry Phelps Brown[53] who pointed out that the problem of the low productivity of British industry goes back to the end of the last century; and he went on to say this:

> Most employees are not made to behave as they do because they belong to a trade union: they belong to a trade union because they want to behave as they do . . . This is, to draw together and adopt rules of common action for mutual protection against the pressures of the market.

This is true and important. Yet it must remain the special function of the economist to try to estimate the cost of keeping an uneconomic factory going, or to remind Ministers, when they want to intervene in a particular industry, of the need to think in real terms about the value of the economic resources that will be required, and the prospective return on these resources, measured over specific periods of time.

Economic problems make people angry nowadays, and no wonder. But economics remains a vital and challenging subject, in which, as Sir Donald Macdougall has said 'constant rethinking is necessary in the light of new situations, new information and new techniques'.[54] Even the pure theorist is needed, not least because his vision of the world seldom turns out to be absolutely 'pure'; it may well prove to have some new and significant connection with practical realities. The great Alfred Marshall reviewing his career near the end of his life, wondered whether he had been right to become diverted so often from the study of ultimate aims to the more ephemeral questions on which his advice was frequently sought; 'I despised them,' he said, referring to the latter category, 'but the instinct of the chase drew me towards them'.[55] I am certain that no one can be a successful economic adviser who does not retain, among his other professional qualities, something of this entirely healthy 'instinct for the chase'.

Notes

[1] *Administrative Theories and Politics*, 1972, p 215.

[2] 'The Work of an Economic Adviser', *Public Administration*, **46**, 1968, p 3.

[3] The Government Economic Service, *Economic Progress Report*, no 99, June 1978.

[4] 'The Economist in Whitehall', *Lloyds Bank Review*, Apr 1957, p 29.

[5] *The Changing Problems of Economic Management*, Lecture to the Johnian Society, Cambridge, 15 Feb 1978.

[6] *Economist*, 18 Dec 1976, p 9.

[7] *Economist*, 31 Mar 1973, p 57; 28 Apr 1973, p 69; 26 May 1973, p 71.

[8] R. M. Punnett, *Front Bench Opposition*, 1973, p 389.

[9] 'The Machinery of Economic Government', in David Butler, A. H. Halsey, eds, *Policy and Politics: Essays in Honour of Norman Chester*, 1978, p 179.

[10] R. W. B. (Sir Richard) Clarke, Lecture on the Plowden Report *Public Administration*, **41**, 1963, p 20.

[11] Interview with Peter Hennessey, *The Times*, 9 Jan 1978.

[12] T. S. Ward and R. R. Nield, *The Measurement and Reform of Budgetary Policy*, 1976, pp 55–6.

[13] Frank Blackaby, ed, *De-industrialisation*, 1979.

[14] Andrew Shonfield, *British Economic Policy Since the War*, 1958, pp 91 et sec.

[15] *The Inter-War Years and other papers*, Oxford, 1955, p 334.

[16] *Economist*, 13 Feb 1954, pp 439–41.

[17] *Sunday Times*, 20 Nov 1977.

[18] See eg Samuel Brittan, *Steering the Economy*, 1971, p 41.

[19] CP (47)/19 para 34.
This report simply assumed for planning purposes that there would be a balance of payments deficit in 1947 of £218 millions (Table 3) — the true figure turned out to be £442 millions. But of course there was also a 'hard currency' problem distinct from, though overlapping with, the balance of payments problem. It is interesting that D. H. (Sir Dennis) Robertson, a fierce critic of the Labour Government in August 1947 when he said that 'any country which gives its mind to it can create/balance of payments difficulties/for itself in half an hour', took a rather different line over Britain's dollar shortage when he lectured a few years later at the University of Virginia (*Britain in the World Economy*, 1953).
Indeed his 'footnote' to the law of comparative advantage brought him unexpectedly close to the arguments used by Thomas (Lord) Balogh in his book on *The Dollar Problem*, Oxford, 1949.

[20] CM 74(47), 25 Aug.

[21] *Hansard*, **468**, 26 Oct 1949, cols 1333–4.

[22] *Hansard*, **495**, 29 Jan 1952, col 52.

[23] *Hansard*, **507**, 11 Nov 1952, col 880.

[24] J. C. R. Dow, *The Management of the British Economy 1945–60*, Cambridge, 1964, p 86.

[25] Information from Lord Carr of Hadley, then Eden's Parliamentary Private Secretary.

[26] *Observer*, 29 Jan, 1978.

[27] S. Brittan, op cit, p 201.

[28] *Listener*, 1 Dec 1960, 967—9.

[29] Cairncross, op cit.

[30] *Diaries of a Cabinet Minister*, vol 3, pp 850, 904.

[31] Wass, op cit.

[32] 'Economists in Government', *Lloyds Bank Review*, January 1970, p 8.

[33] In F. Blackaby, ed, *The British Economy 1960—74*, Cambridge, 1978.

[34] J. C. R. Dow, op cit, p 99.

[35] W. Fellner *et al*, *The Problem of Rising Prices*, OEEC, 1961, see especially pp 53—63.

[36] Harold Macmillan, *At the End of the Day*, 1973, p 105.

[37] 'Power in Government — A Chinese Puzzle', *University of Leeds Review*, **21**, 1978, 175.

[38] *The House of Commons at Work*, 1971, p 102.

[39] *Listener*, 27 Oct, 3, 10, 17, 24 Nov 1977.

[40] The Power Game, 1976, Ch 2.
    Pace the authors, I am positive in my own recollection that there was only one full Cabinet discussion, though there could of course have been an earlier meeting of ministers chiefly involved, with the Prime Minister in the chair.

[41] *Economic Progress Report*, no 99.

[42] Edmund Dell, *Political Responsibility and Industry*, 1973, p 202.

[43] *The Times*, 31 Jan 1978.

[44] 'Heath on Whitehall Reform', reprinted in *Parliamentary Affairs*, **31**, 1978, 382—3.

[45] *Financial Times*, 1 June 1977.

[46] *Observer*, 16 Jan 1977.

[47] Figures supplied to me by Margaret McCreath.

[48] Henderson, op cit, p 356.

[49] I. M. D. Little, *A critique of Welfare Economics*, Oxford, 1957, p 115.

[50] See, for example, Colin Welch, 'Crosland, Reconsidered' in *Encounter*, Jan 1979, especially the earlier part of the article.

[51] Hugh Heclo and Aaron Wildavsky, *The Private Government of Public Money*, 1974, pp 2—3.

[52] Frank Blackaby, review of Nicholas Kaldor, Essays, *New Society*, 18 Jan 1979, p 147.

[53] *The Times*, 6 Sept 1978.

[54] 'In Praise of Economics', Presidential Address to the Royal Economic Society, reprinted in *Studies in Political Economy Vol II*, 1975, p 278.

[55] Quoted in J. M. Keynes, *Essays in Biography*, 1951, p 176.

Inflation

2

The great inflation revisited

G. D. N. WORSWICK

'Economic problems', Ian Little once wrote, 'being problems of choice, are, of course, insoluble.'[1] Yet there was a time when it did seem that one of the biggest economic problems of this century — mass unemployment in industrial countries — had been solved. So far as the theory went, Keynes was, in any case, not so much framing a choice which had to be made as uncovering a weakness in the capitalist system — Say's Flaw, as one might say — which called for correction. Once identified the correction seemed obvious. Even if the Treasury were to fill old bottles with bank notes and bury them in disused coal mines, leaving it to private enterprise to dig them up again, the outcome was likely to increase the income and wealth of the community. How much better still if we did sensible things such as building houses and the like. Why should anyone wish to oppose such a correction of the system whereby many would gain and none lose?

The Keynesians themselves thought, that, at full employment, the economy would have an inflationary bias, which could be rectified by 'incomes policy' (called wage policy in the 1940s). Some people thought that there would be serious resistance to full employment policies from business leaders, fearful of the consequences of softening the sanction of the sack. The alternative view was that conservatives would welcome the reform programme of Keynes, which would put capitalism on its feet again and take the sting out of root-and-branch socialist programmes. In Britain it was already clear by the mid-1950s that the Conservative Party was willing to direct policy on Keynesian lines. In fact, throughout the post-war years, until the monetarist reaction among some Conservative leaders, Conservative Chancellors have seemed less constrained by arguments of 'sound finance', whether in the context of the budget or of the exchange rate, than one guesses that their Labour opposite numbers would have been in similar circumstances.[2] As for inflation, while it was true that consumer prices continued to rise year by year by between 2 and 4 per cent, the general view was that this did little harm. On the contrary it was argued that a low inflation was a positive good, acting as a safety valve for the conflicting claims on resources of different groups. This attitude is in strong contrast with that

27

which is taken today. While there are wide differences of opinion as to the causes of inflation there is now little difference concerning its effects, which are almost everywhere characterized as harmful for investment, for economic growth and the restoration of full employment.

The Great Inflation, 1939–1951 by A. J. Brown was published in 1955,[3] just at the time when it seemed that the unemployment problem had been solved. This inflation was in Professor Brown's words 'in any sense one of the greatest, if not the greatest, in the history of the world economy' and, as such, was worthy of study. But, as the title implies, it was an episode which had been completed. Now, once more, we have been witnessing a great inflation throughout the world. Do these two inflations belong to the same species? It is interesting to take the explanations which Brown offered for the 1939–51 episode and to consider to what extent they account for the present inflation.

Brown gives tables of changes in wholesale prices and the cost-of-living in many countries for a variety of sub-periods during and after the Second World War. For the purpose of comparison of the scales of the two inflations we choose the span January–June 1939 to August 1948, just over nine years, to represent the first one. Inflation is not a smooth process in which the steady acceleration of prices for some time is followed by an equally steady slowing down. There are bursts of acceleration, alternating with periods of comparative quiescence. There was a sting in the tail of the 1939–51 episode, when commodity prices soared once more with the outbreak of the Korean War, and for the purposes of comparison, we leave this out. Dating the start of the current inflation is not easy. Prices in virtually all the industrial countries had been rising throughout the 1950s and 1960s, but at comparatively low rates ranging from 1 to 5 per cent a year, and there was no clear indication of acceleration. The present episode began somewhere in the second half of the 1960s. In the United States — most important because of its large weight in the world economy — it was the extra expenditure on the Vietnam War coming on top of the fully employed Johnson Great Society which started things off, and 1966 was the crucial year. In France, 'les événements de Mai' of 1968 saw the first of a number of wage explosions in Europe. We choose 1967 (average) as the base year of the second great inflation, and since we are only concerned with orders of magnitude, we complete the period with 1976 (average) a span of nine years, and thus a fraction shorter than the earlier case.

In Table 1 we compare indices of wholesale prices (or their nearest equivalent) for a number of countries for the two periods. The countries are listed in five main groups: 1, North America, 2, Other America, 3, Asia (including the Middle East), 4, Western Europe, and 5, Other. We do not

TABLE 1
Indices of Wholesale Prices

		Aug 1948 as % of Jan–June 1939	1976 as % of 1967
N America	Canada	216	194
	USA	222	183
Other America	Argentina	273	10,341
	Brazil	302	713
	Chile	3951	626,000
	Costa Rica	219	282
	Mexico	268	226
	Venezuela	176	169
Asia (including Middle-East)	Egypt	343	147
	India	358	183
	Iran	500	180
	Iraq	521	159
	Israel	398	451
	Turkey	448	323
Europe	Austria	449	155
	Belgium	390	163
	Denmark	237	199
	Finland	983	250
	France	1930	188
	Greece	25,200	244
	Ireland	230	277
	Italy	5700	264
	Netherlands	280	166
	Norway	185	181
	Portugal	253	230
	Spain	329	203
	Sweden	198	198
	Switzerland	218	142
	UK	226	253
Other	Australia	173	167
	Japan	11,467	176
	New Zealand	178	232
	S Africa	185	218
5 per cent a year		155	155
10 per cent a year		236	236
15 per cent a year		352	352

Sources: 1939–48, Brown, op cit.

1967–76, IMF *International Financial Statistics*, Series 63.

include any of the Communist bloc countries. At the foot of the table we show how much prices would have risen over nine years at steady rates of 5, 10 and 15 per cent per annum. The over-all impression given by this wholesale price comparison is that in North America, Asia and Europe the current inflation has been the smaller. In some Other countries it has been larger, while in 'Other America' experience has been mixed. It is apparent that in the later inflation the experience among the mainly industrial countries has been more uniform, with annual average rates running between 5 and 10 per cent, whereas in the earlier episode there are several instances of very high rates, such as Japan, France, Greece, and Italy. This table is by no means complete and excludes a number of instances of hyper-inflation such as occurred in Hungary and China, but we shall not be concerned with that problem nor shall we examine the special properties of some Latin American inflations.

The comparison in Table 2 of consumer prices for a group of advanced countries gives a somewhat different impression. In eight of the sixteen countries listed the recent inflation was greater than in 1939—48. As perceived by the consumer this has been as great an inflation as before. One interesting difference is that in most cases wholesale prices rose more than the cost of living in 1939—48, while the reverse has been the case more recently.

Inflation, says Brown, is an elusive phenomenon, the word being used to describe different processes or states — price inflation, income inflation, currency inflation, cost inflation, suppressed inflation and so on. In some cases the presence of one implies the absence of another. However, as ordinarily understood, inflation has to do with an inordinate rise in prices. Brown took the view that it was not 'profitable to approach the events of the inflationary period treated in this book with a single theoretical scheme into which they must be fitted'.[4] There was in the 1939—51 episode a great diversity of experience in different countries according to the extent of their involvement in the Second World War, and according to the methods adopted by belligerents to secure real resources and finance for the war sector. Brown distinguishes a number of phases of which the first four cover our nine-year span: 1: Economic mobilization (1939 to end 1942), 2: War economy (end of 1942 until August 1945), 3: Demobilization (August 1945 to June 1946), and 4: The post-war boom (June 1946 to. August 1948). He also distinguishes two types of economy.

The first is characterized by flexible prices of finished goods and of factors of production. Changes in the composition of output are brought about through the response of producers to relative prices. Changes in total effective demand result in changes in output and prices in the same direction. At full

TABLE 2
Indices of Consumer Prices

	Aug 1948 as % of Jan–June 1939	1976 as % of 1967
Australia	143	203
New Zealand	125	222
Canada	157	172
USA	177	170
Austria	450	169
Belgium	381	181
Denmark	167	202
Finland	818	225
France	1578	195
Ireland	176	268
Italy	5160	218
Netherlands	202	190
Norway	158	193
Sweden	154	181
Switzerland	163	160
UK	167	252

Sources: 1939–48, Brown, op cit.
1967–76, IMF *International Financial Statistics*, Series 64.

employment, output can no longer increase and a rise in effective demand is reflected entirely in prices.

In the second type of economy, the prices of finished goods are sticky. They do not respond to changes in effective demand, but only to changes in costs, being fixed with reference to average total costs at some normal level of plant utilization. Wages are assumed to be linked to the cost-of-living. Switches in demand result, in the first instance, in changes in order books and in stocks. If demand increases persist some firms will expand capacity: if demand decreases persist some firms will go out of business. Workers move from one industry to another not in response to relative wage differences but in response to differences in job availability. If demand rises persistently beyond full employment capacity, prices will not rise but stocks will be run down; this Brown calls suppressed inflation.[5] In this type of economy, price inflation can occur only if there is a rise in costs originating either in a fall in productivity, raising labour costs, or from outside the economy through a rise in the price of raw materials.

In the first type of economy monetary stringency would reduce inflation, in the second it would be pointless: its sole effect, if it was effective at all, would be to cause low profits and unemployment. These two types of economy are abstractions: actual economies are hybrids of the pure types, which may more resemble one than the other at different times. In Brown's view, for instance, the United States in 1939 was nearer the first type, and the United Kingdom nearer the second.

There still remain two more pieces of Brown's conceptual apparatus to be described — the price-wage spiral, and the relation between unemployment and money wage increases — but we will hold them over for the moment. Meanwhile we will see how Brown uses his two types of economy to explain certain phases of the war and post-war inflation, and see how much, if any, of this kind of explanation might be valid in the 1970s.

Even before the war began governments had embarked on large, deficit financed, programmes of war expenditures, which were expected to increase, but the contribution of these programmes to inflation was indirect. In the first year of the war the inflationary impulse in Europe came from the rise in the flexible prices of primary products, which could be attributed to devaluations of most European currencies, higher freight charges due to war risk, and a sharp change in expectations. Raw material prices rose ahead of wage costs and, in the main, of retail prices. In the United States, where some imports were actually cheapened by European devaluation, the rise in wholesale prices did not begin until the end of 1940. Increasing expenditure on the armed forces and production for them did not, as it were, pull up the prices of intermediate and finished manufactures. This had happened in Britain in the First World War when buyers for the army and the navy had bid against one another for cloth on the floors of textile mills, but that lesson had been learnt and the purchase of war supplies was comparatively orderly. It was the expectation that the war expenditures would create material shortages which contributed to the immediate jump in the flexible prices of raw materials, and it was these increases which fed through into domestic costs and prices. The UK very soon began placing long-term contracts with primary producing countries, often involving jumps in price of 40 per cent, but as the war went on these initially high prices began to appear relatively cheap. Elsewhere, in areas less directly involved in the war, primary producing countries continued to sell their exports in a relatively free and flexible market. The middle-eastern and Indian inflations were in the main demand determined.

In the second phase — war economy — price inflation was almost entirely suppressed in the belligerent countries by the central allocation of resources reinforced by extensive price controls and rationing. The collapse at the end of the war of the enemy and enemy-occupied economies created special problems which, however tempting, must be set aside and we confine our attention to UK and USA. In these two countries between the end of 1942 and August 1945 wholesale prices rose by 6 per cent and 4 per cent, and the cost of living by 3 per cent and 9 per cent respectively. Behind this virtual elimination of price inflation, there were, of course, increasing pressures of suppressed inflation in the form of accumulations of liquid assets which would be available for spending on consumption and investment in the post-war period. What gave rise to a renewed outburst of open price inflation was precisely the abandonment of price control in the United States in 1946. Many consumer goods, especially food, promptly rose to something like a free market equilibrium. Wages followed this rise in prices and a wage-price spiral was set in motion. As for Europe, the price inflation of this period was mainly triggered by the rise in import prices which depended partly on United States control and partly on the rising demand for industrial raw materials.

How much of this war and post-war story was repeated in the late 1960s and 1970s? The initial conditions were different. In 1939 there was still a lot of slack in most industrial economies, but at the same time there was the prospect of very large war expenditures. In 1967 there was much less slack in Europe, and hardly any in the United States, so that a smaller expansion of war expenditure there was imposed on a tighter economy, and was sufficient to generate some acceleration of price inflation. In a world in which fixed exchange rates still predominated this was duly transmitted to European economies in the same way as in 1946. There was no second phase of tightly controlled war economy, bottling up suppressed inflation for release later on, although perhaps the various episodes of price and wage control in Europe and the United States were pale reflections of it; but there was one element in the recent inflation which has no precedent in the earlier one, namely the succession of 'wage-explosions', notably in France and Britain in 1968 and 1969. More generally over the nine-year span the different relative movements of wholesale and retail prices suggest that the contribution of labour costs was larger relative to raw material prices in the later episode. Nevertheless a further big contribution of commodity price rises, very similar to that of 1939—40 (and again 1950—51 which we excluded from our statistical span) came in 1972—73. A number of industrial economies, including the United States, were enjoying booms at much the same time, and although the scale of the rise in industrial production was not inordinate, it triggered a very sharp rise in commodity prices, a rise clearly fuelled by a change in expectations. As in the earlier episode this rise fed back through import prices onto costs and prices of industrial countries. Moreover just as it was subsiding, it was reinforced by the quadrupling of the oil price at the end of 1973. This part of Brown's mechanism seems to have lost none of its force. During the period 1939—51 price inflation looked as though it might die down briefly in 1948 and again after the end of the Korean boom, when in fact it did remain at a low rate for a decade and a half. During the more recent episode there have been one or two false dawns. Export prices of primary products actually fell in 1976 and again briefly in 1978 after a further rise, but, despite a prolonged period of slow growth in many industrial countries their rate of inflation shows little sign of returning to the levels of the 50s and the 60s. Some of the explanation of this may be found in the remaining sectors of Brown's analysis to which we now turn.

Three chapters in the middle of *The Great Inflation* are devoted to the price-wage spiral. The central idea is most easily grasped by considering a closed economy of the second type which is at full employment. In this economy prices are fixed proportionally to costs (being a closed economy this means labour costs), and wages change only in line with prices. If then wages were to rise and prices were prevented from rising, there would be a shift in the distribution of real income from profits to wages: and vice versa, if prices were raised and wages kept from changing. There would also be a whole string of secondary consequences which Brown analyses in great detail. Wage increases, unaccompanied by price increases, are likely to produce, besides their more permanent distributional effects, a temporary increase in consumption at the expense of stocks. Price increases without wage increases will produce a temporary fall in consumption accompanied by a rise in stocks. Essentially the price-wage spiral is an alternation of distributional shifts from wages to profits and back, each one of which will set the stage for the next. The spiral will tend to converge if entrepreneurs and wage-earners fail to secure the price or wage increases they press for in their search to maintain incompatible levels of real income and the money is not available to finance increase transactions.

With the aid of some ingenious diagrams the relationship between the price-wage spiral and income distribution is further developed — bringing in the rest of the world for example — and the model is used to examine a number of instances from the period. Similarly the factors which might speed up or slow down the spiral and cause it to diverge or to converge are systematically analysed.

34

Perhaps the most significant modification of this model was the observation that full employment had been assumed solely for simplicity of exposition: the spiral could still work at levels of activity below full employment. The question whether unemployment might, nevertheless, reduce the pressure for wage increases, we shall come to in a moment. But first one or two implications of the model should be mentioned. It is easy to see how the case of two parties, entrepreneurs and wage-earners, could be extended to include other parties such as rentiers. Entrepreneurs and wage-earners could be divided into industrial groups and each group of wage earners might seek to preserve its share of wages within its industry, but also to keep wages comparable with those in other industries — the wage-wage spiral. In the two party model, either party can break out of equilibrium into a spiral by spontaneously raising prices or securing wage increases. When foreign trade is introduced industrial costs become the total of labour costs and raw material costs. Raw material prices are flexible and even if they are assumed to fluctuate about an average of zero, they may nevertheless generate a wage-price spiral. When raw material prices fall, so to a lesser extent will the prices of finished goods and wage-earners will be better off, yet they may have no inclination to reduce nominal wages accordingly. On the other hand, when raw material prices rise, so also will the prices of finished goods and real wages will be reduced. If wage-earners react strongly and quickly when raw material prices rise, but only slowly or not at all when they fall, this asymmetry introduces a ratchet which continuously pushes up the level of money wages and the prices of finished goods. There is a hint here of a possible explanation of the different relative behaviour of retail and wholesale prices in the inflation of 1939 to 1951 and more recently.

These chapters on the price-wage spiral are highly suggestive. The normal condition of the economy is not one in which prices are constant, being lifted off the ground from time to time by some expansion of demand, only to fall back when the pressure is removed. Rather it is one of an inter-acting price-wage spiral. Such a spiral may well have a tendency to converge. Even so, as Brown himself suggested for the period 1946—48, 'it does not seem too fanciful to regard it (the chart of prices) as showing an exponential or asymptotic adjustment towards a hypothetical equilibrium level, following upon the shock of de-control'[6] and he went on to suggest that the ceiling to which prices were tending seemed to be three or four times the immediate price adjustment of the month or two succeeding de-control. If the price-wage spiral is convergent, but not too strongly damped, then it may be started up again by random shocks.

What Brown's analysis suggests for our present problems is that inflation is a normal condition of the economy. During the 1950s and early 1960s inflation was dormant, ticking over quietly at an annual average rate of between 2 and 5 per cent in different countries. Since the late 1960s there have been a number of quite large shocks which have revived the price-wage spiral. It is obvious enough that expectations can play an important part in price determination, as Brown fully recognized in the context of the flexible prices of raw materials. It is also conceivable that expectations may influence the size of wage claims, although in the end it is settlements which matter. But a good deal of what has been happening can in fact be accounted for in terms of the reaction to past events of the various parties locked in a price-wage spiral.

Little reference has been made so far to money. There is quite a lot about money in the book but for our purposes we need consider only one aspect. A turn in the price-wage spiral is likely to require additional finance. There are circumstances when the monetary system will supply it without any policy action being required from the authorities. It happened that in the 1950s the velocity of circulation was rising strongly. However, if action by the authorities were needed then either they would increase the money supply to accommodate the inflation or they would refrain from doing so, thereby intensifying monetary stringency. This, in the second type of economy, would reduce output and employment: it would *ex-hypothesi* have little direct effect upon prices of finished goods. However, working through the level of unemployment, it might have an effect on the rate of increase of money wages. In the light of the appearance in *Economica* three years later of A. W. Phillips famous paper, Brown's treatment of this question is of exceptional interest.

The idea that the rate at which wages and prices rise might be related to the level of employment was not new. Brown himself went back to Pigou's *Lapses from Full Employment* which was published in 1945, and he would have found the idea even earlier in Joan Robinson's *Essays in the Theory of Employment* published in 1937. Brown expects to find an influence both of the level of unemployment and of the cost-of-living on the annual rate of change of wages. For UK he uses a wage rate index over two periods 1881—1914 and 1920—51. For USA he uses hourly earnings over the period 1921—48. Nowadays a researcher would probably put the data on tapes and run a variety of regressions. Brown's method, by contrast, is a careful study of the successive cyclical episodes. One merit of this historical treatment is that he can distinguish periods when the large part of wages was tied to the cost-of-living in sliding-scale agreements from periods when they were not. Such differences would obviously affect the interpretation of any equations, if they were not, as so frequently happens, overlooked. He is aware that care should be exercised in drawing conclusions from experience of cycles for what might happen in a steady state. Nevertheless he does ask what the critical sustained level of employment is below which unit labour costs would start rising at a rate which would push up the prices of finished goods. For the period before 1914 he puts this critical level in the UK somewhere between 2 and 5 per cent but by the 1930s the critical level had shifted to 'perhaps 10 or 12 per cent'. In the USA before the New Deal he puts the critical percentage as of the same order of the UK before 1914 — perhaps 4 to 6 per cent — but after 1935 it had become at least as high as it was at the same time in the UK — probably over 14 per cent.

Brown had proposed that the ratchet effect of fluctuating commodity prices on the price-wage spiral might be mitigated by schemes to stabilize commodity prices either on a world-wide basis or, through the use of subsidies, on a national basis. Even so he feared that if unemployment was kept low over long periods there would be an upward creep of wages, and the whole inflationary movement would proceed at a constant rate or perhaps an exponentially increasing one. He thought that society's capacity to tolerate gradual inflation was considerable but he was not at all sure that the rate of inflation would stay at tolerable levels: 'The United States might achieve it; for the United Kingdom the prospect is far more doubtful. The dilemma which the first sustained period of full employment in the history of industrial civilization has revealed seems likely to remain with us for some time.'[7]

The contrast between Brown's painstaking analysis of this problem and that of A. W. Phillips is stark. The latter simply fitted a curve to data of wage rate changes and unemployment in UK for the whole period 1861–1957, and concluded that: '. . . it seems from the relation fitted to the data that if aggregate demand were kept at a value which would maintain a stable level of product prices the associated level of unemployment would be a little under $2\frac{1}{2}$ per cent.'[8] The article was devoid of almost any economic analysis, yet the 'Phillips Curve' swept through the media and the textbooks like a forest fire. No need to bother about 'incomes policies' or modifying the system of collective bargaining and administered prices — it needed a little touch, and only a little touch of unemployment and inflation would go away. It took ten or fifteen years to dispose of that beguiling fallacy.[9] Who knows whether those years might have been better used in coming to grips with the real issues which Brown had exposed. What a pity it is that so many people read only 'the literature' and never seem to have time to read good books!

Brown started without 'a single theoretical scheme', and he does not try to construct one at the end of the work. So it is not a question of testing whether a model which worked for 1939–51 would work again to explain the current inflation. Nevertheless some of Brown's specific ideas about the causes of the earlier inflation seem to have had more recent counterparts. The world has, of course, changed a great deal in the last quarter of a century. During the 1939—51 episode, for much of the time there were pervasive administrative controls of production and trade, and exchange rates changed only in discrete steps. Today trade is much freer, economies have become much more inter-dependent and the major currencies are floating. A new *Great Inflation* would have to be extended to assess the impact of these and other developments. Some parts of the original version, such as the long struggle to escape from the meshes of the Multiplier, might no longer be needed, but throughout the original version there are insights and sequences of analysis which have immediate contemporary relevance. Above all there are the chapters on the price-wage spiral which are still as good a description as one can hope to find of what lies at the heart of the process of inflation.

Notes

[1] In G. D. N. Worswick and P. H. Ady, eds, *The British Economy 1945—50*, Oxford, 1952, p 186.

[2] Politicians often say things in opposition which appear to be inconsistent with the things they do when in office and British politicians are no mean performers of the U-turn. Nevertheless the roll of Butler—Macmillan—Heathcote-Amory—Maudling— Barber has a more expansionary ring than Gaitskell—Callaghan—Jenkins—Healey. The odd men out are Thorneycroft and Dalton although the 'song in the heart' of the latter was not fully reflected in his fiscal policies.

[3] A. J. Brown, *The Great Inflation 1939—1951*, Oxford, 1955.

[4] Op cit p 17.

[5] Kalecki distinguished latent inflation, when stocks were running down, and repressed inflation when stocks had run out and distribution became intermittent, with queues. 'What is Inflation', *Bulletin of the Oxford Institute of Statistics*, 1942. This useful distinction never caught on.

[6] Op cit p 133.

[7] Op cit p 300.

[8] A. W. Phillips, 'The Relation between Unemployment and the Rate of Change of Money Wage Rates in the United Kingdom, 1861—1957', *Economica*, 1958.

[9] Just as economic problems are insoluble, so economic fallacies are immortal. Mr David Attenborough has told us, in his splendid television natural history, that in man's unrelenting war against insects, despite enormous efforts, including the use of fire, radioactivity and the most lethal poisons, not a single insect species has been exterminated. Similarly, despite enormous intellectual efforts by men of reason and sense, no economic fallacy has ever been finally put to rest.

3

The theory of cost inflation[1]

J. K. BOWERS

A rise in the money supply, according to the monetarists, is a necessary and sufficient condition for an increase in the price level.[2] On the face of it, this statement, while yielding a definition of inflation, tells us nothing of its causes and little of its consequences. We may still ask what forces cause the money supply to rise, what are the consequences, and, given a judgement that the welfare implications of at least more than moderate inflation, are adverse, what ought to be done to reduce it?

The statement is not of course the tautology that it seems and indeed, it is still much disputed. Monetarists claim only that there is a long-run stability in the demand for money schedule, while inflation as perceived by policy-makers and the parties to collective bargaining is very much a problem of the here and now. But the proposition derives its import from another: that the money supply is exogenous to the economic system in the sense of being within the control, and at the discretion of, government. If this is true then the responsibility for inflation lies ultimately with government. This will be so whether the source of inflation is excess monetary demand deriving from excessive public expenditure or, as some monetarists now concede to be possible, attempts by trade unions to sustain excessive rates of growth of money wages, either from a refusal to accept the current distribution of income, or the current rate of growth of real GNP. Whatever the source, a slower growth of the money supply will result in a slowing down of the rate of increase of prices and wages. This slowing down will be accompanied by an increase in un-employment. There will be a permanent increase if the current level is below the natural rate (for those who accept the concept); but in addition the disequilibrium dynamics of the economy mean that the path to lower inflation scales the heights of unemployment. A return to lower inflation, that is, requires that unemployment shall rise temporarily above its natural or sustainable level.

It is clear that, until recently at least, British governments have not behaved as though the growth of the money supply was a variable which could be used to control the rate of inflation. Indeed, under the influence of the thinking of the Radcliffe Report,[3] they have not accepted that monetary discipline would have much helped in the matter. But identification of error is not enough; the monetarist must still face the question of why successive governments have, through their monetary policies, generated high and rising levels of inflation, since it is only through the answer to this question that one can evaluate the proposition that an active monetary policy — meaning, in the present context, a slow growth of the money supply bringing down the level of money wage settlements and raising the level of unemployment — is possible.

One answer as given by Brittan[2] in a good neo-classical tradition, is that the money supply has been expanded as a consequence of excess demand in the market for votes. Governments have sought to ensure re-election by initiating and sustaining large public expenditure programmes, avoiding the tax increases necessary to finance them, by seeking to maintain unemployment at unrealistically low levels and by refusing to allow excessive wage settlements to result in unemployment. But the analogy of the election system with factor and product markets is somewhat strained. For a start all consumers have the same amount to spend and must spend it all, if at all, on one commodity. In addition an election has many characteristics of an auction for public goods. Voting for a party does not ensure that you receive the benefits of its programme and voting against it does not prevent you benefiting either. Candidates for elections are not selling a commodity or a service in any meaningful sense, and even if individuals seek election for the personal rewards it brings, political parties do not. To a greater or lesser extent governments are arbiters of conflicting interests and pursue as they see it and define it, the public welfare or the national interest. Whether any have ever fallen from a surfeit of taxation or unemployment is not clear, but at least one has fallen, and several have tottered, through attempting to restrain inflation.

There are good reasons for doubting whether unemployment, or the threat of it, will have any effect on the level of money wage demands if that is the source of inflation. A rise in unemployment entails little[4] or no[5] increase in the probability of becoming unemployed for the majority of the workforce. Rather it entails an increase in the expected duration of unemployment for those who do become unemployed. The majority of those becoming unemployed become so as a result of quitting a job, not from being sacked,[6] so any rise in risk can be offset by a reduction in turnover or an increased emphasis on searching while employed. That turnover has a tendency to be inversely correlated with unemployment is well known.

The group with the highest probability of becoming unemployed, the under 25s, become so largely as a result of voluntary quitting, have a low expected

40

duration even with current levels of unemployment, and probably have little impact on union wage policies. The group with the highest expected duration, the over 55s, have a very low quit rate and hence a low probability of unemployment.

Furthermore, it is now well established that unemployment is concentrated on a small section of the labour force, and particularly on disadvantaged sections of it.[7] The burden of unemployment is particularly borne by the unskilled and by those unfortunate enough to have a past history of unemployment.[8] The concentration of unemployment is shown most starkly in a study by Owen which revealed that 50 per cent of the total male unemployment weeks recorded over the period 1970–74 were experienced by only 3 per cent of the labour force.[9] Thus the group which carries the burden of unemployment is much smaller than the unemployment rate would suggest.

Thus for the bulk of the workforce the threat to job security implied by rising levels of unemployment, is unlikely to have much impact on wage demands. Indeed, far from reducing the level of wage demands and settlements, current levels of unemployment could even increase them. Reduced opportunities for job change means a closure of one avenue for sustaining or increasing the rate of money wage rises. The result may be increased militancy rather than the reverse.

While current levels of unemployment leave the bulk of the workforce largely unaffected, there must presumably be some unemployment level at which the sanction will 'bite' by raising the probability of unemployment. The presumption must be that the disadvantaged groups will become even more disadvantaged before unemployment becomes a threat to most workers, so that, that level could be very high indeed. A. J. Brown's[10] estimate of 10–12 per cent does not seem excessive, particularly when one realizes that this level is already approached, eg on Merseyside, with no apparent effect on the levels of wage demands or settlements. Beveridge's work suggests that increasing duration rather than increasing unemployment inflows was the major component of unemployment increases in the 1920s and 1930s.[11]

If inflation is inequitable, unemployment is much more so, and governments are correct, therefore, in refusing to countenance it as a cure for inflation. Thus, the monetarist solution to inflation does not appear to be a feasible one. The level of damage that will result before monetary discipline starts to work is likely to be severe, and the resulting unemployment intolerable.

If this is so, then even if the control of the monetary supply is politically feasible, and technically so, the costs of its use far outweigh the benefits, and since the costs are borne particularly by a group which is largely not responsible for the problem, to a government which accepts some duty to protect the needs of the weak against the claims of the strong, it is not an exogenous variable in the relevant sense. It might be an exogenous variable to a cynical manipulator in the market for votes if the electoral consequences of unemployment are small while those of inflation large, or to an hypothetical dictator.[12] For the rest the money supply is socially endogenous and a search for a cure for inflation must start from an analysis of its causes.

I propose to concentrate on the rate of increase in money wages. I recognize that a full model of inflation has to take account of other elements of cost and to account also for the translation of wage rises into price rises. Nonetheless in the opinion of many writers and policy makers it is pressure for money wage rises that is the key element in the level of inflation.

In the opinion of some economists, explanations of the rate of inflation lie outside of the realm of economics as traditionally conceived, or at least as conceived by the neo-classical tradition. An example of this sort of view is the paper by Wiles.[13] Thus 'We have moved from wage claims based on the actual situation . . . through claims based on concessions made elsewhere in the economy to claims picked out of the air'. Rising wage claims in Wiles' view are 'explained' by the impact of the 'New Left' with its 'anti-nomianism irrationalism and total disregard for social consequences'; 'by pure historical chance [that] left-wingers have replaced right-wingers at the heads of great unions'; and by comparisons with settlements in foreign countries facilitated by improvements in communications. Less iconoclastic views stress the lack of concensus on the distribution of income between labour and capital, this conflict having been intensified by the decay of the social order entailing a weakening of the inhibitions imposed by the old status order and a breakdown in the accepted rationalizations for income differentials.[14] These views make interesting reading, especially when written by a good sociologist, but they hardly give much comfort to the economist. One is left with the view only that the rate of inflation is indeterminate within very wide limits and that we are in the grip of social forces over which we have no control and about which we have little understanding. The desire for quantification, evaluation and prescription which in this context at least distinguishes the economist from the sociologist[15] is not satisfied.

An alternative but related approach is via the so-called wage-wage spiral. A disagreement over relativities between groups of wage bargainers who are making coercive comparisons, one with another, can generate a perpetual cycle of inflation. If the parties to the comparisons attempt to anticipate their peer-group's response then this can lead to accelerating rather than, in the absence of anticipation, constant inflation.[16] Wage-wage spirals may be started or exacerbated by changes in views about appropriate relativities or by economic forces (Wood calls them anomic) which disturb them. The prediction from such theories is that if observations can be made at a frequency greater than the wage-round, a cyclical pattern of relativities should be observed. What precisely constitutes appropriate coercive groups or bargaining units is open to discussion, but in any case, given a wage-round frequency of one year or so, the existing published data is not appropriate for testing the theory. Furthermore, unless wage settlements are synchronized, fluctuations in relativities will be observed in any case. Distinguishing between regular cycles generated by coercive comparisons with disagreements on appropriate relativities and situations where economic forces are keeping relativities at a constant level is thus extremely difficult. Wood is reduced to citing tangential evidence in favour of his view of the wage-bargaining process.

But as well as providing an index of relative social worth and social status, the wage structure, in theory at least, has the function of allocating labour between sectors. Wood recognizes this in his distinction between anomic and normative forces but many of the other writings on the role of relativities in inflation ignore it because the authors believed that relativities did not fulfil this role. Most theorists who argue for a rational wage structure via the inauguration of some form of job evaluation allot some minor role to the forces of supply and demand and the concept of a 'just wage' contains some allowance for the impact of supply and demand.[17]

Provided that money wages are rigid downwards the re-allocation of labour by changing relativities will generate wage inflation even without defensive reaction to restore relativities.

Consider a two-sector economy with, in terms of employment, a growing 'g' and a static 's' sector. The labour force is homogeneous and total employment is constant.

At a given time the total wage bill

$$= E_g W_g + E_s W_s$$

where E, W are employment and the wage rate respectively. Now transfer ΔE workers from s to g by raising W_g by ΔW. The resulting distribution satisfies both sectors so that an excess demand for labour, after the transfer, does not exist in 's'.

Define

$$\dot{e}_g = \frac{\Delta E}{E_g} \; ; \; \dot{W}_g = \frac{\Delta W}{W_g}$$

The elasticity of labour supply to g

$$l_g = \frac{\dot{e}_g}{\dot{W}_g}$$

The wage bill will increase if:

$$\Delta EW_g + \Delta E\Delta W + \Delta WE_g > \Delta EW_s$$

Manipulation gives the condition as:

$$1 + \frac{1}{l_g}(1 + \dot{e}_g) > \frac{W_s}{W_g}$$

and the wage bill will increase if:

(i) $W_g \geqslant W_s$

or (ii) If these conditions do not hold and $\dot{e}_g$ is small an increase in the total wage bill will occur if $l_g < 1$ provided that $\frac{W_s}{W_g} < 2$.

On a realistic upper limit of $\frac{W_s}{W_g}$ of 1.40, the limiting upper value of l_g is 2.5. With the mean observed annual value of $\dot{e}_g$ of 0.16 (1948—75 *see below*) and $\frac{W_s}{W_g}$ = 1.40 an increase in the wage bill will occur if $l_g < 2.9$.

Thus in general transfers between sectors with downward rigidity of wages can be expected to raise the money wage bill.[18]

Inter-sectoral transfers in employment are small relative to the volume of labour turnover.[19] The reason for this lies in the fact that there is imperfect information in the labour market. But the important source of imperfection is not, as is often suggested, imperfect information about the location and condition of jobs on offer, but rather imperfect information about the net advantages of these jobs. The quoted wage rate, and even the concomitant conditions of employment as presented to the job applicant, do not, and from their nature, cannot, reveal what the job is worth to him, and therefore, what level of wage payment he will require to compensate him for its conditions. The prospective employee can only determine this by sampling. If the conditions as perceived by him are not fully compensated for by the wage rate then he will quit and move elsewhere. The consequence is that employers can usually get as many employees as they wish, but a large proportion will quit within the first few months of employment.

In raising his wage therefore, the employer is operating not on his ability to attract workers, or his recruitment function, but on his ability to retain them — on his quit function. New employees normally take some time to reach full productivity and they often undergo a formal on- or off-the-job programme of specific training as well. A reduction in the quit rate raises the return to the employer from his labour training. On some reasonable assumptions the employer will prefer to raise his employment by reducing quits than by increasing hires. The quit rate declines rapidly with length of service of the employee and reaches a low level after one or two years, so that such a policy with a typical medium level of turnover of 3—4 per cent per month will lead to a quite rapid rise in employment without the need for increasing recruitment.

If maintained for a sufficient period and starting from a position of equilibrium where total hires equal total quits, a rise in relative wages, with constant hires will cause the firm to converge ultimately on a new higher employment level. But given the length of working life of the typical employee, and the fact that most quits, and hence most hires are of younger workers, the period of adjustment will be very long. The expanding firm will aim, therefore, to cut the process off by subsequently reducing its hires. The known facts of labour turnover are compatible with this view, hires show less variance than discharges, but the two series are positively correlated. When plotted against each other they exhibit loops whose direction is in conformity with hires lagging on discharges.[20]

If the increase in the wage differential is subsequently eliminated, the firm will return again to its previous employment level, but because quits decline with length of service it will return at a much slower rate than it grew. An example illustrating this point is given as an appendix. In expanding by reducing quits the firm has altered the length of service structure of its employment and this cannot quickly be altered since long-service employees have low quit rates.

Thus the growing firm will not be under strong pressure to resist a restoration of previous differentials, provided that it has maintained the change in differentials for sufficient time to achieve its new desired employment levels. Unless it wishes to continue to grow, it will not be under an incentive to retaliate. To raise its employment level the firm has thus only to alter differentials for a period whose length depends on the elasticity of the quit rate to the wage differential and the slope of the function relating quit rates to length of service. In the limiting case, if quits only took place in the first period of service, and the firm desired a once and for all increase in its employment, it would only need to increase the wage differential for one period.[21]

The elimination of the differential might of course be resisted by the employees. The writers on the wage structure seem agreed however, that ideas of fairness and appropriateness change only slowly and that changed patterns of demand are not generally accepted as legitimizing alternations in the wages structure,[22] so we may surmise that if retaliation does occur it is likely to be muted and consequent echoes and shocks highly damped.

The upshot of this extended discussion is the hypothesis that allowing for retaliation to restore differentials we may expect the percentage increase in the total wage bill arising from the process of employment re-allocation to approximately equal to the percentage increase in the wage in the expanding sector.

If a firm is trying to expand when total employment is declining, then its problems of expansion will be eased. The decline in employment, implying a decline in job opportunities, will result in a reduction in quit rates, thus reducing the change in differentials necessary to bring about a given increase in employment. The total change in employment is the weighted sum of the rate of growth in the growing sector and the rate of decline in the declining sector. This latter is the independent element to be introduced into an equation explaining the rate of wage inflation resulting from the process of employment change. Thus if $\dot{e}_s$ is defined similarly to $\dot{e}_g$, and $\dot{W}$ (without a subscript) is the change in the total wage bill. We hypothesize that:

$$\dot{W} = f(\dot{e}_g \; ; \dot{e}_s)$$

and specifically

$$\dot{W} = \frac{1}{l_g} \dot{e}_g + l_q \dot{e}_s$$

where l_q is a measure of the response of the quit rate in sector 'g' to changes in $\dot{e}_s$. If $\dot{e}_s$ is measured as positive we predict

$$l_g > 0 \; ; l_q < 0$$

A precise division between a growing and declining sector would require data on employment by establishment. This we do not have. As the best available approximation we have examined employment by Minimum List Heading at successive June counts for the period 1951–75, and divided the MLHs into growing and declining groups by the employment change between successive years. Implicitly, therefore, we have assumed that employment is growing in all establishments classified to MLHs where total employment is growing and vice versa. With this division

$$\dot{e}_g = \frac{E_{t+1} - E_t}{E_t} \quad \text{and} \quad \dot{e}_s = \frac{E_t - E_{t+1}}{E_t}$$

$$E_{t+1} > E_t \qquad\qquad E_{t+1} \leqslant E_t$$

46

The Standard Industrial Classification changes twice over the period covered but since there are between 150 and 200 MLHs in all cases the effect of changes of classification is not detectable in the resulting series of $\dot{e}_g$ and $\dot{e}_s$. Some standard statistical tests were made to confirm this.

$\dot{e}_g$ is plotted as part (a) of Chart 1, and $\dot{e}_s$ as part (b). $\dot{e}_g$ shows large fluctuations but, as revealed by the fitting of moving averages, showed an upwards trend from about 1968. After falling in the early 1950s, $\dot{e}_s$ trended upwards until the end of the 1960s, and fell thereafter. $\dot{e}_g$ and $\dot{e}_s$ are uncorrelated.[23]

The argument so far has proceeded on the implicit assumption that employers in the expanding sector are able to get the extra labour that they require. If the degree of unsatisfied demand varies over time this will impart a bias to our measurement of the inflationary effects of employment transfers. As a measure of this disequilibrium we use the coefficient of variation of vacancy rates measured (for this is all that is available) across industrial orders. A positive coefficient is of course predicted. The variable designated as C(v) is plotted as part (c) of Chart 1. It is calculated for December vacancy rates, ie in the mid-point of the year over which $\dot{e}_g$ and $\dot{e}_s$ are calculated. C(v) was higher in the 1960s than the 1950s and arguably higher still in the 1970s, but relative to any possible trend, the fluctuations are large.

$\dot{W}$ is calculated from the June values of the monthly index of average weekly earnings of manual workers and is defined, comparably with the employment variables, ie

$$\dot{W} = \frac{W_{t+1} - W_t}{W_t}$$

The fitted OLS equation is as follows:

$$\dot{W} = -27.197^{\varnothing} + 3.410\,\dot{e}_g{}^* -0.006\,\dot{e}_s + 24.812\,C(v)^{\varnothing}$$
$$(1.82) \quad\quad (2.52) \quad\quad\quad (0.05) \quad\quad (1.50)$$

$$R^2 = 0.398 \quad\quad\quad DW = 0.88$$

Numbers in parentheses are 't' statistics.
$^{\varnothing}$ = significant at 0.10 probability level on a 't' test.
* = significant at 0.01 probability level on a 't' test.
NB 't' test for the constant is a two-tailed one since the predicted value is zero.

The equation, without any price or lagged earnings change terms, accounts for almost 40 per cent of the variance. All the explanatory variables have the

CHART 1

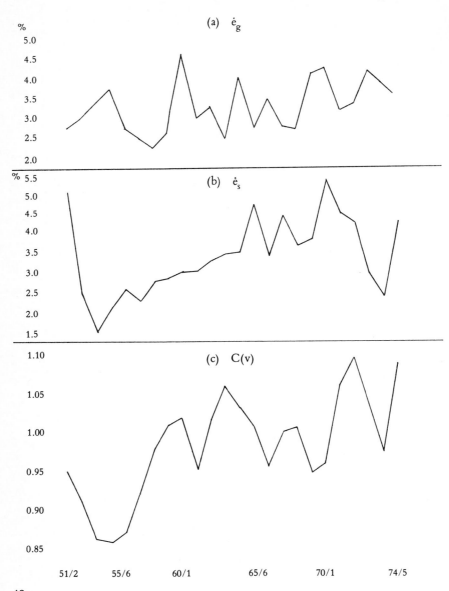

(a) $\dot{e}_g$

(b) $\dot{e}_s$

(c) $C(v)$

right sign but $\dot{e}_s$ is totally insignificant and only $\dot{e}_g$ attains significance at the conventional 5 per cent level. The implied value of l_g is very low at 0.294. This, coupled with the low coefficient on $\dot{e}_s$, suggests that the quit rate is not very responsive to economic forces. The constant term shows a low level of significance. The 't' test is however unreliable since the equation has positive first order serial correlation in the residuals. Inspection of the residuals suggests that the reason for this is that it is under-predicting the level of wage inflation in the 1970s; thus the average value of $\dot{W}$ 1969/70–1974/75 is 15.4 per cent while the average predicted value is 11.6 per cent. The model *is* predicting higher rates of inflation for the 1970s than for the 1950s and 1960s but particularly it is failing to generate the rising values from 1972/73.

The obvious modification, and the simplest, is to allow for an autonomous rise in settlements to compensate for previous price rises. If we include a price change variable calculated in the same way as $\dot{W}$ but lagged by six months (ie computed from December values of the retail price index) we get the following:

$$\dot{W} = -17.279^\varnothing + 2.961\,\dot{e}_g{}^* - 0.628\,\dot{e}_s + 14.567\,C(v)^\varnothing + 0.714\,\dot{p}^*$$
$$(1.73) \qquad (3.33) \qquad (0.86) \qquad (1.43) \qquad (5.27)$$
$$R^2 = 0.735 \qquad\qquad DW = 2.26$$

The introduction of a price term of course raises the problem of whether single equation estimation is correct. If price change is a lagged function of wage change then, provided that the lag of prices on wages is six months or more, the OLS estimators will be efficient.

The introduction of a lagged price term raises the explanation and eliminates the problem of autocorrelation but does not otherwise alter the conclusions previously drawn. $\dot{e}_g$ remains significant and the implied value of l_g at 0.337 is raised only slightly. $\dot{e}_s$ remains insignificant. The size of $C(v)$ falls but its significance level is unaltered. As a regressor it is not well determined but the appropriate way of measuring the dispersion and degree of unsatisfied demand is problematical. The coefficient on $\dot{p}$ implies that about 70 per cent of past changes in prices are compensated for in wage rises over the period. This coefficient is raised to about 0.8 if compensation is assumed to operate only above a threshold of $\dot{p}$ of 10 per cent per annum. That assumption raises the degree of explanation also but it does so by imparting negative autocorrelation to the equation and in any case does not affect the values of the other coefficients.

While the econometric possibilities are not exhausted, enough has been reported for present purposes. It is clear that a wage-price spiral was in progress in the 1970s and this has been the subject of numerous econometric investigations. To explain its genesis one does not need to postulate militant left-wing unions plucking wage demands from the air. The process of transfer of labour between sectors, with the institutional constraints that relativities are altered by wage rises in the expanding sector; that relativities so altered are restored to their previous values by bargaining pressure without setting in being a wage-wage spiral, seems sufficient. Once inflation is into double figures compensatory wage settlements and hence a wage-price spiral is needed to explain events.

APPENDIX

The effect of alterations in the quit rate on the stock of employment[24]

q_1, q_2 and q_3 are respectively the quit rates per period of workers with less than one period's service, between one and two period's service, and more than two period's service. H is the number of hirings per period assumed to take place at the beginning of the period. E is the stock of employment measured at the end of the period made up of E_1, those entering their second period of employment, and E_2 those entering their third or higher period of employment. Thus in a steady state:

$$E_1 = (1 - q_1)H$$

$$E_2 = (1 - q_2)E_1 + (1 - q_3)E_2$$

$$\therefore E = H\left[\frac{(1 - q_1)(1 - q_2) + q_3(1 - q_1)}{q_3}\right]$$

If the initial structure of quit rates is $q_1 = 0.5$; $q_2 = 0.25$; $q_3 = 0.1$, then the steady state employment is:

$$E = 4.25H.$$

Assume that by an increase in its money wage the firm reduces these quit rates to 80 per cent of their previous values, ie $q_1' = 0.40$; $q_2' = 0.20$; $q_3' = 0.08$. This set of values is designated as q'.

The employment stock will converge on a new higher steady state level of:

$$E = 6.6H$$

an increase of about 55 per cent.

To show the speed of adjustment a simulation of the model is given in Chart 2. The level of H has been chosen to give an initial steady-state employment stock of 1000.

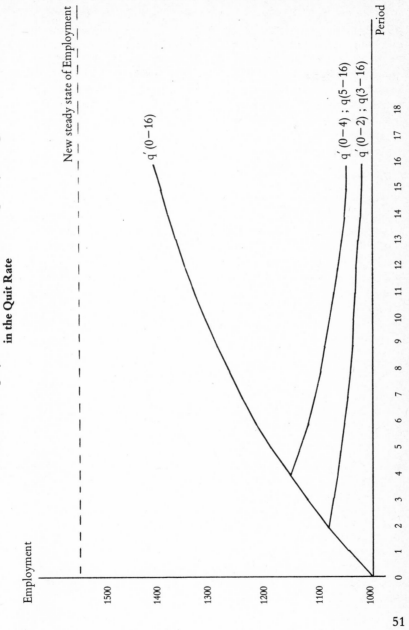

CHART 2

The Effect on Employment of Permanent and Temporary Changes
in the Quit Rate

New steady state of Employment

Employment

1500

1400

1300

1200

1100

1000

$q'(0-16)$

$q'(0-4)$; $q(5-16)$

$q'(0-2)$; $q(3-16)$

0   1   2   3   4   5   6   7   8   9   10   11   12   13   14   15   16   17   18   Period

The adjustment to the new level is very slow with only half of the adjustment made in the first eight periods.

We now consider what happens when the wage differential is eliminated and the quit rates returned to their previous levels after two and four periods. The convergence to the initial employment level is again very slow. It takes six periods to make half the adjustment back in both cases, and fifteen periods for three-quarters of the adjustment. The implication is that the firm can obtain an increase in its employment stock which lasts for a reasonably long time by only a very temporary increase in its relative wage. This is achieved by using the temporary adjustment to secure a change in the length of service composition of its workforce towards employees with a long enough service to have a low quit rate.

Notes

[1] I am grateful to Mike Artis, Dave Deaton, Jerry Turk, and David Worswick for comments on this paper and to Karen Bevins for carrying out the computing. They of course are not responsible for what is written.

[2] Samuel Brittan 'Inflation and Democracy', in Fred Hirsch and John H. Goldthorpe, eds, *The Political Economy of Inflation*, 1978, pp 161–85.

[3] Committee on the Working of The Monetary System. Report. *Command 827*, August 1959.

[4] John Bowers in Royal Commission on the Distribution of Income and Wealth, *Selected Evidence Submitted to the Royal Commission for Report No 6: Lower Incomes*, HMSO, 1978, pp 30, 36–9.

[5] David Metcalfe and Stephen Nickell in Royal Commission on the Distribution of Income and Wealth, op cit, pp 310–28.

[6] When adjusted for those not qualifying for statutory payments, who are not recorded in the official statistics, redundancies constitute at most 10 per cent of total job terminations. On the assumption that all redundancies result in unemployment registrations they constitute at an upper limit 20 per cent of the inflow to the unemployment register. But most of the redundant workers not receiving statutory payments are part-time workers and young workers who probably exert little influence on union wage demands. Statutory redundancies (ie those for whom payment is made) constitute less than 5 per cent of total job terminations. Redundancies are furthermore probably mainly associated with plant closures and bankruptcies. Excessive wage claims are unlikely to have much to do with these. The comment draws on a continuing study on labour hoarding in British industry by J. K. Bowers, D. Deacon and J. Turk, based at the SSRC Industrial Relations Research Unit, University of Warwick.

[7] See — J. K. Bowers and D. Harkess, 'The Duration of Unemployment by Age and Sex', *Economica*, NS 46, 1979; J. Stern, *Who Bears the Burden of Unemployment?* Paper delivered to the Annual Meeting of the British Association for the Advancement of Science, Section F, Bath, September 1978; Metcalfe and Nickell, op cit.

[8] Stern, op cit; M. J. Hill in Royal Commission on the Distribution of Income and Wealth, op cit, pp 195–207.

[9] Susan Owen, 'The Inequality of Male Unemployment and Sickness', University of Cardiff mimeo, 1978.

[10] A. J. Brown, *The Great Inflation, 1939–1951*, Oxford, 1955.

[11] W. Beveridge, 'An Analysis of Unemployment II', *Economica IV*, 1937.

[12] Interestingly, Brittan, op cit, doubts whether the control of inflation, which he assumes is only possible via the control of the money supply, is compatible with the maintenance of democracy.

[13] P. Wiles, 'Cost Inflation and the State of Economic Theory', *Economic Journal*, **83**, 1973, pp 377–98.

[14] John H. Goldthorpe, 'The Current Inflation: Towards a Sociological Account', in Hirsch and Goldthorpe, op cit.

[15] See the exchange between Goldthorpe and Brittan, loc cit.

[16] For a careful and stimulating analysis of the wage-wage spiral see, Adrian Wood, *A Theory of Pay*, Cambridge, 1978, Chapter 5.

[17] See eg Michael Fogarty, *The Just Wage*, 1961, Appendix. The need for wage flexibility to permit the re-allocation of labour is a perennial problem for incomes policies. Failure to cope with it has been a large contributory factor in the breakdown of policies and attempts to allow for flexibility a factor in their ineffectiveness.

[18] A Paasche index will indicate a higher rate of inflation than a Laspeyres index by the amount $\Delta E \Delta W$ which by assumption is positive. These indices in principle yield an alternative technique to that used for estimating l_g but the data is not immediately available for their calculation.

[19] See eg J. K. Bowers, 'Labour Mobility and Economic Depression', University of Leeds, School of Economic Studies Discussion Paper, no 28, 1975.

[20] See, J. K. Bowers, P. C. Cheshire and A. E. Webb, 'The Change in the Relationship Between Unemployment and Earnings Increases: a Review of some Possible Explanations', *National Institute Economic Review*, no 54, 1970.

[21] This is not quite correct since after a considerable period of time the firm would need to compensate for a higher volume of retirements from its new larger labour force. But if its new employees are younger ones this complication has no practical import.

[22] For a good discussion of the evidence see Adrian Wood, op cit.

[23] $r = 0.071$.

[24] I am grateful to Mr D. Deaton for devising and computing this example.

4

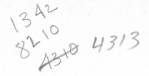

Inflation, real wages and the terms of trade[1]

M. J. ARTIS and M. H. MILLER

Introduction

Friedman's comments on the Phillips curve (see, eg Friedman, 1968) reminded economists of the perils run by theories of wage inflation which neglect to take account of the behaviour of real wages in analysing the process of wage inflation. By introducing inflation expectations into the Phillips curve, Friedman sought to rescue this approach from the assumption of money illusion. Whilst Friedman's suggestion has been widely adopted in empirical work in the UK and elsewhere, an alternative approach which emphasizes even more clearly the role of real wages (by putting lagged real wages explicitly into the Phillips curve) has also commanded considerable, and growing, attention. Two notable proponents of this view are Sargan (1964) and latterly Hicks (1974). It is this approach, termed here 'the real wage hypothesis', which together with the augmented Phillips curve appears to dominate current empirical work on the subject.

Thus, in what follows, what we have attempted to do is, first, to describe some of the existing estimates corresponding to each of these two hypotheses and briefly to indicate the kinds of problem which confront those who have tried to implement them. Second, we explore some of the properties of a wage-price system where the determination of wages is characterized by one or other of these two hypotheses; in particular, we look at the consequences for inflation and real wages of exogenous price and demand shocks in an open economy. Finally, we have drawn together some conclusions reflecting the relative strengths and weaknesses of these two rival views of wage behaviour.

Empirical results

Considering the large volume of empirical work on wage inflation, the fact that 'useless' results are typically not published, and the profusion of variables employed, including alternative versions of the dependent wage inflation variable, the task of drawing up a representative summary is not straight-forward. However, in Table 1, we have listed the results of a number of recent studies, in as standardized a form as seems feasible.[2] The notes accompanying

E

the table elucidate the sources and variable definitions; in the text we have endeavoured to draw out what seem to us to be the outstanding characteristics of the results.

Estimates of the *augmented Phillips curve* are represented in the table by results quoted from the studies by Nordhaus, Henry, Sawyer, Smith (1), Parkin, Sumner and Ward, and most recently, Sumner. In its expectations-augmented form, verification of the Phillips curve requires both that a measure of the excess supply of labour (usually unemployment) carry a significant negative coefficient and, if people are rational, that the coefficient on the inflation expectations term be unity. It is not at all clear that the data are consistent with these restrictions as is attested by the results quoted in the table from the studies by Nordhaus and Henry, Sawyer, Smith.

There are, however, problems in measuring both the variables to which the estimated coefficients attach. Thus it is no longer widely accepted that unemployment is a good measure of excess supply in the labour market; and there are different views as to the best proxy for inflation expectations.

Since there is no direct measure of the amount of inflation anticipated when wage bargaining takes place, the results reported represent both a test of the investigator's theory of the generation of such expectations, and a test of the impact of such expectations on wage bargaining. The studies reported in the table have adopted two alternatives in respect of measuring inflation expectations. Nordhaus and Henry, Sawyer, Smith (1) assume that such expectations are a moving average of past inflation; by contrast, the two studies with which Sumner's name is associated rely on data derived from survey sources (eg Carlson and Parkin, 1975). Clearly, both the differences between studies, and the discrepancies between the results actually obtained and the corresponding theoretical restrictions may be due to the nature of the inflation expectations proxy which is used. This does not conclude the difficulties to which the inclusion of expectations may give rise, however. In particular, different price indices are relevant for the expectations held by employers as for those held by employees; even at the aggregate level in an open economy discrepancies between the relevant price indices are enforced by the presence of imports and exports and indirect taxes. The Parkin, Sumner and Ward study makes the greatest concession of those quoted in Table 1 in the direction of attempting to resolve this problem, by providing for the separate specification of expectations of domestic inflation by wage earners and of inflation in export and home prices by employers, as well as including expectations of tax rate changes. Elsewhere, Parkin (with Duck, Rose and Zis, 1976) has explored an alternative method of handling this problem involving aggregation to a 'world' level.[3]

Friedman's restatement of the Phillips curve provided for a 'natural' rate of unemployment corresponding to that level at which steady state inflation would proceed, if labour market participants were free of money illusion; lower levels of unemployment would be accompanied by (or, looked at the other way round, would be purchased at the cost of) accelerating inflation; and conversely for levels of unemployment exceeding the natural rate. Both the terminology and the context of the argument suggest that the natural rate of unemployment, though not a constant, will be fairly stable in the short run. Nonetheless, empirical estimation of augmented Phillips curves has only proceeded with any degree of success when the natural rate has itself been allowed to increase over the estimation period (ie during the 1960s). Estimates which derive this shift as a residual (using dummy variables as required to give the right sign on unemployment and a coefficient of unity on inflation expectations) are obviously not very convincing; the more recent studies, however, have relied on an explanation sympathetic to the literature on the 'search' theory of unemployment, viz that the real value of unemployment benefits (relative to the real wage) has increased sharply over the period, notably since the first introduction of earnings-related benefits in 1966 and as a consequence of the subsequent up-rating of this element of the dole. The equation quoted from Sumner's most recent study, in particular, depends crucially on the role of the benefit/earnings ratio. Thus, Sumner first estimates (over the whole period) an equation for unemployment in which the benefits/earnings ratio (B/E) appears and on the basis of these estimates subsequently produces a series for 'adjusted unemployment', which is provided by the equation predictions when the ratio B/E is set at its mean value. Sumner then uses the adjusted unemployment series in an augmented Phillips curve to provide the estimate quoted in the table.[4] Implicit in the adjustment of the unemployment figures is an increase in the natural rate of unemployment of some 1.5 percentage points over the period to 1974/75 bringing it to a value of some 5.1 per cent in these last two years.

Doubts must surely be expressed both about the magnitude of this increase in the natural rate of unemployment and about its exclusive attribution to the behaviour of the variable B/E. However that may be, it is worth noting that the behaviour of unemployment as a labour market indicator is a matter of concern to other investigators who have approached the question from a different viewpoint: it would be quite wrong to imply that the problem has only to be faced by those who wish to fit augmented Phillips curves; thus, in so far as formulations of the real wage hypothesis have also required a labour market demand indicator they also are confronted, as we shall see, by the need to account for the aberrant behaviour of unemployment *vis-à-vis* alternative indicators of the labour market.

Certainly the latest, and possibly the most successful of the Phillips curve estimates quoted in the table is that estimated by Sumner, according to which the slope of the short run Phillips curve may be approximated by the value -1. But it will be seen that, by contrast, the two studies listed immediately below carry 'perverse' coefficients on unemployment, and although the restricted equation from Parkin, Sumner and Ward (PSW) study suggests a significant and correctly signed coefficient, their unrestricted estimates suggested an insignificant effect. The performance of inflation-expectation variables is also mixed; although insignificant in Nordhaus' study, the coefficient estimate in Henry, Sawyer, Smith (1) approximates the 'required' value of unity, whilst the restricted value of unity placed on the sum of the coefficients on the three expectational variables in the PSW equation was supported by an approximately similar result in the unrestricted estimate of their equations. There is no direct test of the expectational hypotheses available from the Sumner study (see notes to Table 1), although for purposes of the forecasting exercise conducted with the equation Sumner assumes the absence of money illusion and also notes that in unrestricted estimates the hypothesis that the sum of the price coefficients is unity 'is rejected by the narrowest of margins' (Sumner, 1977, p 18).

The over-all performance of augmented Phillips curve estimates is thus clearly less than resoundingly successful in respect of the principal requirements of the hypothesis. A proponent might argue his case on the need for very careful and detailed specifications, whilst appealing to the ample scope for error afforded by the undoubtedly difficult problem presented by the range of available data (see below). A less sympathetic observer would be more inclined to argue from the lack of robustness of the approach to differences in specification that the hypothesis itself is not empirically sustained by recent UK experience.

Formulations of the *real wage hypothesis* are represented in Table 1 by equations drawn from two studies by Sargan and from those listed by Apps, Artis, Henry, Sawyer, Smith (2), and Johnston and Timbrell. The earliest estimates following this approach were in fact produced some ten years ago, by Sargan (1964) — shown as Sargan (1) in the table — and by Gillion (1968), but little notice seems to have been taken of them at the time. The recent flurry of work in this area and the sympathetic descriptions of wage behaviour to be found in, for example, Hicks (1974) thus represent a line of argument which has not yet been digested by the profession, and the hypothesis has not, so far, met with the kind of theoretical acceptance accorded to the Phillips curve.

The basic assumption of the real wage hypothesis is that money wage inflation is to be related to the discrepancy between a *'target'* or *'bargaining-equilibrium' real wage rate* and the *actual real wage*. Unemployment, or other labour market indicators, are allowed to modify the outcome either by affecting the *'target'* ('bargaining-equilibrium') itself or by slowing down the *rate* at which a discrepancy between actual and target real wages works its way into money wage inflation. In addition it is possible, but not essential, that inflation expectations could 'gear up' any money wage rate increase otherwise arrived at. On this basis, the estimating equation for the real wage hypothesis will look like an augmented Phillips curve with the addition of a term in the lagged real wage.

This general formulation, however, lends itself to significant variations. First, in some studies (although not those of Sargan) the 'bargaining-equilibrium' or 'target' real wage is denoted in after-tax terms, which introduces a direct linkage between tax rate changes and wage inflation. Secondly, the relationship may be reformulated so as to link money wage inflation to a 'catch-up' variable which expresses the amount by which real (pre- or post-tax) wages have failed to grow in line with the target over a specified (limited) period: this formulation in effect confines the extent to which past unsatisfied wage demands linger on in determining wage inflation and may also be expressed in asymmetrical form, where only downward deviations from target are registered in the catch-up variable. (As in Johnston and Timbrell's study: see notes to Table 1.)

A difficulty with the approach in general is the specification of how the target or bargaining-equilibrium real wage is generated. In most applications the functional form employed implies that the target real wage is generated by a log-linear time trend with modifications due to unemployment and incomes policy (alternatively, these variables are regarded as modifying the rate at which frustrated real wage demands are translated into wage inflation).

Thus, a general form of the estimating equation employed — where of variables whose meaning is not obvious, λ is the retention ratio (or one minus the average tax rate) and F is a dummy for incomes policy — is (with g denoting a growth rate):

$$gw = a_0 + a_1 g\lambda + a_2 gp^e + a_3 \, time + a_4 \left(\frac{\lambda w}{p}\right)_{-1} + a_5 F + a_6 U$$

where *a priori* expectations are that:

$$a_1 < 0 \qquad\qquad a_4 < 0$$
$$a_2 > 0 \qquad\qquad a_5 < 0$$
$$a_3 > 0 \qquad\qquad a_6 < 0$$

The distinguishing characteristic of the real wage hypothesis is that the coefficient on the lagged real wage term should be significantly negative, a prediction which is borne out with the exception of the equation due to Apps in the equation results noted in the table. Since the effect of inflation on real wages is captured by this term, it appears less crucial that the expectation term should be significant than is the case for the augmented Phillips curve (we comment more extensively on this point in the next section), and it is clear that the inflation-expectation term does not feature consistently in the real wage equations reported.[5]

Despite the fact that the real wage approach in most formulations shares with the Phillips curve an assumption that labour market conditions count in the determination of wage inflation, it is equally clear that the unemployment variable does not feature strongly in the estimated equations. The chief exception is that due to Artis, where two dummy variables were introduced to mark the points at which the relation between vacancies and unemployment was found to have changed. The contribution that these made to the increase in the 'zero-inflation rate of unemployment' over the period is of the order of 1.6 points, a contribution quite close to the effect attributed by Sumner to the increase in the B/E variable.

In any event the slope of the 'short run Phillips curve' implicit in these estimates is shallower than traditional in the literature as approximated by the Parkin, Sumner and Ward and Sumner equations reported in the table (it will be recalled that the wrong signs are evident in the Nordhaus and Henry, Sawyer, Smith (1) equations). A tabulation of the point estimates of the short-run effect of a one-percentage-point increase in unemployment on the rate of wage inflation — assuming that unemployment starts at 2 per cent — establishes this:

Sumner	-0.9470^* ('adjusted' unemployment)
Parkin, Sumner and Ward	-1.9973^*
Henry, Sawyer, Smith (1)	$-0.04 \ (= -0.0008 \times 100/2)$
Apps	$-0.48 \ (= -0.0048 \times 100)$
Sargan (1)	$-0.60 \ (= -0.0120 \times 100/2)$
Sargan (2)	$-0.38 \ (= -0.00768 \times 100/2)$
Artis	$-1.60 \ (= -0.016 \times 100)$

* indicates significance at customary levels

The structural stability of equations in the 'real wage' vein has been little investigated, but, where it has, it has usually been found wanting (Artis, 1976b). However, a significant difference is made to this conclusion when real wages are taken after tax.[6] Whether deductions from wages by way of tax should have the same 'weight' as deductions inflicted by way of a rise in prices has, again, been little investigated, although the result quoted from Apps was an attempt to answer the question by partitioning the lagged after-tax real wage into two components. It is difficult to believe however, that the implication of the resultant estimates that price rises have no effect and tax increases have strong effects is other than a statistical quirk. The problem still remains to be sorted out.

It is apparent in other ways also that estimates of the real wage hypothesis are as yet unsatisfactory. The approach probably requires modelling the process of generating the real wage target in more sophisticated ways, more decisive tests of the relative significance of taxes and prices, and some attempt to assess the importance of the 'social wage' as a potentially offsetting factor.

Some common problems
Neither the collection of equations representing various attempts to implement the augmented Phillips approach nor the collection of real wage equations could be said to contain estimates which are particularly robust with respect to what might appear to be minor modifications of the specifications used, and it cannot be said that there are as yet well-established results in this area; on the contrary, there are, as has been indicated, a number of outstanding unsettled problems. Incorporated in Table 1 are equations taken from the major macro models (HMT, LBS, NIESR), initially included for the sake of completeness and in order to demonstrate the type of approach employed by the major forecasting agencies. Indicative of the state of the art, however, it has to be noted that only one of these equations (the LBS equation) is employed in current forecasting (and interestingly, it predicts the *real wage* as defined).

Quite apart from differences of interpretation and setting aside for the moment those considerations that would suggest that wage inflation has a considerable 'political' component unamenable to econometric analysis, the raw material itself presents a number of difficult problems. The difficulties of measuring expectations, vital to some views of the inflation process, have been adverted to above and in any case are well known; also mentioned earlier are the problems of identifying a satisfactory measure of excess supply and demand in the labour market. Aside from these two major difficulties, further problems are presented by the intermittent, but nearly continuous intrusion of incomes policy, the effects, after-effects and anticipation of which seem likely to confuse the picture considerably, whilst the basic data series themselves have increasingly come under criticism. Most theories of inflation implicitly address themselves to wage *settlements*, but the raw data of empirical wage inflation

61

	Constant	U	U^{-1}	U^{-4}	$\dot{U}$	$\dot{P}^F$
Parkin, Sumner, Ward Restricted Estimates 1965 I — 1971 IV	5.9108 (1.6465)	−1.9973 (0.8086) All	—	—	—	0.29 (0.11
Sumner 1952–1965 Annual	6.3668* (0.9902)	−0.9470 (0.3546)	—	—	—	*
Henry, Sawyer, Smith (1) 1949 I — 1974 II	8.364 (1.08)	—	−13.674 (2.052)	7.016 (1.474)	−0.0083 (0.0073)	0.93 (0.05
Nordhaus 1955 — 1971 Annual	0.0543	—	−0.151 (0.389)	—	—	0.60 (0.89
Henry, Sawyer, Smith (2) 1948 I — 1974 IV	−0.0059 (0.026)	$(\ln U)_{-1}$ 0.00083 (0.0066)	—	—	—	0.58 (0.13
Apps 1949 II — 1974 IV	0.0278 (0.031)	−0.0048 $(0.0068)^{-1}$	—	—	—	0.36 (0.15
Sargan (1) 1947 — 1960 Quarterly	—	$(\ln U)_{-1}$ −0.0120 (0.0058)	—	—	—	—
Sargan (2) 1949 IV — 1968 IV	0.2818 (0.1059)	$(\ln U)_{-1}$ −0.00768 (0.00468)	—	—	—	−0.00 (0.00
Johnston-Timbrell 1959 — 1971 Annual	−3.900	—	—	—	—	0.84 (0.18
Artis 1950 — 1974 Quarterly	0.973 (0.319)	−0.016 (0.0044)	—	—	—	—
NIESR	0.040	−0.238	—	—	—	0.39
London Business School†	−0.8698	—	—	—	—	—
HM Treasury	0.68566	—	—	—	—	—

Standard errors are shown in parentheses; for detailed definition of variables and sources see the note following.

* Consumers' inflation expectations incorporated in constant term (see note).

† Dependent variable real earnings rather than money earnings (see note).

ps Curve and the Real Wage Hypothesis

$\dot{P}^E_E$	$\dot{P}^E_F$	Trend	$\ln(W/P)_{t-1}$	Other variables				$\bar{R}^a$	DW
				(D62)	(D66)	(T_1)	(T_2+T_3)		
027	0.2029	—	—	0.4607	−1.0612	−0.7056	−0.2944	0.432	1.689
948) $+\theta\Delta q$	(0.2280)			(1.55886)	(1.5160)	(0.1142)	(0.1141)		
142 273)	—	—	—	(D62) −1.0300 (0.7153)	—	—	—	0.776	1.480
—	—	—	—	—	—	—	—	0.830 SE	0.758
—	—	—	—	—	—	—	—	1.46	—
—	—	0.00066 (0.00031)	$\ln RNE_{-1}$ −0.1097 (0.055)	—	—	—	—	0.469	1.466
—	—	0.00014 (0.00044)	$\ln(E/P)_{-1}$ −0.0622 (0.0582)	$\ln\lambda$ −0.269 (0.0796)	—	—	—	0.507	1.46
—	—	0.00133 (0.00036)	$\ln(W/P)_{-1}$ −0.271 (0.073)	—	—	—	—	R 0.00496	—
—	—	—	$\ln(W/P)_{-1}$ −0.0699 (0.0278)	$(Y/h)_{-t}$ 0.0507 (0.0216)	—	—	—	R 0.439	1.73
—	—	—	—	(C_4) 1.105 (0.373)	(n/N) 3.72 (3.41)	—	—	0.758	1.50
—	—	0.001 (0.0004)	$\ln(\lambda w/P)_{-1}$ −0.182 (0.062)	(S_1) 0.012 (0.0064)	(S_2) 0.014	Incomes Policy Dummies	—	—	—
—	—	—	—		$(\dot{W}_{t-1})$ 0.524	—	—	—	—
—	—	0.004249 (0.0005)	—	(RNDI/ GDP) 1.0318 (0.1266)	(PRDM) 0.6238 (0.06)	(DV$_2$) 0.0076 (0.0014)	—	0.991	1.58
(proposed)	—	0.00746	—	$\ln \dfrac{YI}{95(1.0075)}t$		—	—	—	—

63

Notes

PARKIN, SUMNER and WARD (eq 3, p 34 of Inflation Workshop Paper No 7402).

$$\dot{w}_t = 5.9108 - 1.9973\,U + 0.5027\,\dot{P}_E^e + 0.2029\,\dot{P}_F^e + 0.2944\,\dot{P}^e - 0.7056\,T_1$$
$$- 0.2944\,(T_2 + T_3) + 0.4607\,D62 - 1.0612\,D66 + \epsilon$$

dependent variable is change in weekly wage rates $\dot{w}_t = \ln(W_t/W_{t-1}) \times 400$.

$\dot{P}_E^e$ = employers' price expectations (adaptive formation).

$\dot{P}_F^e$ = foreign price expectations (adaptive formation).

$\dot{P}^e$ = consumers' price expectations (Carlson-Parkin).

T_1 = employers' national insurance contribution as proportion of average wage.

$(T_2 + T_3)$ = employees' national insurance contribution as proportion of average wage, plus rate of income tax paid by a married man with one child under 11, one 11–15, earning the average wage.

D62 = dummy variable for pay pause, 1961 III — 1962 II.

D66 = dummy variable for freeze and severe restraint 1966 III — 1967 II.

Quarterly data, quarter on quarter (as for $\dot{w}_t$).

SUMNER (eq 6, p 18 of discussion paper).

$$\Delta W = 6.3668 - 0.9470\,AU + 0.5142\,(\Delta p_w + \hat{\theta}\Delta q) - 1.0300\,D62 + \epsilon$$

dependent variable is percentage change of average wage/salary.

AU = adjusted unemployment rate, adjusted on the basis of changes in benefit/earnings ratio.

$\Delta p_w + \hat{\theta}\Delta q$ = expected rate of inflation held by firms plus 'weighted' rate of change of output per head.

D62 = dummy variable for 1962.

No variable for consumers' inflation expectations is incorporated into this equation. Since the coefficient on Δq was restricted to equal the product of the weighting term $\hat{\theta}$ and the coefficient on producers' inflation expectations, the coefficient on the composite term $\Delta p_w + \hat{\theta}\Delta q$ can be treated as the coefficient on Δp_w alone. Assuming that consumers on average correctly forecast inflation in the estimation period (of 3.006 per cent) and suffered no money illusion, the net-of-expectation component of the constant term can be computed at $6.3688 - 3.006\,(1 - 0.5142) = 4.9065$.

Annual data.

HENRY, SAWYER, SMITH (1) (eq 2, Table 2, Henry, Sawyer and Smith, 1976)

$$\dot{w}_t = 8.364 - 13.674\,U^{-1} + 7.016\,U^{-4} - 0.0083\,\dot{U} + 0.932\,\dot{P} + \epsilon$$

where dependent variable is the rate of change of weekly wage rates, rates of change being defined as the first central difference, centralized over four quarters ie

$$\dot{x} = \frac{x_{t+2} - x_{t-2}}{(x_{t+2} + x_{t-2})/2} \times 100.$$

U = number unemployed, UK, excluding school-leavers, seasonally adjusted.
Quarterly data.

NORDHAUS (for UK from Table 7, p 446, Nordhaus, 1972)
$\Delta \ln W_t = 0.0543 - 0.151 \, U^{-1} + 0.608 \, \Delta \ln P_t + \epsilon$
where dependent variable is hourly earnings per worker in manufacturing industries.
U = civilian unemployment rate.
Annual data.

HENRY, SAWYER, SMITH (2) (Table 9, p 69, Henry, Sawyer and Smith, 1976)
$\Delta \ln W_t = -0.0059 + 0.589 \, \Delta \ln P_{t-1} + 0.00083 \ln U_{t-1} - 0.1097 \ln RNE_{t-1} + 0.00066t + \epsilon$
where dependent variable is rate of change of nominal wages.
P_t = consumer price index ($\Delta \ln P_{t-1}$ proxying $\dot{P}^e$)
U = number unemployed, UK, excluding school-leavers, seasonally adjusted.
RNE = real after tax average earnings.

APPS (Apps, 1976)
$\Delta \ln w_t = 0.0278 + 0.368 \, \Delta \ln P_{t-1} - 0.0048 U_{t-1} + 0.00014t - 0.0622 \ln(E/P)_{t-1} - 0.2691 n \lambda + \epsilon$
as for Henry, Sawyer, Smith (2) with RNE broken down into gross real earnings (E/P) and the retention ratio λ.
Quarterly data.

SARGAN (1) (eq 17, p 44, Sargan, 1964)
$\Delta \ln W_t = -0.0120 \ln U_{t-1} - 0.271 (\ln W_t - \ln P_{t-1}) + 0.00133 \, t + \epsilon$
where dependent variable is first difference of weekly wage rates.
U = percentage index of number wholly unemployed (base 1948).
P = index of retail prices.
Quarterly data.

SARGAN (2) (eq 1A, p 53, Sargan, 1971)

$$\Delta \ln W_t = \underset{(2.66)}{0.2818} - \underset{(2.51)}{0.0699} (\ln W_{t-1} - \ln P_{t-1}) + \underset{(2.35)}{0.0507} \ln (Y_{t-1}/h_{t-1})$$

$$- \underset{(1.64)}{0.00768} \ln U_{t-1} - \underset{(1.63)}{0.00329} \ln (P_{t-1}/P_{t-4}) + \underset{(1.88)}{0.0553} Q_{1t}$$

$$+ \underset{(0.65)}{0.00202} Q_{2t} - \underset{(0.46)}{0.00134} Q_{3t} + \epsilon$$

where

W_t = official wage-rate index.

P_t = official retail price index.

Y_t = real GNP.

h_t = total man hours — number of men × average weekly hours.

U_t = percentage unemployment.

Q_{it} = seasonal dummy for ith quarter.

When the productivity variable is replaced by a linear trend, the implied desired growth of real wage is 1.65 per cent pa (see eq on p 55, Sargan, 1971).

Quarterly data.

JOHNSTON and TIMBRELL (eq 2A, p 92, Johnston and Timbrell, 1974)

$$\dot{w} = -3.990 + 3.72 (n/N) + 0.848\dot{p} + 1.105 C_4 + \epsilon$$

where dependent variable is the annual percentage change in weekly wage rates for all manual workers in all industries and services.

n/N = proportion of workers receiving a wage increase.

$\dot{p}$ = actual change in RPI.

$$C_4 = -\sum_{j=1}^{3} (x_{t-j} - 3\%)$$ is a catch up variable and measures extent to which

increase in net real wage falls short of 3 per cent. Positive values are omitted from the summation.

Annual data.

ARTIS (eq 3.1, Artis *et al*, 1977)

$$\Delta \ln W_t = 0.973 - 0.016 \, U_t + 0.001t - 0.182 \ln \left(\frac{\lambda w}{p}\right)_{t-1} + 0.012 S_1 + 0.014 S_2 + \epsilon$$

seasonal and incomes policy dummies were included but not shown.

Dependent variable is the change in nominal earnings.

U = percentage unemployed.

$\left(\frac{\lambda w}{p}\right)$ = real net earnings.

S_1 = dummy for shift in U−V curve, 1968.

S_2 = dummy for shift in U—V curve, 1971.
Quarterly data.

NIESR (NIESR, *Discussion Paper No 7, 1977*)

$$\frac{WR - WR_{-4}}{WR_{-4}} = 0.040 - 0.238 \frac{UNEMP}{UNEMP+EMP} + 0.392 \frac{CPI_{-1}-CPI_{-5}}{CPI_{-5}}$$

$$+ 0.524 \frac{WR_{-1} - WR_{-5}}{WR_{-5}} + \epsilon$$

where WR = wagerate.
UNEMP = unemployment (GB'000s).
EMP = employment (GB total).
CPI = consumer price index.
Quarterly data.

LONDON BUSINESS SCHOOL

$$\frac{AEM}{PIMO} = 0.8698 + 1.0318\left(\frac{RNDI}{GDP}\right) + 0.6238 \, PRDM + 0.004249 \, TIME$$
$$+ 0.0076 \, DV2 + \epsilon$$

where
AEM = average earnings in manufacturing (index).
PIMO = wholesale price index of manufactured output (index).
RNDI = real national disposable income.
GDP = gross domestic product (non-oil, where the future is concerned).
PRDM = productivity in manufacturing industry (index).
TIME = trend incremented by unity each quarter, beginning 1955 Quarter I.
DV2 = V shaped dummy to allow for 1967—69 incomes policy with 1966 Q4
DV2 = 0 1968 Q2 = —5 other values interpolated along.
Quarterly data.

HM TREASURY (HM Treasury, *Macroeconomic Model Technical Manual*, 1976, 8a.3)

$$\ln ERPR = 0.68566 + 0.00746t + \sum_{i=0}^{11} \alpha_i \ln \frac{YI}{95(1.0075)t} + \sum_{i=0}^{9} \beta_i^* \ln PR + \epsilon$$

where
ERPR = average earnings in private sector (£).
t = time trend (= 1 in 1970(1)).
YI = index of GDP at factor cost (1970 = 100).
PR = retail price index (January 1974 = 100).
The long run coefficients on GDP and retail prices are 0 and 1, ie $\Sigma \alpha_i = 0$ and $\Sigma \beta_i = 1.0$.
Quarterly data.

analysis is the wage index, a situation which has impelled some investigators in the direction of collecting settlement data and others towards the introduction of a variable to measure the frequency of settlements. Finally — although the list is not supposed to be exhaustive — aggregation itself is a largely uninvestigated difficulty, especially since so much discussion of wage-setting emphasizes the importance of relative wages, an emphasis sometimes so over-whelming as to obscure the determination of aggregate, or average wages. In the light of these problems, it is perhaps not too surprising that econometric modelling has not been very successful. Since the data do not, in any case, discriminate between the Phillips curve and the real wage approach we have in our next section examined the wider implications of the two approaches when embodied in a small model determining wages, prices and the exchange rate.

The response of wages and prices to a rise in the price of imports or a shift in demand
In this section, we analyse some of the properties of the two rival hypotheses, the 'augmented Phillips curve' and the 'real wage hypothesis'. We focus attention on the response of a system characterized by one of these two wage hypotheses *first* to an exogenous shock emanating from a rise in import prices and *second*, to a rise in demand. The analysis is carried out on two alternative assumptions about the exchange rate, which is taken to be either fixed or floating, and on alternative assumptions about the values of key parameters in the equations. The results are tabulated in Tables 2—5 below.

I. *The 'Augmented Phillips Curve' with fixed exchange rates* (see Table 2 and Chart 1(a))
The structure of the system examined here can be given by the three equations:

1. Wages $\Delta w = f(u^* - u) + \alpha\pi \cdot$
2. Prices $\Delta p = k\Delta w + (1-k)\Delta m$.
3. Expectations $\pi = \gamma L\Delta p + (1-\gamma)L\pi$.

Glossary of symbols used in the simulation exercises
u = fraction of the labour force unemployed (so $u = 0.05$ denotes 5 per cent unemployment).
w = the log of an index of money wage rates.
p = the log of an index of retail prices.
m = the log of an index of import prices.
π = a measure of the rate of inflation anticipated.
t = the log of the ratio of import prices to domestic prices ($= m-p$).

L = the lag operator ($p(T-1) = Lp(T)$, where T is time).
$\Delta = 1 - L$ (so $\Delta w = 0.05$ denotes an exponential growth rate of wages of 5 per cent, corresponding to a period-on-period growth rate of $100 (e^{0.05} - 1) = 5.13$ per cent).

Given the definition of the variables (see glossary) it can be seen that the augmented Phillips curve equation (1) is complemented by a price equation which is linear in the logs of wage and import costs, with weights of k, 1−k, respectively (cf for example, Sargan, 1964, p 48). The inflation expectations equation (3) is the familiar distributed-lag/error learning formulation.

The system (1) — (3) can be reduced to:

$$(4)\ \Delta p = \left(\frac{1-(1-\gamma)L}{1-(1-\gamma+k\alpha\gamma)L}\right)\ ((1-k)\,\Delta m + kf(u^* - u))$$

where the paths of both import prices (m) and unemployment are taken to be exogenous. It is apparent from the reduction that, but for a scale factor, the price response of the system to a once-over increase in import prices (Δm positive for one period, zero thereafter) is identical to that produced by a *temporary* reduction of unemployment (u reduced for one period, then returning to its former value). Similarly, the response to a sustained inflation of import prices (continued positive value of Δm) is identical, but for a scale factor, to that produced by a *permanent* reduction in unemployment (u being reduced and held at its lower value).

As a 'stylized' value for f, we have adopted a figure of unity;[7] and the value of k, for the United Kingdom, can reasonably be put at around 0.8. On these estimates therefore, a 10 per cent rise in import prices will have the same price effects as a reduction of approximately $2\frac{1}{2}$ percentage points in the rate of unemployment.[8] It is these coefficient values which have been used in the simulation of the system using (4), to produce figures both for the long-run effect and for the short-term path of prices up to five periods, which may be thought of, not implausibly, as years. Also shown are the long-term results for real wages.

The key parameter variations are those for α, the coefficient of expected inflation in the wage equation and for γ, the elasticity of inflation expectations. These are each given alternative values of $\frac{1}{2}$ and 1.

In the top panel of Table 2, the results are shown for a once-over import price increase of 10 per cent (or for its inflation equivalent, *a temporary fall* in unemployment of about $2\frac{1}{2}$ percentage points. In all cases the price index rises in the first year by 2 per cent (one fifth of the import price rise), but with additions to the price level continuing in subsequent periods. The value of α can

TABLE 2

The Augmented Phillips Curve under Fixed Exchange Rates

I. The inflationary consequences of higher import prices and lower unemployment.

(a) A once-over rise in import prices of 10 per cent *or* a temporary reduction in unemployment by approximately $2\frac{1}{2}$ percentage points (for one period).

	Short-run effects on inflation					Long-run effect
	Period					
	1	2	3	4	5	On the price level
$\alpha=\frac{1}{2}$ $\gamma=\frac{1}{2}$	2.0	0.4	0.3	0.2	0.1	3.3
$\gamma=1$	2.0	0.8	0.3	0.1	0.1	3.3
$\alpha=1$ $\gamma=\frac{1}{2}$	2.0	0.8	0.7	0.6	0.6	10.0
$\gamma=1$	2.0	1.6	1.3	1.0	0.8	10.0

(b) A continuing inflation in import prices of 10 per cent *or* a reduction in employment by approximately $2\frac{1}{2}$ percentage points.

	Short-run effects on inflation					Long-run effect
	Period					
	1	2	3	4	5	On inflation
$\alpha=\frac{1}{2}$ $\gamma=\frac{1}{2}$	2.0	2.4	2.7	2.9	3.0	3.3
$\gamma=1$	2.0	2.8	3.1	3.2	3.3	3.3
$\alpha=1$ $\gamma=\frac{1}{2}$	2.0	2.8	3.5	4.2	4.8	10.0
$\gamma=1$	2.0	3.6	4.9	5.9	6.7	10.0

II. Real wage consequences in the long run.

	Once-over 10 per cent rise in import prices (i) *or* temporary reduction in unemployment (ii)			Continuing 10 per cent inflation in import prices (i) *or* permanent reduction in unemployment (ii)		
	Price	Real wages			Real wage growth	
Effect on:	level	(i)	(ii)	Inflation	(i)	(ii)
$\alpha=\frac{1}{2}$ $\gamma=\frac{1}{2}$	$3\frac{1}{3}$	$-1\frac{2}{3}$	$\frac{5}{6}$	$3\frac{1}{3}$	$-1\frac{2}{3}$	$\frac{5}{6}$
$\gamma=1$	$3\frac{1}{3}$	$-1\frac{2}{3}$	$\frac{5}{6}$	$3\frac{1}{3}$	$-1\frac{2}{3}$	$\frac{5}{6}$
$\alpha=1$ $\gamma=\frac{1}{2}$	10	0	$2\frac{1}{2}$	10	0	$2\frac{1}{2}$
$\gamma=1$	10	0	$2\frac{1}{2}$	10	0	$2\frac{1}{2}$

be seen to determine the long-run result, with the value of γ affecting only the speed of adjustment. When the value of α is taken as unity the eventual cumulative increase in prices is 10 per cent: where the initial impetus was a rise in import prices, wages eventually rise by a matching amount so that in the end all prices and wages rise by 10 per cent. The path followed by wages and prices after the rise in import prices is shown in Chart 1(a). Where the initial impetus is provided by a reduction in unemployment, money wages rise by more than the 10 per cent, their effect on the price index being tempered by the constancy of import prices. Consequently, the real wage implication of the two stimuli are quite different from one another, as shown in the bottom panel of the table (Table 2.II).

With a value of α of one half, the inflation consequences are, not surprisingly, less marked, as expected inflation is only half recouped: real wages do not rise so much as they did before (unemployment reduction) or actually fall (import price rise), see Table 2.I(a) and Table 2.II.

For a given value of α, it can be seen that the effect of varying γ from $\frac{1}{2}$ to 1 is to raise the rate at which the long-run effect is approached, the greater elasticity of adjustment of expectations to inflation experience implying a further feed-through into wages and subsequent price rises. This can be seen most clearly in Chart 1(a).

While all the results shown in the top panel of the table indicate that inflation disappears in long-run equilibrium after the full price rise adjustment has occurred, the centre panel of the table (2.I(b)), which gives comparable results for a *permanent* reduction in unemployment or steady inflation in import prices, indicates that long-run solutions here *do* involve positive rates of inflation. The results in the centre panel of the table are obtained simply by cumulating those shown in the top panel, as the inflationary effect of a sustained import price inflation, for example, can be obtained as that of a succession of 'once-over' rises in import prices; and if import prices keep rising, so will domestic prices.

Turning to the 'long-run' effects of unemployment on inflation, it is notable that — even when α is assumed to have a value of unity — an apparent 'trade-off' between unemployment and inflation is indicated by these results. The reason for this is the openness of the economy and the fact that, under the fixed exchange rate assumption, *import* prices are not impelled to rise further by the processes of wage inflation and price mark up that characterize the domestic sector. This is clarified by considering that, if the coefficient on unemployment in the Phillips curve is (minus) unity, then a $2\frac{1}{2}$ per cent fall in unemployment must raise the rate of wage inflation by $2\frac{1}{2}$ per cent but will raise the rate of

CHART 1(a)

**Path of Prices (P) and Wages (W) due to a Once-Over Rise in Import Costs of
10 per cent: Augmented Phillips Curve, Fixed Exchange Rates**

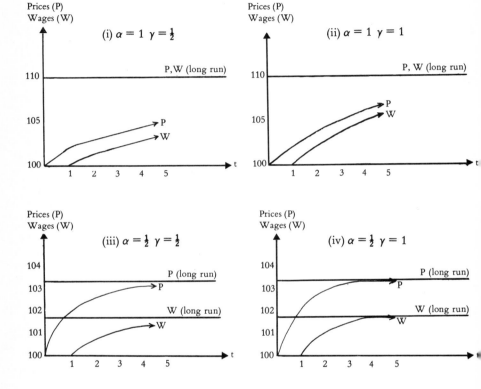

price inflation by only 2 per cent if import prices remain unchanged and the
exchange rate is fixed. (So with $\alpha = 1$, and $\gamma = \frac{1}{2}$ wage inflation in the next
period will only increase by four-fifths of $2\frac{1}{2}$ per cent, a process which is
repeated and approaches a limit of $12\frac{1}{2}$ per cent wage inflation). Clearly though,
by the same token, the 'long-run' solutions for this case are somewhat
misleading since they conceal the fact that a long-run trade-off between
inflation and unemployment, purchased by the assumption of a fixed exchange
rate, must imply a steadily deteriorating trade account and reserve position. The
exchange rate would have to give in time, so what happens when the exchange
rate is assumed to float is considered next.

II. *The Augmented Phillips Curve with floating exchange rates* (see Table 3 and Chart 1(b))

To allow for the consequences of a floating rate the three equations examined above are simply complemented by a fourth, which embodies the assumption that the exchange rate floats downward to the full extent of domestic price inflation. Thus import prices rise not only because of exogenous changes in the terms of trade (denoted by Δt) but also on account of domestic inflation, so:

  4. Exchange rate $\Delta m = \Delta_p + \Delta t$

The determination of inflation now becomes

$$\Delta p = \left(\frac{1-(1-\gamma)L}{1-(1-\gamma+\alpha\gamma)L} \right) \left(\left(\frac{1-k}{k} \right) \Delta t + f(u^* - u) \right)$$

This expression exhibits the same equivalence — so far as the impact on inflation is concerned — between *permanent* shifts in the relative price of imports and *temporary* shifts of unemployment (or *permanent inflation* in imports prices and *permanent* shifts in unemployment) as before.

Once again, the equivalence for inflation impacts does not carry over to the real wage, the long-run implications for which are noted in the bottom panel of Table 3.

Since, in this case, the exchange rate floats down to offset domestic price rises, there is no longer the opportunity there was in the fixed exchange rate case for domestic wage inflation to improve the terms of trade and hence increase real wages. In the floating rate case, domestic wage increases cannot therefore mitigate the initial real loss caused by a deterioration in the terms of trade, nor can they yield terms of trade gains when inflation is demand-induced. These implications are reflected in the results shown in the bottom panel of the table.

In the top two panels, the short-term path for prices and the long-run effects are shown, calculated with the same 'stylized values' as were employed in the case of Table 2 (ie $k = 0.8$, $f = 1$).

Although the floating exchange rate prevents domestic wage earners from achieving real wage gains by raising wages, the observed inflation comes from their attempts to do so. If $\alpha = 1$, and the inflation expectation elasticity (γ) is fixed, this implies that steady state inflation results from a once-over rise in import prices (or a reduction in unemployment even if it is only temporary); if α, the inflation expectations coefficient in the wage equation, is less than unity, then the rise in prices eventually ceases and no inflation ensues: here, the amount of the eventual price rise depends on α, and the speed with which it is achieved depends on γ. On the particular values assumed in Table 3.I(a), an initial rise in import prices of 10 per cent raises total prices by $2\frac{1}{2}$ per cent in the

TABLE 3
The Augmented Phillips Curve under Floating Rates

I. The inflationary consequences of higher import prices or lower unemployment.

(a) A once-over rise in import prices of 10 per cent *or* a temporary reduction in unemployment of approximately $2\frac{1}{2}$ percentage points (for one period).

| | Short-run effects on inflation | | | | | Long-run effect |
| | Period | | | | | On the price level* On inflation† |
	1	2	3	4	5	
$\alpha=\frac{1}{2}$ $\gamma=\frac{1}{2}$	2.5	0.6	0.5	0.4	0.3	5.0*
$\gamma=1$	2.5	1.3	0.6	0.3	0.2	5.0*
$\alpha=1$ $\gamma=\frac{1}{2}$	2.5	1.3	1.3	1.3	1.3	1.3†
$\gamma=1$	2.5	2.5	2.5	2.5	2.5	2.5†

(b) A continuing inflation in import prices of 10 per cent *or* a permanent reduction in unemployment by approximately $2\frac{1}{2}$ percentage points.

| | Short-run effects on inflation | | | | | Long-run effect |
| | | | Period | | | On inflation* On acceleration of inflation† |
	1	2	3	4	5	
$\alpha=\frac{1}{2}$ $\gamma=\frac{1}{2}$	2.5	3.1	3.6	3.9	4.2	5.0*
$\gamma=1$	2.5	3.8	4.4	4.7	4.8	5.0*
$\alpha=1$ $\gamma=\frac{1}{2}$	2.5	3.8	5.0	6.3	7.5	1.3†
$\gamma=1$	2.5	5.0	7.5	10.0	12.5	2.5†

II. Real wage consequences in the long run.

| | Once-over 10 per cent rise in import prices (i) *or* temporary $2\frac{1}{2}$ per cent reduction in unemployment (ii) | | | Continuing 10 per cent inflation in import prices (i) *or* permanent $2\frac{1}{2}$ per cent reduction in unemployment (ii) | | |
Effect on:	Price level* Inflation†	Real wages (i)	(ii)	Inflation Acceleration of inflation†	Real wage growth (i)	(ii)
$\alpha=\frac{1}{2}$ $\gamma=\frac{1}{2}$	5*	$-2\frac{1}{2}$	0	5*	$-2\frac{1}{2}$	0
$\gamma=1$	5*	$-2\frac{1}{2}$	0	5*	$-2\frac{1}{2}$	0
$\alpha=1$ $\gamma=\frac{1}{2}$	$1\frac{1}{3}$†	$-2\frac{1}{2}$	0	$1\frac{1}{3}$†	$-2\frac{1}{2}$	0
$\gamma=1$	$2\frac{1}{2}$†	$-2\frac{1}{2}$	0	$2\frac{1}{2}$†	$-2\frac{1}{2}$	0

CHART 1(b)

**Path of Prices and Wages due to a 10 per cent Rise in Import Costs
(Augmented Phillips Curve) Floating Exchange Rates**

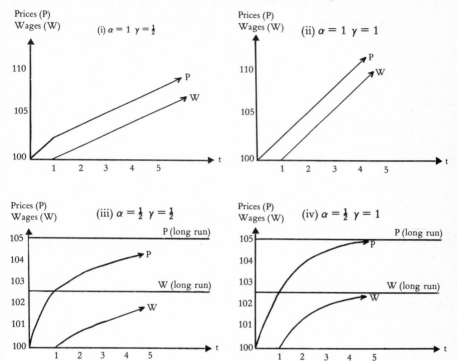

first instance and reduces real wages by a corresponding amount. Ensuing inflation depreciates the exchange rate without reversing this loss in real wages as the attempt to anticipate further price rises by wage increases passes through prices into the exchange rate. The way the path of prices and wages depends on α and γ is in Chart 1(b). In the case where the initial increase in prices is caused by a temporary fall in unemployment, there is no real wage loss (or gain): but the inflationary spiral which this sets in train is just the same. See Table 3.II.

Similar considerations apply *mutatis mutandis* where the increase in import prices is taken to be a *continuing* one, or the reduction in unemployment a *permanent* shift (Table 3.I(b)). The results for this case, as in the analogous section of Table 2, are simply a cumulation of the results already obtained for the 'once-over' or 'temporary' price and demand shocks. In the case where import price rises are the stimulus, real wages decline by $2\frac{1}{2}$ per cent per period and, provided that $\alpha < 1$, result in state steady inflation (of a value dependent upon the actual value of α); in the case where $\alpha = 1$, the result is a steadily *accelerating* inflation (of a value dependent upon γ). For the case where the stimulus is provided by a shift in unemployment, real wages do not change; inflation ensues at a steady rate, provided that $\alpha < 1$, or at an accelerating rate where $\alpha = 1$.

These results confirm that the floating rate open economy exhibits similar behaviour to the closed economy. There is no long-run trade off between inflation and unemployment if $\alpha = 1$; the trade off detected in this case for the fixed exchange rate example no longer applies since there it depended upon the ability to exploit a fixed price of imports (with respect to domestic wage and price behaviour), an opportunity not available in the floating rate regime. With $\alpha < 1$, trade offs between unemployment and inflation do exist, as they do in the familiar closed economy case.

The absence of a trade off means that it is not possible (if $\alpha = 1$) to reduce unemployment permanently at the cost of only a limited increase in induced inflation; as the results show, accelerating inflation would ensue in such a case. Nevertheless, the inflationary consequences of a rise in import prices can be countered by a rise in unemployment (temporary if the import price rise is a oneshot affair, permanent if import prices continue to inflate). In other words, it is as if, in a closed economy, the 'natural rate' were increased; the event giving rise to the increase would spark inflation if actual unemployment is not raised in line with it.

III. *The real wage hypothesis — fixed exchange rates* (Table 4)

In this section we examine the consequences of allowing the lagged real wage to enter the equation determining the rate of increase of money wages. The real wage term enters because money wages are seen as adjusting in response to a gap between the bargaining-equilibrium real wage — which depends on unemployment — and the actual real wage. Although Sargan, who proposed this approach, has in the past found that the presence of lagged real wages tends to render the estimated coefficient on past inflation insignificant (see Table 1) we include a coefficient on expected inflation in the equation. (More recent research by Sargan finds inflation expectations significant even when lagged real wages are included.) The wage equation becomes:

(1) $\quad \Delta w = \beta(f(u^* - Lu) - (Lw - Lp)) + \alpha\pi$

which, together with the price mark-up and expectations equations

TABLE 4

The Sargan Real Wage Model under Fixed Exchange Rates

I. The inflationary consequences of higher import prices or lower unemployment.

(a) A once-over rise in import prices of 10 per cent *or* a permanent reduction in unemployment by approximately $2\frac{1}{2}$ percentage points.

	Short-run effects on inflation					Long-run effect
	Period					
	1	2	3	4	5	On the price level
$\alpha=\frac{1}{2}$ $\gamma=\frac{1}{2}$	2.0	1.2	1.1	1.0	0.9	10.0
$\gamma=1$	2.0	1.6	1.3	1.0	0.8	10.0
$\alpha=1$ $\gamma=\frac{1}{2}$	2.0	1.6	1.7	1.7	1.6	10.0
$\gamma=1$	2.0	2.4	2.5	2.3	1.9	10.0

(b) A continuing inflation in import prices of 10 per cent *or* a continuing reduction in unemployment by $2\frac{1}{2}$ percentage points per period.

	Short-run effects on inflation					Long-run effect
	Period					
	1	2	3	4	5	On inflation
$\alpha=\frac{1}{2}$ $\gamma=\frac{1}{2}$	2.0	3.2	4.3	5.3	6.2	10
$\gamma=1$	2.0	3.6	4.9	5.9	6.7	10
$\alpha=1$ $\gamma=\frac{1}{2}$	2.0	3.6	5.3	6.9	8.5	10
$\gamma=1$	2.0	4.4	6.9	9.2	11.1	10

II. Real wage consequences in the long term.

	Once-over 10 per cent rise in import prices (i) *or* permanent $2\frac{1}{2}$ per cent reduction in unemployment (ii)			Continuing 10 per cent inflation in import prices (i) *or* continuing $2\frac{1}{2}$ per cent reduction in unemployment (ii)		
	Price	Real wages			Growth of real wages	
Effect on:	level	(i)	(ii)	Inflation	(i)	(ii)
$\alpha=\frac{1}{2}$ $\gamma=\frac{1}{2}$	10	0	2.5	10	0	2.5
$\gamma=1$	10	0	2.5	10	0	2.5
$\alpha=1$ $\gamma=\frac{1}{2}$	10	0	2.5	10	0	2.5
$\gamma=1$	10	0	2.5	10	0	2.5

(2) $p = kw + (1-k)m$
(3) $\pi = \gamma L \Delta p + (1-\gamma)L\pi$

implies a path for the price level described by

$$p = \frac{k\beta f(u^* - Lu)(1-(1-\gamma)L) + \{(1-(2-\beta-\gamma)L) + (1-\beta)(1-\gamma)L^2\}(1-k)m}{1-(2-\gamma-\beta(1-k) + k\alpha\gamma)L + (1-\gamma-\beta)(1-k)(1-\gamma) + k\alpha\gamma)L^2}$$

In the long term we can see (by setting $L = 1$) that the price level is determined by the level of unemployment and by the level of import prices, thus:

$$p = \frac{k\beta f(u^* - u)}{1-k} + m$$

This differs from the Phillips Curve approach in two respects; first of all, changes in import prices are reckoned to lead to equiproportionate changes in the price level even if $\alpha < 1$; and, second, a permanent decrease of unemployment is reckoned to change the price *level* by a finite amount, and not to lead to any persistent inflation.

The reason for these results can be easily perceived with the aid of Chart 2. In the upper left-hand panel we show the relationship between the real wage and the wage/import price ratio, while in the upper right-hand panel the equilibrium relationship between the real wage and the level of unemployment is shown as EE. In the lower panel the rate of change of money wages is related to the gap between the equilibrium real wage (given by EE) and the actual real wage determined by the terms of trade.

If we ignore the role of inflation expectations and for simplicity think of the wage equation in continuous terms (so $Dw = \beta(f(u^*-u)-w+p)$) the long-run unit elasticity of the price level with respect to import prices can be confirmed as follows. From an initial equilibrium at u_o, m_o, w_o, p_o, import prices rise to m_1. The *initial* impact is to reduce real wages from A_0 to A_1 which shifts the wage adjustment curve upwards (by $\beta(A_0-A_1)$) in the lower panel. But as wages and prices rise, as they will if unemployment is held at u_0, wages will gradually catch up with import prices, real wages will return towards A_0 and the wage adjustment curve will drift back towards its initial position. The process will stop only when wages and prices have moved up into line with import prices.

In similar fashion we see that if unemployment is 'permanently' reduced from u_0 to u_2 then inflation should only continue until real wages have been increased to A_2 and the wage import price ratio has shifted to w_2-m_0. The wage adjustment schedule will shift 'permanently' downwards in this case, reflecting the rise in the actual real wage to A_2.

These processes depend upon import prices remaining fixed with respect to

78

CHART 2
Reactions under the Real Wage Hypothesis: Fixed Rates

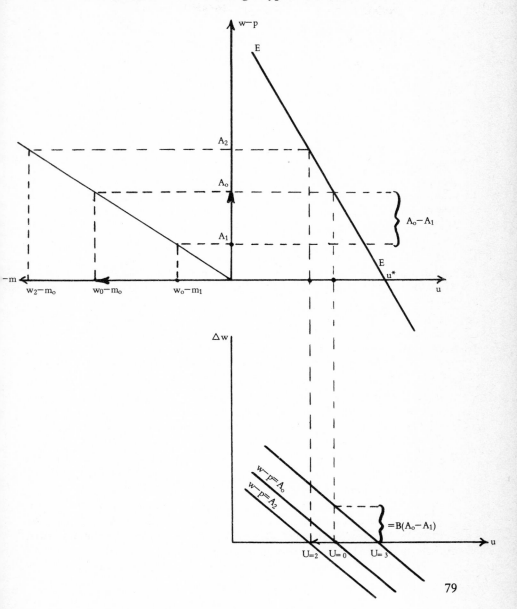

79

domestic wage and price behaviour; this allows for money wage advances to produce increases in real wages. The time paths for the first five periods following a 10 per cent change in the price of imports and following a $2\frac{1}{2}$ percentage point reduction of unemployment given by equations (1) to (3) above are shown in Table 4. In calculating these paths, f is set equal to 2 which, with $\beta = \frac{1}{2}$, gives $\beta f = 1$; otherwise, the value of k(0.8) and the alternatives considered for α and γ are as before.

To get continuing price increases under a fixed exchange rate this real wage approach calls for continuing inflation in import costs (or continuously decreasing unemployment); when prices continue to increase inflation expectations can hardly be ignored, but we note the equations above predict that no matter how fast the rise in import prices the long-run equilibrium is such that wages grow at the same rate and the real wage is restored. Thus if import prices start growing by 10 per cent per annum, they will initially depress real wages but money wages will soon grow and by increasing for a while at *over 10 per cent* will 'catch' up with import prices.

The inflationary consequences of continuing changes in import prices and unemployment are given in Table 4.I(b) (though the example of unemployment falling steadily by $2\frac{1}{2}$ percentage points per period is obviously not realistic).

IV. *The real wage hypothesis: floating rates* (Table 5)

As for the Phillips curve, to allow for a floating rate we simply add an equation for import prices in domestic currency of the form $m = p + t$. The resulting function for inflation is

$$\Delta p = \frac{(1-(1-\gamma)L\beta f(u^*-Lu) + \{(1-(2-\gamma-\beta)L + (1-\gamma)(1-\beta)L^2\}\left(\frac{1-k}{k}\right)t}{1-(1-\gamma+\alpha\gamma)L}$$

This implies that in the long run *inflation* depends on the level of unemployment and the level of the terms of trade according to the formula

$$\Delta p = \frac{\beta f(u^*-u)}{1-\alpha} + \frac{\beta}{1-\alpha}\left(\frac{1-k}{k}\right)t$$

The effect of unemployment on inflation is now strictly analogous to that under the augmented Phillips curve approach because real wages will not be affected by changes in unemployment. The floating of the rate implies that domestic money advances cannot 'buy' real wage increases, as they could in the fixed rate regime. The term βf in the formula corresponds to the slope of the short-run Phillips curve (which is why we have chosen parameter values for β, f to give the same slope as for the short-run Phillips curve of sections 2.I, 2.II above). As in the comparable result for the augmented Phillips curve, α is

80

critical here, but we note that estimated real wage equations tend to generate values for α which are much lower than those estimated when real wages are omitted. To that extent the risk of demand pressure causing hyper-inflation is lessened if one takes a 'real wage' view of UK inflation.

The prediction of the real wage approach that a once-for-all change in the terms of trade causes permanent inflation (which could be eliminated by a permanent increase in unemployment) is less easy to accept. The logic is straightforward: a 1 per cent rise in the terms of trade will cut real wages by the factor $\frac{1-k}{k}$ which will induce wage and price inflation of $\beta\left(\frac{1-k}{k}\right)$ if α is zero,

TABLE 5
The Sargan Real Wage Model under floating Exchange Rates

I. The inflationary consequences of higher import prices or lower unemployment.

(a) A once-over rise in import prices of 10 per cent *or* a reduction in unemployment by approximately $2\frac{1}{2}$ percentage points.

| | Short-run effects on inflation | | | | | Long-run effect |
	1	2	Period 3	4	5	On inflation*
$\alpha=\frac{1}{2}$ $\gamma=\frac{1}{2}$	2.5	1.9	2.0	2.1	2.2	$\Delta P = 2.5$
$\gamma=1$	2.5	2.5	2.5	2.5	2.5	$\Delta P = 2.5$
$\alpha=1$ $\gamma=\frac{1}{2}$	2.5	2.5	3.1	3.8	4.4	$\Delta^2 P = 0.625$
$\gamma=1$	2.5	3.8	5.0	6.3	7.5	$\Delta^2 P = 1.25$

(b) A continuing inflation in import prices of 10 per cent *or* a continuing reduction in unemployment by approximately $2\frac{1}{2}$ percentage points per period.

| | Short-run effects on inflation | | | | | Long-run effect |
	1	2	Period 3	4	5	On acceleration of inflation* On acceleration of acceleration†
$\alpha=1$ $\gamma=\frac{1}{2}$	2.5	4.4	6.4	8.6	9.8	2.5*
$\gamma=1$	2.5	5.0	7.5	10.0	12.5	2.5*
$\alpha=1$ $\gamma=\frac{1}{2}$	2.5	5.0	8.1	11.9	16.2	0.625†
$\gamma=1$	2.5	6.3	11.3	17.5	25.0	1.25†

continued overleaf

Table 5 continued

II. Real wage consequences in the long term.

	Once-over 10 per cent rise in import prices (i) *or* permanent 2½ per cent reduction in unemployment (ii)			Continuing 10 per cent inflation in import prices (i) *or* continuing 2½ per cent fall in unemployment (ii)		
	Inflation*	Real wages		Acceleration of inflation* Acceleration of	Real wages	
	Acceleration†	(i)	(ii)	acceleration†	(i)	(ii)
$\alpha=\frac{1}{2}$ $\gamma=\frac{1}{2}$	2.5*	−2.5	0	2.5*	−2.5	0
$\gamma=1$	2.5*	−2.5	0	2.5*	−2.5	0
$\alpha=1$ $\gamma=\frac{1}{2}$	0.625†	−2.5	0	0.625†	−2.5	0
$\gamma=1$	1.25†	−2.5	0	1.25†	−2.5	0

and by $\frac{\beta}{1-\alpha}\left(\frac{1-k}{k}\right)$ in the long run when α is above zero. Wages are forever increased to eliminate the once-for-all loss of real wages but this simply depreciates the currency and guarantees inflation, which, when it gets built into wage claims, accelerates the inflationary spiral.

This picture of labour condemned by its own real wage targets to an impossible task of trying forever to push up its real wage, for ever unsuccessfully, does seem implausible, for, unlike Sisyphus, those who set wages can by their own choice avoid the hopeless task (by reducing the target real wage in line with the loss due to the deterioration in the terms of trade).

V. *A comparison*

A useful way of comparing the real wage and the augmented Phillips curve approaches has been suggested by Freedman (1977) and we end this section with the illustration. Taking the real wage hypothesis *without* price expectations.

$$\Delta w = \beta f(u^*-Lu) - \beta Lw + \beta Lp$$

and collecting terms in w we have

$$(1-(1-\beta)L)w = \beta f(u^*-Lu) + \beta Lp$$

so, on dividing and differencing, we have

$$\Delta w = -\frac{\beta f(\Delta Lu)}{1-(1-\beta)L} + \frac{\beta L\Delta p}{1-(1-\beta)L}$$

which is similar to the *augmented* Phillips curve, except, of course, that it is (a moving average of) the *change* in unemployment which appears together with the distributed lag on inflation.

Conclusions

The simulations of the previous section were performed under strict limitations that should obviously be relaxed in a more comprehensive treatment. In particular, there was no lag in the price equation and no allowance for the influences of the level of activity to affect the mark-up of prices over costs in the short or long run.[9] Trend terms were ignored. Nevertheless we believe the simulations are useful in demonstrating some contrasts between the augmented Phillips curve and the real wage approaches which we take up in this section.

It was apparent that if real wages are included in the wage equation, then a coefficient of unity on inflation expectations is often not required to avoid 'money illusion'. Under fixed exchange rates, for example, the proportionate response of wages and prices to a rise in import costs is ensured by the lagged real wage term independently of the value of α. Under floating exchange rates a once-only adverse change in the terms of trade will cause permanent wage price inflation even if $\alpha = 0$. If we consider instead a change in the level of unemployment, we find that under fixed rates the consequential increase in real wages is independent of the value of α. Under floating exchange rates we noted that, in this case, the real wage hypothesis became, in the long-run, identical to the augmented Phillips curve, *because* there were no changes in real wages in these circumstances: but if that is so, then clearly we need not require α to be unity in these circumstances in order to ensure no change in real wages.

Another feature which emerges from the simulations is the implausibility of the consequences arising under both approaches of assuming a unit coefficient on price expectations in the face of a change in the terms of trade change with floating rates. The augmented Phillips curve with no money illusion ($\alpha=1$) implies that there will be *permanent* inflation as a result of such a once-over shock to the terms of trade unless there is a temporary rise in unemployment to eliminate the inflation expectations generated thereby. If real wages are also included in the wage equation then this inflation will accelerate, unless the unemployment level is *permanently* increased!

There is, however, a wide degree of support among economists for the idea that inflationary expectations should enter the Phillips curve with a coefficient of unity. The basis of this support is presumably that this is seen as necessary to prevent inflation eroding real wages. But the simulations show firstly that setting $\alpha=1$ is not necessary for this purpose and secondly that this coefficient restriction is not sufficient to ensure sensible reactions to exogenous changes.

Putting $\alpha=1$ ensures that the domestic suppliers of labour and capital refuse to take a cut in real incomes when the terms of trade shifts permanently against them, even though most economists would expect real factor incomes to fall in these circumstances. Hence we would conclude that *both* the augmented Phillips curve and the real wage approach need to be amended to portray a more realistic response. For the real wage hypothesis the necessary change has been discussed in the text — a downward shift in the 'equilibrium' real wage (which guides wage settlements). For the Phillips curve what appears to be called for is a temporary suspension of price sensitivity in wage settlements. Agents must *not* seek a wage increase in line with price increases coming from the increased import prices. If wage earners are in this way assumed to analyse the factors behind a particular price increase and to react differently to different factors, then proponents of this approach will not have to argue, as they otherwise must, that 'the natural rate of unemployment' temporarily increases when the terms of trade shift.

We conclude that neither of the two varieties of the wage equation followed mechanically is adequate for handling a change in the terms of trade and both require some (judgemental?) modification. As *between* the two approaches to wage determination, we note first that in published econometric work the inclusion of lagged real wages tends to drive down the coefficient estimated on inflation expectations. But we have already observed that including real wages is in theory a reasonable substitute for a low value of α for protecting real wages. In these circumstances we would adopt an eclectic attitude to the estimated coefficients on inflation expectations and the real wage in the wage equation, being content with $\alpha < 1$ if real wages are significant.

Notes

[1] An earlier version of this paper was presented to the Academic Panel of HM Treasury. We are grateful for the research assistance of Paul Temple, Rod Apps and Phil Murphy.

[2] The original results were quoted, variously, with t-ratios or standard errors accompanying the reported coefficients. In the interests of comparability, the results quoted in the table have been standardized as standard error statistics re-calculated where necessary from coefficient and t-ratio estimates.

[3] For a criticism of this approach, see Artis, 1976a.

[4] As indicated there, the estimation period for the wage equation in Sumner's study expires in 1965. Sumner subsequently simulates the following decade with the equation and bases his judgements of relative success with it on an examination of the (modest or explicable) forecast errors so obtained.

[5] The equation quoted for Artis omits such a term altogether since in previous trials it was found to carry an insignificant or (occasionally) wrong-signed coefficient.

[6] Cf Artis, 1976b and Henry, Sawyer and Smith, 1976.

[7] Such a value is suggested by the coefficient quoted for the more successful study of the augmented Phillips curve due to Sumner in Table 1.

[8] Strictly speaking, a reduction of the fraction of the labour force unemployed by 0.025 is equivalent to an increase in the *exponential* growth rate of import prices of 10 per cent, which will yield a period-on-period increase of more than 10 per cent. The fall in unemployment corresponding to a period-on-period increase of 10 per cent in import prices is given by $(1nl - 1)/4 = 0.0238$, ie 2.38 percentage points. It is for this reason that the figure of $2\frac{1}{2}$ percentage points is qualified as 'approximate'.

[9] If lags are introduced in the price equation then real wages and correspondingly profits become much more variable at least in the short run. In these circumstances it is not difficult to see how money wage increases may, by squeezing real profits, cause an investment collapse and a rise in unemployment.

References

R. Apps, 1976, 'Real Wage Equation: Some Further Results and Further Problems', mimeo, University of Manchester.

M. J. Artis, 1976a, 'Comment on Duck, Parkin, Rose and Zis', qv.

M. J. Artis, 1976b, 'Is there a wage Equation?', mimeo, University of Manchester.

M. J. Artis, P. Temple and L. Copeland, 1977, 'Wage Equations', mimeo, University of Manchester, June.

J. A. Carlson, and J. M. Parkin, 1975, 'Inflation Expectations', *Economica*, NS 42.

J. Duck, J. M. Parkin, D. Rose, and G. Zis, 1976, 'The Determination of the rate of change of wages and prices in the Fixed Exchange Rate World Economy 1956—1971', in M. Parkin and G. Zis, eds, *Inflation and the World Economy*, Manchester.

C. Freedman, 1977, 'Models of Inflation: a taxonomy of effects', *Bank of Canada Technical Report*, no 8, March.

M. Friedman, 1968, 'The Role of Monetary Policy', *American Economic Review*, 58.

C. Gillion, 1968, 'Wage-rates, earnings and wage-drift', *National Institute Economic Review*, no 46.

S. G. B. Henry, M. C. Sawyer and P. Smith, 1976, 'Models of Inflation in the United Kingdom: an Evaluation', *National Institute Economic Review*, no 77, 60—71.

J. R. Hicks, 1974, *The Crisis in Keynesian Economics*, Oxford.

J. Johnston and M. Timbrell, 1974, 'Empirical Tests of a Bargaining Theory of Wage Rate Determination' in D. E. W. Laidler and D. Purdy, eds, *Inflation and Labour Markets*, Manchester.

W. D. Nordhaus, 1972, 'The Worldwide Wage Explosion', *Brookings Papers on Economic Activity*, 2, 431—64.

M. Parkin, M. T. Sumner and R. Ward, 1976, 'The effects of excess demand, generalized expectations and wage-price controls on wage inflation in the UK, in K. Brunner and A. H. Meltzer, eds, *The Economics of Price and Wage Controls*. Supplement to the *Journal of Monetary Economics*, 2, 193—221.

J. D. Sargan, 1964, 'Wages and prices in the United Kingdom: a study in econometric methodology' in P. E. Hart, G. Mills and J. K. Whitaker, eds, *Economic Analysis for National Economic Planning*.

J. D. Sargan, 1971, 'A study of wages and prices in the UK 1949—1968' in H. G. Johnson and A. R. Nobay, eds, *The Current Inflation*.

J. D. Sargan, 1977, 'Some difficulties in estimating the impact of the level of activity on the wage-price spiral', mimeo.

M. T. Sumner, 1978, 'Wage Determination', in Michael Parkin and Michael T. Sumner, eds, *Inflation in the United Kingdom*, Manchester.

HM Treasury, 1976, *H.M. Treasury Macroeconomic Model Technical Manual*, Section 8a, 'Wages and Salaries (including wage costs)'.

5

Can we measure the rate of inflation?
C. E. V. LESER

The economist or statistician is often asked at what rate the inflation is currently proceeding, or how much an amount such as £1000 at a previous time would be worth at present-day prices. Such a question tacitly assumes that it is possible to quote a single figure describing the inflation rate at any given time. This assumption has not been left unchallenged; the diversity of price movements has been studied for example by Geary and Pratschke (1968) for Ireland, by Stigler and Kindahl (1970) and by Hester (1973) for the United States.

The measurement of price movements over a period as long as a century is generally recognized to face considerable difficulties because of the substantial transformation of production and expenditure patterns over such a period. Measurement of the current inflation rate meets with difficulties of another kind, arising out of ambiguities with regard to the dates on which the calculation is based. It makes a difference whether the figure quoted refers to the last twelve months or represents the change in, say, the last three months converted into an annual rate. Furthermore, the choice of indicator used may obviously make a considerable difference to the result obtained.

The last point is illustrated in Table 1, which shows annual percentage changes in a wholesale price index and in a retail price index for the British economy. The long-term increase is only slightly higher for retail prices than for wholesale prices, but in the short-run there are some sharp discrepancies between the series, particularly in recent years.

The present analysis is confined to movements in retail prices within intervals of one year or longer, and it is designed to furnish answers to the following questions: (a) To what extent do individual price movements follow the general trend, and to what extent do they imply changes in relative prices? (b) How is the spread of price changes related to the overall inflation rate? (c) In what way are the changes in the ratios of prices to each other translated into differences in price indices appropriate for various sections of the community?

The basic data used are the published individual components of the general index of retail prices in January each year from 1962 onwards. The annual

TABLE 1

Annual percentage change, wholesale price index for output of all manufactured products and general index of retail prices, 1957/58 to 1976/77

1st quarter of year	% change from previous year	
	Wholesale prices	Retail prices
1958	0.6	3.6
1959	0.8	2.1
1960	0.1	− 0.4
1961	2.5	2.2
1962	2.9	4.8
1963	1.2	3.1
1964	1.8	1.5
1965	3.8	4.5
1966	3.3	4.3
1967	1.5	3.7
1968	3.0	3.0
1969	3.9	6.2
1970	4.9	5.0
1971	9.9	8.7
1972	5.5	8.0
1973	6.6	8.0
1974	15.7	12.8
1975	27.3	20.3
1976	17.6	22.5
1977	19.9	16.5
Average	6.4	6.9

Derived from: Central Statistical Office, *Economic Trends*, Annual Supplement, no 3, HMSO, 1977, pp 97–9.

percentage changes in prices can therefore be treated for all practical purposes as indicating the price change during each calendar year. An average of these price changes can be deduced from the published retail price index for all items, but it does not tell the whole story of what happens in the field of prices.

The impression that, in times of inflation, all goods and services rise in price at approximately the same rate may be widespread, but, as will be seen, it is not in accordance with facts. Not only are falling prices for some commodities frequently observed even in times of rapid inflation, but the price rises which occur are very different in magnitude. Seen in relation to the overall price increase, some commodities therefore become cheaper and others dearer. The extent of these relative — or deflated — price movements may be measured by their standard deviation, which is also the deflated standard deviation of actual percentage price changes.

If, for example, in a two-commodity world, one commodity increases in price from 100 to 114 and another equally important one from 100 to 126, then the average percentage price increase is 20 with a standard deviation of 6. After deflation by 1.20, the indices 114 and 126 become 95 and 105, respectively, with standard deviation 5, which is also 6 deflated by 1.20.

Detailed price information is published for 37 subgroups of the retail price index (38 from 1968 and 39 from 1975 onwards), comprising virtually the

TABLE 2

**Summary measures for percentage price changes each year,
37—39 retail price sub-indices, 1962—77**

Year	Mean	Standard deviation	
		actual	deflated
1962	2.8	4.7	4.6
1963	1.9	2.9	2.8
1964	4.7	3.1	3.0
1965	4.4	3.9	3.8
1966	3.7	3.7	3.5
1967	2.7	3.5	3.4
1968	6.1	3.6	3.4
1969	4.9	3.3	3.1
1970	8.4	3.6	3.3
1971	8.2	5.3	4.9
1972	7.8	7.0	6.4
1973	11.9	8.5	7.6
1974	19.7	13.9	11.6
1975	23.5	12.7	10.3
1976	16.6	6.6	5.7
1977	10.0	10.8	9.8

whole field of expenditure covered by the index. If the derived percentage changes are averaged with the help of the weights for each year used in the official index number construction, then the average price change implied by the official all items index is obtained, subject only to slight inaccuracies resulting from the rounding of the published data. The standard deviations of actual and deflated price changes may be obtained using the same weights, and Table 2 gives the results.

The inflation rate, as represented by the increase in prices averaged over the various commodities, is seen to be on a rising trend until 1975 and subsequently falling. The rise in the inflation rate has not, however, been steady but proceeded in the form of steps taken in 1964, 1968 and 1970, following which the rate remained steady or even dropped; only between 1972 and 1975 was the rise sustained for several years.

Furthermore, there is clear indication of a wide spread between the price movements for individual items of expenditure. This is evidenced by the fact that in the years 1962, 1963, 1967, and 1977 the standard deviation of price changes exceeded the mean; in 1965, 1966 and 1972 it equalled the mean or fell only little below it. In seven out of sixteen years during the observation period, relative price changes are therefore of about the same magnitude as the general trend of upward price movement.

It is also clearly seen that the dispersion of price changes increases and decreases along with their average. Denoting the mean by $\overline{X}$, the actual standard deviation by S and the deflated standard deviation by S^*, the relationship may be quantified by means of linear regression equations, as follows (with standard errors)

$$S = 1.91 + .485\ \overline{X} \quad , \quad r^2 = .752$$
$$(.074)$$
$$\text{or } S^* = 2.25 + .374\ \overline{X} \quad , \quad r^2 = .691$$
$$(.067)$$

They suggest a standard deviation of about 2 per cent with zero inflation; with a 10 per cent average inflation rate, the standard deviation would be about 7 per cent for actual and 6 per cent for relative price movements.

In the long run, of course, the overall price rise overshadows the changes in relative price levels, but the latter nevertheless remain substantial. Table 3 illustrates this point by showing the price indices for 38 subgroups in January 1978 recalculated with January 1962 as base, together with their values after deflation by an overall price index, which in this case is a Laspeyres-type index and not identical with the official all items index. The mean and standard deviation, obtained by using base year weights, are also given.

TABLE 3

Price indices January 1978 (January 1962 = 100)

Expenditure item	Actual index	Deflated index
Bread, flour, cereals, biscuits, and cakes	443	119
Meat and bacon	440	118
Fish	597	161
Butter, margarine, lard, and cooking fat	378	102
Milk, cheese and eggs	388	104
Tea, coffee, cocoa, soft drinks, etc	363	98
Sugar, preserves and confectionery	468	126
Vegetables, fresh, dried, and canned	426	115
Fruit, fresh, dried, and canned	395	106
Other food	361	97
Alcoholic drink	314	85
Tobacco	317	85
Rent	321	86
Rates and water charges	440	118
Charges for repairs and maintenance, etc	431	116
Coal and coke	482	130
Gas	260	70
Electricity	456	123
Furniture, floor coverings and soft furnishings	345	93
Radio, television and other household appliances	197	53
Pottery, glassware and hardware	326	88
Men's outer clothing	314	85
Men's underclothing	355	96
Women's outer clothing	243	65
Women's underclothing	281	76
Children's clothing	281	76
Other clothing	229	62
Footwear	285	77
Motoring and cycling	308	83
Fares	506	136
Books, newspapers and periodicals	580	156
Medicines, surgical goods and toilet requisites	267	72
Soap and detergents, soda, polishes, etc	352	95

continued overleaf

Table 3 continued

Expenditure item	Actual index	Deflated index
Stationery, travel and sports goods, toys, etc	314	85
Postage and telephone	426	115
Entertainment	311	84
Other services	470	127
Meals out	458	123
Mean	371.4	100.0
Standard deviation	84.0	22.6

In the period under consideration, the general price level was nearer to quadrupling than to trebling, and its increase was equivalent to about $8\frac{1}{2}$ per cent per annum. But at one end of the price increase range, fish and reading materials rose in price almost sixfold and thus became relatively dearer by more than 50 per cent, whilst electrical goods less than doubled their price and hence became almost 50 per cent cheaper in relative terms. The commodities which became relatively more expensive also include most food items, coal and electricity, fares and most services, whilst gas and all clothing items became relatively cheap.

But does it matter whether a given inflation rate is produced by a virtually uniform rate of price increases over the whole field of expenditure or by widely differing rates of price rises, possibly even combined with some price falls? It may matter very much, and that for two reasons. One the one hand, differences between price changes of individual goods allow substitution of goods which have become relatively cheaper for those which become relatively dearer. On the other hand, large differentials of this kind lead to at least a prima facie belief that individual households will be differently affected by the price rises.

The implication of the first point is that with a wide dispersion of price movements, a Laspeyres-type price index tends to exaggerate the increase in the cost of commodity bundles yielding equal satisfaction. The higher the degree of inflation, the greater the dispersion and therefore the larger the extent to which substitution can cushion the consumer from the effect of price rises. The method adopted in constructing the official index reduces but does not completely eliminate this possible bias.

Now it is true that, apart from the automatic change of weights following relative price changes, there has been a reduction in the budget shares of most foodstuffs, coal and coke, and fares, whilst the shares of motoring and durable household goods have risen. In consequence, a Laspeyres-type index for January 1978 with January 1962 as base is 371.4, whilst a Paasche-type index comes to 348.9 and the official index to 363.5. These changes in expenditure patterns may, however, be accounted for less by substitution than by the increase in real income over the period, as well as by the acquisition of motor cars and changes in methods of home heating.

The second point concerns an aspect of inflation which is perhaps less familiar than the over-all rise in prices and which will be dwelt upon here at some length; it is the limited relevance of a single price index for different sections of the population. If all prices increased at approximately the same rate, it would be a relatively simple matter to compensate all consumers for their loss of purchasing power by a uniform percentage in nominal money incomes, provided only that real output and real income of the nation do not fall. But if there are wide disparities in price movements, a universal percentage increase in money incomes is likely to leave some sections of the community worse off in real terms, unless there is an appreciable growth in output and real national income per head, since household budgets are likely to vary substantially in composition.

As far as differences in incidence of price changes concern readily identifiable population strata such as different income groups or households of different composition, they can in theory at least be compensated by adjustments in tax allowances or child benefit. In practice this would be very difficult and would in any case not be applicable to households with similar measurable characteristics but different spending habits. It therefore seems prima facie likely that large changes in relative prices, with gains for some sections of the community and losses for others, would lead to shifts in real income and consequently to social unrest. To what extent the existing income distribution is considered as satisfactory or in need of change is a large and separate question, which it is not possible to discuss adequately in the present context.

To what extent do patterns of household expenditure differ? And do the differences tend to cancel out as regards their effect on average price changes, or do they leave substantial net effects? In other words, are the goods and services which became relatively dear as a whole and those which become relatively cheap as a whole more or less evenly represented in most household budgets, or is the share of one or the other group of expenditure items particularly high in some household groups?

In order to find an answer to the question, average expenditure patterns of various income groups for households consisting respectively of one adult, of a man and woman, and of man, woman and two children have been extracted from the 1961 Family Expenditure Survey. Households containing a man, woman and one child were also analysed, but the results for this group show no appreciable difference from those for households with two children and are therefore not shown here. The classification was brought into line with the retail price index subgroup as far as practicable. Services excluded from the index were omitted, but upward adjustments were made for alcoholic drink and tobacco as well as some food items, in order to compensate for under-recording.

Within each household composition group, the budget shares of the commodity subgroup were assumed to be linear functions of the logarithms of total household expenditure, apart from a disturbance term; the model is the same as that applied by Leser (1976) to broad commodity groups. In addition, total expenditure within each household was assumed to be lognormally distributed; on this basis total expenditure at the levels of first decile, median and ninth decile of all households were obtained. By means of simple linear regressions, the budget shares were calculated for households at these expenditure levels, which may be briefly described as low income, medium income and high income households. The budget shares were then used as base year weights, to be applied to the retail price subindices to obtain price indices for various sections of the population. These price indices are of Laspeyres type and therefore somewhat higher than they would be if constructed by the method adopted for the official index, but the comparisons to be made are not thereby affected. The annual price indices were finally converted into year-to-year percentage changes.

Table 4 compares households of different types which are approximately equally well off; their weekly expenditure on all goods and services in 1961 amounted to £6.87, £13.89 and £17.71 respectively. The price rises are those which the households experienced, assuming that their expenditure patterns did not change apart from the direct effect of relative price changes; admittedly this assumption is not perfectly realistic. The inter-household differences were quite appreciable in some years and not invariably in the same direction. However, the typical pattern is that of one-adult households experiencing the highest rate, and households with children the lowest rate, of price increases; this was the case in ten out of the sixteen years in the observation period.

When looking at the long-term effects, the period from the beginning of 1962 to the end of 1977 has been split into the first twelve and the last four years as well as being considered as a whole. This division coincides with the re-basing of the official retail price index with its sub-indices, but more

94

TABLE 4
Price increases for medium income households of different composition, 1962—77

Year	% price increases for average household of		
	one adult	man and woman	man, woman and two children
1962	3.6	2.8	2.7
1963	2.4	1.9	1.7
1964	4.7	4.8	4.6
1965	4.5	4.3	4.2
1966	4.3	3.8	3.5
1967	3.1	2.7	2.6
1968	5.6	6.0	6.0
1969	5.6	5.2	5.2
1970	8.7	8.5	8.4
1971	9.2	8.6	8.5
1972	8.5	8.0	7.6
1973	12.1	12.2	12.4
1974	17.7	19.1	19.6
1975	24.9	24.4	24.2
1976	18.0	17.9	18.2
1977	10.1	10.0	9.8
Whole period (both years inclusive)			
1962—73	101.2	94.6	92.1
1974—77	91.0	92.3	92.7
1962—77	284.3	274.1	270.2
Annual average			
1962—73	6.00	5.70	5.59
1974—77	17.57	17.75	17.82
1962—77	8.78	8.59	8.52

significantly it yields two sub-periods in each of which prices as a whole nearly doubled. Measured not in number of years but in 'inflation time' we could say that the periods 1962–73 and 1974–77 are of equal length.

For the period as a whole, the average inflation rate was highest for one-adult households and lowest for households with children; it amounted to 8.8 per cent for one-adult households, 8.6 per cent for man-woman households and 8.5 per cent for couples with two children. The differential was wholly concentrated on the first of the two sub-periods; the tendency observed was halted after 1973 and indeed slightly reversed, though this reversal is fully accounted for by the experience of the year 1974 alone.

In the same way as Table 4 makes comparisons across household types, Table 5 effects a comparison between similar households at different income and expenditure levels. For one-adult households, total weekly expenditure in 1961 amounted to £4.10 at the first decile and to £11.51 at the ninth decile; for man and woman, the corresponding figures are £8.69 and £22.17; for couples with two children, the expenditure totals are £13.35 and £23.51 respectively.

The differences in the incidence of price inflation on low-income and high-income households are quite substantial in some years for the households without children. For households with children, the differences are less marked; this is partly explained by the fact that the difference in total household expenditure is smaller among these households than among those without children. The differentials are not invariably in the same direction, but on the whole the low-income households appear to have been confronted by a more sharply rising cost of their budget than the high-income households. This tendency was particularly marked in the years up to 1973; in the more recent years, it was much diminished for the household containing two or more persons, and even slightly reversed for the one-adult households. All in all, the average inflation rate over the sixteen years ranges from 8.4 per cent for couples in the high-income range to almost 9 per cent for low-income single-adult households, probably mostly pensioners. In other words, the cost of the 1961/62 budget has almost quadrupled in these sixteen years for the least favoured section of the population; in the more favourably placed sections, the factor by which the cost was multiplied is nearer to $3\frac{1}{2}$ than to 4.

It can also be shown that the differences in inflation rates experienced in a given year, irrespective of their direction, are generally greater, the higher the overall inflation rate. If the unweighted mean of the six inflation rates is compared with the range of the six rates for each of the sixteen years, a positive correlation becomes evident. The correlation coefficient is $+.543$, which is significant at the 5 per cent level even when a two-tailed test is used. This

TABLE 5
Price increases for households of different income levels, 1962–77

Year	one adult		man and woman		man, woman and two children	
	Low income	High income	Low income	High income	Low income	High income
1962	4.4	2.9	3.5	2.1	3.0	2.4
1963	2.5	2.3	2.1	1.7	1.8	1.7
1964	4.8	4.6	5.1	4.5	4.7	4.5
1965	4.3	4.6	4.3	4.3	4.2	4.1
1966	4.6	4.0	4.0	3.6	3.6	3.7
1967	3.4	2.9	2.9	2.5	2.8	2.5
1968	5.2	6.0	5.7	6.2	5.9	6.1
1969	6.1	5.1	5.5	4.9	5.2	5.1
1970	8.5	8.9	8.4	8.7	8.4	8.4
1971	9.8	8.6	9.2	8.1	8.8	8.2
1972	9.1	8.0	8.4	7.7	7.6	7.5
1973	12.7	11.5	12.6	11.7	12.7	12.2
1974	16.9	18.5	18.3	20.0	19.8	19.5
1975	25.1	24.6	25.1	23.6	24.5	23.9
1976	19.1	16.9	18.9	17.0	18.8	17.5
1977	9.5	10.8	9.7	10.4	9.5	10.1
Whole period (both years inclusive)						
1962–73	106.9	95.6	99.6	89.6	94.1	90.2
1974–77	90.7	91.3	93.0	91.5	93.8	91.5
1962–77	294.6	274.2	285.2	263.0	276.2	264.3
Annual average						
1962–73	6.24	5.75	5.93	5.48	5.68	5.50
1974–77	17.52	17.61	17.87	17.64	17.99	17.64
1962–77	8.96	8.59	8.79	8.39	8.63	8.41

% price increase for households of

confirms the conjecture that high rates of inflation may bring about noticeable shifts in real income even if money incomes after direct taxation remain in the same proportion.

As pointed out, the inter-household differences in inflation rates experienced are not always in the same direction, and they may well tend to cancel out in the very long run. But human memories tend to be short in some circumstances, and a high incidence of inflation in any given year may be keenly felt even though previous years have brought about relatively favourable treatment.

Of course, the impact of price inflation and of differentials in inflation rates cannot be assessed in isolation but should be seen in combination with the growth of money incomes. Up to 1973, whatever the redistributive effect of differential price rises may have been, it is unlikely to have brought about a fall in living standards for any major section of the community at any time, since the real national product and the standard of living were almost universally rising. This was not so after 1974, not only because price inflation proceeded at a higher rate than previously, but also because output and real incomes were stagnating. Even a uniform increase in disposable money income would therefore have entailed falling living standards for some sections. It is well known, however, that increases in money incomes after tax were not uniform and indeed produced serious anomalies, which further aggravated the situation.

To summarize: it has been demonstrated that price inflation is not a simple process of all prices increasing in the same proportion, but that it tends to be accompanied by considerable changes in the ratios between prices of different goods and services. Consequently, the impact of inflation may be felt very differently by different consumers. Adjustments in prices upwards or downwards take place even with a stable overall price level, but an important feature of inflation is the fact that the relative price movements tend to be the larger, the more rapidly prices are rising. These relative price changes may mitigate but may also aggravate any changes in relative money incomes which may arise in times of inflation.

This brings us back to the question 'can we measure the rate of inflation?'. The answer does not appear to be a simple yes or no. Clearly we can measure the broad trend of inflation, but at the same time there are differences in its impact on different members of the community, and not only on pensioner households, whose particular problems have been officially recognized by the construction of special index numbers. The measurement of price inflation remains an important task, but its solution consists perhaps in constructing a band of inflation rates, rather than quoting a single rate and claiming it to be universally applicable.

98

References

R. C. Geary and J. Pratschke, 'Some Aspects of Price Inflation in Ireland', Dublin: Economic and Social Research Institute Paper No 40 (1968).

D. D. Hester, 'Inflation and the Recent American Happening', in M. Parkin and A. R. Nobay, eds, *Contemporary Issues in Economics*, (Manchester, 1973), pp 142–69.

C. E. V. Leser, 'Income, Household Size and Price Changes 1953–1973', *Oxford Bulletin of Economics and Statistics* (1976), pp 1–10.

G. J. Stigler and J. K. Kindahl, *The Behaviour of Industrial Prices* (New York: National Bureau of Economic Research, 1970).

99

6

Antipodean contrasts in incomes policy
WILLIAM BROWN

Incomes policy has, in recent years, become the principal weapon with which successive British governments have sought to combat inflation. Few policy instruments can have proved so double-edged. Yet, despite the politically perilous nature of attempts to control wages and salaries, there is every prospect that governments will feel obliged to grapple with them more often than not for the foreseeable future. Although valuable lessons have been learnt during Britain's short and stormy experimentation with incomes policies, we are still far from a satisfactory formula. This study seeks to establish what might be learnt from Australia, whose experience of incomes policy goes back far longer than that of any other major industrialized country.

A superficial knowledge of the incomes policy which the practice of compulsory arbitration has brought to Australia gives it an immediate appeal in a Britain harassed by turbulent and inflationary collective bargaining. How sublime it would be if we could import a commission of judicial arbitrators, empowered to intervene in any dispute, take evidence from each side, and issue a legally binding settlement. Better still, such a commission could stand back from the pressures of industrial life, ponder what the economy could afford, and announce the annual pay increase that was to go to all employees. In fact, as we shall see, this popular Australian conception of their policy is very far from reality. The Australian Conciliation and Arbitration Commission has to tread a political path of daunting complexity, and to operate more as the midwife than the aborter of collective bargaining pressures.

At times during its seventy-five years' history the Commission (and its predecessor, the Court) have been less than successful; some of their decisions economists can only judge to have been bizarre. But it has been a history of continual evolution in the light of often bitter experience, and the Commission has emerged from it to appear, at least at present, as the master of a remarkably effective incomes policy. This achievement is the more impressive for having been rescued from almost total wreckage in the early 1970s when unco-ordinated collective bargaining and its accompanying spiralling inflation gave Australian wage determination a distinctly British appearance.

Although authorities as well-informed as Professors H. A. Turner and Sir Henry Phelps Brown have, in recent years, urged that Britain should seriously consider adopting aspects of Australian wage fixing institutions, there are grave dangers in seeking to emulate another country's practices.[1] The grass may appear greener elsewhere, but, as Mr Heath's Industrial Relations Act demonstrated, it may not transplant. The differences in labour law and, in consequence, in trade union and employer organization, have been so different in the two countries for so long that no simple legislative grafting could succeed. But, despite that, the fundamental problem of co-ordinating bargaining pressures is common to both countries. Both have a similarly high proportion — slightly over a half — of their employed labour force in trade unions. Australia's workforce is no less likely to take strike action than Britain's.[2] At times when they have become accustomed to high rates of inflation both workforces have shown themselves willing to resort to strike action in an attempt to protect relative pay positions that have come to be accepted as 'fair'. The legislative setting may be different but the fundamental political conundrum is the same.

In what follows we sketch out the haphazard evolution of Australian incomes policy up to the point when, in September 1978, the Commission was able to publish the most detailed and carefully reasoned set of 'Wage Fixation Principles' the country had yet seen.[3] These Principles are then used as the basis for a discussion of the varied forces revealed by seventy-five years' experience of struggling with incomes policy.

The emergence of Australian incomes policy

A national incomes policy was a quite incidental and unpremeditated consequence of efforts to reduce industrial strife in Australia at the turn of the century. State governments had already made some legislative moves to enable third parties to intervene in strikes and lock-outs when the Constitution of the newly federated Commonwealth of Australia gave it, in 1900, power for 'conciliation and arbitration for the prevention and settlement of industrial disputes extending beyond the limits of any one State'.[4] Subsequently, in 1904, the Commonwealth Conciliation and Arbitration Act established what was then called a Court but is now the Australian Conciliation and Arbitration Commission which currently has a President, ten Vice-Presidents (all of Federal Judge status) and twenty-two Commissioners. Individual members of the Commission which currently has a President, ten Vice-Presidents (all of Federal and arbitrating and finally, with varying degrees of agreement from the protagonists, issuing an award that is enforceable at law. Currently more than 90 per cent of all Australian employees are covered by arbitrated pay awards, and more than half of these are awards of one or other of the separate state authorities.[5]

On the face of it, this is a recipe for turbulent *ad hoccery*, with different tribunals at state and federal level making awards at complete odds with one another. But it has not, for the most part, worked out that way. Tribunals quickly learnt that forces of comparison between different groups of employees were such that, if a measure of consistency between pay awards was not observed, the objective of avoiding disputes would be undermined. In order to avoid irritating anomalies they tended to look to previous decisions for guidance.[6] They resisted vigorously attempts that various governments made to settle politically embarrassing disputes by *ad hoc* arrangements outside the machinery of the Act. As Henry Higgins, the dominant figure of the early years observed, 'a tribunal of reason cannot do its work side by side with executive tribunals of panic'.[7]

Gradually the Court, and the Commission after it, centralized its procedures and widened the scope of its awards. Full Benches of three or more members (including two of Presidential status) listened to appeals against tribunal judgements and heard any case that was felt to be of particular national significance. These hearings gathered importance after the Second World War, some landmarks being general awards on standard hours and annual leave in the 1940s, on skilled workers' pay 'margins' in 1954, and annual reviews of basic wages in 1956 that were developed into an annual National Wage Case in 1969.[8]

But it was not simply a desire for bureaucratic tidiness and the avoidance of anomalies that led to the increased co-ordination of tribunal decisions. There was also a concern with the social function of wages and with the need to have some sort of moral principles upon which to base the justification of an award. It was thus early established that the 'basic wage' should reflect the minimum needs of a family. In the same spirit it was decided that real wages should be protected by what would now be called 'indexation'; that is, the automatic adjustment of the basic wage in response to movements in retail prices, a practice followed from 1922 until 1953 and recommended, with qualifications, in 1975. Other examples of the use of fundamental principles are the notion of 'comparative wage justice' whereby the same wage should go to people doing the same job (to which we shall return) and equal pay between the sexes. Isaac has shown that in espousing these principles tribunals did not 'invent' them, but rather crystallized the prevailing views in Australian society. 'In this respect the development of arbitration principles in the settlement of industrial disputes may be likened to the development of common law by the early courts which were guided in their judgements by custom and practice.'[9]

A consistent adherence to some set of moral principles in determining pay is difficult enough in itself. It is all but impossible when confronted with, on the one hand, the uneven collective bargaining power of the workforce and, on the other, the economic objectives of the government. The first of these we shall consider in the next section. The second has been a recurring problem for decades. Wages are so crucial a variable in economic management that it is hardly surprising that elected governments have questioned the control over them exercised by tenured judges. Indeed, given the quite dotty basis upon which tribunals have on occasion made decisions, government nervousness is wholly understandable; Australian economic history can attribute many scars to their worships.[10] In attempts to obtain greater compliance from the tribunals the 1904 Act has been tinkered with several times. But the current version, urging that ' . . . all questions of what is right and fair in relation to an industrial matter having regard to the interests of the persons immediately concerned and of society as a whole' is still open to varied interpretation.

British governments have usually been forced to intervene in pay determination by currency crises or, latterly, by fears of hyper-inflation. Australian governments have become restive with the tribunals through less urgent anxieties about loss of foreign competitiveness and wages outstripping industry's 'capacity to pay'. Such considerations brought about cuts in arbitrated award rates in the 1930s and brought the end of indexation in 1953, with the result that real wages actually declined during the later 1950s. During the 1960s, employers, academics and government alike urged a divided Commission to put aside the objective of protecting real wages for that of keeping pay increases in line with national productivity growth, until the Commission's obvious lack of control over wages made the debate somewhat unrealistic. With its regaining the initiative in 1975 as a result of the reintroduction of indexation, the Commission has come under a barrage of government criticism and abuse. In its 1978 Principles, however, it has resolved to stand firm, in the belief that the orderly fixing of wages on the basis of the protection of their real value is vastly preferable to a scramble of highly inflationary collective bargaining that it fears would occur even under the shadow of high unemployment. The contemporary British experience is likely to reinforce that view. But however independent the Commission may appear to have become in the late 1970s in running its own incomes policy, it is, as its reasoned awards make clear, acutely aware that governmental tolerance is not unlimited. A Commission too insensitive to a government's economic analysis could find itself legislated beyond recognition.

Post-war experience in Australia and Britain

Whatever its legal setting, any incomes policy in an economy with well-established trade unions finds difficulty in achieving what Phelps Brown refers to as 'that unity in diversity which contemporary pay settlements require'.[11] In this respect the Australian and British post-war experiences have much in common. For both, the great change came with the relatively full employment of the 1950s and 1960s, which made labour stronger and employers more ready to bid up for it. This gave rise to a weakening of the industry-wide, multi-employer coalitions that had hitherto kept a united front on wages, and to a consequent growth of what was termed 'wage drift' in both countries. Their parallel experience bears useful comparison.

In Britain the development of collective bargaining outside the framework of multi-employer agreements, although usually somewhat furtive, had become so far advanced by the late 1960s that a Royal Commission under Lord Donovan, reporting in 1968, urged that it should be acknowledged and formalized.[12] This happened in the course of the following decade. Multi-employer agreements were increasingly relegated to the position of providing no more than 'safety nets' of minimum wages, increases in which left the bulk of wage-earners in the industry unaffected.[13] The complementary shift towards single-employer pay bargaining at workplace or corporate level proceeded so fast that, by 1978, it provided the most important level of pay determination for 67 per cent of manual and 72 per cent of non-manual employees in manufacturing industry.[14] This gave rise to tidier and more easily controlled internal pay structures. It also gave rise to far greater professionalism in company industrial relations management and in shop steward organization. The wage drift that had plagued incomes policies in the 1960s became both practically and semantically defunct. Perhaps surprisingly, the newly authoritative shop steward organizations with their company pay agreements proved very disciplined, adhering remarkably closely to the limits of both Conservative and Labour incomes policies in the 1970s until the withdrawal of TUC support from Labour's policy in 1978.[15]

Thus the central problem of Britain's incomes policy had been transformed. It was no longer one of mopping up wage drift from a confusion of multi-level bargaining. Instead a machinery had to be found within which the newly disciplined private sector and the newly truculent public sector could negotiate

105

pay with sufficient co-ordination to prevent its real value vanishing. It is to this new problem that recent Australian experience is particularly germane.

Arbitrated awards in Australia, despite their ubiquity, were never intended to be more than minimum rates. It is an indication of the success of the arbitration system for the first half of this century that, as with the multi-employer agreements in Britain, their rates provided almost the sole source of earnings. The coming of full employment weakened this position. Employers gradually began to augment award rates with what were called 'overaward payments' which were sometimes tied to a condition such as good time-keeping, but increasingly as time passed were simple cash additions with no strings attached. By the late 1950s increases in overaward payments were providing a fifth of all earnings increases in the equivalent of the engineering industry.[16] By the early 1960s this had risen to a third, and by the end of that decade overward payments were contributing almost a half of all earnings increases.[17] Workplace wage bargaining was usurping the arbitration system.

The rapidly emerging collective bargaining was different from its British counterpart. Partly because of the legal status given to full-time union officials by the arbitration system, shop stewards gained little of the authority and permanence they have achieved in Britain. A high, and growing, proportion of overaward payments were registered with either state or federal arbitration authorities, sometimes being described as 'paid rate awards'. Insofar as they were agreed between unions and management before the arbitration process, negotiated pay rates were called 'consent awards'.

As in Britain, multi-employer arrangements were coming under strain. They were tending to fragment into awards covering more specific sectors of industry than hitherto.[18] Furthermore, there was a marked swing to awards covering single employers, especially in multi-national companies and in the new growth industries such as mining and chemicals which were rapidly overtaking traditional manufacturing industry as the wage leaders during the 1970s. This swing to single-employer arrangements could not, however, be as whole-hearted as that occurring in Britain. The legal status of multi-employer awards inhibited their graceful retreat to a 'safety net' role whereby increases in award might be absorbed by existing overaward payments so as not to influence earnings. Indeed, in the early 1970s the influential engineering industry sought to take the steam out of overaward bargaining by granting large increases in the award rate under 'consent' arrangements. Thus Australia entered the 1970s with pay increases being generated in a quite uncoordinated way at national, industry and workplace levels. It was not surprising (and the table provides the

Unemployment, earnings and prices, Australia and UK 1964–78

	Australia				United Kingdom		
	% unemploy-ment		% change earnings	% change prices	% unemploy-ment		% change earnings	% change prices
1964	1.2	1963–64	7.4	4.0	1964	1.6	1963–64	6.4	4.4
1965	0.8	1964–65	4.7	4.0	1965	1.4	1964–65	7.8	4.4
1966	1.3	1965–66	6.6	2.4	1966	1.4	1965–66	4.4	3.5
1967	1.5	1966–67	5.8	3.3	1967	2.2	1966–67	5.6	1.8
1968	1.4	1967–68	7.5	2.6	1968	2.4	1967–68	8.1	5.7
1969	1.6	1968–69	8.4	2.8	1969	2.4	1968–69	8.3	5.2
1970	1.4	1969–70	11.0	4.9	1970	2.5	1969–70	13.8	7.5
1971	1.8	1970–71	10.9	7.2	1971	3.4	1970–71	9.5	9.3
1972	2.4	1971–72	9.0	4.1	1972	3.8	1971–72	15.8	6.9
1973	1.8	1972–73	16.2	13.7	1973	2.6	1972–73	12.7	10.4
1974	3.4	1973–74	25.4	16.2	1974	2.6	1973–74	25.3	19.5
1975	4.5	1974–75	14.4	14.0	1975	4.2	1974–75	21.2	25.5
1976	4.2	1975–76	12.4	14.4	1976	5.7	1975–76	12.4	15.3
1977	5.5	1976–77	9.6	9.3	1977	6.2	1976–77	10.1	13.6
1978	6.2	1977–78	7.6*	7.3*	1978	6.1	1977–78	15.0*	6.1
Notes:	(1)		(2)	(3)		(4)		(5)	(6)

Notes:

(1) Unemployed persons over fifteen years of age. Data for November.

(2) Percentage change from calendar year end of average weekly earnings per employed male unit.

(3) Consumer Price Index for December expressed as percentage change.

(4) Unemployed persons annual average.

(5) Percentage change from last quarter of average earnings of all employees in Great Britain.

(6) Percentage change from last quarter of Retail Price Index for all items.

* Estimate.

Australian data from Australian Bureau of Statistics *Monthly Bulletin of Business Statistics*, and predecessors. British data from Department of Employment *Gazette*.

statistics) that inflation was increasing rapidly by the time the economic boom came to an abrupt halt in mid-1974.

The steady increase in collective bargaining was accompanied by a changing role for the Commission. It adopted less a 'judicial' and more an 'accommodative' attitude to arbitration, concerned more to interpret power relationships than principles.[19] Contributing to this was the general refusal, in the late 1960s, of unions to pay the fines resulting from illegal strike action. The procedures of the tribunals became more informal and their written judgements more brief, and many commentators thought it natural that they should move into a more passive role comparable to Britain's Advisory, Conciliation and Arbitration Service.[20]

But however seductive were the new found freedoms of collective bargaining, the inflationary consequences were much the same as they had been in Britain. Fragmented and multi-level bargaining around an ever-rising 'going rate of increase' was generating unemployment at home and devaluation overseas. It was to general relief that, in April 1975, the Commission strode in with a package of indexaton supported by strict principles. The success of this package is belied by the figures in the table; currency devaluation and changes in government taxation and funding policy have forced the consumer price index considerably higher than it would otherwise have been. Given the very uneven impact of the current recession upon different industries, and given the proven ability of unions to spread pay increases from prosperous to parlous industries on grounds of comparability, there is little doubt that the Commission's policy has been highly effective in restraining prices while protecting real incomes.

In its new assertiveness, the Commission is drawing upon threequarters of a century of experience and producing a subtle blend of its judicial and accommodative roles. In attempting to discern what Britain can learn from this, we shall consider first the machinery and then the implicit principles of wage determination that underlie what the Commission has called its 'fragile package'.

The machinery of consensus

The 'fragile package' laid down no norms or guidelines but instead provided for regular adjustments to allow for increases in the consumer price index, periodic reviews to allow for increases in national productivity, and a variety of rules for dealing with exceptions. Quite apart from the delicacy of these contents its fragility was a consequence of the weak formal authority of the Commission. It has no explicit powers over federal tribunals let alone those belonging to state arbitral authorities. The willingness of individual tribunals to follow its lead,

108

even to the extent of refusing to register 'consent' agreements that breach the indexation principles, has been a measure of its authority. So also has been the willingness of the Prices Justification Tribunal to oppose price increases that stem from pay increases outside the indexation principles. The Prices Justification Tribunal occupies a similar (and similarly insecure) position to the British Prices Commission, which has also on occasion refused to sanction price increases associated with abnormally large pay settlements. Despite the noises of the government of Malcolm Fraser to the contrary, sanctions against illegal strikes are as weak as they have ever been. In short, the success of the policy depends upon a high level of consensus over the authority of the Commission and the fairness of the package.

The main devices for achieving consensus have been joint conferences and public hearings. Indexation, and the subsequent refinement of its accompanying principles, was preceded by a series of private conferences at which members of the Commission met with representatives of state and federal governments and of the employer and trade union confederal bodies. On the trade union side, the Australian Council of Trade Unions is considerably weaker than the roughly comparable Trades Union Congress in Britain, and its sister peak councils covering public, salaried, and professional workers are no stronger. It has, however, an effective and articulate leadership which has given it considerable authority in the country as a whole. The Australian employer confederations are in considerable disarray, although the emergence of the Confederation of Australian Industry in late 1977 (almost forced into the world, as the Confederation of British Industry had been a decade earlier, by a government desperate for a single employers' representative) gives hope that things may improve. These occasional conferences, under the chairmanship of the Commission President, Sir John Moore, have effectively provided an opportunity for the centralized negotiation of the rules of pay determination. Although they have not achieved unanimity, and although they have not bound the Commission, they have left it with a clear notion of what was feasible, besides performing an educative role for the protagonists.

A more regular form of joint participation in the administration of the policy is provided by the Anomalies Conference. This is a body made up of members of the Commission and of the peak trade union and employer councils which considers exceptions to the indexation principles. The procedure is that specific anomalies may be brought by the peak councils for rectification by the Conference. They are discussed with the employers concerned and, if agreement is reached, an order for rectification is made. If agreement cannot be reached, the anomaly is passed up, with a degree of Presidential discretion, for

109

consideration by a full bench of the Commission. In the three years up to September 1978 about 100 cases had been considered. Clearly, if it is to be a genuine filter rather than a blatent loophole, the strictness of the Anomalies Conference is central to the integrity of the whole policy. We shall touch on the criteria whereby cases are judged to be 'anomalies and special and extra-ordinary problems' later. Suffice it to say that the procedure appears to have avoided abuse so far, probably mainly because the trade union peak councils have seen it to be to their advantage to guarantee the 'rarity and isolation' of cases because they have wished to preserve the principle of indexation from government interference.

Public hearings are held when the National Wage Case is heard. Under the original rules these were quarterly, but with the slowing of inflation in 1978 they were changed to twice a year. The peak union and employer councils and the government present their cases in a quasi-legal manner. The whole performance receives considerable attention on the various news media, as do the reasoned judgements that the Commission issues in due course and the subsequent criticisms that this provokes. To the outside observer the whole procedure appears to be an impressive debate about social objectives and economic recipes. It is given added spice by the vigour with which the government of the day, jealous of the Commission's influence over pay, wades in on its analysis.

These mechanisms are doubtless far from perfect and may receive further alteration as experience accumulates. There is no point in arguing for their importation to Britain. But, insofar as they appear to enjoy considerable success, they provide some lessons which may be applicable to British institutions.

The first lesson is that there is considerable advantage in the body operating an incomes policy being genuinely independent of government. In the short term it is immune from cyclical electoral pressures while in the longer term its form is ultimately open to alteration by a truly outraged Parliament. Its independence increases the chance of its acting as a power broker between employer and employee organizations in a way they find they can live with. The ideal of an agreed analysis of what the country can 'afford' and how it should be divided may be as far as ever from attainment, but the chance of a compromise acceptable to employers and unions is increased.[21]

Secondly, it is possible to involve representatives of unions and employers so intimately in the administration of an incomes policy that they participate in both judicial and accommodative roles while still maintaining their independence. The judicial role is that of fixing the 'rules of the game', the wage principles to be discussed in the next section, and of interpreting them in the case of awkward anomalies. The accommodative role is that of recognizing that industrial power waxes and wanes and that exceptional cases may have to receive once-and-for-all shifts in relativities in solemn recognition that there should not be consequent repercussions. In this respect the Anomalies Conference has much in common with the procedure for special treatment proposed by the late Pay Board.[22]

The third lesson is that it is possible to operate a voluntary policy of this sort without draconian sanctions, so long as the confederal representatives of unions and employers are sufficiently committed to it. Or, more realistically, that they are sufficiently afraid of the bargaining turmoil, hyper-inflation and possibly government intervention that might follow on its collapse. The crises of 1974—75 had this effect, at least temporarily, in both Britain and Australia. The Australian experience is that it is even possible to ride out the shudders generated by the occasional maverick employer who for some reason breaches the agreed principles in making an excessive pay offer. Clearly, however, the greater employer solidarity is, the less the fragility of the package.

Finally, the determination of a country's pay strategy through a centralized process over which the government has no final say does at first sight appear to usurp the powers of Parliament. Australian governments continually complain of this. But the Australian practice is at heart the centralization of collective bargaining, albeit through the formidable midwifery skills of the Commission, and thus has much in common with the successful Swedish practice.[23] Any Parliament that seriously desired to determine the relative pay levels of its electorate would be certifiably insane. It is vastly preferable that collective bargaining should proceed under a co-ordinated procedure and negotiated principles than that a mass of fragmented bargains should over-leap each other in fear of falling behind. It is natural for a Parliament to grasp at any economic policy lever it can, but by seeking to usurp the role of confederal collective bargainers it is likely to do neither itself nor the economy any good.

The principles
The Commission described the process it has been engaged in with employers and unions since 1975 as 'the formulation of a whole set of wage principles and their systematic application over a wide range of occupations and industries throughout the country'.[24] Given the general inadequacy of theories of wage determination, it is a daunting task. The array of economic and social forces that had to be considered was much the same as has confronted successive British incomes policies.

(i) Cost of living

No country has had a tradition of protecting wages against inflation as long as Australia's. In making the central feature of its 1975 policy the indexation of pay somewhat arbitrarily abandoned in 1953, the Commission returned to a conception of 'fair play' with deep roots. At first quarterly and then half-yearly, increases were awarded based upon the increase in the retail price index of the previous period. About half of these have been full percentage indexation and the remainder based upon some formula of partial indexation, sometimes with a flat-rate element to favour the lower paid as in the British '£1 plus 4 per cent' of 1973. Generally it was not intended that this should apply to overaward payments, a stipulation which in itself encouraged a growth in 'paid-rate awards' and thus a reduction of multi-level bargaining.

Indexation has been heavily criticized by the government, which feels that a time of high unemployment is a good opportunity to adjust overseas terms of trade through a fall in real wages. But with the industrial incidence of unemployment very uneven, with strong forces of comparability between sectors, and with the exchange rate largely determined by the low employment minerals sector, the Commission is in strong disagreement. Without indexation there would be no chance for consensus.

In retrospect, it is remarkable how little British incomes policies have paid heed to the preservation of real incomes. Cost-of-living increases were not only ignored in the policies of the 1960s, they were expunged from the few industry agreements that allowed for them. In reviewing that experience, Clegg concluded this to have been a fundamental error and argued that indexation should be the spine of future policies.[25] The advice was not followed. The 'threshold payments' of 1974 were a partial lunge toward indexation inherited from Mr Heath's unsuccessful attempts to gain a consensus for his last policy. Subsequent Labour policies paid heed not to the rate of inflation recently experienced but to that which they hoped to achieve.

The apparent success of the Australian policy reinforces the strength of Clegg's argument. Since he spelt it out in 1971, two developments have increased its relevance. Wage claims have more than ever been geared to pessimistic inflationary expectations, a tendency that can probably only be countered by retrospective guarantees to protect real wages. Secondly, the clarification of British bargaining structures sketched out earlier has made it far easier to apply indexation without the dangers of double-counting that result from multi-level bargaining.

(ii) Productivity

The recurrent debate as to whether national wage increases should be related to prices or to productivity was referred to earlier. By coming down in favour of indexation, the Commission has implicitly rejected the productivity criterion, although the 1978 Principles pledged it each year to 'consider what increase in total wage or changes in conditions of employment should be awarded nationally on account of productivity'. Action on this principle has been held up by the effective stagnation of the Australian economy. Even if it had not, the intractable problems of measurement make it likely that the Commission would have been highly cautious in granting general increases on this basis.

In common with the ACTU, the Commission has set its face firmly against allowing particularly large pay increases to go to industries of high productivity growth, their view being that the benefits of new technology should accrue to the nation as a whole and not just to those fortunate enough to be immediately associated with the innovation. This criterion for pay increases reminds the British observer of the rise and fall of productivity bargains as a permissible ground for exemption from pay policy norms. Productivity bargaining never had so strong a vogue in Australia and is not seen to be so serious a potential loophole as it became in Britain in the late 1960s. Consequently, the Commission sees limited payments for changes in working practice as acceptable so long as they are carefully monitored and controlled.

The tricky problem presented by changes in the nature of work which in Britain was often associated with productivity bargains has tended in Australia to be described as 'changes in work value' and to focus on the nature of the labour input rather than the resulting change in productivity. The record of Australian arbitrators in dealing with changes in work value is less than impressive. In a country where formal job evaluation is rare, tribunals have produced impressionistic judgements about changes in relative work content that have often released tidal waves of comparisons elsewhere. A work value judgement widening the skill differential in the engineering industry in 1967 led to abrupt and hotly disputed alterations to pay structures throughout most of the rest of manufacturing.

The danger of breaches to the policy arising through work value cases is particularly acute because so much rests on the judgement of the particular tribunal involved. Well aware of this, the Commission stresses that 'the change should constitute a significant net addition to work requirements to warrant a wage increase' and that such cases should be rare and apply to a restricted number of jobs in an award. As if aware of the weakness of the work value principle, the Commission re-emphasizes the importance of preventing increases in pay arising from its application from spreading through a contagion of comparability. In Australia as in Britain, comparability has presented a recurrent problem.

(iii) Comparability

It appears to be a feature of wage determination systems that make extensive use of third-party intervention — whether through arbitration or through incomes policy — that they come to rely heavily upon arguments related to comparisons. When distanced from the crude priorities of collective bargaining power, arguments become couched in the language of 'fairness' with its inevitable concern with what other people are earning. Thus in Australia a principle as vague as it is revered is that of 'comparative wage justice'. Under this 'universal test which', according to the Commission, 'means all things to all men', employees doing the same job are considered to be entitled to the same wage irrespective of employer, region or industry. The fact that 'comparative wage justice' is denied by the actual conduct of the labour market does not seem to diminish its potency as an argument, or excuse, in arbitration hearings. Related to this is the notion of the 'flow-on', whereby increases granted in one place repercuss elsewhere. Australians tend to explain this reverence for comparison with reference to ancient national traditions of 'mateship' and equality, but Hancock has shown the practice of 'flow-ons' to be essentially a post Second World War phenomenon.[25] It is hard to escape the conclusion that the ritualizing of comparisons has less to do with popular morality than with the line of least resistance for arbitrators when confronted with powerful workforces.[27]

Comparability has always been an important feature of collective bargaining in Britain,[28] but it has been a complicated notion which incomes policies have found hard to cope with because of their need for generally applicable rules. The National Board for Prices and Incomes studiously avoided all use of the comparability criterion that Parliament had made available to them in an attempt to prevent chain reactions of pay increases fuelling inflation.[29] Their successor, the Pay Board, realized that to do this was to deny a basic conception of 'fairness' and instead introduced a subtle distinction between different forms of comparison. Those made between pay levels within bargaining units, which it termed 'differentials', were more important to the workers concerned than those made between pay levels in different bargaining units, which it named 'relativities'.[30] In addition they were fundamentally more accessible to negotiated alteration without repercussions. The lineage of this observation can be traced to the work of Kerr and a number of social psychologists to the effect

114

that individuals worry more about parochial inequities and tend to ignore the more distant ones over which they are unlikely to have influence.[31] The policy implications have yet to be followed up, however, and meanwhile there is every sign that almost unlimited comparison is becoming as acceptable in Britain as it became in Australia. We have a Standing Commission on Pay Comparability in the Public Sector, and the Employment Protection Act (1975) permits, presumably on grounds of 'fairness', resource to the law in pursuit of terms and conditions in line with the general level observed for 'comparable workers . . . in the trade, industry or section . . . in the district' who are employed 'in circumstances similar to those . . . in question'.[32]

One way of overcoming comparability problems is to isolate anomalies as special cases. Attempts to do this in Australia with 'work value' cases have been described. A category with which Britain has had similar experience is what are termed 'catch-ups' that is, cases of groups whose pay suffered because they had yet to settle for the year when the lid of the pay policy slammed shut. The procedure that the Commission allowed for evaluating such cases proved less partisan than the 'anomalies' procedure of the British Pay Board which found in favour only of civil servants.[33] A more dangerous ground for excepton was allowed under the Principles when they were revised in 1978. 'Inequities' are now said to occur 'when employees performing similar work are paid dissimilar rates of pay without good reason' so long as a significant factor is not taken to be 'an historical or geographical nexus'. There must be a fear that the jargon introduced to plug potential leaks in the policy might itself cause fresh erosions.

For all the semantic refinement, British thinking on the empirical nature of comparison probably remains ahead of the Commission's Principles. The most important and most instructive defence against the uncontrolled use of comparisons remains the Anomalies Conference with its capacity for shifting the strains of policy enforcement into intra-organizational bargaining not unlike the way in which the Social Contract shifted much of the strain onto its creator, the TUC. A major test of the new Australian institution will be whether it can reduce the emotive allure of 'comparative wage justice'.

(iv) The labour market
It is a paradox that so much concern with the price of labour should have been informed by so little consideration of labour market theory. Apart from discussion of the appropriate general level of wages, the concerns of incomes policies have been more with politics and social psychology than with conventional economics. It is a tribute to the best exponent of labour market

115

theory, Sir John Hicks, that he long ago appreciated the paradox. Writing in 1955, he noted that:

> it has never been the general rule that wage-rates have been determined simply and solely by supply and demand. Even on pure grounds of efficiency, it is desirable that the wage that is offered should be acceptable, acceptable both to the worker himself and to those with whom he is to work. There has in consequence always been room for wages to be influenced by non-economic forces — whether by custom (which, economically speaking, means supply and demand the day before yesterday), or by any other principle which affects what the parties to the wage bargain think to be *just* or *right*. Economic forces do affect wages, but only when they are strong enough to overcome these *social* forces. Now what happened as a result of the spread of public regulation, was that the social forces grew in strength.[34]

The formulators of British incomes policies in the 1960s did make provision for exceptional pay increases 'where it is essential in the national interest to secure a change in the distribution of manpower'[35] but the National Board for Prices and Incomes rapidly decided that it was a dangerously elastic loophole in times of relatively low unemployment and the provision was barely touched. With less agonizing over the economic heresy of their actions, Australian policy-makers have also largely ignored the allocative implications of wage structures. International studies that have been made suggest that by comparison with Britain and the United States this has not markedly affected relative pay either between industries or within occupational labour markets.[36]

Nowhere has this shunning of market theory been more evident than in the setting of differentials between skill levels. During times of rapid inflation both British incomes policies and Australian awards have tended to compress percentage skill differentials as a means of protecting the lower paid workers against loss in real earnings. But, in confirmation of the perceived 'fairness' of the policy, collective bargainers operating at the same time have tended to increase the compression by an even greater amount.[37] Even coolly considered Commission judgements on the size of skill margins have tended to overlook questions of skill shortages in preference to subjective impressions of job difficulty and comparability.

There is, however, a limit to the extent to which the body operating an incomes policy can overlook market forces. The rise and fall in economic fortune of individual industries and firms is likely to be reflected in due course in the bargaining power of their workforces. During the period of collective bargaining in Australia in the early 1970s, wages in the declining manufacturing industry fell back from those in the more prosperous chemicals

116

and mining industries. Both in Australia and in Britain the spread of single-employer awards or agreements is likely to increase the variation in pay levels between individual firms. Any incomes policy will store up trouble for itself in the long-run if it does not pay attention to changes in product market conditions. Whether the Australian Anomalies Conference is sufficiently flexible to do this will be an important determinant of its life expectancy.

Conclusion

Pay is a complex social phenomenon operating in a broad market setting. The British government has been forced by economic circumstances to intervene in pay determination with extreme reluctance. The Australian Commission has been forced in the same direction by its statutory obligation to administer compulsory arbitration. There is no case for the introduction of compulsory arbitration to Britain. But the features of the current Australian incomes policy which appear to give it at least partial success do not depend uniquely upon the use of arbitration. In the independence of its Commission, the use of indexation, and the heavy involvement of unions and employers in negotiating the policy rules, Australia has evolved some institutions that may be well worth emulation.

Notes

[1] E. H. Phelps Brown, 'Industrial Relations and the Law — Lessons from the Australian Experience'. *Three Banks Review*, **LXXX**, 1971; H. A. Turner, 'The Wages of Fear', *New Society*, 1 Feb 1979.

[2] During the period 1970—74 the number of working days lost in Australia and the UK were very similar — an annual average of, respectively, 684 and 606 per 1000 employees. Australian strikes, though on average only a third of the length of those in the UK during this period, were, however, much more frequent, the respective annual number of stoppages per 100,000 employees being 53.4 and 12.4. The different character of Australian strikes can be partially explained by their use as 'signalling' devices in the arbitration process rather than as simple instruments of coercion. Figures from H. A. Clegg, *Trade Unionism under Collective Bargaining*, Oxford, 1976.

[3] Australian Conciliation and Arbitration Commission, *Wage Fixation Principles: Decision*, ACAC Mis 240/78 MD Print D8400, 1978.

[4] *The Commonwealth of Australia Constitution Act, 1900*, para 51 (xxxv).

[5] Discussion of various aspects of the legislation is to be found in J. E. Isaac and G. W. Ford. *Australian Labour Relations: Readings*, Melbourne, 1971.

[6] K. J. Hancock, 'The First Half-Century of Australian Wage Policy', Industrial Relations Society Conference, Canberra, mimeo, 1978.

[7] Quoted in Hancock, ibid.

[8] K. J. Hancock, 'Wage Policy and Inflation: Australia's Experience under Compulsory Arbitration', *The Australian Economic Review*, 1971.

[9] J. E. Isaac, 'Lawyers and Industrial Relations', in A. D. Hambly and J. L. Goldring, eds, *Australian Lawyers and Social Change*, Sydney, 1976.

117

10 Some vivid examples from the post-war period are to be found in B. d'Alpuget, *Mediator: a Biography of Sir Richard Kirkby*, Melbourne, 1977.

11 Phelps Brown, op cit.

12 Royal Commission of Trade Unions and Employers Associations, *Report*, HMSO, 1968.

13 W. A. Brown and M. J. Terry, 'The Changing Nature of National Wage Agreements', *Scottish Journal of Political Economy*, **XXV**(ii), 1978.

14 Industrial Relations Research Unit, *The Changing Contours of British Industrial Relations*, Oxford (forthcoming).

15 W. A. Brown, 'Incomes Policies and Pay Differentials', *Oxford Bulletin of Economics and Statistics*, **LVIII**, 1976; W. A. Brown, 'Engineering Wages and the Social Contract', *Oxford Bulletin of Economics and Statistics*, **LXX**, 1979.

16 J. E. Isaac, 'Wage Drift in the Australian Metal Industries', *Economic Record*, **XLI**, 1965.

17 W. A. Brown and D. Fuller, 'The Impact of Overaward Pay upon the Australian Wage Structure', *Australian Bulletin of Labour*, **VI**, 1978.

18 J. H. Portus, *Australian Compulsory Arbitration 1900–1978* (forthcoming).

19 J. E. Isaac, 1976, op cit.

20 J. R. Niland, *Collective Bargaining and Compulsory Arbitration in Australia*, Sydney, 1978.

21 The merits of an uncontroversial analysis of economic prospects are pressed in the Confederation of British Industry's *Pay: the Choice Ahead*, 1979.

22 Pay Board, Advisory Report 2, *Relativities*, Cmnd 5535, 1974.

23 G. Edgren, K. O. Faxen and C. E. Odhner, *Wage Formation and the Economy*, 1973.

24 ACAC, op cit, 1978.

25 H. A. Clegg, *How to Run an Incomes Policy and Why We Made Such a Mess of the Last One*, 1971.

26 Hancock, op cit, 1978.

27 W. A. Brown and K. F. Sisson, 'The Use of Comparisons in Workplace Wage Determination', *British Journal of Industrial Relations*, **XIII**(i), 1975.

28 B. Wootton, *The Social Foundations of Wage Policy*, 1955.

29 H. A. Clegg, op cit.

30 Pay Board, op cit.

31 C. Kerr, 'Wage Relationships — The Comparative Impact of Market and Power Forces, in J. T. Dunlop, ed, *The Theory of Wage Determination*, 1957.

32 Employment Protection Act (1975), Schedule 11.

33 Pay Board, Advisory Report 1, *Anomalies*, 1973.

34 J. Hicks, 'The Economic Foundations of Wage Policy', *Economic Journal*, 1955.

35 *Prices and Incomes Policy*, Cmnd 2639, 1965.

36 D. B. Hughes, 'The Wages of the Strong and the Weak', *Journal of Industrial Relations*, **XV**(i), 1973; W. A. Brown, J. Hayles, D. B. Hughes, and L. Rowe, 'Local Labour Markets under Different Wage Fixing Arrangements', *British Journal of Industrial Relations* (forthcoming).

37 Brown and Fuller, op cit.

118

Industrialization and Development

7

Reflections on innovation

ALEC CAIRNCROSS

Innovation in the broad sense includes any element of novelty introduced into the established order of things. The novelty may be in ideas or attitudes or customs or institutions or methods of doing things or in things themselves. It is an innovation in any country if a new law is passed and in some countries it is an innovation if the laws are strictly enforced. There are countries where it would be an innovation if cows ceased to be sacred, and there have been others where it was an innovation if a man could make more money than his neighbours without having his house burnt down or suffering other mischief.

I need hardly dwell on the infinity of problems we should have to consider if innovation were so broadly defined that it covered all forms of change: intellectual, social and economic as well as technical. We have quite enough to discuss if we limit ourselves to technical change, provided we recognize that innovations in technique interact with other types of innovation and are themselves influenced by the cultural environment in which they occur. Indeed, the main problems posed by technical innovation are precisely those that derive from this interaction. If we ask why technical change is faster in one country than another, or even in one industry than another, the chances are that we shall find ourselves obliged to look beyond technology and beyond economics to cultural factors and the restraints imposed on the process of innovation by such factors. Attitudes may be more hostile to new techniques or less responsive to financial incentives in one place than another, and the commercial pursuits that give rise to innovation may be viewed with favour in one place and positive disfavour in another.

If, for the moment, we do not pursue these interactions but confine ourselves to the essentially technical forms of innovation, we have next to ask whether innovation should be taken to include every step in the process by which some new product reaches the market-place or some new process comes to be adopted commercially. Some economists have sought to distinguish innovation from invention, on the one hand, and imitation, on the other. But is there a clear line of division between these three things? I think not.

When invention takes place, for example, it may take the form of a new idea for some mechanical contrivance of which there is not even a working model, much less a carefully engineered product ready to be marketed at a known cost. An obvious example is the Gillette razor blade, which was conceived by Gillette in a kind of vision while he was shaving and which required for its eventual production some years later several major additional inventions. Here at least 'the' invention can be segregated from its subsequent commercial exploitation. But the later inventions necessary to roll steel to the thinness necessary for the production of razor blades cannot be segregated in this way. They involved expenditure to exploit Gillette's idea in much the same way as expenditure on advertising the blades after they were in production. So does it make sense to regard the first invention as excluded from the commercial innovation and the later ones as included?

The fact is that there are various stages in the introduction of a new product or process, from the original concept, if there was one to the construction of a working model; the erection of a pilot plant, the design and re-design of the finished product and its marketing on a commercial scale; and the distinction between invention and innovation has very little to do with the number of stages or their allocation between the one and the other. The true distinction is between the technical and commercial aspects of the whole operation. On the one hand there are problems of design and satisfactory performance; on the other, there are commercial problems that need enterprise and business ability. It is possible, but unlikely, that the two kinds of problem present themselves in sequence so that the invention takes place before innovation begins. The more common situation is one in which the two sets of problems are present throughout. Although some inventions are not prompted in any way by commercial considerations and may even be largely fortuitous, most inventions take place as a response to a known requirement in the market-place, and all are of economic significance only if a commercial application can be seen to exist. At the same time, the innovation, or introduction to the market place, is founded on calculations of profit that generally lead to modifications in the original design or process and these share the characteristics of invention. There are, so to speak, mini-inventions up to the point of actual manufacture.

It is not inevitable, therefore, as some earlier writers on innovation were inclined to suppose, that the different roles are performed by different agents: that an inventor comes on the stage looking for an innovator or entrepreneur who may or may not present himself. But that does happen quite frequently; and many private persons who have hit on a good idea offer it for sale to a going concern. Or a small business incapable of meeting the financial and other costs of developing an invention may sell it to a larger business with the necessary resources. Most inventions covered by patents are probably handled in some such way. Professor Jewkes has shown in his *The Sources of Invention* the continuing importance of the individual inventor and the small business in some of the most important inventions of the twentieth century. It has also been pointed out by Professor McKeown that about two-thirds of the basic innovations made by engineering companies come from outside the company and that, even inside the company, 'the technical solution to a minor innovation problem' usually comes from personal know-how. Nothing in my argument is inconsistent with these contentions. On the contrary, the very language used by Professor McKeown in speaking of 'basic innovations' where most people would say 'major inventions' and 'the technical solution to a minor innovation problem' where others would say 'mini-invention' shows the difficulty of distinguishing between invention and innovation except as different aspects, technical and commercial respectively, of a single process of introducing new products and processes to the market-place. Each aspect may be dominated by a single individual, one an inventor and one a business man, because new ideas and bold decisions are most likely to come from individuals. But they may also involve a great deal of discussion and experimentation by teams engaged in research and development or boards of management pursuing a corporate strategy. We should not try to settle which is the typical case by mere terminology.

What applies to invention and innovation applies also to invention and imitation. The process by which an invention comes into general use can again be broken up into stages, the pioneering work of the innovator being followed by its diffusion as the original invention is more and more widely copied. This sequence of events is often so depicted that the whole process of diffusion can be represented as one of imitation, devoid alike of the originality of the inventor and the enterprise of the innovator. But in practice this is rarely how things fall out. The work of the pioneer is normally incomplete and capable of further improvement; and the improvements are likely to be made by the so-called imitators in an effort to compete with the pioneer. The process of diffusion, in other words, is likely to involve fresh invention and fresh enterprise as successive modifications are made to the original design, usually by competing businesses. Once the first step has been taken, it may be followed by others just as big. In any event, if the original invention is taken up in a different country, to meet the requirements of a different market, it is likely to have to undergo quite substantial changes because of differences in the cost of materials, labour and capital, different climatic and cultural conditions, different scales of manufacture, different consumer preferences, a different balance between home and export requirements, and so on. Adaptation by imitators to meet these differences may require fresh acts of invention on the one hand and will certainly require acts of enterprise, which is the essential feature of innovation, on the other. So the imitators can claim to be, in some sort, innovators, too. Just as there are likely to be mini-inventions once an innovator gets to work on an invention, so there are likely to be minor innovations once an imitator starts to copy an innovation.

It may make these propositions more concrete if I take some familiar examples. Take, first, the motor industry. Who invented the modern motor car? Nobody did. The idea of powering a road vehicle with a steam engine was obvious enough in the railway age and must have occurred to many people. But that is a far cry from the mass market for petrol-driven private cars that exists today. Along the way one can point to a whole succession of inventors who gave us the various engine components, introduced rubber tyres, improved the suspension, and so on. One can also recall major innovators like Henry Ford who invented none of these things but were just as important to the evolution of car design. Each car company may have imitated the others in manufacturing something called a motor car; but no two companies made exactly the same car and each claimed to offer the public better value for their money than its competitors. Innovation was a competitive process in which the ideas of inventors provided one of the motive forces and in which those ideas were themselves a response to competitive pressures.

If we turn from motor cars to locomotives and aircraft we find much the same state of affairs. One may be able to point to the first occasion on which a powered vehicle operated on railway tracks or took-off in flight. But it is, broadly speaking, true to say that nobody invented the locomotive or the aircraft. A succession of men contributed to their conception and development. Their contributions were hardly ever made in isolation from commercial pressures. Each new invention was developed and brought into use where it was thought to serve some commercial purpose and not otherwise, except in the case of military aircraft where non-commercial influences predominated. Once the state becomes directly involved, as in the Advanced Passenger Train and Concorde, other factors enter, for good or ill. But the historical experience in the days when these things were left to private enterprise was one of a response by inventors and innovators alike to the requirements of consumers as registered or at least tested in the market.

Another example is provided by the steam engine itself. Most people seem to think that it was invented by James Watt. In fact, Watt did no such thing. He made an improvement of great importance to the economic use of steam-power by introducing the condenser. But the steam engine had been in course of development for a long time before Watt and continued to be developed by others long after Watt, until the thrust for a given input of fuel was several times greater than in the early Watt engines. Nothing so clearly brings out the incremental character of the innovative process or the combination of technical and commercial skill that it involves as the history of the steam engine.

Let me dwell for a moment on this incremental aspect of innovation. Those of you who were brought up on the history of the industrial revolution will remember this as a familiar theme in the development of the cotton industry. Each invention created new needs and opportunities and generated fresh inventions in response to those needs and opportunities. One invention brought forth another. But there is a less familiar aspect of the matter. One major invention — the kind that nobody can overlook and that sticks in the memory — takes a long time to digest. As it is absorbed a succession of mini-inventions takes place: either minor improvements or consequential changes elsewhere in the economy. Just as a stone cast in a pool sets up ripples along the surface, so an invention has effects that go on spreading out as more and more businesses get to work to improve or take advantage of the invention, and in doing so make fresh inventions that are less dramatic but may be of even greater importance.

When, therefore, some of us have insisted, like Dr Gibbons, on the importance of 'cumulative progressions of small-scale technological improvements', it is presumably this technical aftermath of major inventions that we have principally in mind. Some years ago the National Institute for Social and Economic Research examined the rate at which a number of important new innovations such as the float-glass process, the LD steel-making process, and so on, were adopted in each of the main industrial countries. They found that the British record in those instances was no worse than that of other countries. But if the issue was whether innovation was as rapid in Britain as elsewhere this evidence was not, in my view, decisive. As I pointed out:

> Where there is a dramatic change in technique of which everyone is well aware, and where there is a large saving to be made by adopting it, there are good reasons for expecting one country to show the same alacrity in innovation as its neighbours . . . But it cannot be assumed that for the myriad of small improvements in industrial products and practice that make up the main stream of technological advance the same laws hold good as apply to the conspicuous leaps forward that seize the public imagination.[1]

And I went on to suggest that it might be because this flow of small improvements is comparatively sluggish in Britain that this country was lagging behind industrially.

This brings me to the practical significance of my argument so far. We can take it for granted that the transformation in our material standard of living over the past two centuries is largely the result of innovations in the techniques in use. These innovations have allowed us to produce a wider variety of goods at steadily diminishing real costs. Innovations of the kind we have been discussing are simply one aspect — probably the most important aspect — of rising productivity. Productivity in turn is the main source of economic growth. Practically all economic growth that cannot be attributed to larger inputs of labour and capital must be due to large outputs per unit of input, ie to higher productivity and to the innovations yielding that higher productivity. The obstacles to growth about which we continue to hear so much in this country, are likely therefore to take the form of obstacles to innovation. And any worthwhile theory of economic growth is likely to have as its principal component a theory of innovation.

If we want to understand economic growth, therefore, we would do well to begin by studying innovation. Similarly, if we want to see our material standard of living rise faster we should consider what might be done to encourage innovation.

So far, so good. But what has this to do with the rather semantic analysis with which I began? If there were a sharp line of division between invention and the commercial adoption of the invention by an innovator, and invention were exogenous and unrelated to commercial needs, it would be natural for a government to concentrate on innovation and let invention look after itself. No doubt it would still offer the inventor patent protection with a view to encouraging more invention (but, historically speaking, patents were in fact introduced for the benefit of Elizabethan innovators who were not inventors). An individual government might also be expected to reason that since, in the nature of things, most inventions of any importance are bound to be made abroad, it would be wise to reconcile itself to this presumption and devote its energies to promoting the adoption and diffusion of inventions of foreign origin. But for some obscure reason governments of industrial countries rarely act this way.

Now what difference does it make if invention and innovation are bound up with one another so that invention is soaked in market influences and innovation is almost impossible without extensive mini-invention? If the normal situation is not one of technical certainty and commercial uncertainty, but of *general* uncertainty, then the link between the men who understand

126

technique and the men who understand business becomes of crucial importance. Technical flair has to be married to good business judgement. A successful business has to have at its disposal the necessary *technical* expertise to re-design a new product in the light of market possibilities and engineer it into production; and it has also to have strong commercial management that can form an accurate judgement of market trends and at the same time communicate the significance of these trends to its technical staff.

It is this union of two different kinds of expertise that is the most intractable element in innovation. It is not at all clear what governments can do, if anything, to strengthen the link between the two. They can do much to improve the supply and availability of engineers and chemists; they can try to improve the financial rewards to enterprise; and they can help to make funds more freely available for investment in new products and processes. But to the extent that innovation is *more* than taking a commercial risk through new investment, financial assistance is of limited value.

It is at this point that more radical voices are raised and a much wider role for the state is claimed. There will be those who point out that I have not so far made any reference to the growth of R and D, the new importance of so-called science-based industries, the possibility of re-structuring industry to allow the state to put its full weight behind promising new knowledge. I have indeed carefully refrained from using the words 'research and development', 'science' or 'science-based', 're-structuring' and 'knowledge'. I have also made no reference so far to 'technology'. These are all words calculated to give rise to confusion in any discussion of innovations in technique.

Let me look first at the part played in innovation by science. There is a large literature that gives great prominence to the influence of science. I have never myself found much historical evidence of the direct influence of science before the twentieth century, and I confess also to some distrust of science when it becomes white-hot. Most inventions until comparatively recently have been the work of men with a quite limited background in science, and those responsible for the commercial application of inventions have usually had still less familiarity with modern science. The traditional sequence, contrary to the common English belief, is that the scientist tries to understand the invention *after* it has been made. Even today many important inventions make no great demand on scientific knowledge. The invention of the jet engine, we have been reminded, required no more than a cadet's knowledge of engineering.

This may seem puzzling to those who are dazzled by computers and Concorde, moon rockets and nuclear reactors. There is obviously a growing range of activities in which further progress calls for a thorough and expert knowledge of the latest scientific thinking. This makes science a very important input into those activities, just as familiarity with the properties of various paints has always been a very important input into the activity of painting. The innovator, like the painter, has to know enough to judge what materials to use and what knowledge to draw on. In the activities where science counts for much, he must himself be enough of a scientist to co-ordinate the work of scientists with the work of other specialists and build the indispensable bridge between the technical experts and the commercial and financial experts.

The interests of the scientist are fundamentally different from those of the innovator. The one asks 'what is the truth of the matter?' The one is concerned to understand, the other to produce. The two face quite different sets of problems and the difference tends to be blurred when people add, almost absent-mindedly 'and technology' after 'science', as if subscribing to a take-over bid by science for technology. Whatever technology is, it is not science and usually it is rather messy and unscientific. It is much more akin to innovation, since the technologist, too, is concerned with production and with how to set about producing. The technologist has to equip himself with all that modern science can usefully teach him, but he has also to learn on the job what works and what does not work. It is this know-how and personal skill, acquired by experience, and often incommunicable except by example, that is the hallmark of a good technologist. The scientist, on the other hand, deals in a different kind of knowledge that can be made public in communications to *Nature*, written down and transmitted without his personal intervention, living a life of its own independent of its discoverer.

Turning out more scientists is not, therefore, the high road to more rapid innovation and economic growth. It may be helpful in a limited range of activities that make great use of scientific discovery, but even this is far from certain. The main 'science-based' activities relate to chemical processes and various aero-nautical and electrical engineering products. The contribution of scientists to these activities, so far as it takes the form of new scientific knowledge, is usually freely available or available, if patented, at a price. It is the engineering side of the business, the design of the finished equipment or process plant, that is the more difficult to copy. Indeed, if innovation in science-based activities had all the rigour and calculability of pure science, it is hard to see why the post-war record of Britain in those very activities should have been so disappointing. It is precisely because innovation is an encounter with the unknown — with the difficulties of getting things to work satisfactorily and on competitive terms, of judging market trends and assessing alternative techniques under conditions of great uncertainty — that science cannot guarantee success. The fact that scientists have played so important a part in putting a man on the moon should not blind us to their limitations in less ambitious projects where cost is a first consideration and the list of established alternatives already on the market a long one. Nor should we overlook Professor McKeown's contention that it was not science as such but 'engineering know-how, skills and organization that brought about . . . jet propulsion, nuclear power generation, communication satellites, and space travel'.

Just as there is a mistaken belief that science holds the key to innovation, so it seems to me there is an almost equally mistaken belief that innovation can be reduced to something like routine, thanks to R and D Michael Fores has pointed out that there is a good deal of hocus-pocus in R and D since in engineering at least it is nearly all development and practically none of it is research. Development is a way of taking some of the uncertainty out of innovation by trying things out on a smaller scale or in prototype before going into production. It is obviously a useful method of procedure where large capital funds are about to be committed, and it is of growing importance because of the increasing frequency with which innovation requires large indivisible investments. But in many industries quite modest expenditures on development are adequate. The necessary design work can be carried out with a staff to which no one thinks of applying the R and D label. In the motor car industry, for example — and not just the British motor car industry — R and D is negligible. The same is true of the building industry, shipbuilding and a host of industries making consumer goods.

Of course one cannot take for granted that these industries have nothing to gain from research and development undertaken by themselves, or that they gain nothing from research and development in other industries. It is entirely possible that, just as most of the major inventions used in one country originate in some other country, so most of the major advances in technique affecting one industry are made in another industry. The use of steam power in the nineteenth century had perhaps more effect on manufacturing industry than any other single invention; but the steam engine was not pioneered in any of the manufacturing industries that used it. Similarly, in more recent times the use of plastics or container transport or computers has had major effects on industrial practice and productivity in a wide range of industries. The textile industries, for example, have been revolutionized by the introduction of synthetic fibres, to the original development of which they contributed nothing. The industries in which innovation raises productivity, as recorded in the statistics, may be quite different from those that originate the innovation. So if one is looking at the source of major advances in technique and not at their subsequent influence

129

or at the long process of trial and error and mini-invention by which industry after industry profits from these advances, it is conceivable that research and development plays a very important role.

There is no doubt of the significance of this role in, say, the development of a new synthetic fibre which may cost up to £500 m. The development of a new aeroplane or a new computer can also be extremely expensive. If we reflect on the last two examples, the first thing to strike us is that they are essentially similar to the motor car case discussed earlier. The aeroplane and the computer have already been invented so that development means no more than the introduction of a new model. It is equally striking how far removed from an exact science is the process of trial and error by which such development takes place. We have yet to find a way of reducing major technical changes to routine. All we can say is that technical change, in the nature of things, is highly dependent on engineers and chemists and hence on the engineering and chemical industries, which already account for half the manufacturing labour force in all the leading industrial countries. What proportion of that half is or should be engaged in R and D is partly a semantic question and partly a matter of the kind of development work likely to be worthwhile.

To imagine that heavier expenditure on R and D will by itself speed up industrial innovation is, to say the least, highly optimistic. There is something like an inverse correlation between national R and D expenditure and the rate of economic growth. But I should not want to draw any conclusions from that since a great deal of development work is simply excluded from the statistics because of the way the figures are compiled; and in any event a great deal of the R and D in the United Kingdom, in the United States and the USSR has very little to do with advancing productivity in civil industry and is expenditure incurred at government expense to meet military and semi-military requirements. Similarly when Mr Stevens draws attention to the case of Sony as a firm which 'became rich without any R and D and now that they are rich . . . have a hell of a big R and D department' I should hesitate to conclude that Sony were wrong before or after they became rich. What was not worthwhile when they were quite small may be well worthwhile now that their capital commitments are much larger. The growth of an individual firm's R and D budget may be an interesting phenomenon to study in its own right. But we should beware of concluding that larger R and D budgets all round would give a corresponding fillip to industrial innovation.

In addition to science and R and D, there is a third recipe for more rapid innovation that is sometimes suggested. This takes the form of making changes in the structure of industry. Some people point to the inventiveness of small companies and would like to see industry made more competitive. Mr Stevens wanted new divisions within existing large companies to reproduce the conditions favourable to innovation in smaller companies. On the other hand, some people would like to see a more monopolistic structure because monopolies may hope for larger rewards from innovation if there is no danger of a swarm of imitators cutting into their profits. On this view, the state with its wider interests and more secure monopoly powers might be thought to be a more enthusiastic innovator than any private company. All of these contradictory views have been urged at one time or another with some show of reason.

The issue may not superficially appear a particularly important or interesting one. But if innovation is the key to economic growth and the form of industrial organization has a major influence on it, there is a great deal at stake in finding the most propitious industrial structure. If the state is likely to foster innovation more successfully than private industry, the case for widespread nationalization is enormously strengthened; and conversely if the state is likely to slow down innovation or make a mess of it, the case for relying on private industry becomes much more attractive. Similarly it is important to know how far competition promotes or discourages innovation, or, at least, under what conditions, and with what degree of competition, innovation is most likely to prosper.

It is generally agreed that there is no simple connection between market structure and innovation. Empirical studies yield conflicting conclusions and are often based on doubtful indicators of innovative input (such as R and D) or output (such as patents). Most writers lay emphasis on the importance of profits as a spur to innovation, on the need for competent management and on willingness to take risks. But when the more specific question is asked: 'what forms of competition are likely to favour innovation?' there is no clear answer. It goes without saying that, where innovation involves very large capital outlays, the firms concerned must be correspondingly large and there may not therefore be room in the market for more than two or three — perhaps only for one. In the chemical industry, for example, the investment necessary to develop a new fibre may be beyond the means of firms smaller in size than ICI. In nuclear power engineering, where an equally heavy outlay on development is necessary, the scope for competition is just as narrow.

But it would be a mistake to assume that the only choice, even in such cases, was between a purely monopolistic form of organization and a highly competitive one. Industrial organization is highly flexible and there are all kinds of devices for preserving some element of competition and some scope for

131

private enterprise. A state-run or state-controlled monopoly like the Atomic Energy Authority may take responsibility for some of the more uncertain stages in development or for development costs beyond the means of private firms, leaving subsequent production to competing firms. Use can be made of the familiar institution of the holding company, so common in the private sector and so rare in the public sector. Or a division of function may be worked out on the model of the Admiralty's arrangements for placing orders for warships before the First World War, when shipyards competed in design and subsequent orders for a ship to the winning design were placed with several of the competing yards.

This brings me to the role of the state in innovation, which was the subject of my Presidential Address to the British Association some years ago. I have not changed my view that governments are usually overconfident, clumsy and wasteful in their approach to industrial innovation and have little understanding of what it requires. The experience of Communist countries amply confirms this view, but it is not necessary to go outside this country for evidence. However, in a mixed economy, there is simply no escape from direct state involvement in innovation in those industries which are already nationalized, as well as in those that sell to the government or buy from the government or receive government support in one way or another; and this adds up to a large slice of the total economy.

The state's contribution to innovation is too vast a subject to discuss at the tail-end of a paper, and the same is true of innovation in Britain and the circumstances limiting it. But perhaps I might venture one concluding reflection on this theme before I sum up.

It seems to me that the most important single influence on innovation is the reward which it brings. Without an adequate reward, managements will be inclined to refrain from changes that carry the risk of loss and that might stir up opposition or discontent. In order to face the costs of change they need the prospect of some additional gain. Of course they may be insensitive to such a prospect because they are already making large profits; but as a rule they have an eye to the future and will not want to see competitors steal a march on them. What every management knows, however, is that the full gains from innovation are unlikely to come to the innovator. Some will be taken by the state in extra taxation; some will go to the consumer, either because of the need to lower prices in order to extend the market or because competition brings the price down; some will also go to the wage-earner, if the routine of his work is disturbed and he makes a successful claim for higher wages; and only the residue comes to the innovator and his company.

If one wants to understand why innovation is inhibited in Britain it is this four-way split from which one ought to start. I have yet to see a systematic comparison between Britain and other countries or between one type of investment and another. But there are certainly big differences, not least in the extent to which wage-earners can insist on a share in the prospective gains. If a businessman does not innovate but sinks more capital in exactly the same plant and produces by exactly the same methods as before, he forfeits no part of the return on his capital in higher wages. But the moment he innovates, he finds himself engaged in a dispute over manning ratios or piece-rates or in some other tug-of-war with his employees over the share they feel entitled to claim from the higher profit to be expected from the innovation. I am told that this tussle is peculiar to the United Kingdom. I would argue that it is a good deal more common in the United Kingdom than in other countries, and that it helps to account for the slower rate of innovation and growth in this country.

I can now sum up my arguments:

(i) Innovation is not something different from trying to become more efficient: it is simply one aspect of it. Even new products can be regarded as ways of helping the consumer to satisfy his wants more efficiently.

(ii) Just as one tries harder to improve efficiency if there is money in it and if one has an idea how to set about it, so innovation is a *commercial* response to available ideas and markets.

(iii) Innovation calls for enterprise and for adequate rewards to encourage enterprise.

(iv) At the heart of successful innovation lies good management, co-ordinating the activities of technical, commercial and financial staff and ensuring the right personal contacts and communication. There are several linkages that are of crucial importance, eg between research and development and production, between development engineers and marketing and financial experts, and so on.

(v) The social system and environment must be propitious to new ideas and their adoption. At the most elementary level there must be easy communication between different people and different groups: freedom to exchange ideas, to talk and read and experiment. The spread of technical ideas rests more heavily on personal contacts over wide areas than on any single factor. At a higher level there must be the necessary expertise to draw upon: engineers, well-trained and open to new ideas; and managers with the experience required. Those who have the drive and persistence indispensable to innovation (who may not be the most attractive personalities) should be able to count, if not on public recognition and support, at least on acquiescence and freedom from being penalized. If we want golden eggs we should not persecute geese.

(vi) In a highly centralized system, there is more power to enforce innovation but less likelihood of spontaneous innovation. There is a need in any form of organization to mobilize initiative behind innovation and to decentralize those functions that are either charged with responsibility for innovation or offer most scope for it.

(vii) If we want faster innovation we should not neglect to reward it. It is not easy to do so directly, but a great deal of legislation, reduces the reward to the innovator. Wage bargaining also tends to remove part of the profit from innovation.

(viii) We should always recollect that it is far easier to copy than to create, and that the rate of diffusion is far more important than the rate of generation of new developments. We should never be afraid to borrow, since in the end that is what everybody but the pioneer has to do. And if we want faster innovation in this country (which I sometimes doubt), we might start off the borrowing process by finding out how other countries manage to move ahead so fast and borrow from their experience.

Note

[1] *Inflation Growth and International Finance*, 1975, p 63.

8

Common markets in developing countries[1]

A. M. EL-AGRAA

The theory of economic integration has evolved, almost exclusively, from discussion of post Second World War European developments: the European Economic Community (EEC), the European Free Trade Association (EFTA) and COMECON — their Eastern European counterpart.[2] This is in spite of the fact that the East African Common Market (EACM) was one of the pioneers in this field.[3]

The first rigorous attempt at a consideration of economic integration in the context of development was made by Professor Brown[4] and most of the subsequent work has concentrated on the estimate of the gains and losses from such associations.[5] The most notable exceptions are the contributions by the late Professor Johnson[6] and by Cooper and Massell.[7]

This essay develops a three-country version of the model used by Brown to highlight some of his conclusions and to add a significant new conclusion. The theory of economic integration and development in particular and of economic integration in general will then be examined in the light of this new conclusion.

1. The theory of economic integration[8]

It used to be the accepted tradition that economic integration is beneficial and should be encouraged.[9] Viner challenged this tradition by pointing to the harmful 'trade diversion' effects of a 'customs union'. He emphasized that 'trade diversion' should be compared with 'trade creation' before an economic judgement can be passed on a 'customs union'.[10] Cooper and Massell then demonstrated that a unilateral tariff reduction will always be superior to a 'customs union'.[11]

Developments from there on took two different paths. Johnson reversed the Vinerian conclusion: 'trade diversion' is beneficial for the countries concerned while 'trade creation' may be good or bad.[12] The other developments centred on the terms of trade effects[13] and the (so-called) dynamic effects.[14] Cooper and Massell demonstrated that two countries acting together can do better than each acting alone.[15]

As far as developing countries are concerned it was immediately realized[16]

K

135

that the static resource reallocation effects have little relevance. The theory suggested that there would be more scope for 'trade creation' if the countries concerned were initially very competitive in production but potentially very complementary and that a customs union would be more likely to be 'trade creating' if the partners conducted most of their foreign trade amongst themselves.[17] These conditions are unlikely to be satisfied in the majority of the developing nations. Moreover, most of the effects of integration are bound to be 'trade diverting' since most developing countries seek to industrialize.

On the other hand, it was also realized that an important obstacle to the development of industry in the less developed nations is the inadequate size of their individual markets.[18] It is therefore necessary to increase the market size so as to encourage optimum plant installations — hence the need for economic integration. This would, however, result in industries clustering together in the relatively more advanced of these nations — those that have already commenced the process of industrialization.[19]

Brown, using a two-country model, argued that even though the clustering together of industries might be a natural development, the other parties to the union would gain from such an association and that the benefits could be more equitably distributed if some fiscal arrangements were introduced for this purpose.[20]

These developments have led to the conclusion that economic integration in the advanced world is a very different matter from that in the developing world.[21] This conclusion is examined by a three-country version of Brown's model.

2. A three-country version of Brown's model

In order to simplify the analysis I shall assume the following:[22]

(a) Factors or production are perfectly mobile within each country but lack the freedom to move across national borders. The union is not allowed to introduce measures to divert resources to the industrializing partner.[23]

(b) There is a plentiful unutilized supply of all factors of production.

(c) The newly introduced industrial output is to be sold as a substitute for a product imported from the rest of the world.[24] This product will be sold at a price equal to the import price plus the customs duty.[25]

(d) Each of the partner nations receives customs revenue from those commodities which are consumed within its territories as well as the revenue from direct and excise taxes collected accordingly.

(e) The governments' budgets are to remain balanced throughout, so that any change in government revenue must bring about an equal change in government expenditure. This change in expenditure must fall on goods and services so that transfers are unaltered.

(f) No change in investment takes place in any of the partner countries.[26]

The newly produced output of manufactured goods by the partner that has already commenced industrialization will be indicated by P. The tax-free value of the imports displaced by this new product is $P(1-t)$, where t is the *ad valorem* marginal rate of duty in the three partner countries: 1, 2 and 3. Country 1 is the partner that has already started industrializing.

x_1 and x_2 of P are consumed in countries 1 and 2 respectively while the remainder $P(1 - x_1 - x_2)$ is consumed in country 3. Thus the consumption of P in countries 2 and 3 together is equal to $P(1 - x_1)$.

m_1, m_2 and m_3 are the total marginal propensities to import (mpi) of countries 1, 2 and 3 respectively. These mpi are composed of three parts each: a_1, a_2 and $[m_1 - (a_1 + a_2)]$ are country 1's mpi from countries 2, 3 and the rest of the world respectively; a_3, a_4 and $[m_2 - (a_3 + a_4)]$ are country 2's mpi from countries 1, 3 and the rest of the world respectively, and; a_5, a_6 and $[m_3 - (a_5 + a_6)]$ are the mpi of country 3 from 1, 2 and the rest of the world respectively.

t^* is the direct marginal tax rate.

The change in income in each country due to the newly introduced industrial output is measured in each country by:

$$Y = C + Td + X - M^{27}$$

where Y is the change in income at factor cost, C is the change in consumption at market price, Td is the change in direct tax revenue, X is the change in exports at market price and M is the change in imports at factor cost.

The change in direct tax revenue is related to the change in income by t^*, the direct marginal tax rate $(Td = t^*Y)$, Consumption is relaaed to disposable income by c, the marginal propensity to consume (mpc) $[C = c(Y - Td) = cY(1 - t^*)]$.

Td appears in the equation because the change in consumption expenditure is related to disposable income. Hence the government must receive income tax revenue. Since it is assumed that the budget is balanced, tax receipts must be spent on goods and services. Therefore, Td represents the government sector.

There are two parts to the change in country 1's exports. The first part is equal to x_2P and $P(1 - x_1 - x_2)$, the sum of the two being $(1 - x_1)P$. This represents the substitution of part of the newly produced industrial output in country 1 for imports from the rest of the world in countries 2 and 3. The second part is equal to a_3Y_2 and a_tY_3. These represent the increased exports to countries 2 and 3 induced by their respective income changes.

There are also two parts to the change in imports in country 1: an increase equal to m_1Y_1 due to the increased income in the country, and a reduction equal to $x_1P(1 - t)$ which is the consequence of country 1's substitution of a proportion of the new industrial output for imports from the rest of the world.

Taking all this into account plus the consumption and the direct tax receipts changes one gets:

$$Y_1 = \frac{a_3Y_2 + a_5Y_3 + P(1 - x_1t_1)^{28}}{s_1(1 - t_1^*) + m_1} \tag{1}$$

For country 2 the change in exports is equal to a_1Y_q and a_6Y_e, which are the exports induced by the income changes in countries 1 and 3 respectively. The change in imports is equal to m_2Y_w which is the increased imports in country 2 induced by its income change, and tx_2P which is the amount of import duty previously collected from imports coming from the rest of the world now replaced by imports from country 1. This customs revenue is now received by country 1 as part of the price of the proportion of P consumed in country 2 (assumption c).

This gives:

$$Y_2 = \frac{a_1Y_1 + a_6Y_3 - t_2x_2P}{s_2(1 - t_2^*) + m_2} \tag{2}$$

Following exactly the same procedure as in the case of country 2, one can derive the income change for country 3. Thus the change in exports is equal to a_2Y_1 and a_4Y_2, and the change in imports is equal to m_3Y_3 and $t_3P(1 - x_1 - x_2)$. Hence:

$$Y_3 = \frac{a_2Y_1 + a_4Y_2 - t_3P(1 - x_1 - x_2)}{s_3(1 - t_3^*) + m_3} \tag{3}$$

These equations are untidy in their present form, particularly since one is interested in the income changes in terms of P alone. Eliminating the irrelevant income changes gives:

$$Y_1 = \frac{M(b_2b_3 - a_4a_6) + N(a_4a_5 + a_3b_3) + K(a_3a_6 + a_5b_2)}{D} \tag{1'}$$

$$Y_2 = \frac{M(a_2a_6 + a_1b_3) + N(b_1b_3 - a_2a_5) + K(a_1a_5 + a_6b_1)}{D} \tag{2'}$$

and

$$Y_3 = \frac{M(a_1a_4 + a_2b_3) + N(a_2a_3 + a_4b_1) + K(b_1b_2 - a_1a_3)}{D} \tag{3'}$$

where:
$D = b_1b_2b_3 - a_4a_6b_1 - a_1a_3b_3 - a_1a_4a_5 - a_2a_3a_6 - a_2a_5b_2$;
$M = P(1 - x_1t_1)$;
$N = -t_2x_2P$;

138

$$K = -t_3P(1 - x_1 - x_2);$$
$$b_1 = s_1(1 - t_1^*) + m_1;$$
$$b_2 = s_2(1 - t_2^*) + m_2;$$
$$b_3 = s_3(1 - t_3^*) + m_3.$$

Equations $(1') - (3')$ can be used to formulate the net spill-over ratios:[29]

$$\frac{Y_2}{Y_1} = \frac{M(a_2a_6 + a_1b_3) + N(b_1b_3 - a_2a_5) + K(a_1a_5 + a_6b_1)}{M(b_2b_3 - a_4a_6) + N(a_4a_5 + a_3b_3) + K(a_3a_6 + a_5b_2)} \quad ; \qquad (4)$$

$$\frac{Y_3}{Y_1} = \frac{M(a_1a_4 + a_2b_2) + N(a_2a_3 + a_4b_1) + K(b_1b_2 - a_1a_3)}{M(b_2b_3 - a_4a_6) + N(a_4a_5 + a_3b_3) + K(a_3a_6 + a_5b_2)} \quad ; \qquad (5)$$

and
$$\frac{Y_2}{Y_3} = \frac{M(a_2a_6 + a_1b_3) + N(b_1b_3 - a_2a_5) + K(a_1a_5 + a_6b_1)}{M(a_1a_4 + a_2b_2) + N(a_2a_3 + a_4b_1) + K(b_1b_2 - a_1a_3)} \quad . \qquad (6)$$

These equations are mathematically too complicated to handle. To make deductions from them I shall insert some hypothetical but representative values.[30] The data are given in Table 1 and the resulting income changes in Table 2.

These results lead to the following conclusions:

(a) Y_1 is a multiple of the newly introduced industrial output (the results range from 2.225P to 1.787P) while Y_2 and Y_3 are a small but positive fraction of it (the results range from 0.59P to 0.143P). These results are clearly indicated by the net spill-over ratios, which range from 0.072 to 0.265 (7—25 per cent).[31]

(b) Cases II — VII, considered together, clearly indicate that the higher (the lower) the three countries' marginal propensities to import from each other, the higher (the lower) the income changes, and the higher (the lower) their marginal propensities to import from the rest of the world, the lower (the higher) the resulting income changes (Cases VI and VII).[32]

Within this general conclusion one notices the following:

(i) the higher (the lower) the marginal propensities of the three countries to import from each other, the higher (the lower) the rates of change of the income changes for countries 2 and 3 (Case II). In other words, the net spill-over ratios are at their highest (lowest);

(ii) the higher (the lower) the marginal propensity of country 2 (3) to import from country 1, the higher (the lower) the income change over all. This income change is, however, experienced equally by country 3 (2) — [Cases II and V]. This suggests the result that one would expect: *the crucial factor is the marginal propensity of country 1 to import from the other two countries;*[33]

TABLE 1
Representative Data

Variable	t_1	t_2	t_3	t_1^*	t_2^*	t_3^*	s_1	s_2	s_3	a_1	a_2	a_3	a_4	a_5	a_6	m_1	m_2	m_3	x_1	x_2	$1-x_1-x_2$
Case I	0.2	0.2	0.2	0.1	0.1	0.1	0.15	0.15	0.15	0.05	0.05	0.05	0.05	0.05	0.05	0.3	0.3	0.3	0.75	0.125	0.125
	0.2	*0.1*	*0.2*	*0.1*	*0.05*	*0.1*	*0.15*	*0.1*	*0.15*	*0.1*	*0.1*	*0.1*	*0.1*	*0.1*	*0.1*	*0.35*	*0.3*	*0.3*	*0.75*	*0.25*	*0.0*
	0.3	*0.2*	*0.2*	*0.2*	*0.1*	*0.1*	*0.2*	*0.15*	*0.15*	*0.05*	*0.05*	*0.1*	*0.05*	*0.05*	*0.05*	*0.3*	*0.35*	*0.3*	*0.5*	*0.25*	*0.25*
	0.2	*0.3*	*0.2*	*0.1*	*0.2*	*0.1*	*0.15*	*0.2*	*0.15*	*0.05*	*0.05*	*0.05*	*0.1*	*0.05*	*0.05*				*0.8*	*0.1*	*0.1*
	0.3	*0.3*	*0.3*	*0.2*	*0.2*	*0.2*	*0.2*	*0.2*	*0.2*	*0.05*	*0.05*	*0.0*	*0.05*	*0.05*	*0.05*						
	Cases XIX–XXII			Cases XV–XVIII			Cases XI–XIV			Cases II–V						Cases VI and VIII			Cases VIII–X		

Note: Case I is the basic case; all other cases have the same values for their variables except for the variables specified. For each category, the case number is to be read from top to bottom.

TABLE 2
Results

Result Case	Y_1 P	Y_2 P	Y_3 P	$\dfrac{Y_2}{Y_1}$	$\dfrac{Y_3}{Y_1}$	$\dfrac{Y_2}{Y_1}$
I	1.999	0.195	0.195	0.097	0.097	1.000
II	2.225	0.590	0.590	0.265	0.265	1.000
III	2.022	0.198	0.198	0.098	0.098	1.000
IV	2.002	0.198	0.218	0.099	0.109	0.907
V	1.976	0.192	0.192	0.097	0.097	1.000
VI	1.787	0.167	0.167	0.094	0.094	1.000
VII	1.996	0.174	0.192	0.087	0.096	0.907
VIII	1.999	0.143	0.246	0.072	0.123	0.581
IX	2.102	0.143	0.143	0.068	0.068	1.000
X	1.978	0.205	0.205	0.104	0.104	1.000
XI	2.002	0.218	0.198	0.109	0.099	1.102
XII	1.806	0.170	0.170	0.094	0.094	1.000
XIII	1.996	0.176	0.192	0.088	0.096	0.915
XIV	1.802	0.151	0.151	0.084	0.084	1.000
XV	1.998	0.191	0.194	0.096	0.097	0.985
XVI	2.072	0.204	0.204	0.099	0.099	1.000
XVII	2.000	0.202	0.196	0.101	0.098	1.032
XVIII	2.074	0.213	0.213	0.103	0.103	1.000
XIX	2.003	0.224	0.198	0.112	0.099	1.130
XX	1.821	0.172	0.172	0.094	0.094	1.000
XXI	1.995	0.165	0.191	0.083	0.096	0.865
XXII	1.813	0.138	0.138	0.076	0.076	1.000

(iii) the higher (the lower) country 2's marginal propensity to import from country 3, the higher (the lower) the income change in country 3 and the lower the rate of change of income change in country 1 (Case IV).[34]

(c) As one would expect, the higher (the lower) the marginal propensities to save the lower (the higher) the income changes (Cases XI — XIV). Also the higher (the lower) the income tax rates, the higher (the lower) the income changes (Cases XV — XVIII). This is clearly suggested by the definitional expressions.[35] Moreover, the higher (the lower) the tariff rates, the lower (the higher) the income changes.[36]

(d) The most significant conclusion is that the lower (the higher) the proportion of the newly introduced industrial output consumed by a partner, the higher (the lower) that country's income change (Cases VIII — X). The importance of this conclusion will be discussed in the following section.

3. Interpretation of the conclusions

Most of these conclusions are quite consistent with Brown's except for the generalizations made possible by the use of a three-country model. Conclusion (d) is, however, not mentioned by him.[37] Here, country 3 (2) decides not to partake in this union (Case VIII). This decision is reflected in its continuing to import from the outside world rather than consume any part of the newly introduced industrial product. As a result, country 3 experiences an income change much larger than it would as a member of the union (Case I). The income change is $0.246P$ as against $0.195P$, giving a net spill-over ratio of 0.123 as against 0.097.

This result can be shown mathematically. Suppose that country 3 decides not to partake in this common market, then:

For Y_1, the components are as before. Hence

$$Y_1 = \frac{a_3 Y_2 + a_5 Y_3 + P(1 - x_1 t_1)}{s_1(1 - t_1^*) + m_1} \tag{1}$$

For Y_2, M_2 becomes:

$$m_2 Y_2 + t(1 - x_1)P$$

all the other components remaining the same as before. Hence

$$Y_2 = \frac{a_1 Y_1 + a_6 Y_3 - t_2 P(1 - x_1)}{s_2(1 - t_2^*) + m_2} \tag{16}$$

For Y_3, M_3 becomes:

$$m_3 Y_3$$

all the other components remaining the same. Hence

$$Y_3 = \frac{a_2 Y_1 + a_4 Y_2}{s_3(1 - t_3^*) + m_3} \tag{17}$$

Comparing (17) and (3) it is obvious that Y_3 as given by (17) is greater than Y_3 as given by equation (3) by a multiple of

$$t_3 P(1 - x_1 - x_2).$$

The multiplier is given by

$$\frac{1}{s_3(1 - t_3^*) + m_3}.$$

The point that needs emphasizing, therefore, is that *the crucial consideration is not whether or not Y_2 and Y_3 would be negative or positive, but whether or not they would have been greater had countries 2 and 3 decided to stay out of the union.* The results clearly show that countries 2 and 3 are better off staying out of this association.

Could one then argue [from conclusion b(ii)] that since it is country 1's marginal propensity to import from 2 and 3 which is the most significant element then it is to the benefit of 2 and 3 to join a union with 1? It is quite obvious that such an argument would be absurd — these 'spread' effects are the outcome of the three countries' normal relationships (apart from this new industrial output) and unless country 1 suddenly decides to exercise some compulsion on 2 and 3, there is no reason why these normal relationships should be disturbed. Moreover, it is to the benefit of country 1 to have a market for disposing of its surplus industrial output.

Hence, both these considerations point to the fact that it is country 1 which benefits most from this association.

A reappraisal

I have demonstrated that there is no economic justification for a customs union of developing countries based on protected industrialization, ie a trade diverting association. One could of course argue that such a union would be desirable if fiscal arrangements were established with the aim of distributing the gains equitably or of locating the industries in a more scattered fashion.[38] Both would be reasonable suggestions but they are not of direct relevance here.

My immediate concern is with the proposition that the theory of economic integration as developed for the advanced world has very little relevance to the developing world. There are three basic considerations for a *purely* economic justification of customs unions: (i) the static resource reallocation effects, ie the 'trade creation'/'trade diversion' effects, (ii) the terms of trade effects and (iii) the (so-called) dynamic effects — economies of scale and external economies. I have demonstrated that there is no difference between advanced and developing nations as far as (i) is concerned: trade diversion is bad because the country concerned is bound to lose (*a multiple* of the loss of) its tariff revenue.

As for the terms of trade effects, these can only come about if the members of the union can charge higher export prices and/or bargain for lower import prices. here one is thrown into the world of monopoly/monopsony or oligopoly/oligopsony where any outcome is perfectly feasible, particularly if retaliation by the injured parties is allowed for.[39] I cannot, however, see any differences between advanced and developing countries in this respect, and if the

143

immediate past is anything to go by, it is the OPEC countries that seem to have gained from such action. Needless to say, OPEC is not a customs union.

As for scale economies, it is equally obvious that there is more scope for them in a union of developing countries than in the EEC or in EFTA; they are the basic necessity for integration and development.[40]

When it comes to external economies, it is also obvious that there is much more scope for them (and absolute need for development purposes) in the developing than in the advanced world: a pool of skilled labour, the provision of technology and infrastructure are the basic necessities of industry and they are lacking.

It therefore appears that the body of theory developed for economic integration in the advanced world is *more appropriate* for developing countries.

Conclusion

This essay supports Johnson's[41] preference for a political economy of integration. There is *essentially no theoretical difference* between economic integration in the advanced world and in the developing world. However, there is a major difference in terms of the type of economic integration[42] that is politically feasible: the need for an equitable distribution of the gains foom industrialization and the location of industries is an important issue. This suggests that any type of economic integration that is being contemplated must incorporate as an essential element a common fiscal authority and some co-ordination of economic policies. But then one could equally well argue that *some degree* of these elements is necessary in any type of integration.[43]

Notes

[1] I would like to acknowledge the help of Messrs J. F. Brothwell, D. Harkess and B. P. M. McCabe The responsibility for the views expressed is, of course, entirely mine.

[2] The literature to date is certainly biased towards common markets in advanced economies — of the references cited by Lipsey, 1960, Corden, 1965 and Krauss, 1972.

[3] cf J. F. Due and P. Robson, 1967, p 553. One should emphasize, however, that the EACM was formed for colonial administrative convenience rather than as a voluntary association of independent nations — A. Hazelwood, 1967, chapter 1 and 1975, chapter 3.

[4] A. J. Brown, 1961.

[5] cf B. F. Massell, 1963, W. T. Newlyn, 1965 and 1966, A. Hazelwood, May 1966 and August 1967, R. N. Wood, November 1966, D. Ghai, 1967, P. Robson, 1968, F. Kahnert and others, 1969, A. Hazelwood, 1975.
Newlyn's (1965) contribution contains some interesting ideas on the methodology of estimating these gains and losses, eg his concept of the 'shiftability' of industry.

[6] H. G. Johnson, 1965. The ideas put forward in this article are general enough to cover integration at all levels of economic development. No reference to this article is made in any of the literature on economic integration and development. It must be added, however, that it has made little impact on the theory of economic integration in developed countries.

144

[7] C. A. Cooper and B. M. Massell, 1965.

[8] For a comprehensive survey of the literature see Lipsey, 1960, Corden, 1965 and Krauss, 1972.

[9] The logic behind this ran thus: free trade maximizes world welfare; a customs union is a move towards free trade; a customs union therefore increases world welfare even though it does not maximize it.

[10] 'Trade creation' takes place when a partner country replaces its own expensive production by imports from a less costly partner. 'Trade diversion' occurs when the *initial* amount of cheap imports that used to come from the rest of the world is replaced by costly imports from the partner. I am deliberately using Johnson's (1974) definition of 'trade diversion' so as to avoid the non-problem of a trade-diverting welfare-increasing customs union.

[11] Cooper and Massell, 1965, *Economic Journal.*

[12] Johnson (1965) argues as follows: protection is a rational 'maximizing' response of governments which perceive national economic welfare (real income) as reflecting not only consumers' interests (ie the consumption of private goods) but also producers' interests [ie the consumption of a 'public good' which takes the form of a collective preference for industrial production (and employment) independent of the direct satisfaction from the consumption of industrial products].

[13] cf Arndt, 1968 and 1969, and Petith, 1977.

[14] B. Balassa (1962) and T. Scitovsky (1958) were the first to use the term in the context of economic integration. Corden (1972) shows that scale economies can easily be tackled within the traditional framework.

[15] Cooper and Massell, 1965. This conclusion is not as clear-cut as is suggested because one of the necessary pre-conditions is that non-optimum tariffs are being used.

[16] A. J. Brown, 1961, p 34.

[17] cf R. G. Lipsey, 1960 and J. E. Meade, 1956.

[18] cf A. J. Brown, 1961 and A. Hazelwood, 1967 and 1975.

[19] cf A. J. Brown, 1961, A. Hazelwood, 1975, P. Robson, 1969. This is the so-called 'back-wash' effect.

[20] A. J. Brown, 1961. This is the so-called 'spread' or 'multiplier' effect.

[21] A. Hazelwood, 1975, P. Robson, 1969, F. Kahnert and others, 1969.

[22] These are the same assumptions made by A. J. Brown, 1961, pp 88–9.

[23] The association is therefore a customs union rather than a common market; in a common market there should be free factor mobility across the borders of partner countries.

[24] The customs union is therefore purely trade diverting.

[25] This amounts to assuming that the customs union has an external tariff rate equal to the initial (equal) rate(s).

[26] This might seem like a very strange assumption particularly when a new industrial output is to be introduced. It will be apparent, however, that the relaxation of this assumption will actually reinforce the conclusions of the analysis rather than render them invalid.

[27] '. . . since that part of extra government expenditure which is financed by indirect taxation is offset by the subtraction of the extra revenue required to reduce income to a factor cost basis', A. J. Brown, 1961, p 89. Expressed in symbols: $Y_{f.c.} + M_{f.c.} + Ti = C_{m.p.} + G_{m.p.} + X_{m.p.}$ (i) where $G_{m.p.} = Ti + Td$ (ii). Substituting (ii) into (i), simplifying and rearranging one gets: $Y_{f.c.} = C_{m.p.} + Td + X_{m.p.} - M_{f.c.}$

[28] Readers interested in the derivation of this and the following equations should contact the author.

[29] The term 'net spill-over ratio' was coined by Newlyn in his article, 1966, p 131.

[30] The hypothetical data is consistent with that used by Brown in his article and is subject to the same limitations cited there. I have, however, chosen a range of values so that most possible situations can be examined.

[31] This result is clearly consistent with Brown's: '. . . the country in which manufacturing arises to displace imports into the free trade area experiences a rise in income equal to twice the new manufactured output, the rest of the area experiences a rise in income equal to about a tenth of the new manufactured output' (p 90).

[32] This result is also clearly specified by Brown: '. . . the higher this marginal propensity to import, the greater B's share in the total income increase for the free trade area' (p 91).

[33] Brown calculates the crucial value for country 1's marginal propensity to import from country 2 (and 3 here) — this is the value for a_1 (and a_2) which produces Y_2 ($=Y_3$) equal to zero. The equivalent values for the model used in this chapter are given in the appendix: Table 1. They are not discussed at length at this stage for reasons that will shortly become apparent and also because it 'does not seem very likely that the marginal propensity of one country to import from a neighbour to which it is bound in a free trade area will be so small as to bring about this result', Brown, p 91.

[34] This result is consistent with the previous conclusion and with the concept of the multiplier in general.

[35] This is because any income tax revenue is spent by the government to counteract the effect of the difference between 'earned' and 'disposable' income on consumption. But it is well known that a government expenditure financed by equal taxation has a multiplier effect, particularly in such a highly simplified model.

[36] This follows from assumption (c): the higher the tariff rate, the greater the loss to 2 and 3 from such a union.

[37] Brown does hint at the conclusion but in a different context, 'though the chance of "country B" actually losing national income as a result of A's development is small . . . the chance of its government losing revenue is somewhat greater. There is a direct loss of customs revenue equal to $tc(1 - x)P$', Brown, p 91. It is apparent from the main text that the actual loss must be a multiple of that loss in tariff revenue.

[38] A. J. Brown, 1961, p 91, determines the income changes for the partner countries in the situation when there is a common pooling of revenues and their distribution. The equivalent equations for the three-country model can easily be worked out but they are not really relevant to the argument.

[39] cf Arndt, 1968. Petith (1977) finds evidence for terms of trade improvements in the EEC, but specifies that no retaliation has in fact occurred during the period examined.

[40] It has been argued quite coherently that it is the market size that is an important factor in economic development, cf A. J. Brown, 1961, A. Hazelwood, 1967, 1975 and R. F. Mikesell, 1960. Moreover, the discussion between H. G. Johnson and J. Williamson (1962) has questioned that there is great scope for scale economies in the EEC, cf Johnson, 1957, 1958, J. Williamson, 1971 and A. J. Brown, 1961.

[41] H. G. Johnson, 1965.

[42] B. Balassa (1962) describes different types of economic integration (free trade areas; customs unions; common markets; economic unions; political unions) which some authors seem to have taken too literally. Some co-ordination is necessary even for integration at the commodity level as was the case in the European Coal and Steel Community.

[43] cf the recommendations of the Raisman Committee (1961) for the EACM.

References

S. W. Arndt, 1968, 'On Discriminatory vs non-preferential Tariff Policies', *Economic Journal* (EJ), 78.

S. W. Arndt, 1969, 'Customs Unions and The Theory of Tariffs', *American Economic Review* (AER), **LIX**. Also reprinted in Robson, 1971.

B. Balassa, 1962, *The Theory of Economic Integration*.

A. J. Brown, 1961, 'Economic Separatism versus a Common Market in Developing Countries', *Yorkshire Bulletin of Economic and Social Research* (YB), 13.

C. A. Cooper and B. F. Massell, 1965a, 'A New Look at Customs Union Theory', *EJ*, 75.

C. A. Cooper and B. F. Massell, 1965b, 'Towards a General Theory of Customs Unions in Developing Countries', *Journal of Political Economy* (JPE), 73. Also reprinted in Robson, 1971.

W. M. Corden, 1965, *Recent Developments in the Theory of International Trade*, Princeton University, International Finance Section.

W. M. Corden, 1972, 'Economies of Scale and Customs Union Theory', *JPE*, 80.

J. Haldi, 1967, 'Economies of Scale in Industrial Plants', *JPE*, 75.

A. Hazelwood, 1966, 'The "shiftability" of Industry and the Measurement of Gains and Losses in the East African Common Market', *Bulletin of the Oxford University Institute of Economics and Statistics*, BOUIES, 28.

A. Hazelwood, 1967, *African Integration and Disintegration*.

A. Hazelwood, 1975, *Economic Integration: The East African Experience.*

A. Hazelwood, 1976, 'The East African Common Market: Importance and Effects', (BOUIES), 28.

H. G. Johnson, 1957, 'The Criteria of Economic Advantage', *BOUIES*, 19.

H. G. Johnson, 1958, 'The Gains from Freer Trade with Europe: An Estimate', *Manchester School*, 73.

H. G. Johnson, 1965, 'An Economic Theory of Protectionism, Tariff Bargaining and the Formation of Customs Unions', *JPE*, 73.

H. G. Johnson, 1974, 'Trade-Diverting Customs Unions: A Comment', *EJ*, 81.

F. Kahnert, P. Richards, E. Stoutjesdijk, P. Thomopoulos, 1969, *Economic Integration Among Developing Countries*, Development Centre of the OECD, Paris.

M. B. Krauss, 1972, 'Recent Developments in Customs Union Theory: An Interpretive Survey', *Journal of Economic Literature*, 10.

R. C. Lipsey, 1960, 'The Theory of Customs Unions: A General Survey', *EJ*, 70.

B. F. Massell, 1973, *East African Economic Union: An Evaluation and Some Implications for Policy*, The Rand Corporation, Santa Monica.

J. E. Meade, 1956, *The Theory of Customs Unions*, Amsterdam.

R. F. Mikesell, 1960, 'The Theory of Common Markets as Applied to Regional Arrangements among Developing Countries', in R. Harrod and D. Hague, eds *International Trade Theory in a Developing World*. Reprinted in Robson, 1971.

W. T. Newlyn, 1965, 'Gains and Losses in the East African Common Market', *YB*, 17.

W. T. Newlyn, 1966, 'The Shiftability of industry and the Measurement of Gains and Losses in The East African Common Market: A Reply', *BOUIES*, 28.

H. C. Petith, 1977, 'European Integration and the Terms of Trade'. *EJ*, 87.

Raisman Report, 1961, Colonial Office, *East Africa: Report of the Economic and Fiscal Commission*. Cmnd 1279.

P. Robson, 1967, J. F. Due, 'Tax Harmonisation in the East African Common Market', in C. S. Shoup *Fiscal Harmonisation in Common Markets*, vol II, New York; and D. A. Lury, *The Economies of Africa*. Ed P. Robson, 1971, Ed *International Economic Integration.*

T. Scitovsky, 1958, *Economic Theory and Western European Integration*, Stamford.

T. Scitovsky, 1963, 'International Trade Theory and Economic Integration as a means of Overcoming the Disadvantages of a Small Nation', in E. A. G. Robinson, ed *Economic Consequences of the size of Nations.*

J. Viner, 1950, *The Customs Union Issue*, Carnegie Endowment for International Peace, New York.

J. E. Williamson, 1962, Taped discussion with H. G. Johnson on Britain and the EEC.

J. E. Williamson, 1971, 'On Estimating the Income Effect of British Entry to the EEC', Surrey Papers in Economics.

147

TABLE 1

Critical a_1 and a_2 Values to Produce (i) $Y_2 = 0$ (ii) $Y_3 = 0$ (ii) $Y_2 = Y_3 = 0$

	$Y_2 = 0$ $a = a_1$	$Y_3 = 0$ $a = a_2$	$Y_2 = Y_3 = 0$ $a_1 = a_2 =$	a_2 if not equal to a_1
I	0.0084	0.0084	0.0128	
II	−0.0079	−0.0079	0.0128	
III	0.0084	0.0082	0.0128	
IV	0.0084	0.0041	0.0128	
V	0.0084	0.0085	0.0128	
VI	0.0100	0.0100	0.0143	
VII	0.0084	0.0088	0.0128	
VIII	0.0195	−0.0028	0.0256	−0.0000
IX	0.0210	0.0210	0.0242	
X	0.0057	0.0057	0.0104	
XI	0.0084	0.0079	0.0128	
XII	0.0099	0.0099	0.0141	
XIII	0.0084	0.0088	0.0128	
XIV	0.0103	0.0106	0.0141	
XV	0.0084	0.0085	0.0128	
XVI	0.0079	0.0079	0.0124	
XVII	0.0084	0.0082	0.0128	
XVIII	0.0077	0.0077	0.0124	
XIX	0.0020	0.0076	0.0064	0.0128
XX	0.0098	0.0095	0.0140	
XXI	0.0147	0.0091	0.0192	
XXII	0.0175	0.0175	0.0211	

9

Market limitation and industrialization in Arab countries[1]

M. M. METWALLY

The aim of this study is to demonstrate that the long-run solution to the economic development problem of most, if not all, the Arab countries lies in industrialization. However, in their attempt to industrialize on an adequate scale, these countries could be faced with a serious problem of market limitation. The study shows that to overcome this problem, some form of economic integration between the Arab countries may prove necessary.

I

The Arab world comprises all Arab-speaking countries, namely: Algeria, Bahrain, Egypt, Iraq, Jordan, Kuwait, Lebanon, Libya, Morocco, Oman, Qatar, Saudi Arabia, Sudan, Syria, Tunisia, United Arab Emirates, Yemen Arab Republic, and Yemen People's Democratic Republic. These countries stretch from the Atlantic Ocean in the west to the Persian Gulf in the east. They occupy a total area of approximately 4,341,000 square miles or roughly 1.5 times the size of the USA and half the size of the USSR. In 1976, the population of the Arab countries exceeded 140 million people, or approximately two-thirds of the population of the USA. However, their total GDP was less than 10 per cent of that of the USA.

The standards of living as well as the general economic structures of the Arab countries differ significantly from one economy to the other. It is possible, however, to distinguish three groups according to the main industrial sources of GDP which fall into three categories. (i) Oil producers where oil contributes over 60 per cent of GDP, (ii) Semi-oil producers, where 30 to 40 per cent of GDP originates in the oil sector and (iii) Non-oil producers whose oil production does not contribute significantly to GDP (ie no more than 5 per cent).

The structure of the economies of the three groups is shown in Appendix A. The data given in this appendix are, for the majority of countries, unpublished information obtained from primary sources (ie from the official agencies of

149

these countries in answer to my enquiries in November 1977). These data were checked, whenever possible using available UN publications. The following few points can be made in the light of the information given in Appendix A.

(a) The degree of wealthiness or the standard of living (as measured by GNP per head) differs significantly between the three groups. The average GNP per head of the oil producers is over 13 times that of the non-oil producers and about 6 times that of the semi-oil producers. The data suggest, however, that less than 10 per cent of the total Arab population had an average GNP per head which exceeded $2000 in 1975. On the other hand, over 70 per cent of the total Arab population had an average income in the same year less than 5 per cent of that of the USA. Just how unequally distributed is GDP between the different Arab countries can be seen from the fact that in 1975, the one million Kuwaitis had a larger total income than the thirty-seven million Egyptians. It is misleading therefore, to speak of the Arabs as being rich; one must be more specific. And even among the rich oil producers, many observers report a high degree of inequality of income and wealth.

(b) With the exception of Tunisia, the average annual rate of growth of population is quite high. This would be of concern to those non-oil producers who are poorly endowed with natural resources relative to their present population. This applies to Egypt, Syria, (North) Yemen, and to a lesser degree to Morocco and Sudan. Malthus' doctrine applies fairly well to some of these countries. Egypt's economic problem, for example, can be summed up as 'over-population'. Its density of population is one of the highest in the world. Almost all observers agree that there is a large surplus rural population. This already very serious situation is being aggravated by rapid population growth which is a real obstacle to economic development and the spread of public services in Egypt.

(c) The data on GNP per head apparently show that the oil producers are highly developed. This is an outstanding example of the deficiency of this indicator as a single measure of development. None of the Arab countries has reached a stage of 'take off into self-sustained economic growth' if to such a concept one can give a practical meaning. The rate of net productive investment to GDP in most of these countries is far below 10 per cent per annum over a long period. It is even lower in the group of oil producers.[2] Moreover, in none of them is there an industry or sector whose expansion and technical transformation would induce a chain of Leontief input-output requirements for increased capacity and the potentiality for new production functions in other sectors to which the economy will progressively respond. The production and exportation of petroleum in the oil producers would seem to have had no effect in changing the structure of these countries apart from enabling them to pile up reserves and pay for 'fat' import bills.

(d) None of the Arab countries can be considered industrialized. The net value of manufacturing production per head in any one of them is less than $100 per annum. The percentage of GDP originating in the manufacturing sector in 1975 was much higher in the non-oil producers than in the oil producers, but did, not as a rule, exceed 15 per cent. The only exceptions were Egypt (20.1 per cent) and Syria (19.8 per cent). Moreover the proportion of active population engaged in manufacturing industry in any one of them was less than 15 per cent of the total active labour force in 1975. Furthermore, the exports of finished manufactures of most of the Arab countries are almost negligible.

But, although they can not be considered industrialized, they differ significantly in their degree of industrialization. Egypt has already established a wide variety of industries. In contrast, most oil producers import over 80 per cent of their requirements of manufactures.

The Arab economies seem to be foreign trade oriented. The proportion of exports to GDP is quite high. This is particularly true of the oil producers. Also, the majority of the Arab countries earn foreign exchange by the exportation of one or two staple products. The marginal propensity to import is high in most of them, and because of the 'demonstration effect' the long-term average propensity to import is increasing. Furthermore a foreign labour force still plays a major role in carrying out economic activities, particularly in the oil producers who could afford to build adequate schools for learning and training.

The data of Appendix A suggest that the great majority of the non-oil producers and the two semi-oil producers have a problem of underemployment (or disguised unemployment) as can be seen by comparing the percentage contribution of the primary sector to both GDP and total active labour force. These countries may be divided into two categories: (1) Those who do not (or are not likely to continue to) enjoy a rich endowment of natural resources in relation to their population (Egypt, Iraq, Morocco, Syria, Tunisia, North Yemen, and South Yemen). The solution of underemployment and/or unemployment in these countries can only be found in industrialization. (2) Those who do (and are likely to continue, though perhaps at an increasing cost, to) enjoy a rich endowment of natural resources in relation to their population (Algeria and Sudan). These countries should attempt to diversify their economies to maintain reasonably steady prices in the face of variations in demand to avoid instability in income earned in export industries and, thereby to maintain a greater degree of stability in general money incomes and prices as well as in external purchasing power and real expenditure, particularly real investment.

The data of Appendix A also suggest that the oil producers are selling their assets without seeking to establish viable alternatives. This can be seen by comparing the contributions of different sectors to GDP and total active labour force. The development strategy of selling one's assets and piling up reserves has dangerous consequences. First, petroleum is an exhaustable resource. Second, there is the threat raised by the development of new technology which could result in the creation of a competitive substitute in the not too distant future. Third, there is the question of the adequacy of the reserves and the forms in which they could be held in the future. Finally, it may not be possible to persuade over 90 per cent of the labour force to move into what may still be labelled as 'the service sector' or even to ask them to retire at an early age; financing this by the returns from the reserves. Hence for these oil producers too the solution probably lies in industrialization.

II

The above suggests that for most, if not all, Arab countries industrialization is the best hope for achieving self-sustained economic growth.

In their effort to industrialize, the Arab states are likely to face a problem of market limitation. This problem arises from the empirical observation that the efficient scale of producing manufacturing products is not very much smaller in less industrialized countries than it is in industrialized countries whose markets for the same products are much wider than the markets of the underdeveloped countries. In spite of the huge differences between the two types of economies, the same size of plant tends to prevail in the same industries. Technical factors determining the size of plant in manufacturing industries tend to play more or less the same role in determining the scale of operations in industrialized and less-industrialized countries. In the latter, however, indivisibilities and/or

---

Sources: USA, Census of Manufacturers, 1972, Bureau of Census.
UK, Census of Production, 1971, Board of Trade.
Pakistan, Census of Industrial Production, 1973, Department of Commercial Intelligence and Statistics.
Egypt, Census of Industrial Production for 1974, Government of UAR, Department of Statistics and Census.
India, Census of Manufacturers for 1972.
Spain, Estadisticas De Production Industrial I, 1972.
Iran, Industrial Statistics, 1973, Government of Iran.
Iraq, Industrial Statistics, 1973, Government of Iraq.

TABLE 1

A Comparison between 'Typical' Size of Plant in Different Countries
(Size Measured in Terms of Numbers Employed)

Industry	Median employee in UK	Median employees in corresponding industries in specific countries as a percentage of median employee in UK						
		USA %	India %	Egypt %	Spain %	Pakistan %	Iran %	Iraq %
Canning and preserving of fruits and vegetables	374	48	53	94	65	63	44	94
Grain mill products	218	79	72	63	41	109	82	79
Sugar	865	96	143	261	264	255	95	NA
Beer	301	174	68	82	116	76	48	NA
Soft drinks	84	58	116	152	96	118	104	109
Tobacco and cigarettes	2220	106	121	129	133	119	105	106
Cotton spinning	376	87 }	659	614	NA }	401	290	NA
Cotton weaving	209	395 }			NA }		136	NA
Woollen and worsted	254	101	473	469	130	315	349	NA
Rayon, nylon, etc, and silk	592	429	NA	272	350	NA	111	NA
Leather footwear	263	135	290	91	99	92	94	123
Make-up textile goods	109	81	88	95	NA	74	77	101
Sawmills and plywoods	91	103	104	156	64	91	92	104
Wooden containers	75	107	115	99	85	NA	95	103
Manufacture of furniture	163	171	77	82	66	78	74	90
Paper and board	545	85	174	133	92	127	NA	NA
Leather tanning	127	241	153	102	94	91	44	93
Rubber	1113	97	98	101	96	65	47	NA
Paints and varnishes	266	73	120	105	NA	74	58	NA
Soap	1300	61	82	87	49	43	31	68
Matches	241	209	369	102	109	298	103	NA
Petroleum refining	2285	123	NA	133	NA	132	NA	175
Glass	799	101	83	100	72	102	62	NA
Cement	682	48	165	177	109	182	106	118
Fertilizers	270	71	405	673	329	390	136	129
Iron and steel	2369	215	682	139	174	123	NA	NA

1. Where the median size is indeterminant because of open ends, the average size of the largest class was taken as an alternative.

2. NA = Not available.

TABLE 2
A Comparison between 'Typical' Size of Plant in Different Countries (Size Measured in Value-Added)

Industry	Median-output plant size in specified countries as a percentage of median-output plant size in UK %				
	USA	Egypt	India	Pakistan	Iraq
Fruits and vegetable processing	172	62	37	36	55
Grain milling	195	73	48	44	67
Sugar refining	418	161	76	63	NA
Soft drinks	244	136	NA	79	NA
Beer	1233	104	NA	NA	NA
Tobacco and cigarettes	301	153	117	119	117
Cotton spinning and weaving	1709	795	381	224	NA
Woollen and worsted	325	310	374	281	NA
Rayon, nylon, etc, and silk	982	267	215	NA	NA
Made-up household textiles	417	82	92	97	72
Footwear (except rubber)	239	174	NA	88	111
Timber	376	76	135	140	85
Wooden containers	185	82	88	NA	97
Furniture and upholstery	326	72	NA	NA	81
Paper and board	295	87	82	84	NA
Leather tanning	854	90	43	44	73
Rubber	777	159	NA	103	NA
Fertilizer	98	802	174	156	NA
Paints and varnishes	267	64	111	108	NA
Soap	310	77	117	107	90
Matches	915	820	356	325	NA
Glass and glassware	476	148	72	81	NA
Cement	190	104	82	78	NA
Petroleum refining	248	61	49	60	139
Iron and steel	1004	126	350	127	NA

Sources: See sources to Table 1 and note 3.

154

discontinuities in the productive process exert a stronger influence in determining the 'optimum' size of plant than in the more industrialized countries. This has resulted in most of the less-industrialized countries being unable to establish even one plant to produce those items for which technical factors put a lower limit on plant size and the minimum economic scale of production is so large that one plant can easily meet the whole national market.

Table 1 gives the size of plant with median employee (the size below and above which 50 per cent of total employees are found) in specific countries for each manufacturing industry as a percentage of the corresponding size (measured in terms of number employed) in the UK. The table shows that the median size is roughly the same in other countries as in the UK for most industries. The size appears to be greater for some industries (eg sugar, textiles, paper, matches, petroleum, cement, and fertilizers) in the less industrialized countries than in UK. The same conclusion seems to hold true when size is measured in terms of value-added.[3] The results are shown in Table 2. It is clear from the data in this table that the median-output plant-size (measured by output) is generally much greater in the United States than in any of the other countries considered — a fact resulting from higher output per man rather than from larger numbers being employed in the typical American plant. On the other hand, prevailing outputs from median-output plants are not very much smaller in less-industrialized countries than in UK.

The available evidence suggests, therefore, that to industrialize on an efficient scale, an Arab country must possess a present market wide enough to justify the establishment of at least one plant of a size that is typical of advanced countries. None of the Arab countries seems to be in this position. For example, a comparison between the present size of the Egyptian domestic market for a large number of manufactures (as measured by apparent consumption, ie domestic production + imports—exports over the period 1972—75) and the typical scale of production in UK in 1975 (Table 3) shows that the market is too small to justify the establishment of even one plant of economic size in most categories of manufactures. Only in food and clothing does the Egyptian market appear to be large enough to justify the establishment of plants of size that is typical in UK.

The Egyptian (domestic) market, measured by its total population, total GDP, income distribution, and habits of consumption, is probably much larger than the domestic market for any other Arab state.[4] Thus the problem of market limitation in other Arab countries may be expected to be more inhibiting to their industrialization than it is in the case of Egypt. Indeed, in some of the Arab states, the domestic market for certain food products is too small to justify

TABLE 3

A Comparison between Size of Egyptian (Domestic Market) and Typical Size of Plant*

Article	Typical scale of production in UK industry in 1975	Present size of the Egyptian domestic market (1972–75)
1. Rubber tyres and tubes (th)	1800	400
2. Steel (th tons)	710	250
3. Pig iron (th tons)	812	270
4. Steel sheets and strips (th tons)	220	110
5. Primary aluminium (th tons)	70	4.5
6. Copper (worked) (th tons)	23	10
7. Zinc (tons)	9000	6000
8. Ball and roller bearing (th dollars)	15,000	620
9. Electric motors (th dollars)	35,000	2200
10. Electric transformers (th dollars)	30,000	1400
11. Typewriters (th)	350	10
12. Electric domestic washing machines (th)	300	4
13. Electric domestic vacuum cleaners (th)	400	4
14. Electric domestic refrigerators (th)	250	18
15. Agricultural tractors (40 to 50 hp) (assembly only)	3000	1700
16. Agricultural tractors (all types) manufacturing (th)	72	4
17. Passenger cars (assembly only) (th)	71	8.9
18. Passenger cars (manufacturing) (th)	330	8.9

* (1) The typical size of plant is defined here as the average size in the range in which 50 per cent or more of the industry's employment is concentrated. The employment of the typical plant in relation to total industry employment would give a rough measure of production in the typical plant in relation to total national production of the industry in question. From the last relationship one can determine the production of the typical plant, which we call the typical scale of production in the industry in question.

(2) The size of the Egyptian domestic market is measured by average consumption (domestic production plus imports-exports) during the period 1972–75. The data used were obtained from the Egyptian Ministry of Planning and the Department of Census and Statistics.

the establishment of even one plant of a size that is typical in advanced countries. This is particularly true for such industries as sugar refining, biscuits, chocolate, and confectionery. Thus, the number of manufacturing industries that can be economically established (even if only one plant is established in any industry) within the present market limitations in any Arab country is too small to provide employment opportunities for a large number of the unemployed and underemployed labour force.

III

One wonders whether it would be possible to produce the given manufactured product at a reasonably low per unit cost by means of a small-scale process not widely used, if at all, in industrial countries, yet suitable to the present size of the specific country's domestic market. If we were to hazard a generalization from the scanty data available on the matter, it would be that:

(a) A fairly large proportion of advanced countries' manufacturing industries requires large-scale operation for the sake of efficiency and the possibility of achieving the same (or nearly the same) degree of efficiency by producing on a smaller scale does not appear to be great.

(b) There is a substantial number of manufacturing industries in which operation at one-half or even one-fourth of optimal scale imposes very slight total unit cost disadvantages. On the other hand there appears to be at least a minority of industries in which the penalty of operating at smaller scales is very severe.

(c) While it might be true that in a large number of manufacturing industries many processes allow almost no flexibility whatever, there are probably many cases in which alternative factor combinations are applicable in major processing operations. Even in those industries where basic processes are technologically inflexible, certain ancillary operations may lend themselves to alternative techniques.

Thus there is no exclusive evidence to support the pattern of development referred to at the beginning of this section.

For well-known reasons, the possibility of industrialization through exportation is not great. First, the newly developed industries would not be able to compete with those of the mature industrialized countries. Even if the Arabs were to use the best available techniques of production and produce at a scale large enough to enjoy all available economies, they would still lack the know-how which results from experience. Secondly, the Arabs are not likely to possess, at least in the near future, the marketing ability and technology needed to invade the export markets. Thirdly, and perhaps most importantly, the export markets are, to say the least, semi-closed. This is because the markets of the developing economies are either dependent on imports from traditional suppliers who are usually developed countries with whom they have established long-term trade and credit patterns, or are protected to encourage the products of their own infant industries (since most of these countries are also trying to industrialize). The markets of the developed countries are usually protected against imports of cheap manufactures to secure the jobs of the employees of the native (inefficient) industries. The story of textiles is very well known.

The policy of industrialization through 'build-and-wait', based on the assumption that as development proceeds and the level of income rises, plants which are not justified at lower income levels may become justified, may not prove effective for any individual country whose present size of market is much too small.

The only avenue left seems to be co-operation with neighbours.

Static analysis of the effects of customs unions would not help much in evaluating the gains from establishing a common market among the Arab countries and, in fact, shows an exceedingly weak case for any proposed form of integration among them.

Trade between the Arab countries is a very small proportion of their total trade. Intra-regional trade among them is estimated at about 7 per cent of total trade in 1975 as compared with 50 per cent in Western Europe and 30 per cent in the European Economic Community. It is only in the case of Syria, Lebanon and Jordan that the share in each other's trade is significant. Furthermore, the ratio of foreign trade to gross national product is very high in most Arab countries. Imports in all of them are quite high in proportion to gross national product while, of those imports, only a small fraction comes from the Arab world. It seems, therefore, that according to the orthodox theory, the case of discriminating in favour of the outside world would be much stronger than that for discriminating in favour of the Arab countries. Also in most of them exports are a high proportion of gross national product. Hence, abolition of duties and other restrictions on existing intra-regional trade could hardly have a marked effect on the level of economic welfare of the Arab countries. The benefits of customs unions will, according to this theory, be greater for industrialized countries than for less-industrialized countries but will increase for the latter as they succeed in developing. The static analysis also suggests that for some Arab countries it would be more beneficial to form a customs union with a highly developed trading partner, more especially if that partner has a low ratio of trade to domestic expenditure. It would, for instance, be more beneficial for a country like Egypt to form a customs union with a highly developed country than with other Arab countries, since she trades more with highly advanced areas than with Arab countries and has a relatively low ratio of trade to gross national product. This would ensure an unimpeded market for her products in industrialized countries. But Egypt is poorly endowed with natural resources in relation to her population and must industrialize or be doomed. In such a case, it is precisely against the industry of a highly developed area that an underdeveloped country, especially one which is beginning to industrialize, requires to be protected.

The static analysis, however, ignores the economies of scale which, for small- and medium-sized countries, are quite decisive. From the point of view of static cost comparison at a given time, the scale economies in the protected industries are irrelevant. As long as costs in the protected industry are above world prices, the economy would increase its welfare by importing the protected goods and expanding its exports to finance them, given that the opportunity cost of producing these exports remains low. But given the desire for industrialization in the interest of long-run development, the day when these industries become competitive will be reached sooner if a customs union creates a bigger market. And, if the much-needed imports must be secured by expanding exports which face inelastic demand, marginal costs of imports would be very high and may become prohibitive. Trade diversion then becomes a source of considerable gain.

The total Arab market is much bigger than the market of any individual Arab state. This can be seen in Table 4. In a large number of cases, manufacturing is not possible within the Egyptian market, but in the Arab market the same plant, operating at optimum scale is feasible. Thus, for Arab countries, the argument for an aggregation of markets to provide an outlet for the product of at least one efficient, modern manufacturing plant is extremely powerful. Economic intergration will permit the Arab countries to obtain important scale economies. Although the creation of an Arab Common Market has to be judged primarily in terms of its effectiveness in promoting new investment and the establishment of new industries, its short-run impact on productive efficiency should not be overlooked. One of the paradoxes of less-industrialized countries is that, while they obviously need many more factories and industries, they may not fully utilize the industrial capacity they already have.

It is true that the present size of the Arab market is too small to justify economic production of such articles as electric motors and transformers, washing machines, refrigerators, vacuum cleaners, cars and so on, as can be seen in Table 4. But plans for the creation of a customs union usually involve relatively long time periods to fruition so that the initial impact, and perhaps the most important one, is on expectations regarding further market opportunities rather than on existing conditions. What are most relevant are the effects on investments which will determine production patterns a decade or two in the future as compared with what might have been in the absence of the creation of the regional trading arrangements.

TABLE 4

A Comparison between Size of Arab Market and Typical Size of UK Plants

Article	Typical scale of production in UK industry	Present size of Arab market	No of plants possible within present Arab market
1. Rubber tyres and tubes (th)	1800	3700	two
2. Steel (th tons)	710	1910	two or three
3. Pig iron (th tons)	812	2100	two or three
4. Steel sheets and strips (th tons)	220	305	one
5. Primary aluminium (th tons)	70	12	none
6. Copper (worked) (th tons)	23	21	one
7. Zinc (tons)	9000	11,500	one
8. Ball and roller bearings (th dollars)	15,000	4100	none
9. Electric motors (th dollars)	35,000	7200	none
10. Electric transformers (th dollars)	30,000	9600	none
11. Typewriters (th)	350	40	none
12. Electric domestic washing machines (th)	300	51	none
13. Electric domestic vacuum cleaners (th)	400	17	none
14. Electric domestic refrigerators (th)	250	77	none
15. Agricultural tractors (40 to 50 hp) (assembly only)	3000	5100	two
16. Agricultural tractors (all types) manufacturing (th)	72	22	none
17. Passenger cars (assembly only) (th)	71	83	one
18. Passenger cars (manufacturing) (th)	330	83	none

Sources: The typical scale of production in UK is the same as in Table 3. The Arab market was estimated by calculating average apparent consumption for each Arab economy during the period 1972–75 and summing up. Apparent consumption = domestic production + imports-exports. The data on these items were obtained from individual countries and from UN: *Commodity Trade Statistics.*

The Arab domestic market may widen sufficiently in the near future to justify economic production of those articles that cannot be produced efficiently at the present. We projected the future demand for those products which do not have adequate markets at the present. For the rational formulation of demand projection it was important to obtain a well organized description of actual demand behaviour. Income and prices are the main factors that might be expected to produce variations in the observed patterns. Other factors such as family size, geographical location, social class, and climate are not necessarily less important and there are certain formal methods (including the analysis of variance and the use of dummy variables) for detecting whether such factors have a significant bearing on the pattern of demand for a given consumption item.

We shall consider consumption as a function of income only. If there are no discontinuties, it would be possible to have a consumption-income relationship embodying two properties: (a) an initial income level below which the commodity is seldom bought, and (b) a saturation level which provides an upper limit to the consumption of the commodity. These two properties imply that income elasticity gradually diminishes as income increases, possibly from values higher than unity down to an ultimate value of zero.

We have used the following two formulae in projecting the future market:

$$\textit{Equation} \qquad\qquad \textit{Proportional rate of growth}$$

$$(1) \quad x = c\int_{-\infty}^{t} \frac{1}{\sqrt{2\pi}}\, e^{-t^{2}/2} dt \qquad\qquad \frac{r\beta\lambda\,(\alpha y^{\beta})}{\Delta\,(\alpha y^{\beta})}$$

where $t = \ln\alpha + \beta\ln y$

$$(2) \quad x = c\int_{-\infty}^{z} \frac{e^{z}}{1 + e^{z}}\, dz \qquad\qquad r\beta\, \frac{e^{z}}{1 + e^{z}}$$

where $z = \alpha + \beta\ln y$

x and y denote per capita consumption (of a given commodity) and income respectively: α and β are constant parameters to be estimated.

The rate of growth is given by $\dfrac{dx}{dt}\, \dfrac{1}{x}$ where $\dfrac{dx}{dt} = \dfrac{dx}{dy}\, \dfrac{dy}{dt}$. Income (y) is assumed to grow at a constant rate r, or $y = y_{0}e^{rt}$ and thus the (proportional) rate of growth is given by $\dfrac{dx}{dy}\, .\, \dfrac{ry}{x}$.

161

The method of maximum likelihood was used to estimate the parameters of the two equations.[5]

A comparison between data of Table 5 and the 'typical size' of plant shows that the Arab market in the near future would be large enough to justify economic production of certain luxuries as well as other manufactured articles for which the present market is too small to justify economic production. By the year 2000, the Arab market for commodities such as passenger cars, washing machines, domestic refrigerators, typewriters, ball and roller bearings, and aluminium will be large enough to justify the establishment of plants of economic size.

A common market between the Arab countries through the pooling of markets would encourage appreciably the development of large-scale manufactures. This would hasten growth. So too would the intensification of competition if its effect was to increase the efficiency of operation of existing industries and hence to initiate a higher sustained growth of productivity.

The above powerful arguments may not convince the Arab countries to put aside their political differences and consider carefully their new frontier. The backwash effects of an Arab Common Market or an Arab Customs Union cannot be ignored. But these effects never outweigh the advantages to be gained from a concerted action.

TABLE 5
Projection of Future Demand for Specific Products

Article	Size of domestic Arab market by 2000	
	Model 1	Model 2
1. Primary aluminium (th tons)	—	—
2. Ball and roller bearings (th dollars)	42,000	38,500
3. Electric motors (th dollars)	39,000	36,000
4. Electric transformers (th dollars)	41,200	39,300
5. Typewriters (th)	169	176
6. Electric domestic washing machines (th)	361	385
7. Electric domestic vacuum cleaners (th)	310	319
9. Tractors (th)	110	86
10. Passenger cars (th)	590	540

Notes

[1] I am grateful to my colleague R. Gunton for valuable comments. Any remaining errors are my responsibility.

[2] This may suggest that the 'poor Arabs' are trying to build their productive capacity while the 'rich Arabs' are relying on their accumulated reserves.

[3] Size measured in terms of value-added was obtained from size measured in terms of employment using the following method:
  (i) calculating the value-added per worker in each size-class by dividing total value-added by total employment and assuming it to be that prevailing in the mean establishment in the size-class concerned.
  (ii) plotting graphically the value-added per worker corresponding to the mid-value of each size-class. From this graph we get the approximate value-added per worker corresponding to the limits of each size class.
  (iii) multiplying the value-added per worker corresponding to the limits of each class by these limits we get the approximate size as measured by value-added.

[4] Although incomes per head are much higher in oil producers than Egypt, the size of the domestic market for manufactures in these economies is smaller than the Egyptian domestic market. This is so because the population of the oil producers, with the exception of Saudi Arabia, is very tiny. Also the severe inequalities in the distribution of income and wealth, the lack of an industrial base and the slow development of consumption habits for many manufactures result in a relatively small domestic market.

[5] Δ (t) in equation (1) designates the area and λ (t) the ordinate of the log-normal distribution function at the value of $t = \ln(\alpha y \beta)$. For the estimation of equation (1) see J. Aitchison and J. A. C. Brown. For estimation of equation (2) see P. R. Frisk.

References

J. Aitchison and J. A. C. Brown, 1957, *The Lognormal Distribution*, Cambridge.

J. S. Bain, 1954, 'Economics of Scale, Concentration and the Condition of Entry in Twenty Manufacturing Industries', *American Economic Review*, **44**.

J. S. Bain, 1956, *Barriers to New Competition*, Harvard.

B. Balassa, 1962, *The Theory of Economic Integration*.

K. M. Barbour, 1972, *The Growth, Location and Structure of Industry in Egypt*, New York.

G. Barthel, 1972, *Industrialisation in the Arab Countries of the Middle East*, Berlin.

R. S. Bhambri, 1962, 'Customs Unions and Underdeveloped Countries', *Economica Internazionale*.

A. J. Brown, 1961, 'Economic Separatism Versus A Common Market in Developing Countries', *Yorkshire Bulletin of Economic and Social Research*, **13**.

A. J. Brown, 1963, 'Common Market Criteria and Experience', *The Three Banks Review*.

G. P. Casadio, 1976, *The Economic Challenge of the Arabs*, Basingstoke.

C. A. Cooper and S. S. Alexander, 1972, *Economic Development and Population Growth in the Middle East*, Elseview.

M. N. E. Farrag, 1963, 'An Arab Customs Union, A Study of Some of its Potential Effects on Production and Trade', unpublished PhD Thesis, London School of Economics.

F. S. Florence, 1950, *Investment, Location and Size of Plant*, Cambridge.

P. R. Frisk, 1958, 'Maximum Likelihood Estimation of Tornquist Demand Equations', *Review of Economic Studies*, **26**.

K. Grundwald and J. Banall, 1960, *Industrialisation in The Middle East*, New York.

Z. Y. Hershlay, 1975, *The Economics of the Middle East*, Leiden.

S. Hunaykaty, 1975, 'Countries of the Arab World Industrialised', *The Arab Economist*.

S. Kachachi, 1974, *Industrial Development and Projects, Industrial Planning in Iraq*, Ministry of Planning, Baghdad.

R. Knauerhase, 1975, *The Saudi Arabian Economy*, New York.

R. G. Lipsey, 1960, 'The Theory of Customs Unions: A General Survey', *Economic Journal*, **70**.

R. Mabro, 1974, *The Egyptian Economy 1952–1972*, Oxford.

R. Mabro and S. Radwan, 1976, *The Industrialisation of Egypt, 1939–1973*, Oxford.

A. Maizels, 1963, *Industrial Growth and World Trade*, Cambridge.

R. A. Merklein, 1975, 'Can Middle East Producers Preserve their Petro-Wealth?', *The Arab Economist*.

M. M. Metwally, 1965, 'A Comparison Between Representative Size of Plant in Manufacturing Industries in Industrialised and Less-Industrialised Countries', *Yorkshire Bulletin of Economic and Social Research*.

A. Musrey, 1969, *An Arab Common Market*, New York.

L. E. Preston and K. A. Nashashibi, 1970, *Trade Patterns in the Middle East*, American Enterprise Institute for Public Policy Research, Washington DC.

A. Robana, 1973, *The Prospects for an Economic Community in North Africa*, New York.

E. Said and F. Suleiman, 1973, 'The Arabs Today: Alternatives for Tomorrow', *Forum*.

R. Stephens, 1973, *The Arabs' New Frontier*

UN, 1958, *The Development of Manufacturing Industry in Egypt, Israel and Turkey*, New York.

UN, 1958, 'Problems of Size and Plant in Industry in Underdeveloped Countries', *Industrialisation and Productivity Bulletin*, no 1.

G. V. Vassilion, December 1973, 'Trade Agreements between EEC and Arab Countries of the Eastern Mediterranean and Cyprus', University of Reading.

R. Wilson, 1977, *Trade and Investment in the Middle East*.

Appendix A

Structure of the Economies of the Arab Countries

Countries	Population (millions) 1975	GNP (million $US) 1975	GNP per head ($US) 1975
Group A (Non-oil producers)			
Egypt	37.23	11,505	309
Jordan	2.70	1197	443
Lebanon	2.87	2599	905
Morocco	17.31	7606	439
Sudan	17.73	4293	242
Syria	7.35	5082	372
Tunisia	5.61	3971	688
Yemen (North)	6.67	1380	207
Yemen (South)	1.69	302	179
Total: Non-oil producers	99.16	37,935	382
Group B (Semi-oil producers)			
Algeria	16.78	10,721	659
Iraq	11.12	13,198	1187
Total: Semi-oil producers	27.90	23,919	857
Group C (Oil producers)			
Bahrain	0.26	1107	4258
Kuwait	1.00	12,571	12,571
Libya	2.44	13,395	6000
Oman	0.77	1648	2140
Qatar	0.09	988	10,975
Saudi Arabia	8.97	37,333	4162
United Arab Emirates	0.22	2558	11,628
Total: Oil producers	13.75	69,600	5062
Grand Total: (All Arabs)	140.81	131,454	938

TABLE A2

Countries	Average annual rate of growth population	Average annual rate of growth of GDP at constant price	Net investment as a percentage of GDP
	1965–75 (%)	1965–75 (%)	1965–75 (%)
Group A (Non-oil producers)			
Egypt	2.2	2.4	7.4
Jordan	3.3	3.8	6.6
Lebanon	2.2	4.7	7.2
Morocco	2.2	4.3	6.3
Sudan	2.5	2.8	4.8
Syria	3.3	7.4	7.5
Tunisia	1.8	7.4	6.2
Yemen (North)	2.9	2.3	4.7
Yemen (South)	3.3	3.8	4.2
Total: Non-oil producers	2.4	3.2	6.9
Group B (Semi-oil producers)			
Algeria	3.2	5.8	8.3
Iraq	3.3	8.2	5.1
Total: Semi-oil producers	3.2	6.3	6.2
Group C (Oil producers)			
Bahrain	3.4	11.2	6.1
Kuwait	6.2	14.4	5.3
Libya	4.2	16.8	5.0
Oman	3.1	18.6	8.0
Qatar	2.4	20.2	4.1
Saudi Arabia	3.0	13.9	7.4
United Arab Emirates	3.0	19.1	5.3
Total: Oil producers	3.4	16.2	5.8
Grand Total: (All Arabs)	2.2	7.8	6.1

TABLE A3
Percentage of GDP by Sector

Countries	Agriculture & fishing (%)	Mining & quarrying (%)	Manu-facturing (%)	Others (%)	Agriculture & fishing (%)	Mining & quarrying (%)	Manu-facturing (%)	Others (%)
Group A (Non-oil producers)								
Egypt	27.0	1.0	20.1	51.9	45.8	0.2	14.1	39.9
Jordan	13.3	1.8	11.8	73.1	30.0	0.8	7.2	62.0
Lebanon	12.4	—	15.0	72.6	17.8	0.2	14.9	66.1
Morocco	27.6	9.5	14.8	51.9	50.0	1.1	10.8	39.1
Sudan	40.0	0.4	14.1	45.5	66.5	0.1	9.6	23.8
Syria	22.0	4.8	19.8	53.4	49.0	0.6	11.9	38.5
Tunisia	24.4	14.3	13.2	48.1	32.4	1.7	14.9	49.0
Yemen (North)	68.5	0.9	3.0	27.6	74.5	0.2	0.8	24.5
Yemen (South)	26.5	16.7	5.2	51.6	58.0	1.4	4.6	36.0
Total: Non-oil producers	24.2	4.6	16.2	55.0	50.6	0.5	11.3	47.6
Group B (Semi-oil producers)								
Algeria	9.8	34.5	13.0	42.7	50.4	0.9	6.4	42.3
Iraq	10.3	41.0	11.9	36.8	52.6	0.7	6.9	39.8
Total: Semi-oil producers	10.1	38.1	12.4	39.4	51.3	0.8	6.7	41.2
Group C (Oil producers)								
Bahrain	1.2	68.6	2.7	27.5	3.6	2.6	6.9	86.9
Kuwait	0.2	67.9	3.6	28.3	2.5	1.6	8.0	93.9
Libya	1.8	66.8	2.9	28.5	24.6	2.1	4.8	68.5
Oman	2.4	62.2	0.3	35.1	4.2	2.8	3.9	91.1
Qatar	1.1	71.4	0.9	26.6	8.9	2.6	3.6	84.9
Saudi Arabia	4.0	63.3	7.6	25.1	40.9	3.2	5.1	50.8
United Arab Emirates	0.8	69.7	0.8	28.7	7.2	2.5	4.3	86.0
Total: Oil producers	2.7	65.2	5.4	26.7	31.6	2.8	5.2	60.4
Grand Total: (All Arabs)	10.4	42.7	9.8	37.1	48.9	0.8	9.8	40.5

Appendix A *(continued)*

TABLE A4

Countries	Exports as % of GDP (1975)	Imports as % of GDP (1975)	Manufacturing exports as % of total exports (1975)	Manufacturing imports as % of total imports (1975)
Group A (Non-oil producers)				
Egypt	23.0	35.1	18.2	53.7
Jordan	27.7	70.1	6.9	56.9
Lebanon	27.9	44.9	27.6	58.6
Morocco	27.4	39.1	7.1	61.1
Sudan	13.8	21.4	2.0	65.4
Syria	25.5	40.4	19.3	62.1
Tunisia	31.2	36.0	3.8	69.0
Yemen (North)	4.6	23.6	0.6	66.3
Yemen (South)	36.2	69.4	0.3	62.5
Total: Non-oil producers	24.0	36.8	12.3	60.2
Group B (Semi-oil producers)				
Algeria	41.1	30.2	6.7	60.4
Iraq	57.9	43.3	3.0	63.8
Total: Semi-oil producers	50.4	37.4	4.7	62.3
Group C (Oil producers)				
Bahrain	81.3	69.2	0.2	74.6
Kuwait	80.8	22.5	0.6	76.4
Libya	64.6	30.6	0.1	79.2
Oman	66.2	50.6	0.1	78.5
Qatar	76.9	59.4	0.1	81.3
Saudi Arabia	84.8	16.5	0.1	77.9
United Arab Emirates	82.4	61.3	0.1	79.7
Total: Oil producers	79.5	24.2	0.1	78.2
Grand Total: (All Arabs)	58.2	30.2	4.5	70.1

TABLE A5

Countries	Exports directed to Arab countries as % of total exports (1975)	Imports originating in Arab countries as % of total imports (1975)	Trades with Arab countries as % of total trade (1975)
Group A (Non-oil producers)			
Egypt	16.6	5.3	11.1
Jordan	62.5	26.5	33.8
Lebanon	49.3	24.2	27.4
Morocco	11.1	2.1	5.1
Sudan	15.8	8.6	10.6
Syria	39.6	21.4	27.5
Tunisia	9.4	5.3	8.8
Yemen (North)	18.2	17.0	6.7
Yemen (South)	26.8	5.4	5.2
Group B (Semi-oil producers)			
Algeria	5.2	3.6	3.2
Iraq	8.9	16.8	7.4
Group C (Oil producers)			
Bahrain	5.2	2.8	3.4
Kuwait	2.7	8.4	4.0
Libya	3.3	6.3	9.1
Oman	3.6	4.0	2.8
Qatar	4.1	3.2	4.0
Saudi Arabia	4.0	19.6	4.2
United Arab Emirates	3.0	6.1	2.3

Sources of Appendix A

1 Primary statistics obtained from the *Ministries of Economy and Department of Statistics*
2 IMF *International Financial Statistics*
3 UN *Statistical Year Books*
4 UN *Commonwealth Trade Statistics*
5 UN *Demographic Year Books*
6 UN *Year Books of National Accounts*

Trade and Integration

10

A model of export-led growth with a balance of payments constraint[1]

A. P. THIRLWALL and R. J. DIXON

There are two main reasons for believing in the importance of export-led growth; one uncontroversial, the other more contentious. The first is that export growth can lift a balance of payments constraint on demand and therefore permit faster growth if factor supplies are available to be utilized. The second is that export growth may create a virtuous circle of growth by virtue of the link between output growth and productivity growth. A number of models of this genre have appeared in the literature in recent years (eg Lamfalussy (1963), Beckerman (1962), Kaldor (1970), Dixon and Thirlwall (1975)), and we survey them later. There is a problem with these models, however, and that is they do not incorporate an explicit balance of payments equilibrium condition or constraint, which means that the equilibrium growth rate specified may be inconsistent with the long run requirement of payments balance.[2] The implicit assumption seems to be that provided it is exports that are the engine of growth, as distinct from domestic demand, the balance of payments will look after itself. Indeed, it is assumed in some models that the initial export growth and trade surplus generates such favourable responses in the economy that the balance of payments surplus actually grows. No consideration is given to the possibility that the rate of growth of income determined by the model may generate a rate of growth of imports in excess of the rate of growth of exports, thereby imposing a constraint on the export-led growth rate if balance of payments equilibrium must be preserved. Import behaviour in export-led growth models seems to have been neglected. This is not to pour cold water on export-led growth models. If the balance of payments is constraining the actual growth rate before the capacity rate is reached, then growth led by export demand, as opposed to other elements of demand, will raise the constraint; and if the actual growth rate can reach the capacity rate, the capacity rate itself may be raised. But it cannot be taken for granted in export-led models that there is no constraint on growth at all. If balance of payments equilibrium is a requirement, the equilibrium growth rate in an export-led growth model must reflect this requirement, otherwise the model may be useless for predictive purposes.

Models of export-led growth are typically very unspecific about the precise relationship between the rate of growth of exports and income, and how much income growth might be associated with a given growth of exports. It is clear from the historical and contemporary evidence, however, that exports tend to grow faster than income, which must make one immediately suspicious of models, for predictive purposes at least, which set the rate of growth of income equal to the rate of growth of exports. There is no doubt a variety of explanations as to why the rate of growth of exports typically exceeds the rate of growth of income through time, but a balance of payments constraint, related to the characteristics of goods traded, is one powerful explanation. It is intuitively obvious, and will be shown formally later, that if the income elasticity of demand for imports is greater than unity, and there is no continual compensating improvement in price competitiveness, an equality between the rate of growth of exports and income would generate a higher rate of growth of imports than exports, and income growth would sooner or later have to be curtailed. Thus, as long as the income elasticity of demand for imports is greater than unity, which it appears to be for most countries, the ratio of export growth to income growth will almost certainly show an historical tendency to exceed unity. Indeed, one could go further and say that if the income elasticity of demand for imports exceeds unity the export sector *must* expand relative to the total economy if growth is to be sustained. This simple truth has important policy implications for developing countries, and all countries, that wish to raise their growth rate but which at the same time are confronted with a high income elasticity of demand for imports. If the growth rate is specified as $y_t = \gamma(x_t)$, where x_t is the growth of exports, and $0 < \gamma < 1$, it will be shown later that γ does indeed approximate to the reciprocal of the income elasticity of demand for imports for a number of countries.

In this paper we first briefly consider the importance of export-led growth and survey the main models. The balance of payments equilibrium condition is then specified and incorporated into an export-led growth model already developed by the present authors in a previous paper (1975). On the basis of the international evidence, a fundamental law of growth is then propounded which states that a country's long run growth rate will approximate to its rate of growth of exports divided by the income elasticity of demand for imports. Finally, the link between balance of payments constrained growth and deindustrialization is discussed with particular reference to the United Kingdom.

174

The importance of export-led growth

The importance of export-led growth is best discussed and understood within the framework of the relationship between the balance of payments equilibrium (constrained) growth rate (y_B) on the one hand and the actual and capacity rates of growth (y_A and y_C) on the other.[3] The possible sets of relationships between y_B, y_A and y_C are outlined below:

(i) $y_B = y_A = y_C$: balance of payments equilibrium and full employment
(ii) $y_B = y_A < y_C$: balance of payments equilibrium and growing unemployment
(iii) $y_B < y_A = y_C$: increasing balance of payments deficit and full employment
(iv) $y_B < y_A < y_C$: increasing balance of payments deficit and growing unemployment
(v) $y_B > y_A = y_C$: increasing balance of payments surplus and full employment
(vi) $y_B > y_A < y_C$: increasing balance of payments surplus and growing unemployment.

It is a fundamental proposition in economics that in the long run when all resources are fully utilized, a country's actual growth rate cannot exceed its capacity rate as determined by the rate of growth of the labour force and the productivity of labour: the Harrodian natural rate of growth. For countries with perpetual balance of payments and unemployment difficulties, the lure of export-led growth lies in the possibility of moving from situation (iv) to at least (i) if not (v), where the balance of payments equilibrium growth rate lies above the capacity growth rate thus allowing the actual growth rate to equal the capacity growth rate without balance of payments difficulties arising. In this situation, so the export-led growth advocates argue, the buoyancy of demand at full employment will then raise the capacity growth rate. There are a number of possible mechanisms through which this may happen: the encouragement to investment which would augment the capital stock and bring with it, perhaps, technical progress, the supply of labour may increase by the entry into the workforce of people previously outside or from abroad; the movement of factors of production from low productivity to high productivity sectors, and the ability to import more may increase capacity by making domestic resources more productive. In this spirit, Cornwall argues persuasively in a recent book (1977) that the major explanation of growth rate differences between countries is differences in the pressure of demand to which supply adjusts, although for reasons we shall consider later (and question) he does not believe that the balance of payments has been a constraint on demand.

As far as the British economy is concerned it is difficult to know what a faster rate of growth of exports might do for the capacity growth rate because export

175

performance in the past has never been good enough to escape a balance of payments constraint before the capacity growth rate has been reached. Britain has approximated to situation (iv) above. It is frequently argued, however, that *if only* Britain did not run into balance of payments difficulties before full employment is reached, demand would not have to be contracted, investment would remain high, and that these conditions in the long run would raise the capacity growth rate closer to that of other countries. While the argument is speculative, it would be surprising if Britain's growth record relative to other countries since the Second World War did not have something to do with the characteristics of its trading position compared to other countries, particularly its low rate of growth of exports combined with a relatively high income elasticity of demand for imports. Certainly part of Japan's phenomenal success must be related to the fact that, as our later calculations show, its growth rate consistent with balance of payments equilibrium has exceeded by a considerable margin its actual growth rate which has continually pressed on its capacity rate. Kaldor (1974) has argued that the main cause of unemployment in the UK throughout the last century, barring periods of acute depression, has not been over-saving but insufficient exports relative to the level of imports which would be required at full employment: 'despite commitment to full employment from 1944 it took a very long time — in fact until 1967[4] — before it was realized that the true effect of the new system (ie commitment to full employment) was simply to transmute the chronic pre-war unemployment problem into the chronic post-war balance of payments problem'. Kaldor goes on to say that what the UK has really suffered from has been the slow growth of exports, an historical fact which can be explained by the industrialization of other regions of the world which have constantly narrowed the markets for British goods. Kaldor is a strong believer in the importance of export-led growth, maintaining that the common feature of all industrial economies is that their economic growth has been invariably led by a faster growth of exports which has given a higher rate of growth of industrial productivity. He claims that the UK could have grown at 5 per cent per annum had it achieved export growth of 10–15 per cent per annum.

To sum up, we can make two propositions about the importance of export growth. First, that up to the capacity growth rate, a country's actual growth rate is fundamentally determined by its rate of growth of exports (in relation to the rate of growth of imports) if it is to maintain balance of payments equilibrium. Secondly, it is probable that a country's capacity rate is also partly determined by its export performance because of the link between high demand and the response of factor supplies, and because faster growth itself generates

176

faster productivity growth. This is the idea of a virtuous circle of growth led by exports, which we now develop.

Models of export-led growth[5]

In the European context Lamfalussy (1963) was one of the first economists to propound an export-led growth theory to account for differences in the growth performance of Western European countries. In Lamfalussy's model, export-led growth is important for three main reasons: (i) the rate of growth of exports, as a determinant of demand, is likely to be an important determinant of investment; (ii) growth requires imports, and if exports do not rise as fast as import requirements, growth will be constrained by the balance of payments, and (iii) the smaller the domestic market the greater the importance of external demand in enabling economies to reap economies of scale in production to make enterprises viable that would otherwise not be so. Lamfalussy envisaged a virtuous circle commencing with higher exports leading to more investment, which in turn leads to a higher rate of growth of productivity, lower export prices and thus higher exports. There is, however, no explicit treatment of the balance of payments in the model.

Beckerman (1962) sees a similar virtuous circle in export-led growth, but his model also lacks a balance of payments constraint. Demand determines investment and growth; an important component of demand is exports (and it is only this component of demand that can help to balance the import requirements at a higher level of demand); a high level of demand and investment is favourable to growth which contributes to greater competitiveness and further export demand. Beckerman claims that the growth of exports is closely related across countries to the growth of competitiveness, and that differences in competitiveness are mainly a function of differences in productivity growth. While not wanting to prejudge the cause of the relationship, there is certainly a close relationship across countries between the rate of growth of output and the rate of growth of exports. The rank correlation between the two variables for the selection of countries in Table 1 later is 0.84. As Caves (1970) rightly noted, Beckerman's model in its original form lacks an equilibrium condition. Also the export demand function is very *ad hoc* making the *rate of growth* of exports a function of the *absolute* difference between domestic and foreign prices. We will make use of the more conventional multiplicative export demand function, which makes the rate of growth of exports depend on the difference between the rate of growth of domestic and foreign prices. This also gives the model an equilibrium condition. The (modified) Beckerman model runs as follows: export growth is a function of the difference in the rate of growth of domestic

177

and foreign prices; faster export growth leads to faster productivity growth; faster productivity growth contributes to a lower rate of growth of wage costs per unit of output *if wages do not rise in line with productivity*; a lower rate of increase in wage costs per unit of output leads to a lower rate of domestic price increase, and a lower rate of domestic price increase leads to a faster rate of growth of exports. The virtuous circle is complete. If the model is formulated algebraically, using linear relations, with signs correctly specified in the model, we have:

$$x = a_0 - b_0(p_d - p_f); a_0 > 0, b_0 > 0, \tag{1}$$

where x is the rate of growth of exports; p_d is the rate of growth of domestic prices; p_f is the rate of growth of foreign prices, and a_0 represents the rate of growth of exports determined by other factors (eg the growth of world income).

$$r = a_1 + b_1(x); b_1 > 0 \tag{2}$$

where r is the rate of growth of labour productivity.

$$w = a_2 + b_2(r); 0 < b_2 < 1 \tag{3}$$

where w is the rate of growth of wages,

and $p_d = w - r$. \hspace{1cm} (4)

Substituting (2) and (3) into (4), and the result into (1), gives an expression for the equilibrium rate of growth of exports of:

$$x = \frac{a_0 - b_0(a_2 - a_1 + b_2 a_1) + b_0(p_f)}{1 + b_0 b_1 (b_2 - 1)} \tag{5}$$

Notice that the virtuous circle of export-led growth depends crucially on the rate of increase in wages being less than the rate of increase in productivity (ie $b_2 < 1$). If $b_2 = 1$ there would be no 'circular' process; that is, no induced rate of growth of exports from the initial expansion of exports itself. Balassa (1963) has also argued that if wages respond to the level of employment, the virtuous circle may be choked. He is concerned that if $b_2 < 1$, Beckerman's model may lead to diverging country growth rates which are not observable in practice. The model is easily modified by relating changes in wages to the level of unemployment, using a Phillips curve relation. This makes for stability by causing wages and prices to rise faster in regions where export growth is high than in regions where export growth is sluggish and unemployment high. Divergence of growth rates may take place until full employment is reached but then the virtuous circle would break down. Beckerman replies (1963) that wage rate increases between countries bear little relation to unemployment rate differences. This is clearly an empirical matter. A lot would seem to depend on the extent to which labour supply can adjust to demand across countries. The recent work of Cornwall (1977) suggests that labour is very flexible and that demand and growth have not been constrained in Europe in the post-war period by a lack of factor supplies. Beckerman stresses an economy obtaining its initial advantage in trade through a favourable movement in relative prices; that is, through some competitive shock such as devaluation. It will be shown later, however, that using the modified Beckerman-type model, a once-for-all devaluation cannot raise the rate of growth of exports permanently. Continual devaluation (or depreciation) would be necessary.[6] By contrast, we stress the importance of countries obtaining their initial trading advantage in goods with a high income elasticity of demand in world markets, which affects the term a_0 in equation (1).

Before proceeding to develop our own model, incorporating a balance of payments equilibrium condition, a brief examination of Caves' (1970) comments on the empirical content of the individual functions making up the export-led growth models of Lamfalussy and Beckerman may be useful to clarify the argument. He makes two major points but neither, in our view, are substantial enough to alter one's view on the importance of export growth for simultaneous balance of payments equilibrium and a high rate of growth of income. First Caves asks 'what is special about the growth of exports compared to the growth of any other component of aggregate demand of equal size?' Beckerman himself gives the answer when he argues that if other items of demand are expanded businessmen may fear that demand growth will not continue smoothly because of the balance of payments implications of the expansion of other types of demand. Caves seems to recognize this as the crucial point, but then says 'but it does attribute to business enterprises an aversion to demand fluctuations induced by public authorities that defies easy credibility'. Caves appears to be questioning the influence of the level of demand on investment. But if investment is sensitive to the pressure of demand in relation to capacity output, the point made by the export-led growth school remains valid if export-led growth raises the rate of growth at which a balance of payments constraint becomes operative. Caves' second point concerns the relationship between higher export growth and a higher rate of productivity growth. He contends that there may be a link between export and output growth on the one hand and productivity growth on the other, but the direction of causation is anything but clear. This question relates to the controversy over the Verdoorn relationship.[7] Suffice it to say that while productivity growth is obviously a source of output growth, there are also good economic reasons why higher output growth should be a stimulus to productivity growth (see Dixon and Thirlwall (1975), p 209). The question is

179

not whether there is a relationship but whether the estimate of the relationship is biased because of its two-way nature.

Another recent critic of the idea that growth is constrained by the balance of payments is Cornwall (1977) who argues that the forces that lead to the rapid growth of output, eg technological change and entrepreneurial dynamism, also work to relieve a country of a balance of payments constraint. He rightly observes that the developed countries with recurring balance of payments difficulties have also been the slow growers, but wants to argue from this that it is the slow growth that has caused the balance of payments difficulties — rather than the other way round. It is hard to accept this view. It is not the case that all of the forces that lead to rapid output growth in a country necessarily improve the balance of payments. Technological change may be expected to improve productivity at home and also increase the desirability of a country's goods abroad, but this is only one of many factors behind the growth of output. Cornwall's argument does not fit the British experience where, if anything, productivity growth and the capacity growth rate have risen, and yet the balance of payments constraint has not improved because the forces making for the rise in productivity have not improved the demand characteristics of the goods exported.

As we indicated earlier, Kaldor is a strong devotee of the export-led growth school and has become one of its major protagonists. He has presented many verbal models, one of which (1970) the present authors have formalized elsewhere (1975). We shall briefly elaborate the model again, and then incorporate a balance of payments equilibrium condition. Kaldor's argument is essentially the Hicksian view (1950) that it is the growth of autonomous demand which governs the long run rate of growth of output. In open economies, export demand is the main component of autonomous demand, so that the rate of growth of exports governs the long run rate of growth of output to which investment and consumption adjust. Kaldor is not explicit on the form of the export demand function but seems to be suggesting the conventional multiplicative function. We adopt this, and relate the quantity of exports to prices measured in foreign currency to capture the effect of exchange rate changes.

$$X_t = \left(\frac{P_{dt}}{E_t P_{ft}}\right)^{\eta} z_t^{\varepsilon} \tag{6}$$

where X_t is the quantity of exports; P_{dt} is the domestic price of exports; P_{ft} is foreign prices; Z is the level of world income; $1/E$ is the foreign price of home currency; η is the price elasticity of demand for exports ($\eta < 0$); ε is the income elasticity of demand for exports ($\epsilon > 0$), and t is time. The rate of growth of exports may be written:

$$x_t = \eta(p_{dt} - p_{ft} - e_t) + \epsilon(z_t), \tag{7}$$

where lower case letters represent rates of change of the variables. The rate of growth of income outside the economy (z_t); the rate of change of foreign prices (p_f), and changes in the exchange rate are taken as exogenous. The rate of growth of domestic (export) prices (p_d) is assumed to be endogenous, however, and is derived from a pricing equation of the form:

$$P_{dt} = (W/R)_t (T)_t \tag{8}$$

where W is the level of money wages; R is the average product of labour, and T is $1 + \%$ mark-up on unit labour costs. From equation (8) we can write the approximation:

$$p_{dt} = w_t - r_t + \tau_t \tag{9}$$

The third relation in Kaldor's model, which gives a virtuous circle of export-led growth, is the dependence of the growth of labour productivity on the growth of output, which is Verdoorn's Law referred to earlier:

$$r_t = r_{at} + \lambda(y_t) \tag{10}$$

where r_{at} is the rate of autonomous productivity growth and λ is the Verdoorn coefficient. Equation (10) makes the model 'circular' since the higher the rate of growth of output the faster the rate of growth of productivity, and the faster the rate of growth of productivity the lower the rate of increase in unit costs and hence the faster the rate of growth of exports and output. It is also the Verdoorn relation which gives rise to the possibility that once an economy obtains a growth advantage it will keep it. Suppose, for example, that an economy obtains an advantage in the production of goods with a high income elasticity of demand in world markets, which raises its growth rate above that of other economies. Owing to the Verdoorn effect, productivity growth will then be higher and the economy will retain its competitive advantage in these goods, making it difficult for other countries to establish the same commodities. The income elasticity of demand for imports must assume key importance in an important determinant of comparative export performance. Likewise, the income elasticity of demand for imports must assume key importance in an export-led growth model with a balance of payments equilibrium condition. The lower the income elasticity of demand for imports the higher the growth rate consistent with balance of payments equilibrium, other things remaining the same. In models with cumulative causation (Myrdal (1957) and Hirschman (1958)), in which some economies produce goods which are expanding fast in demand while other economies produce goods which are sluggish in demand, it is the difference between the income elasticity characteristics of exports and imports which is the essence of the theory of divergence between 'centre' and 'periphery' and between industrial and agricultural economies. This is also the essence of Kaldor's view that the opening up of trade between economies may create growth rate differences which are sustained or even widened by the process of trade, viz the United Kingdom in the European Economic Community.

Combining equations (7), (9) and (10) gives an expression for the rate of growth of exports of:

$$x_t = \eta(w_t - r_{at} - \lambda y_t + \tau_t - p_{ft} - e_t) + \epsilon(z_t) \tag{11}$$

Kaldor's model, formalized above, also lacks a balance of payments equilibrium condition, and therefore could overpredict the sustainable rate of growth depending on the assumed relationship between x_t and y_t. Let us now specify the balance of payments equilibrium condition, therefore, and incorporate it in the model. Doing this also enables us to compare the more simple version of export-led growth models which stresses the relaxation of the balance of payments constraint with the more involved models incorporating the notion of a virtuous circle.

The balance of payments equilibrium condition
Starting from initial balance of payments equilibrium, the condition for a moving equilibrium through time is that the rate of growth of exports equals the rate of growth of imports. Let the initial equilibrium be defined as:

$$P_{dt}X_t = P_{ft}M_tE_t \tag{12}$$

where M_t is the quantity of imports, E_t is the domestic price of foreign currency, and P_{dt}, X_t and P_{ft} are defined as before. Taking rates of change of the variables, gives the condition for a moving equilibrium through time of:

$$p_{dt} + x_t = p_{ft} + m_t + e_t \tag{13}$$

The quantity of imports demanded may be specified as a multiplicative function of the price of imports (measured in units of domestic currency in order to incorporate exchange rate changes); the price of import substitutes (which we assume to be approximated by the domestic price level), and domestic income. Thus:

$$M_t = \left(\frac{P_{ft}E_t}{P_{dt}}\right)^{\psi} Y_t^{\pi} \tag{14}$$

where Y_t is domestic income, ψ is the price elasticity of demand for imports

$(\psi < 0)$, and π is the income elasticity of demand for imports $(\pi > 0)$. The rate of growth of imports may be written as:

$$m_t = \psi(p_{ft} + e_t - p_{dt}) + \pi(y_t). \qquad (15)$$

Substituting equation (15) into (13), the condition for balance of payments equilibrium through time is:

$$p_{dt} + x_t = p_{ft} + \psi(p_{ft} + e_t - p_{dt}) + \pi(y_t) + e_t, \qquad (16)$$

and thus the rate of growth of income consistent with balance of payments equilibrium is:

$$y_B = \frac{x_t + (1 + \psi)\,[p_{dt} - p_{ft} - e_t]}{\pi} \qquad (17)$$

An increase in x_t will raise the balance of payments constraint on growth. Within this framework, we are free to specify any export demand function we choose. In the simplest case, without going on to develop a virtuous circle model of export-led growth, equation (7) could be used. Substituting (7) for x_t in equation (17) gives:

$$y_B = \frac{(1 + \eta + \psi)\,[p_{dt} - p_{ft} - e_t] + \epsilon(z_t)}{\pi} \qquad (18)$$

Alternatively, if we use the specification of the rate of growth of exports in equation (11), which contains the idea of a virtuous circle of growth led by exports, and substitute in equation (17) we obtain:

$$y_B = \frac{(1 + \eta + \psi)\,[w_t - r_{at} + \tau_t - p_{ft} - e_t] + \epsilon(z_t)}{\pi + \lambda(1 + \eta + \psi)} \qquad (19)[8]$$

Both models showing the importance of exports, and incorporating the balance of payments equilibrium condition, have interesting properties, some of which are very familiar. In both equations (18) and (19), domestic prices rising faster than foreign prices will lower the equilibrium growth rate if the sum of the (negative) export and import price elasticities exceeds unity. Secondly a depreciation of the currency, ie a rise in the home price of foreign currency $(e_t > 0)$, will improve the equilibrium growth rate if the sum of the two elasticities exceeds unity in absolute value. This is the famous Marshall-Lerner condition for a successful devaluation $(|\eta + \psi| > 1)$. Notice, however, that the improvement in the growth rate can only be once-for-all unless depreciation is continuous. In subsequent periods when the exchange rate settles at its new level, the growth rate would revert to its former level (as $e_t = 0$). Thirdly, the equilibrium growth rate varies positively with the growth of world income, and inversely with the income elasticity of demand for imports. The difference between the two export growth models is that the virtuous circle version of the model (equation (19)) will give a higher equilibrium growth than otherwise would be the case if the bracketed term in the denominator of the equation is negative; in other words, if the Marshall-Lerner condition is satisfied. If it is not fulfilled, the growth rate consistent with balance of payments equilibrium will be lower than it otherwise would have been. If, of course, there is no virtuous circle through the Verdoorn effect, so that $\lambda = 0$, the two models are the same: that is, equations (18) and (19) are identical.

A fundamental law of growth
It is interesting to look at the data for various countries to see if the balance of payments equilibrium growth rate, as specified above, is a good predictor of actual growth experience, and whether any simple growth law can be formulated based on some simplifying (though not necessarily unrealistic) assumptions. From equations (18) and (17), it will be noticed that if in the long run there is no change in relative prices measured in a common currency, so that $p_{dt} - p_{ft} - e_t = 0$, or if the sum of the (negative) export and import price elasticities is unity the balance of payments equilibrium growth rate reduces to:

$$y_B = \frac{x_t}{\pi} \qquad (20)$$

Likewise from equations (19) and (17) if $|\eta + \psi| = 1$, the balance of payments equilibrium growth rate is:

$$y_B = \frac{\epsilon(z_t)}{\pi} = \frac{x_t}{\pi} \qquad (21)$$

In support of the simplifying assumption that in the long run the relative prices of foreign and domestic goods measured in a common currency are likely to remain unchanged; either the law of one price could be invoked, or in the event of exchange depreciation it could be argued that depreciation will force up domestic prices equiproportionately. There is no shortage of plausible models outlining this possibility (see Ball, Burns and Laury (1977) and Wilson (1976)). It would be harder to support the simplifying assumption that the sum of the export and import price elasticities approximates to unity. Arthur Brown himself did pioneering work (1942, 1951) on the elasticity conditions for a successful devaluation and surveyed the evidence, and at that time did not suffer unduly from elasticity pessimism (unlike some of his contemporaries). And today, most people would probably concede from the evidence that, while the import price elasticities may be quite low, the sum of both elasticities is

184

probably substantially in excess of unity. The pessimism over depreciation stems from the doubt that relative prices can be altered by exchange rate changes.[9]

To apply equation (19) to data for a number of countries would require a substantial amount of information that we do not have available. We therefore decided to apply the simplest growth rule of all, enunciated in equation (20), which makes the growth rate equal to the ratio of the rate of growth of exports divided by the income elasticity of demand for imports. The simple rule gives such a remarkable approximation to the growth experience of several countries over the post-war period, as to almost take on the status of a fundamental law. Two different sets of data on the growth of output and exports were used, one for the period 1953—76 (Kern (1978)), and the other from a different source for the period 1951—73 (Cornwall (1977)). We have slightly more faith in the latter data since it is undistorted by the oil price rises of 1973/74, but we have taken the two sources to avoid being accused of choosing the source to suit our argument! On the income elasticity of demand for imports, Houthakker and Magee's estimates (1969) have been taken as applying to the whole of these periods, even though they were only estimated over the period 1951—66. The elasticities are now probably slightly higher, but these dated estimates are still the best consistently estimated international estimates available. The data and results are presented in Tables 1 and 2. The estimated growth rates from applying equation (20) are shown to be quite close to the growth rate actually experienced for most countries and the rank ordering is very strong. For the sample of countries in Table 1 the Spearman rank correlation between the predicted growth rates from applying our simple rule and the actual growth rates is 0.764; and for the sample of countries in Table 2 the rank correlation is 0.891. There is a general tendency for the balance of payments equilibrium growth rate to be higher than the actual growth rate which should show up as a balance of payments surplus. This is clearly at odds with the evidence with the exception of a minority of countries such as Germany, Switzerland and Japan. Japan is a striking example of a country where the gap between its actual growth rate and its balance of payments equilibrium growth rate has resulted in the build-up of a huge payments surplus. Presumably Japan could not grow faster than it did because of a capacity ceiling. Except for the surplus countries where a capacity constraint may have been operative, we must look for other explanations of why the estimated balance of payments equilibrium growth rates are overestimates. As suggested above the assumed income elasticity of demand for imports is probably an underestimate for the period of time stretching into the late 1960s and early 1970s. Other factors excluded from consideration may also be exaggerating the balance of payments equilibrium growth rate, such as rising domestic prices not fully offset by exchange depreciation.

The worrying feature of the results from Britain's point of view is that it has the lowest balance of payments equilibrium growth rate of any country in the sample. It is not much more than one-half of the rate of its major European neighbours. The policy implication is plain. If Britain is to escape the syndrome of slow growth and low productivity (or falling employment) it must raise the rate of growth of exports and/or lower the income elasticity of demand for imports. A country cannot grow faster in the long run than its balance of payments equilibrium growth rate. The balance of payments constraint

TABLE 1

Calculations of the Growth Rate
Consistent with Balance of Payments Equilibrium 1953–76

Country	% change of real GNP (y)	% change of export volume (x)	Income elasticity of demand for imports (π)	Balance of payments equilibrium growth rate from applying equation (20)
USA	3.23	5.88	1.51	3.89
Canada	4.81	6.02	1.20	5.02
West Germany	4.96	9.99	1.89	5.29
Netherlands	4.99	9.38	1.82	5.15
Sweden	3.67	7.16	1.76	4.07
France	4.95	8.78	1.62	5.42
Denmark	3.58	6.77	1.31	5.17
Australia	4.95	6.98	0.90	7.76
Italy	4.96	12.09	2.25	5.37
Switzerland	3.56	7.20	1.90	3.79
Norway	4.18	7.70	1.40	5.50
Belgium	4.07	9.24	1.94	4.76
Japan	8.55	16.18	1.23	13.15
Austria	5.17	11.12	na	—
UK	2.71	4.46	1.51	2.95
South Africa	4.97	6.57	0.85	7.73
Spain	5.94	11.10	na	—
Finland	4.55	6.63	na	—

Source: Kern, 1978, and Houthakker and Magee, 1969.

provides the major explanation of why growth rates differ between countries (Thirlwall (1978)).

The balance of payments constrained export-led growth model used here is certainly a far better predictor of the actual British growth experience than the unconstrained export-led model of equation (19a).[1] When we applied the un-constrained model to the data for the period 1951—66 (Dixon and Thirlwall (1975)) it predicted a growth rate of 4 per cent on the basis of the following values for the variables and parameters: $\eta = -1.5$; $w_t + \tau_t = 0.06$; $r_{at} = 0.02$; $p_{ft} = 0.02$; $\epsilon = 1.0$; $z_t = 0.04$; $\lambda = 0.5$ and $\gamma = 1.0$. Since the actual growth rate over the period was 2.8 per cent, we mentioned at the time that the model may be overpredicting because of a balance of payments constraint — apart from any constraint on capacity. If 4 per cent was a permissible rate consistent

TABLE 2

Calculations of the Growth Rate Consistent with
Balance of Payments Equilibrium 1951—73 using data given by Cornwall, 1977

Country	% change in GDP (y)	% change in exports (x)	Income elasticity of demand for imports (π)	Balance of payments equilibrium growth rate from applying equation (20)
Austria	5.1*	10.7	na	—
Belgium	4.4*	9.4	1.94	4.84
Canada	4.6	6.9	1.20	5.75
Denmark	4.2†	6.1	1.31	4.65
France	5.0	8.1	1.62	5.00
Germany	5.7	10.8	1.89	5.71
Italy	5.1	11.7	2.25	5.20
Japan	9.5	15.4	1.23	12.52
Netherlands	5.0	10.1	1.82	5.55
Norway	4.2	7.2	1.40	5.14
UK	2.7	4.1	1.51	2.71
USA	3.7	5.1	1.51	3.38

* 1955—73
† 1954—73

Source: Cornwall, 1977, p 162.

187

with balance of payments equilibrium the country should have enjoyed a growing surplus, which it did not. Application of the same model, but with a balance of payments constraint (equation (19)), assuming $\pi = 1.51$ and that imports are insensitive to price, gives a growth rate consistent with balance of payments equilibrium of 2.4 per cent. This is closer to the actual growth rate of 2.8 per cent, and the discrepancy between the two rates is consistent with the balance of payments moving into deficit over the period. Making imports sensitive to price would raise the rate slightly. The application of our simple rule in equation (20) gives a balance of payments equilibrium growth rate of 2.6 per cent over the period.

Applying the equations to the post-1966 period gives rather less satisfactory results probably because the period has been one of general economic upheaval, and the model is very sensitive to small variations (errors) in the variables and in the assumed parameter values. When the constrained virtuous circle model (equation (19)) is applied to the data over the period 1967–76 the estimated growth rate is 5.2 per cent compared with the actual growth rate of 1.8 per cent per annum.[10] Since the country moved into substantial deficit over the period, the model is clearly overpredicting. It could be that the income elasticity of demand for imports is much higher than the assumed value of 1.51 or that the price elasticity of demand for UK exports is less than the assumed −1.5. The application of our simple growth rule gives a balance of payments equilibrium growth rate of 2 per cent. This looks much more consistent with the facts, particularly if the income elasticity of demand for imports has risen. A value of approximately 2 would give a balance of payments equilibrium growth rate of 1.5 per cent per annum over the period, which would be consistent with the actual growth experience and the balance of payments on current account moving into deficit. Despite the effort of formulating a fairly sophisticated export-led growth model, incorporating the idea of a virtuous circle led by exports but constrained by the balance of payments, it seems from the empirical evidence that a simpler model will suffice. Specifically, that growth performance, and growth rate differences between countries, can be approximated by the rate of growth of a country's exports divided by the income elasticity of demand for imports. This is not to disparage the idea of the possibility of a virtuous circle. It is to suggest that the link between exports and growth via the Verdoorn effect may not be very important either because relative prices change very little or because the price elasticities of demand for exports and imports are not sufficiently high. The main importance of export growth lies in raising the balance of payments constraint on growth, simply allowing countries to reach their capacity rate.

188

De-industrialization

Some concern has been expressed in recent years that Britain is entering a period of de-industrialization with severe implications for the future level of employment and unemployment.[11] One simple explanation of the de-industrialization process lies in the fact that if the growth of manufacturing output is constrained by the balance of payments below the rate of growth of productivity in manufacturing, then industry is bound to shed labour (Thirlwall (1978)). At the heart of the de-industrialization process would seem to be Britain's weak balance of payments. A similar argument has been put forward by Singh (1977). The relation between the growth of manufacturing output (g_m) and the growth of total income (y) may be expressed as:

$$g_m = \mu(y), \tag{22}$$

where μ is the elasticity of manufacturing output to total income, which is a measure of the income elasticity of demand for manufactured goods. Given μ, and the growth of total income consistent with balance of payments equilibrium, the rate of growth of manufacturing output consistent with balance of payments equilibrium ($\bar{g}_m$) is also determined:

$$\bar{g}_m = \mu(y_B) \tag{23}$$

where y_B can be determined from the application of our simple rule. If $y_B = x/\pi$, the maximum long run rate of growth of manufacturing output is:

$$\bar{g}_m = \frac{\mu x}{\pi} \tag{24}$$

The only ways to increase the long run rate of growth of manufacturing output, given the over-all constraint of the balance of payments, are to raise μ by producing goods with a higher income elasticity of demand; to raise the rate of growth of exports by making all goods more desirable abroad, and to lower π by making all foreign goods less desirable. If $\bar{g}_m$ is less than the rate of growth of labour productivity in manufacturing, less labour will be demanded. What are the facts? For the period 1951–66 we estimate the balance of payments constrained growth rate to have been about 2.4 per cent. For the period since then we are less certain, but our simple rule predicts 2.0 per cent because of the slow-down in the growth of world income. From statistics on the share of manufacturing output in total output (see Table 3), it would appear that μ is virtually unity, with the share of manufacturing output to total output remaining constant over time. This means that the growth of manufacturing output consistent with balance of payments equilibrium is exactly the same as the over-all balance of payments constrained growth rate. Now productivity

TABLE 3

**The Share of Manufacturing Employment and Output in
Total Employment and Output 1950—75**

	Share of manufacturing employment in total employment (%)	Share of manufacturing output in GDP at constant (1963) prices (%)
1950	34.7	29.3
1955	35.9	30.6
1960	35.8	31.0
1965	35.0	31.1
1970	34.7	31.7
1975	30.9	29.1

Source: Brown and Sheriff, 1978.

growth in manufacturing output over the period 1950—64 was 2.7 per cent per annum which is approximately equal to the rate of growth of total output and manufacturing, output, and thus is consistent with the economy retaining labour in the manufacturing sector over this period and the economy moving into payments deficit. Since the mid-1960s, however, productivity growth seems to have accelerated, but the growth of manufacturing output permitted by the over-all balance of payments constraint has not risen commensurately, and hence the decline in employment. The decline in manufacturing employment between 1961 and 1976 is estimated at 1.3 million. The slow growth of the manufacturing sector does not lie in the lack of factor supplies, as once thought (Kaldor (1966)), but in constraints on demand. If demand could be expanded, manufacturing would find its own factor supplies. The problem lies in the characteristics of the goods that Britain produces and sells at home and abroad. The British treat them as 'inferior' goods and the world too.

Notes

[1] The authors are grateful for encouragement and constructive criticism from Professor Kaldor, Dr W. Beckerman, Mr J. Bowers, Mr D. Vines, and two anonymous referees.

[2] Balance of payments equilibrium is defined here in terms of balance on the current account partly for simplicity but also in recognition that *net* long-term capital flows are likely to be relatively small in magnitude and that few countries are likely to be able to finance for ever a growing current account deficit by continual short-term borrowing. There may, of course, be an asymmetry in the system. While it is assumed that a country's long run growth rate cannot exceed that consistent with payments equilibrium, it can be lower.

190

[3] A good textbook treatment of the concept of the balance of payments equilibrium growth rate is to be found in Eltis, 1966.

[4] Kaldor, having once been an advocate of currency depreciation to improve export performance, has belatedly turned against it because of its inflationary repercussions domestically.

[5] This section is meant as a brief survey and no attempt is made to integrate the models or to assess their empirical validity.

[6] This is not true, however, of Beckerman's original specification since the export demand function is additive not multiplicative.

[7] ie the relationship between the rate of growth of productivity as the dependent variable and the rate of growth of output as the independent variable, which when tested empirically gives a coefficient of about 0.5. The law is not simply an empirical generalization, however. In the mathematical appendix of Verdoorn's original article, he also develops a predictive model.

[8] This compares with the equilibrium growth rate derived from the Kaldor model without a balance of payments equilibrium condition, letting $y_t = \gamma(x_t)$, of:

$$y_t = \frac{\gamma\left[\eta(w_t - r_{at} + \tau_t - p_{ft} - e_t) + \varepsilon(z_t)\right]}{1 + \gamma\eta\lambda} \qquad 19(a)$$

Notice that if the price and income elasticities of demand for imports are both unity (ie $\psi = 1$ and $\pi = 1$), and $\gamma = 1$, equation (19) collapses to (19a) because the balance of payments would always be in equilibrium whatever the rate of growth of income and foreign prices. In an export led growth model without a balance of payments constraint, γ must take on that value which preserves balance of payments equilibrium as income and import prices change.

[9] There must also be pessimism, as our models show, that exchange depreciation can improve the balance of payments permanently, unless the depreciation is continuous. Models of trade and growth seem to ignore this fundamental point.

[10] The parameter values and estimates of the variables (rates per annum) used were: $\eta = -1.5$; $w_t + \tau_t = 0.26$; $r_a = 0.01$; $p_f = 0.28$; $\varepsilon = 1$; $z = 0.03$; $\lambda = 0.5$; $\pi = 1.51$ and the exchange rate fell by about 4 per cent per annum over the period.

[11] Aspects of this concern are discussed in the proceedings of a seminar on de-industrialization organized by the National Institute of Economic and Social Research (Blackaby, 1978).

References

B. Balassa, 1963, 'Some Observations on Mr. Beckerman's "Export Propelled" Growth Model', *Economic Journal*, **73**.

R. J. Ball, T. Burns and J. S. Laury, 1977, 'The Role of Exchange Rate Changes in Balance of Payments Adjustment: The UK Case', *Economic Journal*, **87**.

W. Beckerman, 1962, 'Projecting Europe's Growth', *Economic Journal*, **72**.

W. Beckerman, 1963, 'A reply to Balassa', *Economic Journal*, **73**.

F. Blackaby, ed, 1978, *De-industrialisation*.

A. J. Brown, 1942, 'Trade Balances and Exchange Stability', *Oxford Economic Papers*, OS.

A. J. Brown, 1951, 'The Fundamental Elasticities in International Trade', in T. Wilson and P. W. S. Andrews, ed, *Oxford Studies in the Price Mechanism*, Oxford.

C. J. F. Brown and T. D. Sheriff, 1978, 'Deindustrialisation in the U.K.: A Summary of Empirical Evidence and Alternative Explanations', in Blackaby op cit.

R. Caves, 1970, 'Export-Led Growth: The Post War Industrial Setting', in W. Eltis, M. Scott and J. N. Wolfe, eds, *Induction Growth and Trade: Essays in Honour of Sir Roy Harrod*, Oxford.

J. Cornwall, 1977, *Modern Capitalism: its Growth and Transformation*.

R. Dixon and A. P. Thirlwall, 1975, 'A Model of Regional Growth Rate Differences on Kaldorian Lines', *Oxford Economic Papers*, NS.

W. Eltis, 1966, *Economic Growth*.

J. Hicks, 1950, *The Trade Cycle*, Oxford.

A. Hirschman, 1958, *Strategy of Economic Development*, Yale.

H. Houthakker and S. Magee, 1969, 'Income and Price Elasticities in World Trade', *Review of Economics and Statistics*.

N. Kaldor, 1966, *Causes of the Slow Rate of Economic Growth of the United Kingdom*, Cambridge.

N. Kaldor, 1970, 'The Case for Regional Policies', *Scottish Journal of Political Economy*, XIX.

N. Kaldor, 1974, 'The Road to Recovery', *New Statesman*, 1 March.

D. Kern, 1978, 'An International Comparison of Major Economic Trends 1953—76', *National Westminster Bank Review*, May.

A. Lamfalussy, 1963, *The United Kingdom and the Six*.

G. Myrdal, 1957, *Economic Theory and Underdeveloped Regions*.

A. Singh, 1977, 'U.K. Industry and the World Economy: A Case of Deindustrialisation?', *Cambridge Journal of Economics*, I.

A. P. Thirlwall, 1978, 'Britain's Economic Problem: A Balance of Payments Constraint', *National Westminster Bank Quarterly Review*, February.

A. P. Thirlwall, 1978, 'The Balance of Payments Constraint as an Explanation of International Growth Rate Differences', *Banca Nazionale del Lavoro Quarterly Review*.

P. J. Verdoorn, 1949, 'Fattori che Regolano lo Sviluppo della Produttivita del Lavoro', *L'Industria*. Translation by G. and A. P. Thirlwall in *Research in Population and Economics* (forthcoming).

T. Wilson, 1976, 'Effective Devaluation and Inflation', *Oxford Economic Papers*, NS.

11

The theory of economic integration
A. J. JONES

193–213

The purpose of the paper is to present a unified view of the different and often apparently conflicting strands of the most rigorously developed branch of the theory of economic integration, customs union theory. By doing this it is hoped to suggest some pitfalls to be avoided as well as a few insights which might usefully be applied to other branches of the subject.

The analytical framework adopted here will be confined to the standard model of customs union theory derived from the modern theory of tariffs. Thus throughout the argument it will be assumed that the world can be split into three separate economies, the home country, the (potential) partner and the rest of the world. It will also be assumed that all goods produced and consumed in the world can be aggregated into the two composite commodities, the 'importables' (x) and the 'exportables' (y) of the home country.

This simplifying assumption enables the use of various geometrical tools of analysis, but the range of choice between them has been a persistent source of confusion in the development of the analysis. Most of the more rigorous formulations have employed the geometrical techniques of two-commodity space; indifference curves, production and consumption possibility frontiers and offer curves. Such tools do have many advantages. They help to clarify the basic assumptions of the model, welfare conclusions can be shown by direct reference to the properties of indifference curves or consumption possibility frontiers, and the general equilibrium nature of the analysis is evident at all times. On the other hand, they have proved to be rather complex to handle, especially when the economic relationships of all three economies need to be examined and, even in the simplest formulation of the problem, they have been the source of at least one notable red-herring: concern to demonstrate the possible gains that might arise even for so-called 'trade-diverting' customs unions. This problem, however, has been avoided by the use of the demand and supply curve techniques which have provided the other main line of development and which have almost always been the initial source of insights into the subject. Unfortunately, the proponents of the two-commodity techniques have derided these simple methods as representing an inferior, partial equilibrium approach.

Indeed in presentations of customs union theory using only demand and supply curves this limitation has often been apologetically admitted but the impression that the two-commodity general equilibrium model and the demand and supply curve analysis of customs unions necessarily represent different theories is mistaken.

In Fig 1, the home country's (general equilibrium) demand curve for importables (dd_x) can be regarded as being derived directly from the assumptions of the two-commodity model without significant modification.[1] The curve ss_x is similarly derived directly from the production possibility frontier without modification of any assumptions, and is the marginal opportunity cost curve of home country's production of importables. Given the standard assumption (in both approaches) that there is perfect competition in the commodity market, it follows that ss_x can also be regarded as the domestic supply curve of importables. Although the diagram focuses on the market for a single commodity, it nonetheless remains a two-commodity model in which there is only one commodity price variable (the term of trade, p) and in which information about the second commodity is provided by the fact that all areas in Fig 1 are measured in units of y.

This property of the diagram raises a problem which has long been a matter of dispute in economic theory. It will be argued here that any area bounded by dd_x, ss_x, and appropriate terms of trade lines is a measure (in units of exportables) of the change in the gains from trade caused by changes in the international terms of trade or by changes in the policies being pursued by the home country. Thus, in Fig 1, suppose that the international terms of trade are fixed at e^w, and that a tariff on imports leaves the effective foreign supply curve of importables to the home market at $E^tE^t_x$. The effects of the removal of the tariff on both the domestic terms of trade (the fall from E^t to e^w) and the change in the volume of imports (the increase from $x^t_sx^t_d$ to $x^w_sx^w_d$) are readily identified (and have identical counterparts in two-commodity space). The welfare effects are identified as the gross gains from increased trade ($acc''a''$) less the loss of tariff revenue ($acji$). The net gains from trade of this policy change can thus be split into the gains from increased specialization (the production effect aia'') and the gains from increased exchange (the consumption effect cjc''). Like the change in tariff revenue (and its offset due to the change in the domestic terms of trade on the initial volume of imports), the gains from specialization are identified in terms of a commodity measure which has an exact counterpart (which is used in the same way) in two-commodity space. Following Hicks, it is also accepted that the compensating variation provides a commodity measure of the welfare consequences of the consumption effect of a price change. When compensation

FIGURE 1
The 'Small Country' Model

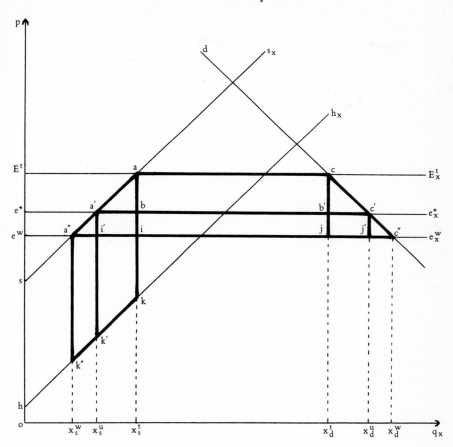

is actually paid or received, this measure is entirely appropriate and dd_x can be interpreted as a compensated demand curve so that the familiar triangle under the demand curve is the exact counterpart of the compensating variation shown in two-commodity space. When tariff changes are being considered, however, it is generally assumed that compensation is not paid, with the result that the simple Hicksian measure (whether in two-commodity space or in diagrams such as Fig 1) can at best be considered an approximation of the appropriate welfare

195

change. In two-commodity barter models (and in n-commodity general equilibrium models in which homothetic preference functions are assumed), however, a precise measure of the consumption effect can be defined. This is provided by the limit of the sum of Hicksian compensating variations obtained when the price change is regarded as a set of small, successive steps with no compensation being paid. Within the limited framework of this model such a measure is well defined and, although it cannot readily be depicted in two-commodity space, it corresponds exactly to the measure of the consumption effect identified above.[2]

The 'small country' model

With these tools of analysis, the presentation of the basic and most widely influential form of customs union theory is straightforward. This model abstracts from the problems of evaluating welfare change in the other economies by assuming that the home economy is 'small' relative to the two foreign economies, which are regarded as offering fixed, but different, terms of trade. As the formation of a customs union with the lower cost source of imports would be identical in its effects to the adaption of a policy of free trade, the analysis focuses on the effects of forming a customs union with the higher cost foreign source of supply. In Fig 1, this information is shown by the fixed terms of trade e^w offered by the rest of the world and e^* offered by the potential partner.

The traditional formulation of this model proceeds by identifying an initial non-discriminatory tariff policy in the home country. In terms of Fig 1, this results in the tariff-inclusive export supply curve of the rest of the world becoming the effective foreign supply curve of importables ($E^tE_x^t$) for the home market. The formation of the customs union is accomplished by the removal of the tariff on imports from the partner and the adoption of a common external tariff at least as high as the prohibitive tariff which the partner is implicitly levying initially on imports of commodity x from the rest of the world. As a result of these tariff changes, the tariff-free export supply curve of the partner ($e^*E_x^u$) becomes the effective foreign supply curve to the home economy. Consequently there is both an increase in the volume of trade (from $x_s^t x_d^t$ to $x_s^u x_d^u$) and the diversion of all trade from being with the rest of the world to being with the partner. The net welfare effects of this change, *compared with the initial policy*, consist of the gains from increased specialization (the production effect, aba'), the gains from increased exchange (the consumption effect, $cb'c'$) and the uncompensated loss in tariff revenue ($bb'ji$). Despite much pedantic confusion over terminology, the first two effects can be combined into the gains from increased trade (ie the 'trade creation' effect) whilst the loss associated with diverting trade to a higher cost source of supply is identified as the 'trade diversion' effect.

Since, in this formulation, both the initial tariff policy and the difference between the two foreign terms of trade are purely arbitrary, it follows that no *a priori* conclusions can be generated about the relative sizes of the trade creation and trade diversion effects. A welcome consequence of this has been the stimulus given to empirical studies of actual proposals for customs unions and free-trade areas. Despite this gain, however, this formulation of the issue of customs union formation must be recognized as containing two crucial flaws.

The first of these is its failure to give explicit consideration to the basis of the determination of government policy and in particular to the existence of constraints on policy choice. It is perhaps a fair criticism of much economic analysis of government policy that inadequate attention has been paid to these issues but, at present, the most helpful approach seems to be based on the assumption that governments seek to maximize a social welfare function given the constraints that might affect policy choice. If all policy instruments are regarded as costlessly and freely variable, it would follow that governments would always employ a policy of optimal intervention, the basic principles of which are (a) that only 'first-best' policy instruments should be used to intervene at the exact points in the economy at which the problems exist which are preventing the market mechanism from producing the socially optimal result and (b) that such policy instruments should be set at the optimal rate in order to offset the problem exactly and so produce the desired result.

Since the basic models of customs union theory abstract from problems of time, uncertainty and money, the analysis here need identify only five policy instruments. Lump-sum income transfers are the first-best method for redistributing income, and this assumption that these are being optimally used provides the basis for the derivation of the social indifference curves on which both demand functions and welfare judgements are based. Similarly taxes (and subsidies) directed at factor use, at production, and at consumption, provide the first-best means of offsetting the externalities and market imperfections which arise, respectively, in the factor market, in production and in consumption. It is the (implicit) assumption of the previous analysis that these are also being optimally employed which enables the demand and supply curves of Fig 1 to be used to convey information about the social as well as the private valuation of the costs and benefits of domestic production and consumption. As with the domestic policy instruments, it then follows that taxes (and subsidies) directed at international trade are also first-best policy instruments whose optimal use arises when (and only when) they are used to offset externalities (such as 'public good' arguments for greater national self-sufficiency) and market imperfections (such as monopoly power) which occur in international trade.

Given this picture of unconstrained optimal policy choice, it is a simple conclusion from Fig 1 that, as no such foreign distortions are postulated in the standard model, the optimal tariff policy is one of free trade. Both the initial tariff and the policy of forming a customs union with the partner country are therefore not rational policy choices and the inconclusive result of the attempt to rank them should occasion little surprise.

This result, however, rests upon the assumption that all first-best policy-instruments are freely and costlessly variable. If this assumption is abandoned, it is helpful to distinguish between constraints on domestic policies and constraints on trade policies. The latter will be considered subsequently but, initially, the argument will follow the attempts to rationalize customs union formation by the assumption of constraints on the use of domestic policies. These will be exemplified throughout this paper by the assumption that the use of production taxes and subsidies is constrained though, by analogy, the resulting analysis could be applied to the loss of any other domestic first-best instrument.

The effect of this assumption is to introduce the possibility that the social and private valuation of costs of domestic production may differ. This is illustrated in Fig 1 by the introduction of hh_x as the socially valued marginal cost curve of the domestic production of importables, whilst ss_x retains its earlier interpretation as the privately valued marginal cost or supply curve. With no constraints on policy choice, optimal intervention would involve the use of a production subsidy which would shift ss_x to coincide with hh_x. Given the assumed constraint, however, the optimal use of tariff policy changes. Imposing a tariff still brings about consumption effect losses and privately valued production effect losses but it is now also necessary to take into account the difference between the social and the private valuation of marginal opportunity costs of production. Thus, in the case of the non-discriminatory tariff policy which raises the effective foreign supply curve of importables to the home market to $E^tE_x^t$, the consumption and privately valued production effects are measured as cjc'' and aia'' respectively, as above. The socially valued production effect, however, is the net gain $a''ikk''$. In the case illustrated, this gain exceeds the consumption loss and, indeed, the diagram has been drawn so that this non-discriminatory tariff represents the (second-best) optimal rate, such that the marginal consumption loss (cj) is just equal to the marginal production gain (ik).

As I have pointed out elsewhere,[3] however, the introduction of constraints on domestic policy choice in the home country is insufficient to enable the 'small country' model to provide a rational justification for the formation of a customs union. A full consideration of this problem involves distinguishing between the optimal effective preferential tariff policy and the formation of a customs union. By introducing two foreign economies into the theory of tariffs, customs union theory identifies two policy instruments for optimal intervention in international trade — taxes (and subsidies) on trade with the partner and taxes (and subsidies) on trade with the rest of the world. Given the 'small country' assumption of fixed foreign terms of trade, the effect of any non-discriminatory policy is for all trade to be with the lower cost source of supply — the rest of the world. To have any effect on the source of trade it is necessary for the home country to adopt an effective preferential policy such that the rate of duty on imports from the partner is at least $e^w e^*$ lower than on the rest of the world. If there are no constraints on policy choice, this preferential policy need not involve the formation of a customs union (or a free-trade area). Thus consider first the adoption of the minimal effective tariff preference to alter the pattern of trade. With a (specific) tariff duty of $e^w E^t$ on imports from the rest of the world, an effective preferential policy is achieved by imposing the (lower) tariff rate $e^* E^t$ on imports from the partner. The result of this is to leave the effective foreign supply curve of importables as $E^t E^t_x$ with domestic consumption and production as with the optimal non-discriminatory tariff. Given the preference, however, $E^t E^t_x$ is no longer solely the (tariff-inclusive) export supply curve of the rest of the world but is also the (tariff-inclusive) export supply curve of the partner. Domestic consumers may therefore buy from either source and, to the extent that imports are diverted from the lower cost source of supply, the sole result of this for the home country is a reduction in tariff revenue. In the limit, if the tariff preference is just sufficient to divert all trade to the partner, the home country's tariff revenue loss is $bb'ji$, ie the 'trade diversion' effect. Compared to the optimal non-discriminatory policy, the granting of such a preference is thus an unambiguous source of loss to the home country. It is, however, superior to the form of preferential policy implied by membership of a customs union.

This can be seen by splitting the formation of the customs union into two steps. The first is the reduction of the non-discriminatory tariff duty to $e^w e^*$. Compared with the optimal non-discriminatory tariff, such a change is inevitably a source of loss, with the consumption effect gain ($cb'c'$) being outweighed by the production effect loss ($i'ikk'$). The second step involves the granting of the effective minimal preference by reducing the tariff on imports

o

from the partner by $e^w e^*$ (ie to zero). This is again assumed to be just sufficient to divert all trade from being with the rest of the world to being with the partner, and again results in the unambiguous loss of tariff revenue which can be identified as a trade diversion effect. With the greater volume of trade involved, however, this trade diversion effect is $a' c' j' i'$ and is inevitably larger than the trade diversion effect associated with the initial preferential policy considered. Accordingly the introduction of constraints on domestic policy choice alone can justify the use of non-discriminatory tariffs but not the formation of a customs union. Indeed the ranking of policy choice in the model so far outlined is (1) the optimal non-discriminatory tariff, (2) the optimal preferential policy, (3) the formation of a customs union.

The introduction of two further assumptions, however, can enable the framework so far outlined to provide a rational explanation of the formation of a customs union. The first of these additional assumptions is that there are also constraints on the choice of tariff policies. This could justify customs union formation even from the viewpoint of the small country so far considered if (a) it was constrained from altering the level of its non-discriminatory tariff to the optimal level, and (b) it was constrained from following an optimal preferential policy but could join a customs union (or free-trade area). The second of these constraints is normally regarded as being widely effective — partly because of the formal provisions of GATT and partly because of the fear of retaliation if forms of preferential policy other than membership of a customs union are adopted. The former constraint, however, although possibly existing where the optimal tariff is higher than the existing tariff, is difficult to convert into a justification for the formation of a customs union since constraints also apply to this route to increased protection. Where the optimal tariff is lower than the existing tariff, no external barriers to unilateral non-discriminatory tariff reduction exist, and the only possible explanation of the constraint must then rest on the rather dubious claim that internal political constraints allow preferential but not unilateral tariff-cutting policies.

Even where the constraint on non-discriminatory tariff change is not operative, however, the case for membership of a customs union can be based on the existence of constraint (b), together with the second further assumption that there exist externalities in international trade in the form of public good benefits associated with the partner (or public good losses associated with trade with the rest of the world). Such public good arguments make preferential trade taxes and subsidies a first-best policy choice and, whilst the constraint rules out optimal preferential policies, it is possible that the policy of membership of a customs union may prove to be a superior second-best alternative to any non-discriminatory tariff. Indeed the original formation of the EEC may be partly explained in these terms, with the public good benefits of greater intra-European trade being viewed as the reduction in the risk of future wars between France and Germany, and possibly also with public good losses being associated with at least marginal imports from the then dominant USA.

Such an example, however, goes beyond the confines of the 'small country' model, since France and Germany (and other countries) can be viewed as potential beneficiaries from this effect, and points to the other crucial weakness of the traditional model of customs union theory: by concentrating on the 'small country' framework it excludes all the external effects that the home country's policy decisions may have on the partner and the rest of the world.

The 'small union' model

To rectify the weakness, it is helpful to proceed initially by retaining the assumption that the terms of trade of the rest of the world are fixed whilst recognizing the existence of the partner as another small country which can be modelled in the same way as the home economy.

The resulting model is depicted in Fig 2 with $e^*e_x^*$ in part (a) of the diagram being drawn as the partner's (tariff-free) export supply curve of x, derived from its domestic demand ($d^*d_x^*$) and supply ($s^*s_x^*$) curves drawn in part (b). If it is initially assumed that both countries are following first-best domestic policies, the optimal tariff policy for both economies is free trade. Equally, acceptance of constraints on the use of first-best domestic policies results in the second-best argument for non-discriminatory use of trade taxes. If both countries can in fact unilaterally adopt the second-best optimal (non-discriminatory) level of trade taxes, any preferential tariff arrangement remains inferior. Thus, in the special case illustrated in Fig 2, the optimal non-discriminatory tariff for both the home and the partner economy would be to raise their internal terms of trade to E^t ($=p^u$). For the home country, an import tariff of the specific rate e^wE^t would accomplish this but the partner would require to combine this import tariff with the same rate of export subsidy to be able to export c^*a^* of x at the terms of trade offered by the rest of the world. The requirement, however, points to a further possible constraint on the use of trade taxes, since the use of export subsidies runs counter to the provisions of GATT and their use may well be constrained by the fear of international retaliation. In such circumstances, even if the partner sets its non-discriminatory tariff at the optimum level, without export subsidies the net outcome would be the inferior self-sufficiency position, r^*.

Compared with this situation the effect of the home country granting a preference to the partner may bring net benefits. This arises because, although the home country necessarily still loses through at least the trade diversion effect, the granting of the preference to the partner has significant welfare effects in the partner economy which may be larger than the net losses for the home economy. In order to simplify the illustration as far as possible, Fig 2 has been constructed so that the optimal preferential policy consists of forming a customs union which has a common external tariff of the same height as the optimal non-discriminatory tariffs in both countries. A consequence of this is that the sole effect for the home country is the trade diversion loss of tariff revenue, acji.[4] The partner, on the other hand, obtains the privately valued gains in specialization and exchange, $c^*a^*r^*$, stemming from its exports of x to the home country plus the socially valued gain, $j^*i^*k^*k^{*'}$, arising from increased production of that commodity. Since the partner's gains exceed the losses of the home country, the formation of the customs union is justified from the viewpoint of the combined membership of the union. The attractiveness of such a policy to the home country, however, would clearly depend on arrangements for a satisfactory quid pro quo to offset the inevitable loss that it suffers. Again it is tempting to apply the analysis to the development of economic integration in Western Europe and, in particular, to the case of the UK application for membership, with commodity x being regarded as agricultural products. The model in Fig 2 then points to the unambiguous trade diversion loss to the UK associated with acceptance of the CAP[5] and thus to the need to identify a substantial gain arising from another aspect of UK membership of the EEC in order to justify UK entry.

One of the most widely canvassed sources of such gains rests upon the existence of economies of scale rather than the constant or increasing costs postulated so far. Surprisingly little rigorous attention has been given to the problem but, following the analysis of Corden,[6] it is possible to examine the case for the formation of a customs union in the presence of economies of scale with the aid of Fig 3.

Instead of the (privately valued) marginal cost curves of earlier diagrams, it is helpful to represent the cost relationships in terms of the average (opportunity) cost of producing commodity x — shown by AC_x for the home country and AC_x^* for the partner. Again for the purposes of illustration, Fig 3 represents a particularly simple case in which the internal demand curves of both the home country and the partner are identical, as shown by dd_x, with dD_x representing the combined demand curve after the union is formed. The given terms of trade of the rest of the world are again shown by e^w and it is assumed that, whatever

202

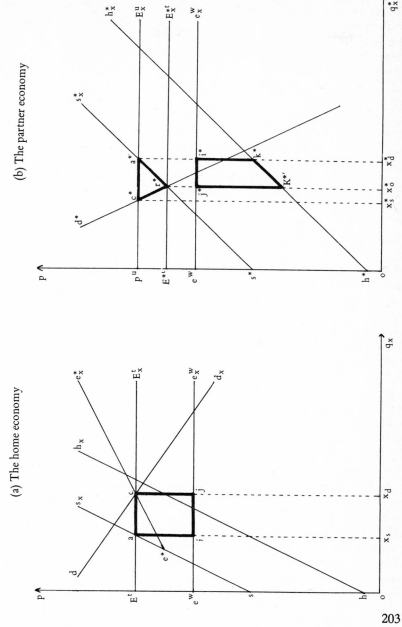

FIGURE 2
The 'Small Union' Model

(a) The home economy

(b) The partner economy

203

the scale of production, neither the home nor the partner industry can produce with (privately valued) average costs at or below this level.[7] As with the previous models, unless the presence of an uncorrected distortion between privately and socially valued costs of production is introduced, the optimal policy for both countries is free trade, with no internal production of commodity x. The introduction of uncorrected distortions between social and private valuations of domestic production, with the assumed unavailability of first-best domestic policy means for dealing with this, can again produce a second-best justification for the use of a non-discriminatory tariff. In the case of falling costs, however, there is only one possible value for the second-best tariff — the 'made-to-measure' tariff. This is defined as the tariff which just enables domestic production to supply the domestic market without the opportunity to obtain monopoly profits, and is thus shown as the tariff rate required to raise the foreign supply price to the point at which domestic average costs equal average revenue (given by the demand curve). Any higher tariff must be inferior since the loss of consumers' surplus and a reduced (socially valued) production effect gain must exceed any monopoly profit. Equally, any lower tariff would be unable to support domestic production and would therefore be inevitably inferior to a policy of free trade. Thus the justification of the made-to-measure tariff as the second-best optimal rate requires only that the socially valued production effect associated with its imposition outweighs the consumption effect loss compared with free trade.

In order to simplify Fig 3, the socially valued average cost curves are not shown but, on the assumption that they are low enough in both economies to justify unilateral tariff intervention, the second-best (made-to-measure) tariff rates are shown as $e^w p_o$ and $e^w p_o^*$ for the home and partner countries respectively. Such tariffs, however, are not optimal from the viewpoint of the combined membership of the union. From the union viewpoint, the optimal tariff policy is for the home and partner countries to form a customs union with a common external tariff set at the made-to-measure rate. In Fig 3 this is shown as $e^w p^u$ with the result that the consumption effect in both economies must be one of gain.[8] Since in the diagram it is the partner's industry which is regarded as having lower costs, it also follows that the partner's industry takes over the whole union market and thus benefits from a socially valued production effect gain. On the other hand, with the usual assumptions about the nature of the distinction between social and private valuations of costs and about the location of national enterprises, it can be shown that, for the home country, the socially valued production effect loss will outweigh the consumption effect gain. Thus again therefore, the possibility of the formation of the customs union being

204

FIGURE 3
The 'Small Union' Model with Economies of Scale

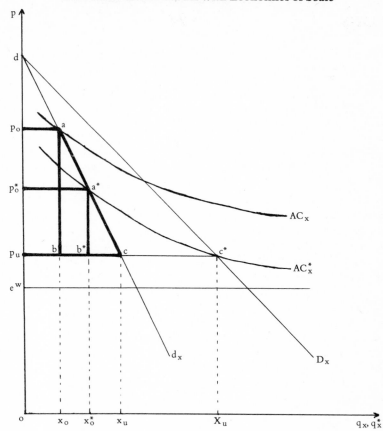

formed depends not only on the net gain to the union as a whole but on an adequate quid pro quo for the home country. The possibility of similar results can also be shown where initial production of x is in either one or neither of the member countries.

On the other hand, if the economies of scale are interpreted as economies accruing to an integrated industry rather than from plant economies of scale or economies of scale internal to a national industry, the possibility exists that, although the partner industry may gain control of the whole market, the location of some of its producing units may move to the home country. Thus, unless the socially valued production effects are necessarily linked with domestic ownership of the industry, it may be that the socially valued production effects might not be so adverse for the home economy and that the net outcome may even be net gain in the home as well as the partner economy, even without the arrangement of a quid pro quo. Nonetheless, in the context of UK membership of the EEC, one is left with the hope that it is the UK which most closely approximates the role of the more competitive partner economy, though the empirical support for such a hope seems sadly lacking.

Of course it might appear even more relevant to point out that the only basis for these gains is the assumed constraint on domestic policies (as well as on trade taxes), and that it would be much better for all economies if sufficient political will was applied to the problem of removing the constraints on domestic policy choice. The economies of scale argument, however, does suggest a potentially more powerful case for economic integration. In the argument up to this point, externalities and market imperfections, other than those which arise directly in international trade, have been regarded as confined to being within each country. If this assumption is relaxed, the possibility exists of private decisions taken in one country having external effects not only within that economy but for other countries as well. From a wider, international viewpoint even the optimal *national* use of first-best policies may then be sub-optimal. In such a case the first-best solution requires the establishment of international authorities with the power to use appropriate first-best policies. The optimal limits of the jurisdiction of such international authorities are determined in principle by the equality of the marginal benefits from 'internalizing' such externalities and the marginal costs associated with setting up (and controlling) such international authorities. Of course, in many cases such costs may be very high, especially in a changing world in which optimal policy intervention will require the capacity for flexible response, and the scope for the delegation of first-best domestic policies to such international authorities has so far proved to be very limited. With international constraints on the use of tariff policies being more readily accepted, however, with the imperfect use of national policies to offset externalities and market imperfections which overflow national boundaries, and with such externalities being more significant among countries with close economic ties, it follows that a second-best case may exist for the formation of a customs union between closely linked economies. Such a case is analogous to the second-best case for the national use of tariffs in the presence of domestic distortions. Given the inability of the partners to adopt appropriate first-best policies to offset distortions which are internal to the union, the optimal use of a second-best instrument, such as the common external tariff, is justified.

The 'large union' model

The final step in the development of customs union theory comes with the relaxation of the assumption of constant terms of trade in the rest of the world, with the resulting implication of the price-making powers of each separate economy. The immediate result of this is to place the argument in the context of oligopolistic interdependence, and therefore introduces the possibility of exploring the problem of tariff-making within the format of whatever theory of oligopoly seems most appropriate. Although the few analyses which have extended the analysis of customs union theory to this (large union) case have not tackled this problem explicitly, the most useful assumption seems to be to treat the rest of the world as being unable to pursue a unified tariff policy in reaction to the decisions of the home and partner countries (thereby reflecting the diverse nature suggested by the naming of the third economy).[9]

Two main versions of the large union model can then be identified. The first of these is illustrated in Fig 4 and extends the earlier arguments, in all of which the partner is treated as an actual or potential exporter of the home country's importables. This places the home country in the position of a monopsonist and, if it were not for the threat of retaliation, the optimal unilateral tariff policy would involve the imposition of different tariff rates on imports from the two sources, so that the home country would, in effect, be acting as a profit-maximizing discriminating monopsonist. With this possibility eliminated by assumption, however, the optimal unilateral policy involves the imposition of a non-discriminatory tariff on imports set at the optimal rate such that the marginal cost of obtaining imports is equated with their marginal value.

In Fig 4, the home country's marginal valuation of imports is shown by the import demand curve, mm_x, whilst the average cost of obtaining imports is provided by the kinked (tariff-free) total foreign supply curve EE_x, which is obtained as the summation of the export supply curves of the partner ($e^*e^*_x$) and the rest of the world ($e^we^w_x$). The marginal cost of obtaining imports is thus shown by $E'E'_x$, and the optimal non-discriminatory tariff (shown here for simplicity as a specific duty) is the non-discriminatory rate which raises the tariff-inclusive foreign supply to $E^tE^t_x$, ie to intersect mm_x at the same point as $E'E'_x$.[10] It follows from this that the tariff-inclusive export supply curves of the partner and the rest of the world are given by $e^{*t}e^{*t}_x$ and $p^w_1e^{wt}_x$ respectively with the internal terms of trade being identified as p^t_o in the home country, p^*_o in the partner and p^w_o in the rest of the world.

As with the earlier illustrations, Fig 4 has been drawn to represent a special case which simplifies the comparison of the optimal non-discriminatory policy with membership of a customs union. From the viewpoint of the union as a

208

FIGURE 4
The 'Large Union' Model

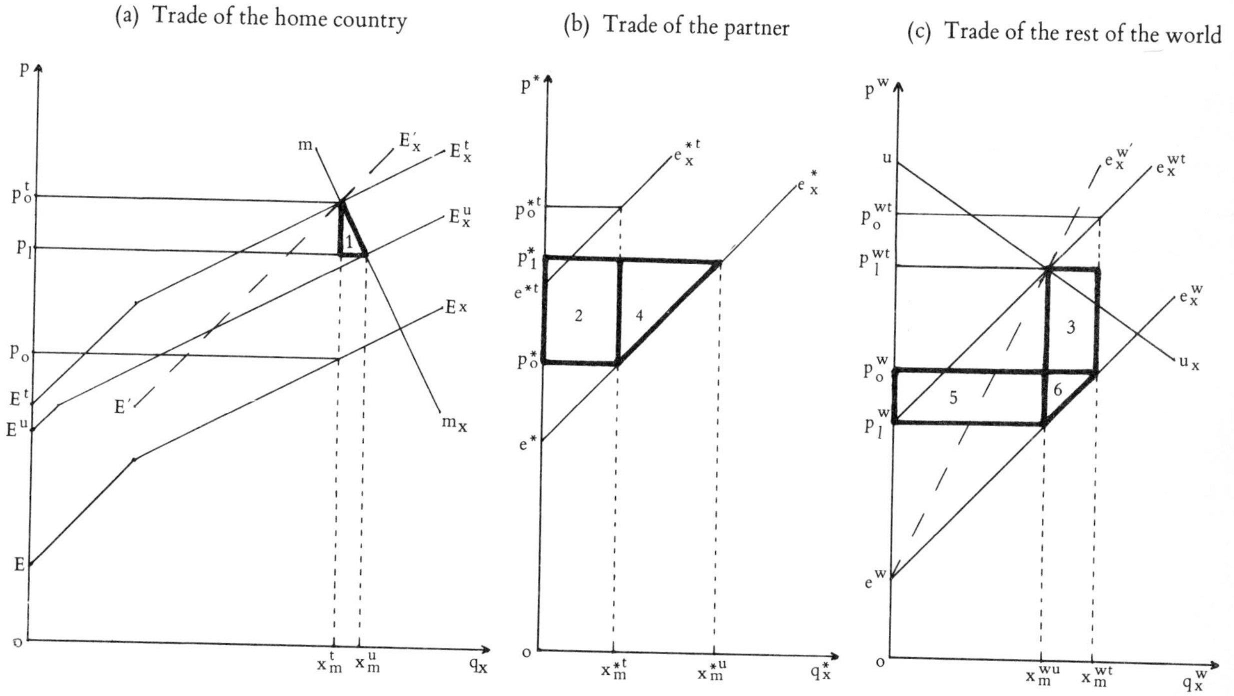

(a) Trade of the home country

(b) Trade of the partner

(c) Trade of the rest of the world

whole, it is the export supply curve $(e^w e_x^w)$ of the rest of the world which represents the average cost of obtaining imports of x, and it is the combination of the home country's import demand curve (mm_x) and the partner's export supply curve $(e^* e_x^*)$ which yields the union demand (and marginal valuation) curve (uu_x) for imports from the rest of the world. By analogy with the optimum tariff argument for the home country alone, it therefore follows that the optimal common external tariff from the viewpoint of the whole union is that which raises the tariff-inclusive export supply curve $(p_o^w e_x^{wt})$ to intersect the import demand curve (uu_x) at the same point as the marginal costs of imports curve $(e^w e_x^{w'})$. It follows further that the initial (optimal) tariff of the home country from its purely national viewpoint is equal (but only in the special case shown) to the optimal external tariff for the customs union judged from the combined viewpoint of the union as a whole. The effects of forming an optimal customs union can thus be compared with the optimal unilateral policy for the home country in this special case, simply by identifying the results which flow from the complete removal of the home country's initial tariff on imports from the partner whilst retaining it on imports from the rest of the world. In terms of the positive effects, this policy change can be seen to shift the (policy-inclusive) total foreign supply of importables to the home market to the kinked curve $E^u E_x^u$, which is constructed as the summation of the tariff-free export supply curve of the partner $(e^* e_x^*)$ and the tariff-inclusive export supply curve of the rest of the world $(p^w e_x^{wt})$. The internal terms of trade of the partner rise to p_1^*. The change in trade for each country can be identified as corresponding to the volume of trade creation for the home country $(x_m^t x_m^u)$, the volume of trade creation for the partner economy $(x_m^{*t} x_m^{*u})$ and the volume of trade diverted $(x_m^{wu} x_m^{wt})$.

The welfare effects are identified by the numbered areas shown in the diagram and they can be named as follows:

1. is the trade creation effect gain for the home country;
2. is the terms of trade effect gain for the partner which is exactly equal to a loss (in tariff revenue) suffered by the home country;
3. is the trade diversion effect loss for the home country and, like (2), corresponds to a loss of tariff revenue on imports;
4. is the trade creation effect gain for the partner,
5. is the terms of trade effect loss for the rest of the world which corresponds exactly to a gain (in tariff revenue) for the home country, and
6. is the trade diversion effect loss for the rest of the world.

Combining these effects produce several different viewpoints, the most obvious of which are those of the rest of the world, which unambiguously loses, and the partner, which unambiguously gains. Less obviously the union as a whole will also gain (providing that the common external tariff is optimal), but the net effects for both the home country and the whole world are uncertain. In the example shown, the home country is in fact a net loser, and this is probably the more likely outcome, since a necessary (but not sufficient) condition for the home country to gain is that the elasticity of the partner's export supply curve should be lower than that of export supply curve of the rest of the world.

This may suggest again that the successful formation of the customs union may depend on appropriate arrangements for international compensating transfers to be made but, whilst not wishing to reduce the significance of such issues, it should be recalled that the comparison is being made with the situation in which the home country has adopted an optimal unilateral policy with no retaliation from the partner. If the partner, however, is also prepared to pursue an active tariff policy, it may be able to pose the threat of causing a greater loss to the home country than that arising from membership of the customs union by itself pursuing a unilateral policy of imposing nationally optimal taxes on international trade without regard to the effect on other economies. As El Agraa has pointed out elsewhere,[11] co-operation in tariff policies can be more attractive than retaliation. In the case of the formation of customs unions, the potential gains for members from co-operation stem not only from the benefits of free trade among members, but also from the gains of being able to exploit their joint power in the face of a passive tariff policy in the rest of the world.

From the global viewpoint, both the unilateral tariff policies of individual countries and the formation of customs unions are inevitably sub-optimal. Whilst the rest of the world is unable to react and to co-operate with the home and partner countries to arrive at a globally optimal solution based on full international co-operation, the possibility exists for groups of countries to obtain aggregate benefit for themselves by pursuing co-operation on a more limited scale. From the global viewpoint, therefore, developments such as the formation of the customs union of the EEC and the hesitant steps towards regional monetary integration must be judged as desirable or not to the extent which they either facilitate or prevent co-operation on a wider international scale.

The 'large union' model has so far been exemplified by a very special case. It is easy to see, however, that the probability that the optimal common external tariff will be different from the optimal non-discriminatory tariff of the home country could be handled by an analysis which split the formation of the customs union into the two steps: (i) the adoption of the initial (optimal) tariff of the home country as the common external tariff and (ii) the change in the common external tariff to the rate which is optimal from the viewpoint of the union as a whole. Step (i) would then involve the same kind of effects as shown in Fig 4 but would not necessarily bring net gain to the union, whilst step (ii) would bring net gains which would modify the effects identified in step (i) without introducing any different sources of welfare change. The only interesting possibility suggested by the extension of the simple case already analysed is that ignorance or external constraints may prevent step (ii). In this case the common external tariff would not be optimal so that the justification for the formation of the union would then depend on the empirical evaluation of trade creation, trade diversion and terms of trade effects. Equally, it can be acknowledged that the initial national tariff may not be optimal, and this possibility could also be taken into account by introducing the further step of considering the effects of the move from the initial tariff to the optimal non-discriminatory level. As in the 'small country' model, however, the gains accruing from such a step should not be attributed to economic integration unless there were effective constraints preventing such unilateral action.

The alternative version of the large union case adds little new to the argument. In such a case the optimal solution from the joint viewpoint of both economies again involves the co-operation required for the establishment of the optimal common tariff on imports — a policy outcome which corresponds to the joint monopoly profit-maximizing solution of oligopoly theory. This can again provide a rationale for membership of a customs union and its application may also be relevant to the EEC, especially in the light of the recent evidence that terms of trade gains may have been a significant consequence of integration in Western Europe.[12]

Summary
This survey of customs union theory suggests four principal conclusions. The first is that the rationale for regional economic integration rests upon the existence of constraints on the use of first-best policy instruments. Thus, in the case of the 'large union' model, the optimality of regional economic integration depends upon the inability or unwillingness of the rest of the world to co-operate successfully with member countries in obtaining globally optimal solutions. In the 'small union' and 'small country' models, further constraints must be recognized — on the domestic use of first-best policy instruments and on the unilateral use of export subsidies and preferential trade taxes. Economic analysis has had little to say about the nature of such constraints, and

presumably the evaluation of any regional scheme of economic integration should incorporate a consideration of the validity of the view that such constraints do exist to justify the pursuit of second — rather than first-best solutions.

Secondly, even when the existence of constraints on superior policy instruments is acknowledged, it is misleading to identify the results of regional economic integration by comparing an arbitrarily chosen common policy with an arbitrarily chosen national policy. Of course ignorance and inertia provide sufficient reasons why existing policies may be non-optimal, but it is clearly wrong to attribute gains which would have been achieved by appropriate unilateral action to a policy of regional integration. Equally, although it is appropriate to use the optimal common policy as a point of reference, it must be recognized that this may overstate the gains to be achieved if, as seems highly likely, constraints and inefficiencies in the political processes by which policies are agreed prove to be greater among a group of countries than within any individual country.

Although the first two conclusions raise doubts about the case for regional economic integration, in principle at least, a strong general case for economic integration does exist. As with the 'large union' model or the 'small union' model in which economies of scale may be in part external to national industries, this case rests essentially upon the recognition of the externalities and market imperfections which extend beyond the boundaries of national states. In such circumstances, unilateral national action will not be optimal whilst integrated action offers the scope for potential gain.

As with the solution to most problems of externalities and market imperfections, however, customs union theory frequently illustrates the proposition that a major stumbling block to obtaining the gains from joint optimal action lies in agreeing an acceptable distribution of such gains. Thus the fourth conclusion is that the achievement of the potential gains from economic integration will be limited to countries able and willing to co-operate to distribute the gains from integration so that all partners may benefit compared to the results achieved by independent action. It is easy to argue from this that regional economic integration may be more easily achieved than global solutions but, as the debate about monetary integration in the EEC illustrates, the chances of obtaining potential mutual gain may well founder in the presence of disparate views about the distribution of such gains and weak arrangements for redistribution.

212

Notes

[1] The only difference arises over the normal treatment of the expenditure of tariff revenue. Most of the formulations employing the two-commodity techniques employ the assumption that this is redistributed to consumers who spend it, in the same manner as factor income, on both commodities. When demand and supply analysis is used, however, it is simpler to regard the tariff revenue as being returned solely in the form of the numeraire commodity (exportables).

[2] For a fuller discussion see A. J. Jones, 'Partial Equilibrium Tariff Theory' Leeds Discussion Paper, forthcoming. See also, M. E. Burns, 'A Note on the Concept and Measure of Consumer's Surplus', *American Economic Review*, 1973, 335—44.

[3] A. J. Jones, 'Domestic Distortions and Customs Union Theory', Leeds Discussion Paper 46.

[4] It can be noticed that, in general, the optimal preferential policy from the joint viewpoint of both members is determined where the marginal net gains to the partner just equal the marginal net losses to the home country. Only in special cases will this involve the formation of a customs union but, given the assumed constraints on other forms of preferential policy, the argument here identifies the crucial comparison between optimal non-discriminatory policies and the optimal available preferential policy — formation of a customs union. It should also be noticed that the general comparison made here is not crucially dependent on the simplification that $e^* e_x^*$ intersects $E^t E_x^t$ at c. If the intersection had been to the left of c (but to the right of a), the sole effect for the home country would have been a diminished trade diversion loss as some trade would have been retained with the rest of the world. On the other hand, if $e^* e_x^*$ had intersected dd_x below c, membership of the customs union would have also involved the further net losses associated with the move away from the terms of trade given by the optimum second-best tariff level — as analysed above in the 'small country' model of customs union formation.

[5] The actual loss may well be higher than this, both because of UK's domestic agricultural policy had proved more able to use first-best policy instruments and because the actual CAP is far from being optimal, even on second-best grounds.

[6] W. H. Corden, 'Economies of Scale and Customs Union Theory', *Journal of Political Economy*, 1972, 465—75.

[7] If average costs of production do fall to the level given by the terms of trade of the rest of the world, domestic production (and exports) of commodity x can be achieved without protection.

[8] Total consumption (equal to total production) in the union after it is formed is shown as X_u, with x_u being national consumption in both member countries. Accordingly, the consumption effect gain for the home country is $p_0 acp^u$ and for the partner is $p^* a^* cp^u$. Of these gains $p_0 abp^u$ and $p_0^* a^* b^* p^u$ are 'cost reduction^o' effects and, in general, may be significantly larger than the triangle-like areas of gain under demand curves which are the sole components of the consumption effect in the increasing opportunity cost models and which are also present in this case, as shown by areas abc (for the home country) $a^* b^* c$ (for the partner). To save cluttering the diagram, the socially valued production effects are not identified but they pose no difficulties being given, in principle, by comparison of the volume of production multiplied by the amount by which socially valued average costs fall below the world price level before and after the formation of the union.

[9] It will continue to be assumed however, that fear of retaliation will restrain both the home and partner from any other policy choices than those of non-discriminatory tariffs and full membership of a customs union.

[10] It can be noted that, in *ad valorem* terms, this optimal rate can be expressed as $(M - A)/A$ where M and A represent the marginal and average cost of obtaining imports respectively. Since it is a well-known result that $(M - A)/A = 1/\eta$ where η is the elasticity of the A curve, it follows that this optimal rate is identified as equal to the reciprocal of the elasticity of the foreign supply curve — a familiar result which has surely attracted more attention than it deserves as its practical significance is at best limited to the case of log-linear functions.

[11] 'On Optimum Tariffs, Retaliation and International Co-operation', *The Bulletin of Economic Research*, **31**, 1979.

[12] H. C. Petith, 'European Integration and the Terms of Trade', *Economic Journal*, **87**, 1977, 262—72.

12

The Common Market after twenty years

D. S. SWANN

The purpose of this paper is to attempt to review what the Community has achieved in the twenty or so years since the Rome Treaty was signed. The limitations of space preclude anything more than what at best might be described as a *tour d'horizon* in which the focus is almost purely on the internal policy of the European Economic Community.[1]

I

The formal creation of the customs union[2] element was achieved ahead of schedule, and no great difficulties have been encountered in persuading the new members to accommodate themselves to it within the negotiated transition periods.[3] However, it is a truism that a true customs union requires that non-tariff barriers also be removed and in this respect the record is a mixed one.

The outstanding non-tariff barrier achievement has been the development of a policy for dealing with cartels and concentrations.[4] Early commentators were sceptical about the ability of the EEC to take a firm stand. This scepticism was partly based on the earlier activities of the High Authority of the ECSC which was disposed to find good reason not to interfere radically in politically sensitive areas and most issues seemed to turn out to be sensitive. In practice the EC Commission has created some quite effective machinery for dealing with antitrust phenomena. In this connection, it is worthy of note that, despite the oft repeated charge of inept bureaucracy, the Commission has on a number of issues devised much more credible ways of dealing with specific problems than has been the case in the UK. For example, under Article 85(1) cartels are prohibited unless they can satisfy the stiff exemption requirements of Article 85(3). But no cartel can be entertained for consideration under Article 85(3) unless it has been duly notified. Contrast that with the fact that nearly twenty-five years after our own major restrictive practices legislation was placed on the statute book, a credible system of enforcement still does not exist.[5]

The Commission has not hesitated to condemn cartels and practices which have impeded the creation of a common market and where, as is often the case, no counterbalancing advantages could be offered. However, flexibility has been shown in recognizing that certain forms of collaborative activity are advantageous and can be exempted. Quite impressive fines have been imposed on miscreants and the Commission has not shrunk from claiming an extra-territorial jurisdiction for EEC antitrust law.

But the picture is not unalloyed. Article 86 (dealing with the abuse of dominance) has not been applied to any comparable extent, although it is possible that this reflects a paucity of genuine cases and/or real difficulty in detecting transgressions. In the latter context any judgement of the efficacy of the Commission should be set against the background that in terms of the number of officials it does not amount to even half of a respectably sized British ministry. (Its 8000 or so officials makes it smaller than Wandsworth Borough Council!) Also it has to work at a distance from the problems which confront it. The main area of failure lies with mergers. Although the *Continental Can* case established that Article 86 was applicable to mergers, that article is a far from ideal merger controlling instrument, since it can only be applied where dominance already exists. An addition to the Rome Treaty, specifically to provide for a control over mergers, was adopted by the Commission in 1974[6] but remains on the Council table and, given the political sensitivity of the issue (witness our own reluctance to allow the Director General of Fair Trading to refer mergers to the Monopolies and Mergers Commission), is likely to languish there for some time to come.

In respect of other non-tariff barriers, achievements are limited and in some cases a degree of retreat is apparent. It might have been expected that in the field of indirect taxes[7] the end of the original transition period (1969) would have witnessed a total resolution of the problems arising. In fact, ten years after, we have little to show on excise duties. In respect of turnover taxes, we have a common system, in the form of the VAT, and more recently a uniform assessment base (an important step prior to the full implementation of the own resources system of the Community Budget) but harmonization of rates seems a long way away. The destination principle and the so-called fiscal frontier therefore persist.

The harmonization of official standards[8] seems to promise significant pay-offs in terms of economies of European scale and the adoption of best national practice, particularly when protecting life and limb. Unfortunately the process of achieving uniform standards is a protracted one and as a result the number of harmonization directives, particularly where the impulsion of the CAP has been lacking, is limited. Added to all this are a number of profound problems. One is that by the time specific directives have been agreed, technological progress has rendered them in varying degrees irrelevant. Also the growing awareness of the problem of pollution and the desire to keep pace with the demands of the consumer lobby have led governments to intervene on an increasing scale in laying down health and safety standards. National Parliaments have been passing environmental, health and consumer laws faster than the Commission has been able to harmonize them. It is also undoubtedly true that these laws, drawn up in consultation with national industries, are often — but not always — designed to block imports. It is also sad to report that even when common standards have been agreed, member states have dragged their feet over implementing them. It should be emphasized at this point that Community common standards usually take the form of directives which indicate particular goals but leave it to member state governments to introduce, or to modify existing, national laws in order to give effect to them.

On the question of state aids[9] the basic posture of Article 92 is that such aids are prohibited, but it then goes on to indicate that some aids are permitted and others may be. Clearly an unqualified prohibition would have been a flat contradiction of the aspirations of the Rome Treaty as revealed in the preamble. The latter clearly recognizes the desirability of removing material disparities as between the different regions of the Community — a prime task for regional policy and regional aids.

In some cases of aid-giving the Community has remained consistent in attitude and has been successful in effect. Export aids have always been regarded as being incompatible with the treaty and the Commission has not hesitated to seek their termination. Regional aid, which the Commission has supervised, did at one stage threaten to get out of hand as states vied with each other in raising the level as a means of attracting footloose investment. However, the Resolutions on aid ceilings of 1971 and 1975 seem to suggest that the matter is at least under some control. However, in respect of other types of aid-giving the Community has been in a state of retreat. One is sectoral aid where the number of industries receiving assistance has steadily mounted in recent years, and in respect of which the Commission has on occasions seemed to resemble the old High Authority in avoiding awkward confrontations. The other is the general aid scheme which, because of its blanket characteristic, has little to be said in its favour. The Commission's attitude has always been that this type of aid should be transmuted into a specific form — ie regional and/or sectoral — so that it addresses itself to some identifiable problem and can be assessed in that context. In the early days general schemes did exist but were a relatively small cloud on the horizon. Since 1974 they have grown at an alarming rate. There is of course nearly always a let-out clause somewhere in the treaty and if the reader cares to search diligently enough he will find that Article 92(3) does allow aids

217

where there is serious underemployment. This the Commission can no doubt invoke in defence of its decision not to directly confront these aids. When and if employment prospects improve a roll-back will be appropriate. Until then judgement will have to be suspended.

There are two other areas where a true common market still awaits realization. One is state monopolies.[10] However, their significance should not be overrated since there are not many of them. Despite very long standing efforts to reform them, they still continue to limit or block imports from other EEC countries and the Commission has been forced to launch cases against them. Public purchasing[11] has been an area whereby national attitudes have been rampant and, if British ministerial speeches are a fair sample, may be expected to continue. It is true that in 1971 public works contracting was opened up to Community-wide competition but there are exemptions. It is also true that in 1976 central and local authority buying was subjected to similar treatment, but it is easy to exaggerate the significance of this development since, for example, public utilities such as transport and energy have been excluded. Moreover, as yet only four countries (UK, Ireland, Denmark, and Luxembourg) have written the directive into their national laws.

II

Because the Rome Treaty envisaged a Community based on a common market (with a small infusion of economic union) rather than a customs union, we find that some of the treaty titles are concerned with the establishment of conditions of free movement of factors. Within the transition period, regulations were introduced by the Six providing for free movement of labour[12] and, indeed, formally complete free movement became a reality in 1968. Considerable efforts have been made to facilitate mobility. Notable among these have been the progressive development of a vacancy clearing system[13] and the establishment of a system of transferability of social security rights.[14] A generous level of social security benefits would be a deterrent to labour mobility if a migrant worker had to sacrifice them on moving to another member state. Here the EEC benefited from the previous experience of the ECSC. An ECSC Convention on Social Security of Migrant Workers was signed in 1957. This ensured that all social security contributions, in whatever state they were paid, counted for benefit eligibility. In 1959 the ECSC Convention was extended to all workers and in 1970 it was further extended to cover self-employed insured persons.

By contrast a considerable amount yet remains to be done before capital movements are absolutely free and undistorted.[15] Before we discuss the main problems, it should be noted that some commentators have pointed to the

218

inhibiting effect of exchange rate fluctuations. The Segré Report (1966)[16] singled this out for attention and obviously if EMU (see below) on the lines of the Werner Plan had succeeded, the problem would ultimately have been taken care of.

The inhibiting and distorting factors which remain are several. Member states have in the past controlled, and it must be emphasized still do control, the conversion of their domestic currencies into foreign currencies in connection with the carrying out of international transactions. They have done so, and continue to do so, partly for short-term balance of payments reasons and also because of the fear (sometimes most strongly felt by trade unions) that job creating investments will be lost. These are motives which have led potential donors to apply controls. It must also be added that potential recipients have added to the problem. That is to say, those members possessing strong currencies have been concerned about the effects of capital inflows on the supply of money and domestic inflation. West Germany has, for example, imposed restrictions on foreigners acquiring its short-term securities and shares.

There has therefore been a reluctance to totally abdicate control over capital movements and some of the considerations discussed above undoubtedly explain why the UK has dragged its feet since accession. In fairness it should be added that the treaty did not demand total liberalization. Rather, Article 68 calls for exchange authorizations to be as liberal as possible and in truth some liberalization has been achieved. Two directives were adopted by Council, one in 1960 and the other in 1962, which laid down the basic ground rules. The original Six unconditionally liberalized capital movements, which were a necessary concomitant of other decisions taken under the treaty. For example, direct investments had to be freed if firms were literally going to enjoy the right to establish themselves in other member states (see discussion of Articles 51—58 below); the acquisition of property and the personal movement of capital were a natural consequence of the free movement of labour already discussed above. Some forms of portfolio investment were also unconditionally freed, although the word unconditionally employed in this context and above did not preclude the possibility that in exceptional circumstances (see Articles 73 and 109) the freeing could be revoked. This still left a substantial list of transactions in respect of which the only obligation was to retain the degree of liberalization then attained. Another way of putting it was that if no liberalization had been achieved then no obligation arose. This did not preclude states from introducing some liberalization and some totally liberalized certain items. There then remained a final category which included short-term movements arising in connection with the purchase of money market paper, etc. No obligation to

219

liberalize arose in this connection. Some of the Six did go on to liberalize, although West Germany, for reasons which have already been discussed, had to back-track.

The Community capital market has however been distorted by other state interventions, and these by their discriminatory nature have undoubtedly offended under Article 67. For example, national laws have precluded banks and insurance companies from acquiring foreign assets. These types of institution have also been limited in their investment activity to certain forms of asset (eg public sector bonds but not equities, etc).

Then again, differences in corporation tax rates have almost certainly distorted the allocation of capital within the Community. However we look in vain for any *explicit* reference to the need for a harmonization of rates, although such a harmonization is consistent with the desire by Article 67 to 'abolish . . . any discrimination based . . . on the place where such capital is invested'. Moreover, the fact that some tax credit systems have only been operated for the benefit of domestic but not foreign investors is undoubtedly the kind of discrimination to which Article 67 refers. The Commission did in 1975 put forward a draft directive designed to give rise to a common imputation system of corporation tax and a common system of withholding tax on dividends — the latter being a tax designed to prevent concealment of taxable income from the tax authorities. The proposal envisaged similar but not identical rates of corporation tax and tax credit and an identical rate of withholding tax. The directive has not been adopted by the Council and even the kindliest commentator would probably, in the light of past experience, incline towards some pessimism as to the prospects for rapid progress in this field.

The Rome Treaty also envisaged the general introduction of the Right of Establishment and the Freedom to Supply Services.[17] This would enable firms and individuals, wishing to carry out their business or profession in Community countries other than their own, to set up permanent operations (factories or offices) or to offer their services without setting up any kind of permanent operation. As early as 1961 two general programmes were adopted by the Council of Ministers which envisaged that these two freedoms should become a reality by the end of the transition period. Unfortunately the enormity of the task, and the smallness of the Commission, meant that this ambitious timetable could not be adhered to. Whereas in trade and industry (subject to some limited exceptions) liberalization was accomplished, serious obstacles were encountered in respect of what may be termed the liberal professions. Here the Commission encountered similar problems to those discussed earlier in respect of goods, namely that it would be necessary to harmonize a mass of national laws relating to admission to professions. The Community has however made some progress in the more complex area. In 1975 two directives and two decisions were adopted by the Council of Ministers designed to make the Right of Establishment and the Freedom to Supply Services a reality in respect of doctors. In 1977 a directive was also adopted providing Freedom to Supply Services (but not the Right of Establishment) in respect of lawyers. It is hoped that further measures relating to other liberal professions will follow.

III

The idea of an Economic and Monetary Union (EMU) was not explicitly envisaged by those who drafted the Rome Treaty and the monetary rules[18] were in fact confined to securing a limited degree of monetary co-ordination.[19]

However in 1969, at the end of the transition period, a summit meeting of the heads of state and government (these meetings are now dignified under the title of the European Council) was held at The Hague. It was decided that the Community should not mark time at the Rome Treaty level of integration but should forge ahead with the objective of carrying the Six to the stage of EMU. This aspiration was underwritten at the Paris Summit of 1972 by the Six and the applicant members.

The grand design was to arrive at a situation in which the exchange rates between member states could be irrevocably locked, not even the traditional band of fluctuation being permitted. Such a situation would certainly permit the member states to sweep away the separate national currencies and to replace them with one Community currency *should they so choose*. Centralized control over (a) economic and monetary policy[20] (as opposed to mere co-ordination of national policies) and (b) the Community's foreign exchange rate, as well as the creation of a Community balance of payments and a Community foreign currency reserve, were all logical concomitants of the bolder policy.

The plan for EMU was set on foot early in 1971 but was effectively shelved at the European Council in Paris in December 1974. The Rome Treaty had not failed, but the Community had failed to develop beyond what the treaty had envisaged. Some commentators have gone further than that and have regarded the episode as not merely one of being pushed back to square one — rather they would argue that if there was any movement at all it was backward.[21]

The origins of the failure are not a matter of great dispute. The idea of irrevocably locking exchange rates and eliminating the band of fluctuation was undoubtedly overtaken by events. In the post-Smithsonian period the climate of opinion switched in the direction of greater exchange rate flexibility and away from rigidity. However, that in itself hardly constitutes a major reason why the scheme fell apart in practice. Its failure was due to an amalgam of factors, which might be summarized as external buffeting and internal lack of co-ordination. Undoubtedly the Community chose an inopportune time to launch EMU since the first stage was characterized by enhanced trade and monetary instability. The Community had to cope with the Oil Crisis and speculative pressures. The plan did require an effective co-ordination of macro-economic policies but the truth is that this never really got off the ground. The problems involved in achieving convergence of the rates of inflation were almost certainly under-estimated.[22]

The plan which eventually emerged was a compromise between the second Barre proposal, which emphasized early locking of exchange rates, thus forcing states to adopt the requisite domestic economic discipline, and the Schiller proposal, which envisaged a progressive development of mechanisms of domestic economic control and an increasing degree of harmony between member state policies, leaving the locking until the end. In the event the Werner Plan, which carried the day, embodied a proposal for parallel progress towards these two goals. As a concession to the Barre point of view, it envisaged (thanks to the Central Bank Governors) a narrowing of the band of fluctuation around the exchange rates between member state currencies (the snake) as compared with the band which was allowed around the rate against the dollar (the tunnel). As a concession to the Schiller position the need to achieve harmonization of domestic policy was also emphasized.

In fact, when the system was inaugurated, the new international situation dictated a fatter snake[23] and a wider tunnel — already the system was being forced to set out from a position which was further away from the ultimate goal. Then a further retreat occurred when the joint float was introduced. Further blows occurred as some member who could not stand the pace decided to float out of this more flexible system.

The failure to achieve cohesion in the field of exchange rates was at least, in some degree, a result of a lack of harmony between member state domestic policies as well as differing economic fortunes and propensities. This was reflected in the disparity of inflation rates. For example, and these figures do not reflect the full extent of national divergence, between 1971 and 1975 West Germany had a 34 per cent inflation whilst the UK notched up 82 per cent.

The flexible[24] snake survived as a not wholly EEC arrangement, with reduced membership. Britain (plus Ireland) and Italy left early. France left, rejoined and left again. Sweden joined and then left. Norway also joined but

222

left towards the end of 1978. In effect the snake became a West German currency area with only Denmark and the Benelux in attendance (Austria was associated).

In reviewing institutional achievements,[25] we should note that the snake participants operated a very short-term credit facility of unlimited amount. In other words, central banks could run up debts in each other's currencies in the process of holding their exchange rates within the permitted range of fluctuation. We should also note that in 1970 the Community introduced a short-term credit facility and followed this up in 1971 with agreement on the creation of a medium-term facility. In 1973 a European Monetary Cooperation Fund (EMCF) was established. Its operations were related to the snake and it was responsible for administering the very short- and the short-term finance systems. It was hoped that the EMCF would also become the focal point of an actual pooling of reserves (as opposed to merely being a credit operator), but this never came to fruition.[26]

In 1977, there was little to suggest that the time was ripe for a revival of EMU, although the President of the EC Commission made this the major plank of his internal platform. In 1978 the need for a monetary initiative was enthusiastically advocated by the West German Chancellor (at the 1978 Bremen meeting of the European Council), closely supported by the French President, and at the European Council in Brussels in December 1978 a new scheme was agreed. Italy and Ireland reserved their positions but ultimately (partly no doubt influenced by the prospect of a transfer of resources — see below) decided to participate. The UK decided that it would not join *the exchange mechanism* immediately but might participate later.[27] The establishment of a European Monetary Fund (FECOM — the French abbreviation) was also included in the agreement and the Brussels communiqué was worded so that the UK could be a member if she wished.

The original West German proposal was very much centred around the idea of a European Currency Unit (ECU), itself a monetary unit paralleling the EUA which, of course, is merely a unit of account. Under the European Monetary System (EMS) agreed at Brussels, each national currency has an ECU-related central rate and these central rates are to be used to establish a grid of bilateral exchange rates. Around these exchange rates fluctuation margins of ± 2.25 per cent will be established. Member states outside the snake will be allowed up to ± 6 per cent margins. The ECU basket formula is also intended to detect divergences between participating currencies. Once a currency has moved to 75 per cent of its maximum permitted divergence, there is a presumption that the authorities concerned will step in to correct the situation.

223

Obviously intervention will include operations in the foreign exchange market but also measures of domestic monetary policy.[28]

The motives lying behind the EMS are mixed. There has been a growing disenchantment with the flexible exchange rate as a device for achieving external equilibrium. There has also been a growing attachment to the idea that a fixed, or relatively fixed, exchange rate has a valuable disciplinary effect on those in a position to determine the internal course of events. Significantly those countries who had remained in the snake were not anxious to see it replaced by a more permissive system. France, although outside the snake, has always been attached to fixed exchange rates. The original West German motive seems to have centred around a desire to deflect some of the pressure on the mark (arising from disaffection with the dollar) on to a composite currency unit. Is it too much to say that some others were attracted by the prospect of a transfer of resources?[29]

IV

Within the Rome Treaty there is a call for the establishment of common policies and notable among them are those concerning transport and agriculture. Although not called for in the treaty the Community has added to these the concept of a common energy policy. How far, we may ask, has the Community progressed along these three paths? The answer is a very differential one.

Transport has been very disappointing. Some hint of difficulties to come is to be found in the treaty itself[30] which, reflecting differences of national emphasis, in effect merely records that there shall be a common transport policy (CTP) and leaves it at that. It was in fact left to the Commission to shape the policy and in particular to Lambert Schaus, the first transport Commissioner. The result was a Memorandum and an Action Programme whose aims, had they been fully achieved, would have produced a very considerable impact nationally as well as internationally. The policy makers were in fact torn between considerable national differences. Some states believed in a fairly rigid control of transport — in some degree in order to protect the railways. Others, notably the Dutch, were more inclined to free competition. The policy attempted to bridge the gap and this is almost certainly the explanation for the espousal of the forked tariff principle. The Commission, rather foolishly, tended to seek to justify the idea of a limited band of transport rate fluctuation as being necessary because of the alleged instability in the transport market, when in fact it was merely a political compromise.

The policy leant towards competition but in a guarded manner. The latter was evident to such an extent that it seemed fair to assess the result as being something of a managed market and thus it was not incongruous to lump it with the CAP. Although competition was to be encouraged it was to be constrained within the fork. The policy was all embracing and would apply to national as well as to international hire and reward traffic — moreover road, rail and inland waterway were all to be involved. If competition, however limited, was to work, the proper allocation of infrastructure costs was essential and the need to set the necessary work in motion was recognized as early as 1964. Equally fair competition required harmonization of technical, social and fiscal conditions. Problems concerned with the subsidization and public obligations of railways had to be dealt with. Support tariffs (banned under Article 80) had to be tackled. National and international transport were regulated not only in respect of price but also in terms of quantitative access to the market on the part of suppliers. The policy did not propose to abandon quotas and licensing but envisaged that they should be rendered more flexible, this was notably the case in international road transport.

This was heady stuff but in practice the mountain laboured and brought forth a mouse. Compulsory forked tariffs, rather generously spread, emerged but not for all modes, national and international, but merely for international road transport. Exceptions were allowed. As for quotas the only real signs of impact were in the field of international road transport. Here a Community Quota (CQ) of international road licences was created — its size seemed derisively small. The arrangement was in fact a whittled down version of the original proposal, which envisaged the progressive elimination of nationally negotiated bilateral quotas and their replacement by a flexible CQ which would be expanded in line with the needs of trade. (It should be noted that the national railways have been opposed to a generous CQ and all the signs are that transport ministers have been responsive to their pleas.) In practice the CQ is merely a limited number of international licences added to the existing national bilateral system. Some limited steps were undertaken in the area of harmonization.

Perhaps the best way to assess the achievements of the period up to 1973 is to read the Commission's Communication to Council (1973). It recognized that the policy had 'not made striking progress' — truly an understatement and went on to propose a new and radically different approach. Stripped of all its political deferences the policy proposed to leave transport rates to find their own level under conditions of inter-modal, inter-undertaking competition. Intervention should progressively decline and be undertaken only in times of real crisis. Transport should bear its infrastructure costs and social and technical harmonization was also crucial. There is merit in all this. How much progress has been made in its implementation? The Commission, following the spirit of its Communication, suggested that international transport should be subject to a *reference* (ie voluntary) tariff system. However it suffered a twofold set-back. The Council decided to include only international road transport and oddly in a common policy, left states to choose between the reference and the compulsory forked tariff systems. On the social harmonization issue, it is apparent that there had been considerable back-sliding on the part of the Six as well as dilatoriness on the part of new members. However, in 1977 a more hopeful situation emerged in the form of a revision of the old arrangements and extended time limits for new members to come into line. The question of allocating infrastructure costs still eludes the Community and deadlock prevails on the subject of harmonization of the weight and dimension of commercial vehicles.

We now come to the subject of the common energy policy. As we noted earlier, none of the Community treaties expressly calls for such a policy. Nor is its achievement facilitated by the fact that energy is covered by three separate treaties.

During the period from 1958 until the early seventies a really powerful compulsion to forge such a policy was lacking, since the energy position was becoming progressively easier as the price of oil fell. It was only by looking into the future that it was possible to produce any telling arguments as to why the Community should positively intervene.

The Community was becoming dangerously dependent on imported oil, and was thus vulnerable. The Commission's concern proved to be valid in more senses than one. In the longer term, energy was going to be scarce. The coal producers argued that the coal industry should be supported until the scarcity became a reality. In practice, perhaps because governments are too concerned about present problems, nothing of great significance emerged. At no point did the Community take a positive decision that coal production should be held at a particular level. Still less did the Community agree (except to a limited degree in respect of coking coal) that since, under the Paris Treaty all were free to draw on Community supplies of coal, all should equitably subsidize the industry's continuance. All that happened was that, in piecemeal fashion, states began to intervene by subsidizing their own coal output, largely it seems to cushion the decline, and Community activity merely consisted of a belated attempt to harmonize the subsidies in the interests of fair competition. By the end of the sixties, the repeated proposals for a common policy were largely reminiscent of Disraeli's 'range of extinct volcanoes'.

It has been argued that the inception of the Community was itself a response not only to the desire to prevent further European dissension but also to the existence of an external threat. If the latter is correct then it was possible in 1973 to expect that the oil price rise and the reality of supply cuts would provide a new and fruitful impetus in the search for a Community approach to energy. Added to that was the growing appreciation of the prospect of long-term scarcity. Has this happened? The answer is yes, to a very qualified extent and in a round-about way.[31]

The Community has addressed itself to the problem of trying to estimate how its demand for energy will grow. It has agreed that the pattern of energy demand must be altered in ways which will make it less dependent on imports. But the necessary action — developing national coal industries, speeding up atomic energy programmes, footing the bill — remains a national responsibility.[32] The Community has conspicuously failed to take any concrete action to provide a guarantee for those footing the bill. The European Council at Rome in 1975 appeared to take on board the idea of a minimum floor price for oil, etc, but the Council does not produce Community law. That is the task of the Council of Ministers, and as yet a floor price has not been adopted.

The Community has, however, agreed on a number of emergency procedures. As far back as 1968 it agreed on a minimum stockholding of oil. Also, given that Community energy supplies are supposed to be available on non-discriminatory terms, it has been necessary to devise arrangements for sharing supplies and reducing oil useage in times of oil crisis. It is, however, highly significant that the Community has not been the prime forum for the development of a common stance on energy policy. Rather the member states (with the exception of France) have preferred to work in other fora. Policies have often been agreed there and have then been imported into the Community arena.

We come now to the CAP.[33] This alongside the industrial common market is overwhelmingly the major product of the Rome Treaty. By contrast with transport in particular it is an area where substantial progress has been made. That is to say, towards the end of the sixties a common price and income support policy had been evolved which covered about 90 per cent of farm output and the produce of more than ten million operatives. However, we have to be careful here since not everyone would regard the creation of policy with such unfortunate features as progress! We shall therefore regard the word progress as referring to a situation where a policy is created as compared with a situation where, in substantial measure or indeed totally, all that can be seen are documentary aspirations.

There are several reasons why, as compared with the other common policies, significant progress has occurred in respect of agriculture. The first is that the CAP was (and still is) a direct descendant of the national policies (of the Six) which preceded it. It is possible to generalize and say that those previous policies tended to favour high market prices as the method of support and achieved the objective by external protection, and by support buying if necessary. There is a contrast here with the CTP where, as we have seen, differences of emphasis were evident from the outset. A second factor has been the political pressure exerted, notably by the French. In the Gaullist period the French made it clear that they were not interested in an EEC without a CAP.

The creation of the CAP might have been accomplished without too many embarrassing surpluses had the spirit which lay behind the resolution of the original grain price dispute also informed all future price decisions. It will be recollected that Germany wanted a relatively high price whilst France was happy with a significantly lower one. To the French the latter still offered an improved prospect whilst it was expected that German output would fall. The French would thus enjoy a healthy piece of trade creation. In practice, it was evident to those observing the evolution of common prices that domestic political pressures were such that farm ministers were not inclined to agree to common levels which would lead to marked domestic contractions of income and output. Common prices in milk, for example, tended to be pitched towards the top end of the national spectrum. When countries did agree to make sacrifices, they used them as an excuse for achieving better (ie more protective) terms elsewhere. Added to all this, we must acknowledge that technological progress has been shifting supply curves to the right. Also the Community support system has been markedly open-ended — in fairness this was not always true of the previous national system.

The result was not one in which low price producers would expand at the expense of the high price producers, within a given degree of self-sufficiency. Rather the degree of self-sufficiency, *which in any case had traditionally been high*, grew markedly in a number of key areas and with it came the now almost legendary mountains and lakes. The cost of disposing of these surpluses and the consequent relatively heavy drain of the farm fund on the Community Budget need no emphasis here. Article 39 of the treaty laid down the objectives of the CAP and they included the need to ensure a fair standard of living for the agricultural community. The way in which the Community sought to achieve this objective has tended to conflict with the other objective of ensuring supplies to consumers at reasonable prices. Prices have, as we have seen, been pitched up but this had not eradicated the low income problem.[34] What those prices have done is to add gold plate to the Mercedes of relatively efficient producers. A more sensible approach would be for prices of offending products to be lowered in real terms and selective and degressive payments to be made to higher cost producers. The efficient would still be adequately rewarded and would be less disposed to add to the surpluses.

Whilst in this critical vein it should also be noted that the CAP is not really common at all. Far too much attention has been paid to common methods of support and, in the days before currency upsets and MCAs, common prices. What has tended to be overlooked is the massive amount of national aid giving. Whilst no one has argued that this is always contrary to the CAP, there is no doubt that such aids could be used to counterbalance effects which might be sought through the agency of prices and they could give rise to unfair competition. The Commission has long expressed a desire to regulate these aids. Its active awareness goes back to at least 1966, yet it appears that the Community is still in the throes of introducing an effective monitoring system.

The Community response to the surplus problem was first to think in terms of structural reform. In practice the package of measures agreed fell well short of the massive programme which Sicco Mansholt had envisaged. Moreover there have been some conspicuous delays in implementing the measures.[35] More recently, thinking has shifted to reform of the support system itself. However, despite the growing acceptance of the need for change on the part of the Commission, and indeed the European Council, little has yet emerged from the rebellious Ministers of Agriculture.

All this is rather critical. Is there nothing praiseworthy in the CAP? One virtue is that it has provided certainty of supply — another of the objectives sought in Article 39. It is also argued that under the CAP agriculture has shed a great deal of labour. It is true that between 1960 and 1975 6.3 million persons left the industry — a net loss of just over 50 per cent of the agricultural labour force. Despite this, food output increased at an average rate of 2 per cent per annum and this was due to the substitution of capital for labour, technological improvements in the capital used, better plants and animal strains. However, it must be pointed out that labour was leaving agriculture quite rapidly before the future shape of the CAP began to be actively discussed. The rate accelerated in the sixties but this was largely before the CAP price system had become fully operational. Actually the rate decelerated in the seventies when the system was in full operation although some of this was undoubtedly due to unemployment in the rest of the economy. There is, however, every reason to expect this quiet decline to continue. It is also essential that the structure of farming should change. Productivity and income tend to be positively correlated with farm size

229

and it is a notable feature that on average farms are small on the Continent as compared with, for example, the UK.

V

That the path to integration should for the most part take the form of competition in trade is made quite clear in Article 3 of the treaty. That article lays down the overriding general objectives and 3(f) requires the establishment of conditions of undistorted competition. But the treaty also contains provisions in which emphasis is laid on measures to cope with the consequences of competition. Social and regional policy are most conveniently viewed in this context.

The social achievements of the Community are not easy to appraise. First we need to determine what was expected. Apart from the generalities in the preamble, in Article 117 the member states are declared to be in agreement that living conditions, in the broadest sense, are to be improved and harmonized. It seems that this was partly expected to proceed directly from the creation of the EEC, which would give a fillip to the process of economic growth. Obviously there were also specific aspects of the treaty, such as free movement of labour, which would for some provide an avenue to a better standard of living. The second part of Article 117 relates to social systems and clearly here social security benefits are a major factor. Again the emphasis is on improvement and harmonization. Although it was expected that the creation of the EEC would favour their harmonization (just how is not explained), it was recognized that such benefits were acts of government and therefore some mechanism was needed which would impel governments in the necessary direction. The treaty did not impose an absolute obligation, or any time limits. There was no parallel with the regimen relating, for example, to internal tariffs. Rather it saw the hoped for evolution proceeding from closer government collaboration, which the Commission had a duty to foster.

What has been achieved? That per capita living standards within the Six have risen sharply since 1958 is not in doubt. As for the harmonization thereof, there is evidence which points to some narrowing in the dispersion of standards — this was revealed in studies leading up to the creation of the European Regional Development Fund (ERDF). As for per capita social security benefits within the Six, these have moved up markedly in real terms. As for social security harmonization, this can have several meanings but if we focus on relative per capita values then there is evidence that the dispersion has narrowed — in particular Italy and the Netherlands, which were at the bottom of the league, have moved significantly closer to the West German level. How much of all this is due to the creation of the EEC it is difficult to say. We must however concede that the trend appears to have been in conformity with the aspirations of the treaty.

It would have been possible for the Community to have created an instrument which was designed to achieve harmonization of standards by means of a positive redistribution of resources, but the Community did not take up that option. Nevertheless there are institutions which could work in that direction. Have they? One possible candidate is the Community Budget. Its objectives are not specifically redistributive but it could have a redistributive effect in practice. In actual fact it tends to work in a very random way. For example, in 1976 in per capita terms West Germany (the richest country) was the biggest net contributor — this sounds promising. Ireland (the poorest) was the biggest net beneficiary. This sounds equally promising. But after that the randomness emerges since the next poorest, Italy and the UK, respectively received a per capita pittance and made a net contribution. The reason for this is quite simple. The Budget is dominated by the CAP, which swallows up about three-quarters of the funds, and the financial implications of the CAP do not automatically favour the poor. This leaves little for the ERDF and the European Social Fund (ESF).[36] The former is particularly biassed towards the poor, but because it (and the ESF) currently enjoy only 10 per cent of the budget, the redistributive effect is swamped. We should not of course forget that, even if these two funds were to command a majority of the budget resources, the redistributive effect would still be small because the budget is trivial in relation to the aggregated GNPs of the member states.

There are two other possibilities. One is the European Investment Bank (EIB).[37] In the past, the bulk (about half) of its very considerable assistance[38] has gone to Italy. Since enlargement the UK and Ireland have been major beneficiaries. This sounds promising; although it should be remembered that EIB assistance is loan based. The other possibility is the transfer of resources arising in connection with the EMS. This could amount to 1000 million EUA per annum for five years. Again this will take the form of loans (from the EIB or via the Community's new borrowing facility — the so-called Ortoli Instrument) but in this case there will be an interest rebate, and this assistance is specifically designed to help the less prosperous participants in the EMS exchange rate mechanism. This may represent the beginning of a growing appreciation of the need to gear Community policy more closely to the need to even out levels of prosperity.

The Community has also made a number of specific if unspectacular contributions to social policy. The activities of the ESF in connection with unemployment and retraining, etc, are well known. Following the Paris Summit of 1972 a whole clutch of measures have been introduced including directives and recommendations on topics such as equality of treatment between male and female workers (access to employment, vocational training, promotion, etc), on the handling of mass dismissals, on the rights of workers in the event of mergers and take-overs, on the length of the working week and annual holidays. Some new institutions have been created including the European Centre for Vocational Training and the European Foundation for the Improvement of Living and Working Conditions. However, in respect of equal pay for equal work there has been some back-sliding. Under Article 119 EPFEW should have been introduced by 1962 but such was the lack of progress that a directive had to be issued in 1975.

We have already touched upon the Commission activities, and some specific actions by the Council of Ministers, in connection with regional policy. Under the treaty the Community's role was largely negative, consisting as it did of a supervision of aid giving, although in the early years the Commission was active in encouraging the study of the regional problem. There were no provisions in the treaty which conferred upon the Community an active role in aiding regional development[39] the regional problem was a national responsibility. In the light of that fact, the creation of the ERDF in 1975 must be regarded as a positive step forward.

VI

The Community has also given consideration to the development of an industrial policy. The Commission has been an enthusiastic advocate but, as yet, the cupboard remains relatively bare. In explaining this failure, and setting aside the point that it is far from clear just what such a policy would imply, two factors seem to have been paramount.

The first is that the treaty does not call for an over-all industrial policy. Reflecting this, when in 1970 the Commission produced its Memorandum on Industrial Policy (the Colonna Report), it admitted that the treaty lacked the legal bases for such a development. This is true but it does need qualification since there are scattered around the treaty a number of legal provisions which are relevant. It has been generally recognized that such a policy includes the creation of a European Industrial base and an important feature of such a policy is the harmonization of technical standards, the opening up of public procurement, etc. Clearly these are explicitly provided for and we have already discussed the progress made. Also, in the context of business penetration (companies establishing subsidiaries for their member states, cross-frontier mergers, etc) Article 220 has considerable potential, since it relates to the abolition of double taxation, the national recognition of companies, the maintenance of legal personality on transfer of registered office and the need to facilitate cross-frontier mergers. Nevertheless the main point remains. For example, a major task of industrial policy is to enable specific industries to cope with structural change. Insofar as contraction is threatened by foreign competition, Community action can cushion the impact by common protective measures (eg the multifibre agreement). But when it comes to the question of which national industry is to contract, and by how much, this is a national responsibility and member states show no enthusiasm for handing it over, however much the Commission, and Viscount Davignon, would rejoice at the prospect.

What we are saying is that the powers conferred upon the old High Authority by the Paris Treaty (now enjoyed by the Commission) in respect of coal and steel[40] were not generalized in the Rome Treaty. Again this needs qualification. It does not mean that the Commission is absolutely powerless when structural adaptation is called for. But it does mean that it has been forced to rely upon, or to threaten to rely upon, indirect methods and not always successfully. Davignon was not prevented from doing anything about the over-production problem of the synthetic fibre industry because he lacked the formal power to close plants down. What he could and did do was to agree with the industry that a capacity reducing cartel should be introduced. Unfortunately for him his plan was frustrated by the Competition Directorate and then by the whole Commission. Again, in the case of shipbuilding, Davignon does not have the power to actually slim the industry down, but what he can do, and has actually done, is to threaten to invoke the powers he does have to terminate the subsidies which have kept the industry going at its present level.

We mentioned that there was a second reason why Industrial Policy has not got very far. This relates to the fact that there have been profound differences of attitude as to the appropriate form that industrial policy should take. It all sounds a little like a repeat of the medium-term programming furore. The West Germans have shown a marked preference for a liberal, market orientated approach to industry whereas the French have favoured a more dirigiste policy. This has been the most important inhibiting factor.

What has been achieved? On the subject of business penetration (as defined above) four main paths have been identified. Against a background of legal and fiscal inhibitions, it has been proposed that (a) directives should be introduced which would eliminate tax-treatment which discriminates against cross-frontier, as compared with domestic, mergers; (b) that directives should be introduced to harmonize national company laws; (c) that matters such as the recognition of legal personality, when a company established in one state operates in another, should be dealt with by conventions; (d) that Community-wide company activity should be facilitated by devices such as the introduction of a Community company law — hence the idea of a European Company or *Societas Europea.*

In fact tax directives have been submitted to Council but have not been approved. Some company law directives have been passed by Council but most remain unadopted. A convention on the mutual recognition of companies was signed in 1968. The European Company Statute has not yet been formally adopted. It is true that a Business Cooperation Centre was established in 1973 but this is a modest affair. Whether the more formal measures to assist in the process of cross-frontier merging will eventually be approved by Council is open to some doubt. Following the *Continental Can* case, and in the light of the draft proposal to control mergers, the tide may have turned.

Industrial policy can also be defined to include scientific and technology collaboration. This policy is still in its infancy, and may remain so.

The Community has also made a start in the field of consumer protection. As yet, the policy has not had time to develop. The proposal for strict liability in relation to product related injury, with producers bearing the development risk, is one which would be a real benefit to those afflicted, although consumers as a body will of course have to pay for it in the form of higher prices.[41]

VII

How then do we assess the Community's performance over all? It does seem important to stress that, in the light of what has gone before, it is possible to over-estimate its achievements. At any moment of time the Community appears to be a hot bed of activity as new goals are handed down by the European Council, as study groups report, as the Commission adopts yet more regulations and directives and so forth. But none of this means anything unless the Council of Ministers is prepared to put its imprimatur on the various drafts, without them having to be watered down, and, having adopted them, the member states really do implement them. It is all too obvious that in a number of areas policies have not progressed very far — draft directives, etc, have gathered dust on the Council table. Putting it another way, it is important to assess the Community by reference to what it actually does and not by what the Rome Treaty, the European Council or the Commission say it ought to do. The ratio of aspiration to achievement is sometimes rather high. Critics will no doubt reply that this is to be expected — the path to concensus at the international level is strewn with difficulties, particularly when majority voting is largely in abeyance.

Our final assessment can best be carried out by seeking to distinguish, perhaps in a rough-and-ready fashion, between those objectives which the Community was obliged and empowered to attain, and those objectives in respect of which in 1958 explicit obligations and powers were not provided at all, or were not sufficiently generously provided.

Let us deal with the obligatory aspect first. At the top of the list was the creation of a customs union. As we have seen, in terms of tariffs and quotas that obligation has been fully met. Does it not also seem reasonable to conclude that, in the more difficult seventies, the treaty obligation to hold fast to that which was attained in the sixties has been a significant factor in helping to prevent a world-wide tidal wave of protection? In respect of non-tariff carriers the record is, however, mixed. Much remains to be achieved and even Community officials readily admit that free trade is not a complete reality. The student is left with the impression that the Commission has been more successful at standing up to firms than at standing up to states — which is not too surprising!

The second highest obligation was to achieve a free movement of factors. Here again the picture is mixed. The position in respect of free movement of labour is highly creditable although progress has been slow in respect of the professions. The position in respect of capital is unsatisfactory. Here the Commission has been contending with powerful national interests. The fact that the treaty is less explicit about the action required in respect of direct as opposed to indirect taxes may be a contributory factor.

In the case of common policies there were explicit obligations only in respect of transport and agriculture. The poor performance in transport is all too evident. In the case of agriculture it is easy to criticize the CAP — in fact to suggest stiff measures in the form of swingeing price reductions. Without doubting that drastic medicine is needed, we should not ignore the political complications. When countries such as France insisted on the completion of the CAP, they were not the originators of the political pressure. They were responding to the pressure of the farming vote. The farming community in such countries was deeply disillusioned with the results of national agricultural policies. They therefore looked to the CAP as the source of salvation. Indeed, the Commission was able to appeal over the heads of national governments in its quest to see the agricultural policy carried to fruition. Having established the policy, it was clearly embarrassing to have to declare redundant those who looked to it for salvation.

In the case of social policy, modest progress has been made. The degree of harmonization has not been great, but it should be remembered that no time limit was set nor was the ultimate goal precisely specified. We should also remind the reader that the EMS agreement may represent the beginnings of a positive commitment to redistributing resources.

We turn now to the areas of policy where obligations and powers were inadequate or non-existent. EMU is an example of the latter. Had this account been written a year earlier, we would have been forced to conclude that the cupboard was bare. The Community had not proved capable of advancing beyond the level envisaged in 1958. Now the situation has changed although at the time of writing the inception of the EMS has been delayed. Obviously the key question is — will this new initiative prove more successful than its predecessor? First we can consider the grounds for optimism. The prime one must be that it is less ambitious than the Werner Plan with all its federalist implications. There is no intention, at this stage, of trying to establish anything as ambitious as a common currency. The present scheme, as the Bremen title clearly indicates, is merely a plan for the creation of a zone of monteary stability — not fixity. Margins of fluctuation are allowed. In the case of non-snake countries these are indeed quite generous. Not only that, but the system also quite explicitly encompasses the possibility of changes in the central parities. All this suggests that substantial instability could occur without the system being declared a failure. The system will also enjoy substantial support facilities.

The pessimist will on the other hand wonder whether, due allowance being made for all this flexibility, the Community has failed to learn from experience. Once again, all the emphasis is being laid on the exchange rate aspect. There is little evidence that member states have evolved any agreement which will lead to a convergence of national policies and national rates of inflation.

One conclusion seems to be reasonably clear. If such a system, with all its built-in allowances for flexibility, cannot be made to work, then we shall almost certainly have reached the end of the road in the search for something beyond the Rome Treaty blueprint.

The achievements in the field of energy are modest. However, given the fact that a common policy was not provided for those achievements must be nevertheless regarded as positive steps beyond the 1958 conception. Equally we have noted that the creation of the ERDF was also a distinct step beyond the original blueprint. Having said that, it has to be admitted that its capacity to make an impact on the regional problem will continue to be severely limited until the CAP ceases to command such a large share of the Community Budget.

In the case of Industrial Policy we have already noted that the Community has made no great impact. This brings us face to face with a point, the significance of which extends well beyond the industrial field. It relates to the difficulties inherent in founding economic policy on a treaty. The problem with treaties is that, having been ratified, they are difficult to change. Their provisions tend to reflect the economic and policy atmosphere existing at the time when they were drafted. In 1956 the prospect was one of expansion and most governments were inclined to leave matters to the market. Now we see problems of excess capacity, some of it stemming from outside competition which did not then exist or exist to any significant degree. National policies can, of course, be readily adjusted. It would not be true to say that the Rome Treaty, having been ratified, cannot now be changed. The European Council is the forum within which the political will can be manifested and Article 235 enables additional powers to be taken. But if the political will is absent, the Rome Treaty ceases to be capable of addressing itself to present problems. The signs are that this has happened in respect of Industrial Policy.

We have noted some of the Community's difficulties and deficiencies. The obvious question which arises is, will they diminish in the future? Such an act of speculation would require a paper all of its own. Nevertheless, there is one possible development which suggests that they will not — that is enlargement. The addition of countries at a significantly lower level of development is going to create a lot of problems. The Mediterranean products' aspect of the CAP is one likely problem area. In addition it is going to be increasingly difficult to co-ordinate and harmonize twelve economies. Also the new members will be in need of aid, and as a result the deficiency of the resources made available to, for example, the ERDF and ESF will become even more obvious.

All that has gone before does not enable us to render any ultimate judgements about the EEC and its worthwhileness for the member states. There are three reasons for this. The first is that the Community has substantial achievements to its credit in external policy. Secondly, as the largest trading bloc in the world, which looks very united to those outside it, it confers upon its members substantial advantages in international bargaining. Thirdly, member states value the Community because its creation has stimulated the extension of integration into the foreign policy field. It is difficult to appraise the success of the political co-operation machinery because it has been set no specific tasks, and there are therefore no bench-marks to measure success or failure. It is also a kind of activity which inevitably is kept out of the public eye. However, the impression which emerges is that in a quiet kind of way it has been successful in bringing positions closer together and indeed in achieving a common front on some issues.

Notes

[1] I am grateful to David Allen and Geoffrey Dennis who have read and commented on this paper. The author is, of course, solely responsible for the end product.

[2] See Articles 3(a), 3(b) and 9—37.

[3] However, it is fair to say that at the moment the Brussels Commission is uneasy about the solidity of the customs union. There are fears that in the future it could be undermined by protectionism and dumping.

[4] See Articles 3(f) and 85—90.

[5] It is also noticeable that EEC antitrust terminology and reasoning has begun to be adopted by antitrust systems in the English-speaking world.

[6] The Paris Treaty included an express power to control mergers.

[7] See Articles 95—102.

[8] See Articles 100—2. Harmonization has been greatly misunderstood in the UK. It is not intended to make everything the same. For example, cars will not have to be identical but will have to meet certain common standards in respect of vital aspects of design and performance. Harmonization can, of course, add to consumer choice by making it easier for foreign suppliers to penetrate the domestic market. Harmonization may also take an optional form. Those who do not comply still being able to enjoy the home market whilst those who comply are admitted to the whole EEC market.

[9] See Articles 92—4.

[10] See Article 37.

[11] Articles 100—2 provide a basis for action.

[12] See Articles 92—4.

[13] See Article 49.

[14] See Article 51.

[15] Articles 67—113 relate to capital movements.

[16] EEC Commission, *The Development of a European Capital Market*.

[17] See Articles 52—8, 59—66. See also Industrial Policy discussed below.

[18] See Articles 103—9 but also 67—73.

[19] However, we should note that the CAP did presume that exchange rates would be fixed. The fact that they did not remain fixed undermined the CAP (discussed below) and led to the creation of MCAs (Monetary Compensating Amounts).

[20] The latter via a Community Central Bank.

[21] EC Commission, *Report of the Study Group, Economic and Monetary Union 1980*, Marjolin Report, Brussels, 1975.

[22] See L. Tsoukalis, *The Politics and Economics of European Monetary Integration*, 1977.

[23] The Benelux snake was thinner than that generally agreed.

[24] In the five years up to November 1978 there were nineteen parity changes within the snake.

[25] In this paper no attempt has been made to describe all the committees which have been established in order to operate various policies.

[26] The introduction in 1963 of a medium-term programming mechanism need not detain us. Although at the time of its proposal it was invested with considerable potential as a focus of some form of indicative planning and as a result created a furore, in practice it has never been more than a relatively innocuous system of medium-term economic forecasting.

[27] Although not as a result of a deliberate Community decision, a development foreshadowed by the Tindemans Report on European Union (1975) has come to pass. It envisaged the possibility of a two-tier Europe. Those who wished to forge ahead with more integration should be allowed to do so. The rest

238

should be permitted to lag behind although they would not be released from the ultimate obligation to come into line.

[28] It is also envisaged that the ECU will be a debt settlement medium and a rival reserve asset to the dollar.

[29] This is discussed below.

[30] See Articles 3(e) and 74—84.

[31] It should be noted that the very first reactions to the Oil Crisis were not Community but unilateral in character.

[32] We must however recognize that JET may prove to have been a highly significant Community initiative.

[33] See Articles 3(d) and 38—47.

[34] Average farm employees' earnings are about 70 per cent of those in industry.

[35] The measures themselves have been criticized, it being argued that they have not had the correct aims — see J.S. Marsh, 'Europe's Agriculture: Reform of the CAP', *International Affairs*, **53**, 1975, 604—14.

[36] The establishment of which was called for in Article 3(i); the governing provisions being found in Articles 123—8. Its original constitution has been beneficially modified.

[37] The establishment of which is called for in Article 3(j); the governing provisions being found in Articles 129—30.

[38] Between 1958 and the end of the 1976 operations inside the Community amounted to 8600 million UA at 1976 prices.

[39] The EIB is not an aid giving body although it has made a notable contribution to infrastructure development in Italy in particular.

[40] However, we should not exaggerate the coal and steel powers. The Commission can introduce various crisis measures to keep prices up (and has done so) but control over investment is largely of indicative planning variety.

[41] ie prices will be raised because of the extra insurance costs borne by producers.

[42] The destination principle provides a tolerable solution without the need for harmonization of rates. In the cases of taxes on income from capital a half-way house solution does not immediately suggest itself.

13

Transport infrastructure investments and
regional development

K. M. GWILLIAM

Introduction

For the last decade A. J. Brown has been recognized as a leading authority on
regional economics. In his work for the National Institute he gave the subject a
more firm foundation both in statistics and in analysis (Brown, 1972). As a
member of the Hunt Committee on the Intermediate Areas (Cmnd 3998,
1969), this authority was directed to the formulation of regional policy. In that
context it was appropriate that his skill and judgement should be applied, in
part, to the economic problems of his native Yorkshire.

Brown's special contribution to the Hunt Committee was acknowledged in
the introduction to the Report. But on a number of issues, both of detail and of
general approach, he was unable to convince his colleagues. His own views on
these matters were consequently spelt out in a minority report. It is to the main
general contention of that minority report that this essay is addressed.

Throughout the main report of the Hunt Committee, and in numerous other
places, the view is expressed that the state of the infrastructure, and particularly
transport infrastructure, is an important determinant of the level of activity and
prosperity of a region. Whilst not disputing that good infrastructure bestows
economic benefits, Brown was concerned to challenge the presumption that
improvement in transport infrastructure was therefore a good and important
instrument in dealing with the problems of regional imbalance. His argument
was that road improvements, at great initial expense, produce only relatively
small reductions in an already relatively small component of the total delivered
costs of the products of the less active regions. If the sum of these small savings
is sufficient to justify the investment, all well and good. But, if not, then the
difference between the capital cost which would be justified by the expected
sum of benefits to traffic, and that actually incurred, must be viewed as the
regional development subsidy. It is the ratio of activity created to this cost that,
Brown argued, should be compared with the similar ratio for direct financial
inducements. His judgement was that this comparison would prove

unfavourable and that road investment, as an instrument of regional policy, was not worthy of particular attention.

The obvious starting point is theoretical. The role of transport costs is similar to that of tariffs, affording protection to 'home' producers against imports. The bilateral reduction of transport costs, like the tariff reduction, accentuates the relative advantage of the lower cost producer. In the absence of complete factor price flexibility or mobility of factors, it may result in reduction of activity levels in some of the trading regions. Even with flexibility it may redistribute real welfare to the disadvantage of some (though not all) of the parties. Hence, at best, transport infrastructure investment as an instrument of regional policy could only be effective in particular circumstances (where the less active region was a relatively efficient producer of tradeable goods) or as part of a package (the rest of which must have the effect of reducing the local production costs in the target regions below those in its potential trading partners' economies). Moreover, the conditions under which transport investment appraisal based on user benefit introduces bias by failing to account adequately for 'development effects' are very restrictive, and unlikely to obtain in densely developed *industrialized* countries (Gwilliam, 1970). Thus, Brown can be seen to have understated his case; not only is there no *a priori* reason to expect transport infrastructure investment to be an efficient instrument of regional policy, it may quite easily be counterproductive in this role.

The body of thought to the contrary is vague but pervasive. It is mostly fuelled by observation of the association between transport infrastructure and economic activity levels in the historical process of development. But such evidence is notoriously difficult to interpret. The 'axiom of indispensibility' — that transport infrastructure investment is a necessary precursor, and hence generator, of economic development — is now viewed much more critically by economic historians who recognize the difficulty of identifying the sequence of cause and effect (Fogel, 1964). In any case, what is true of the early stages of economic development may not be true later on. So it becomes necessary to find some other basis for conclusions about the structural effects on the economy of transport infrastructure investments. The object of this essay is to review a number of areas of theoretical and statistical investigation for conclusions pertinent to this issue.

Transport costs[1]
Insofar as transport improvements produce any structural effects we may at least expect those effects to be broadly correlated with the magnitude of the direct transport cost changes. Thus, an alternative source of evidence on likely

242

structural effects might be found in an examination of the significance of transport costs in the total distributed cost structure of different industries. From this we might hope to be able to deduce some conclusions about over-all magnitudes of effect, and the particular activities most likely to yield greatest structural response.

There appear to be several stages in this relationship on which evidence can be sought. For instance, we may quite independently study:

> (i) what transport costs are incurred by the firm;
> (ii) what proportion of relevant total costs these transport costs account for;
> (iii) how these transport costs are likely to be affected by road infrastructure improvements;
> (iv) how sensitive transport decisions are to variations in these money cost items.

We shall consider these questions in sequence, paying particular attention to the variation between industries.

(i) WHAT COSTS?

When considering firms' reactions to variations in transport cost we might expect our concern to be centred on the private costs of the firm — ie those which are incurred directly and so perceived by the firm. Exactly what this set of costs will consist of depends on the nature of the contractual arrangements between the firm and its suppliers or customers. In the extreme, where the firm is able to obtain its supplies at uniform delivered prices, it will not have to concern itself at all about its location relative to that of suppliers (except insofar as timing, reliability and security of supplies varies with distance). The same does not hold for outputs. If the firm is operating to a standard delivered price it will need to concern itself with the level of transport costs; if it is selling fob it will need to concern itself with the effect of transport costs incurred by others on its market area and share.

There is, in fact, a good deal of evidence to suggest that most manufacturers quote uniform delivered prices (Brown, 1977). The implication is that locations will tend to be more market orientated than the classical location theory would have suggested. Moreover, insofar as the further back one regresses towards primary production in the chain of transactions the less flexible the locational decision becomes for physical reasons, we may expect the structural impacts to be more dominated by ease of access to final consumption markets than by ease of access to raw material supplies.

243

(ii) THE RELATIVE IMPORTANCE OF TRANSPORT COSTS

The main source of information on transport costs for firms in the UK comes from the Census of Production. This source records transport expenditures incurred by firms, and hence, in terms of the argument of the last section appears to give the relevant estimates. These expenditures can be expressed as a proportion of turnover or as a proportion of net output (value added) (Edwards, 1970). Whilst the former basis probably reflects better the way that firms perceive the importance of transport costs, the latter avoids the problem of double counting. On this basis, and taking account of the transport costs incurred by the distributive trades, Edwards was able to estimate that in 1963 transport costs represented 9 per cent of the total costs of producing and distributing manufactured goods in the UK.

As Table 1 shows, though there are substantial differences between the proportions on a gross output and net output, the two bases are highly correlated, and do appear to be stable over time.

At minimum list heading level the variations are somewhat more extreme, ranging from 27.5 per cent of net output in milk products to only 1.09 per cent for watch and clock manufacturers in 1963. For the most part these variations accord with intuition, being largely explicable in terms of the perishability (eg food, drink) or bulk (eg furniture) of the product or the inflexibility of the locations of production (eg bricks). Thus it might appear that those industries which are most susceptible to 'restructuring' because of their high transport cost components are least flexible in location for other reasons. Hence, over all, we should not expect very substantial restructuring effects.

Two caveats need to be entered against this general conclusion. Firstly, even if transport costs are a small proportion of gross output or net output they may still have a significant impact on profit levels (Jones and Townsend, 1958, p 147). A recent study has suggested that transport costs of manufacturing industries amounted to about 25 per cent of pre-tax profits (Chisholm, 1971, p 217—18). Whilst the same may be true of other cost items, the significance of this observation is that it relates to a cost which may be location dependent, and therefore presenting a link of a rather more direct kind between transport cost changes and restructuring effects.

This leads us to our second caveat. Whilst the average proportion of gross costs accounted for by transport in an industrial sector may be low, those transport costs may vary significantly with location. An analysis of the 1963 Census of Production data suggests a range of about 20 per cent in transport costs of manufacturing industry by region (Edwards, 1975, p 122). Adjusting for differences in regional structure would not significantly alter this

TABLE 1
Transport Costs in Manufacturing Industry in UK

SIC order	Industry	% of gross output		% of net output	
		1963	1968	1963	1968
III–XIX	All manufacturing	2.03	2.20	5.22	5.58
III	Food, drink and tobacco	3.02	3.34	12.51	13.74
IV	Coal and petroleum products	1.22	1.31	7.94	8.72
V	Chemicals and allied industries	2.75	2.79	6.19	6.59
VI	Metal manufactures	2.04	1.81	6.37	5.98
VII	Mechanical engineering	1.30	1.35	2.52	2.62
VIII	Instrument engineering	0.76	0.99	1.28	1.72
IX	Electrical engineering	1.30	1.23	2.58	2.47
X	Shipbuilding and marine engineering	0.57	0.82	1.13	1.55
XI	Vehicles	0.82	1.06	2.05	2.58
XII	Metal goods nes	1.49	1.84	3.92	4.13
XIII	Textiles	1.08	1.26	2.93	3.18
XIV	Leather, leather goods and fur	1.16	1.34	3.40	3.82
XV	Clothing and footwear	0.91	1.10	2.09	2.41
XVI	Bricks, pottery, glass, cement, etc	7.28	7.37	13.80	15.39
XVII	Timber, furniture	2.99	3.21	6.72	7.55
XVIII	Paper, printing and publishing	2.63	2.76	5.27	5.47
XIX	Other manufacturing	1.95	2.22	4.11	4.43

Source: Department of Trade and Industry. Census of Production, 1968. Summary Tables.
Note: Since 1968 the Census of Production does not separately state total transport costs.

conclusion. Thus location may cause significant *differences* in transport costs, even if transport only accounts for a small proportion of total costs.

(iii) THE EFFECT OF INFRASTRUCTURE INVESTMENT ON INDUSTRIAL TRANSPORT COSTS

Because of the fixed element of terminal costs, and the fact that some vehicle operating costs are incurred on a time basis, costs of haulage do not vary in direct proportion to the length of haul. In a study of haulage charges for

245

twenty-three commodity groups, Chisholm estimated that the non-mileage related element accounted for nearly 70 per cent of the total cost (Chisholm, 1971, p 238). In a costing study covering both own account and hire and reward sectors, undertaken on 1965 data, it was similarly found that standing charges accounted for between 55 and 75 per cent of road freight transport operating costs (Bayliss and Edwards, 1971, p 102). The standing charge proportion declines as vehicle size increases in the Bayliss and Edwards study, predominantly because average vehicle mileage increases with vehicle size. Whatever the appropriate precise figure, the moral is clear. Improvements in infrastructure, because they do not affect terminal costs cause less than proportionate saving in unit costs of transportation.

(iv) TRANSPORT DECISIONS AND MONEY COSTS

The final step in our argument attempts to relate the benefits that emerge from infrastructure improvements to the transport and locational decisions of firms. A number of studies have suggested that firms are poorly informed about the costs of transport by modes other than those currently in use (Cook, 1967; Sharp, 1970; Bayliss and Edwards, 1970). A similar conclusion emerged when the Department of Trade and Industry inquired into 'Location Attitudes and Experience' (DTI, 1973). Only a minority of firms appeared to take any careful statistical comparison of transport costs into account when deciding on location. Thus the direct money expenditures on transport seem to be of only limited importance either in the locational or transport decisions of firms.

The other side of the same coin shows considerable emphasis on quality of service factors as explanations of transport choices. Only 6 per cent of road transport operators interviewed in a study in Swindon considered transport cost minimization to be their prime objective (Hitchcock et al, 1974, p 11). However, in a series of studies of choice of mode (Bayliss, Edwards, 1970; Sharp, 1971; Hitchcock, 1974) speed and reliability of delivery emerged as the dominant non-price determinants. Unfortunately all of these studies elicited ordinal rankings of the importance of qualitative factors but did not quantify them in any way which allowed them to be aggregated, or compared, with direct cost savings. But, of course, increased speed reduces unit transport costs in several ways — by spreading the time related haulage costs over more ton miles, by reducing the costs of stockholding, by eliminating production hold ups due to delayed deliveries of supplies. Whilst direct attempts to evaluate stockholding and output loss costs suggest that they are low (Law, 1964) firms do appear willing to pay a high premium to be relieved of the risk of their occurrence.

The significance of these conclusions on the determinants of transport decisions is that, whilst transport costs may be a low proportion of total costs, and the effect of infrastructure improvements on transport costs is attentuated by the fixed element of terminal costs and times, the dominating non-cost element — speed of delivery — is the one which is most directly affected by infrastructure improvements. But, for a range of reasons which we have outlined, it is not possible to quantify these relationships. The transport cost studies thus leave us with the impression that the relative speed changes may, in the long term, affect modal choice as well as locational decisions and that any restructuring affect could be primarily related to the achievement of micro locations proximate to high speed transport links rather than in any major inter-regional shifts.

Location theory
Both freight traffic effects and structural effects of transport improvements derive eventually from the decisions made by firms. We must, therefore, explore this already well-cultivated field of theory and research to see what light it can throw on our particular problem.

Classical location theory stems from the work of Alfred Weber. His approach (Weber, 1929) consisted essentially of the micro-economic analysis of the profit maximizing firm in a perfectly competitive environment. With the product price determined by uncontrollable market forces the problem for the firm was reduced to that of seeking the location which minimized the cost of supplying the market chosen. The solution to this problem was to minimize the weighted sum of the distances travelled by inputs, from source to point of production, and outputs, from point of production to market. For the simplest, two factor, case, this could be shown to fall within the locational triangle described by the input sources and the market (Launhardt, 1885). Extending this analysis to a multifactor, multimarket, situation, and allowing for non-linearity in transport costs, forces the solution into a different area of mathematics but does not change its fundamental nature. Transport costs tapering with distance would force the optimum location towards corners of the locational space (Palander, 1935), whilst transhipment costs might force the optimum to a transport node (Hoover, 1948). But the optimum location remains a point of least cost located within the surface described by the points of origin of inputs and destination of outputs.

The nature of the Weberian model changes rather more drastically when we attempt to relax two other fundamental assumptions which it makes, namely,

(i) fixed factor proportions and prices;

(ii) fixed market location.

If input prices vary over space then, even with fixed markets and output prices, profit maximization will cease to be achieved by simple transport cost minimization. The ensuing trade off between transport cost and production cost variations will be further complicated if the proportions of the various inputs to the production process can be varied to take advantage of relatively cheap factors. Hence, the optimum location decision cannot be separated from the choice of optimum combination of inputs (Moses, 1958). Moreover, the existence of economies of scale in production will alter the number, as well as the location, of points of production (Mohring and Williamson, 1969).

Relaxing the Weberian assumption that demand is fixed, and concentrated at a single point in space, also brings new considerations into play. A simple market area model (Palander, 1935) would suggest that firms will then locate relative to their competitors in such a way as to maximize their market share. But the outcome of this process will differ according to the pricing systems used by the competing firms (Richardson, 1969) and the elasticity of the demand facing the individual firm (ie the strength of product differentiation).

In a spatially uniform total market, with plant prices and transport costs equal for all firms, it has been argued that an equilibrium division of the market is secured when each firm is serving a hexagonal market area, the size of the areas, and the number of firms, depending on transport cost levels (Losch, 1954). With a number of different, but interdependent product markets the same theoretical approach suggests a tendency for firms to concentrate at particular locations.

The effects of locational interdependence are not limited, however, to those of static optimization in the face of market transactions. In practice firms will select locations not only on the basis of the existing locations of their competitors, their markets, and their suppliers, but also on how they *expect* these patterns to change. The introduction of this gaming element into locational choice also led Hotelling to conclude that there was a tendency to industrial agglomeration stemming from this source. In his famous analysis of two ice-cream sellers locating on a linear beach he suggested that they would locate themselves side by side in the middle of the beach because only then could they each be sure to capture at least half the market (Hotelling, 1929).

Here, of course, we have entered the field of oligopoly theory. The outcome will depend on the number of competitors and the way in which they interpret each others actions. Determinancy disappears, and even the tendency towards agglomeration has been challenged (Chamberlin, 1936).

248

When we attempt to put this variety of supply and demand considerations together the theory of industrial location which emerges is very complex. The factors affecting location include processing costs, and economies of scale therein, transport costs, market structure and demand elasticities, external economies of agglomeration, and expectations of cost reducing or revenue increasing factors. Transportation is important if freight costs form a large proportion of total costs or vary significantly between locations (Greenhut, 1963). Hence, the effect of reduced transport cost on a particular link in the network on the location of activities and on transport demand may vary very substantially according to the types of products, industries and markets which it affects.

Even in its most developed form this neo-classical micro theory of the location of the profit maximizing firm has been observed to retain two significant omissions from its catalogue of determining factors (Brown, 1977). Qualities of transport service such as speed, safety and reliability are all subsumed hopefully (but inefficiently) under the banner of cost. The concentration on the costs of movement of goods implicitly assume the costs of business travel and of journeys to work to be relatively unimportant. The qualitative aspects of goods movement, and particularly of personal communications and movement, may well, at the end of the day, dominate. Thus, in terms of the observed information on production and transport costs and demand factors, the location of the firm, and the affect of transport cost charges on the firm's activities, may remain indeterminate. There is therefore little we can deduce directly from location theory.

This conclusion is strengthened when one considers more recent developments in the direction of a behavioural theory of the firm. In this vein one may view the location decisions of the firm, like its other decisions, to be products as much of the internal characteristics of the firm as of the external environment in which it operates. Divorce of ownership from control of the firm, the absence of perfect information, and the development within the firm of competing pressures and objectives conspire together to rob us of any determinate response to a changing environment (Cyert and March, 1963).

In particular the firm is seen as no longer exhibiting any clear and stable maximizing behaviour but rather acts to retain 'satisfactory' levels of performance in respect of a number of different, and not necessarily mutually compatible, objectives (Simon, 1969). A number of important effects on location decision making result from this attitude. The personal tastes, and particularly the social aspirations, of managers — the desire to live in pleasant surroundings, to have good educational facilities for their children and so on —

may play a part quite unforeseen in classical theory (Eversley, 1965). The pressure to 'satisfice' rather than maximize may also lead to the acceptance of the first acceptable solution rather than to a prolonged search for the best (Townroe, 1972). By the same token, changes in transport conditions which cause a deterioration in the locational advantage of the firm may only become active in causing locational change when some significant threshold of acceptability is crossed. Locational inertia thus relates not only to the cost of relocation but also to the satisficing levels sought. The avoidance of potentially very profitable, but also risky, locations also follows from the 'satisficing' mentality.

The administrative complexity of the modern industrial undertaking is often matched by the structure of the markets in which it operates. The firm typically produces multiple products and has multiple functions (eg manufacturing, sales, distribution) for each of which dimension an optimum or preferred location might emerge (Keeble, 1971). The reconciliation of these conflicting preferences through the administrative procedures of the firm may be a highly unpredictable process of negotiation and compromise rather than one of calculation. Moreover, these location decisions may be most typically associated with, or even the by-product of, wider strategic choices for the firm. Such strategic decisions are taken intermittently, and may not be at all heavily transport orientated.

The developments of classical location theory and its reconsideration in the context of the behavioural theories of the firm thus leads us to no clear conclusion about the magnitude, or even the direction, of the structural changes consequent upon transport improvements.

Empirical location studies
Whilst both the study of transport costs and location theory might show a confusing range of theoretical possibilities in the likely structural response to transport infrastructure changes, it might still be the case that some dominating influences existed which led to some of the theoretical possibilities being more closely related to the real situation than others. In this section and the next we shall be examining more direct, but less theoretical, evidence, firstly concerning the declared principal factors in location and secondly the heuristic statistical analysis of a number of particular impact situations.

Most empirical location studies concentrate on the factors which firms claim, when approached, to take into account in making decisions. Inevitably there is an element of *ex post* rationalization which may distort the results of such studies. Indeed, in even more sinister vein, managements may positively seek

250

'objective' explanations, however untrue, to obscure the importance of more personal and less businesslike considerations. There is also a problem about the locational scale at which particular considerations operate. Labour supply may determine the general choice of region for an activity, but access to the motorway system determine the location in a more micro sense. Thus the precise way in which the enquiry is formulated may affect the apparent determining factors.

In the UK the two most extensive studies have been those of Luttrell (Luttrell, 1962), which surveyed the reasons for industrial movement in the period 1945—52, and that of the government 'Inquiry into Location Attitudes and Experience' (Department of Trade and Industry, 1973) which covered 543 relocated firms in the early 70s. In these cases, and in other similar studies (Cameron and Clark, 1966; Hayden, 1977) the concern is as much with the reasons which caused firms to seek new locations as with the basis on which new locations were chosen. Whilst it is reasonable to expect these to be related it may well be the case that, once the original reasons for a move had been satisfied, other elements — not considered instrumental in causing the move — take over in determining the new location selected. Such a distinction could also be closely related to the distinction in locational scale which we have already discussed.

The evidence from the locational studies suggests that the need for expansion, closely related to the insufficiency of existing site or labour resources, is the major impetus causing firms to relocate. The earlier studies (Luttrell, 1962; Cameron and Clarke, 1966) found more emphasis on labour supply deficiencies; the later studies (Loasby, 1967; DTE, 1973; Hayden, 1977) found site inadequacies relatively more important. Transport issues, such as traffic congestion or site access for commercial vehicles were not major factors.

When it comes to the choice of a new location the factors appear to vary according to the type of movement. Summarizing the studies Brown argues that for long distance, inter-regional movement the availability of trainable labour is the key locational factor, whilst for short distance, intra-regional, movements it is access to existing local markets which is the important single locational factor. Accessibility to suppliers emerges as being of only minor importance (Brown, 1977). It is interesting to note that in a study of newly located plants carried out in West Germany in 1971 similar results were obtained (Fischer, 1971). Accessibility to a motorway ranked only fourth after labour availability, scope for expansion and low labour costs in the reasons for selection of location.

Unfortunately this conclusion seems to reduce to the tautology that those firms which are very dependent on local markets are unwilling to relocate far from them whilst those who are not so constrained are willing to move further and to consider determining factors other than those of access. Only if one knew, *ex ante*, what proportion of firms fell in each category could one deduce from the empirical location studies any conclusions of direct relevance to the question of the restructuring effects of infrastructive investment.

One important factor which does seem to emerge from these studies is the relative importance of person movements, as opposed to the movement of goods. It has been argued that close and frequent personal contact with customers is a more important stimulus to locations proximate to markets than the costs of distribution of goods (Keeble, 1976). This accounts also for the attraction of London from whence many firms buy, even if the ultimate point of consumption is not in the metropolis. At the micro level the availability of good passenger transport facilities, and particularly public transport, may also be very important in determining whether a location may be viewed as having adequate supplies of trainable labour.

Land use and transport modelling
The last two decades in planning have been the decades of the large-scale models. It is therefore appropriate to consider what they have contributed, or might still be developed to contribute, to the understanding of the effects of transport investment on land use.

Three distinct bodies of work should be mentioned here. Firstly, there is the transport model which, on the basis of land use and income inputs, analyses the way in which movement is generated, the choice of mode selected, the linking between origins and destinations determined, and the resulting traffic assigned to the transport network. Of crucial importance in this structure is the distribution stage which from very simple origins in extrapolatory forecasting devices has developed into the doubly constrained gravity model. But, despite their increasing sophistication, the operational transport models have remained essentially static, forecasting the transport implications of any given land use pattern but not feeding back to incorporate the dynamic effects of transport facilities on land use patterns.

The second relevant area of work is that in location modelling. The seminal work is that of Lowry (Lowry, 1964), which considered the location of market sensitive employment simultaneously with the location of population. The essential ingredient of this model, and many of its derivatives, is that it starts with the existing location of 'basic' employment and locates both household

252

residences and retail and commercial employment as consequent upon this economic base. In the following decade this essentially static model has been developed in a number of important ways. It has been given a time orientation, so that forecasts can be obtained for specific years (Crecine, 1964); the number of household and activity types have been increased (Crecine, 1969); the sophistication of the trip distribution models contained has been increased to allow for differences of attraction between alternative destinations (Goldner, 1972). Particular attention has been paid to residential location, and large-scale models have been calibrated for some conurbations as, for instance, in the Bay Area Simulation Study (CREUE, 1968) and NBER Studies (Ingram *et al*, 1972). More recently effort has been concentrated on attempts to integrate the land-use and transportation model (Putnam *et al*, 1973; Mackett, 1977).

For the purposes of understanding the effects of transport investment on regional development, the modelling approaches we have considered so far have two major deficiencies. First, they are extremely complex and make data requirements that are difficult to satisfy, often without offering forecasts which are capable of interpretation at an operational level (Lee, 1973). Second, they are driven by, rather than produce, forecasts of the levels and locations of 'basic' employment which is the essence of the forecasting problem in the inter-regional allocation context. Hence, if this whole area of work is to be of relevance it needs to be linked to a much more sophisticated, and spatially disaggregated, inter-industry model.

The third relevant area of modelling is thus that of multi-regional input-output models. Regional disaggregation within the Leontieff framework produces no insuperable mathematical problems (Leontieff and Strout, 1963). But the simple addition of a spatial dimension accentuates the problem of interpreting the coefficients of the model when used in a forecasting mode. On top of the assumption of stable technological coefficients one has added an implicit assumption that the geographical origin of particular commodities is also fixed (ie that there is no possibility of substitution between alternative sources of supply and inputs). Whilst there may be a good deal of inertia in the markets for intermediate inputs such an extreme assumption is implausible. In conceptual terms the problem is not intractable. It has been shown that, by using entropy maximizing methods, gravity models of spatial distribution can be integrated with the Leontieff-Strout input-output model to produce a family of commodity flow models (Wilson, 1970), allowing changes in transport costs to change inter-regional linkages. Such an integration would make enormous data requirements and would depend for its validity on the extent to which the gravity model effectively explains the distribution of the flows of homogeneous

253

commodities. These problems have been sufficient to prevent any substantial practical progress to date along this line.

But even if these problems did not exist we should note that our problem is not solved. All that a combined gravity/inter-regional input-output model would do would be to project the implications of existing distributions of activity. It would contain no mechanism for analysing or projecting the level or structure of activity in the regions of the model. In the same way as urban modellers have been led to attempt to integrate a land use model with a transportation model, we should still have to find a basis for analysing and allocating the basic economic activities.

In the urban context this reconciliation has been approached by treating some economic activities as exogenously determined. In the inter-regional context the parallel would seem to lie in treating the location of primary activities (mineral extraction, agriculture, forestry and fishing) as fixed and driving a model from this base. Whether the links between manufacturing location and primary industry are sufficiently deterministic to allow such an approach is, however, very doubtful.

This allocation problem has been approached in different ways. For instance, in a study of the location of development in the Melbourne—Sydney corridor in Australia a mathematical programming formulation is used (Dickey and Sharpe, 1974). The total amount of available land and the total amount of activity to be allocated are treated as constraints; the objective function is the sum of production costs and transport costs (where transport linkages are determined in a gravity formulation). The results of this analysis are interesting as an exploration of the implications of alternative infrastructure and land use control policies. But, because the optimization procedure is a total social cost minimization and does not imply that private welfare is maximized contingently for all sectors, there is no reason to expect it to accurately reflect or predict what *will* take place in a less than completely controlled situation.

Probably the most extensive intra-regional allocation study to date has been that of the North East Corridor in the United States. The model used (INTRA I), builds upon the economic base concept (Isard, 1960) using single equation multiple regression analysis. Base sector employment (agriculture, forestry and fishing, mining, manufacturing, and transport and communication) is related to the levels of employment in the sector, employment in other sectors, population, and accessibility both to markets and inputs. All the independent variables are lagged by one period. Non-basic sector employment was postulated by a function of total population, total employment and

254

employment in the sector in the price period. Very high levels of correlation were obtained (Putnam, 1975).

The fundamental weakness of this formulation is that there inevitably exists a very high degree of serial correlation in the data. Hence the use of the lagged value of the dependent variable as an independent variable robs the formulation of any substantial causal content. To meet this central criticism a later model, INTRA II, was developed with *changes* in the level of sectoral employment as the dependent variable. At the same time, however, indicators of intermediate and final demand for goods in the sector were introduced. Unfortunately, these indicators both contained the change in sector employment supply indirectly in their formulation. Thus, some kind of simultaneous estimation procedure is called for. Without such procedures being employed the single equation estimates of the other independent variables, which included an accessibility variable, lose their reliability. In the single equation structure, as used, the results were totally inconclusive. The sign of the coefficient expressing the effect of accessibility on change in sectoral employment varied from sector to sector, with many of the relationships being statistically insignificant.

It is difficult and invidious to conclude briefly on this field of planning models as a whole. They are clearly expensive, hungry animals. Their most extensive applications have been in urban transport planning with fixed or exogenously determined land uses. In respect of the allocation of activity their results are yet to be proven. Certainly the causal locational factors incorporated in the modelling process are a very sparse sub-set of those which we have considered previously. All of which leads one to conclude that whilst they are undoubtedly interesting vehicles for the examination of complicated sets of assumptions, they are not presently able to interpret observed historical evidence on the location of activities and transport patterns to give reliable predictions of what *will* happen to the location of activities in response to specified changes in transport infrastructure.

Inter-regional freight flow models
Whilst in the long term we may expect some relocation of activities to result from transport improvements, and we may wish to model the complex set of interactions which this implies, this is not the only dimension in which re-structuring the economy may take place. With activities constantly located, the origins of supply for a given location or destinations supplied by it may change. In mathematical terms we may say that, with fixed vectors representing

255

origins and destinations, the matrix of interactions linking the two is not unique and may itself respond to changes in transport infrastructure. What we need for this purpose is a freight transport distribution model.

In the context of urban transport planning models this distribution stage has attracted a voluminous, and very sophisticated, literature (Lamb, 1974). Typically these models express the trips between any pair of zones as a function of the ability of the zone to attract or generate trips and the impedance, in transport terms, between them. The most common form of model, the gravity model, is clothed in statistical respectability in the theory of entropy maximization (Wilson, 1970) and, with certain assumptions, can even be derived from utility maximizing axioms (Niedercorn and Bechdolt, 1969). For person movements the heterogeneity of demands encourages resort to some kind of random utility theory, enhancing the apparent economic respectability of fundamentally heuristic statistical models. These kinds of models have, in the past, been made to fit well to base year data and have also performed tolerably well in a forecasting role.

As a pure matter of record we may observe that urban freight flows have not been modelled in the same way. There are two main reasons for this. Firstly, freight flows are a relatively unimportant contributor to the peak hour congestion which has been the primary focus of most urban modelling activities. Second, a much larger proportion of freight vehicle movements originate or terminate outside the study area and cannot thus be analysed endogenously in a restricted area model. But, in addition, there is the intellectual concern that for freight movements the underlying processes of interaction may not be such as to support the kind of statistical averaging implicit in the gravity model formulation.

When considering inter-urban or inter-regional transport facilities we find freight demands comprising a much greater proportion of the pressure on facilities, and we are able, at this level of aggregation, to close a study area in such a way as to include, rather than exclude, the majority of origins and destinations. The excuses for ignoring freight distribution disappear.

Unfortunately, even with the largest available collections of British data some serious statistical problems remain. For instance, an analysis of the 1962 Road Goods survey was able to study 700,000 journeys (Chisholm and O'Sullivan, 1973). Division of these movements between the cells of a 78 × 78 zonal matrix still gives, on average, over 100 journeys per cell. But when one divides further into only thirteen commodity groups, no statistical reliance can be placed on the results because of the very small mean cell size. For the purposes of an inter-zonal distribution model the situation is made even worse by the loss of 90 per cent of the tonnage which is moved intra-zonally (Bayliss, 1974).

For these statistical reasons we should not expect too much of the attempts to calibrate a gravity model for freight flows. In the event, Chisholm and O'Sullivan did find a slight tendency for more highly valued and processed goods (steel, transport vehicles, and equipment, chemicals) to be less impeded than bulky goods (coal and coke, building materials). In addition, the impedance appeared to be greater in urban than in rural and peripheral areas. But these variations in coefficient values were small, and were quite sensitive to the choice of origin zone.

As we have stated earlier; the gravity model is usually derived stochastically, reflecting a recognition that we are unable to grasp and model all the factors relevant in determining spatial interaction. If, however, we assumed perfect knowledge and perfect rationality, with the whole freight system being operated in such a way as to minimize total freight transport costs, we obtain the classical formulation of the linear programming transportation problem (Hitchcock, 1941). In an earlier study using the same basic data sources as Chisholm and O'Sullivan, the Mathematical Advisory Unit of the Ministry of Transport attempted to apply such a model (Black, 1971). For the commodity group coal and coke the estimated total transport cost obtained from this formulation was only about 70 per cent of actual cost. In this case the excess was explained in terms of the suppressed heterogeneity of the products leading to apparent, but not real, irrational cross hauling. In a later study of the movements of steel strip similar departures from cost minimization were attributed to the continuation after nationalization of personal and business contacts resulting in steel of given characteristics not always being supplied from the cheapest source in transport cost terms (UWIST, 1976). Even with a common ex-works price and transport costs borne by the consignee such results may properly reflect advantages in security and reliability of supply which cannot emerge in a transport cost minimizing procedure. Taking together the effects of product heterogeneity, variations in production costs and in marketing policies we would not expect good understanding of freight flows to emerge from linear programming models.

Whilst this experience pushes freight flow modellers back in the direction of the heuristic statistical device of the gravity model there is still too little reliable application of the model in the freight context to engender confidence in its results. Different applications have yielded impedance factors for specific commodity groups varying substantially not only in magnitude but also in ranking (Bell, 1978).

Impact studies

The conceptual complexity of the relationships involved has meant that neither general equilibrium models, nor the more limited freight flow models, have been calibrated suitably for application to the assessment of specific infrastructure projects. This inability to built realistic models from *a priori* reasoning has led us to resort to argue by analogy. In this approach we attempt to observe directly the changes that occur when a new infrastructure is introduced and to infer from that observation the kinds of effect that we would expect from similar future infrastructure projects.

The most obvious trap in this kind of research is to mistake statistical association for cause and effect. For example, in a study of the effect of the construction of the A7 motorway on population growth in the Rhône Valley, Delaygue observed that the average rate of population growth of parishes in the region was related to proximity to nearest access point to the motorway (Delaygue, 1971). He then concluded that proximity to the motorway was a determining factor of population trends. But all that has been shown is statistical association. The explanation may more simply be that the motorway serves the valley and the valley contains the zones with expanding population; indeed, selection of the optimal route may ensure that as a normal situation (Plassard, 1977). Similar examples of this fallacy can be found in the German analyses of the effects on the rate of growth of industrial turnover of proximity to waterways (Marchal, 1975) and motorways (Frerich, Helms and Kreuter, 1972). Apart from the problem of causation there are also statistical problems associated with this approach. In a study of the effects of the M62 motorway on employment in West Yorkshire it was found that, at the level of aggregation at which employment data is reliable no statistically significant relationship is to be found, whilst at the level at which locational effects might be expected to be most apparent the data was not reliable (Dodgson, 1974).

This leads into a second problem of interpretation which may be equally troublesome. Whilst the precise location may be partly determined by accessibility to transport facilities one really needs to know what the situation would have been in the absence of the facility. Would the activity have taken place in any case and, if so, where? This kind of problem of interpretation is exemplified by the Italian study of the effects of the Autostrade de Sole (Balduini, 1972). In that study the location of 1186 firms, responsible for 53,000 jobs were attributed as results of the motorway over the period 1958—70. But the development of the Mezzogiorno was in any case an objective of policy to which a range of instruments were applied; the survey work does not discriminate between motivations with sufficient precision to allow any firm conclusions to be reached about the *regional* rather than *sub-regional* effects.

A third difficulty in impact studies may be to separate any genuine long-term redistributional effects of a transport investment from the more direct and shorter-term multiplier effects of the investment itself. Whilst, in principle, the two may be distinguished by their relative permanence, in practice some of the multiplier effects may be lagged. If we delay the 'after' stage for a sufficiently long period to be satisfied that delayed multiplier effects had disappeared, and 'genuine' relocation effect had time to take place, we will almost certainly be faced with a sufficient range of other changes of situation to confuse the attribution of causation of any observed effect.

All of these considerations lead to the conclusion that the direct impact studies cannot be regarded as a simple means of settling the issue. On the other hand, it does not follow that nothing can be learned from them. For instance, the Severn Bridge Study (Cleary and Thomas, 1972) showed, not surprisingly, no significant relocation of manufacturing establishments in the three years following the opening of the bridge. But it did show some rapid and substantial adjustments in sources of supply or market outlets which generated substantial amounts of new traffic between Bristol and South Wales. From this one may infer that some welfare benefits accrued which were not associated with observed relocation. What is less clear is to whom these benefits occurred.

For the reasons outlined above the number of impact studies undertaken in Western Europe has been very limited (CEMAT, 1973). In a review of those which have taken place (ECMT, 1975) it was concluded that the effects of new links connecting equally developed regions have been very slight. Furthermore, in the Netherlands, Italy, Portugal, and Norway and Sweden transport infrastructure programmes aimed at rectifying regional imbalances have all failed to achieve their objectives.

This combination of data and interpretation problems has led some recent impact study work to adopt much more modest and partial objectives. It has been argued that any significant restructuring effects associated with transport improvements should be reflected in changes in transport activity. Hence, as an initial guide, a study of the amount of new traffic generated by motorways, for example, should indicate whether any significant effects have been experienced or not. Only if transport responses are significant does one then need to go further to establish whether it is in changes in linkages between basically unaffected activity locations or the relocation of activities which is responsible for the change. In a study of the M62 (Gwilliam and Judge, 1975) it was found that most of the apparent change in traffic was due to changes in routeing and

259

that only a small amount of generated traffic of any kind was left to account for.

Conclusions

The question we set out to explore was whether transport infrastructure investment was an effective instrument of regional development policy. Our conclusion can be presented in three propositions. First, the relevant areas of pure theory give no unambiguous guidance on the likely effect of transport improvements. Second, such propositions as can be derived from simplified theory cannot be subject to proper empirical testing. Third, given these limitations, the sparce evidence available supports rather than undermines Brown's judgement that transport investment has limited impact on regional activity.

Note

[1] I would like to record my debt to R. H. Brown (no relation to A. J. B.) whose excellent unpublished work (Brown, 1977) is substantially drawn upon in the sections on transport costs and location theory.

References

G. Balduini, 1972, *Autostrade et Territorio in quadermi de Autostrade 20*, Rome.

B. T. Bayliss and S. L. Edwards, 1970, *Industrial Demand for Transport*, HMSO.

B. T. Bayliss, 1974, Review of M. Chisholm and P. O'Sullivan, *Freight Flows, and Spatial Aspects of the British Economy: Journal of Transport Economics and Policy*, 8.

M. G. H. Bell, 1978, 'Preliminary Investigations of the Properties of Inter-Regional Road Freight Distribution.' Paper presented to the UTSG Conference, London, January.

I. Black, 1971, 'Some Experience in Modelling Road Freight Flows.' Paper presented to the PTRC Symposium, Amsterdam, May.

A. J. Brown, 1972, *The Framework of Regional Economics in the United Kingdom*, Cambridge University Press.

R. H. Brown, 1977, 'Transport Considerations in the Location of Manufacturing Industry in Conurbations.' Unpublished MPhil thesis. University College London.

G. C. Cameron and B. D. Clark, 1966, *Industrial Movement and the Regional Problem.* University of Glasgow Social and Economic Studies Occasional Papers No 5, Oliver and Boyd, Edinburgh.

CEMAT, 1973, 'Effects of Transport Infrastructure on Regional Development — An Enquiry.' Paper presented to Second European Conference of Ministers responsible for Regional Planning. September.

E. H. Chamberlin, 1936, *The Theory of Monopolistic Competition*, Harvard University Press, Cambridge, Massachusetts.

M. Chisholm, 1971, 'Freight Transport Costs, Industrial Location and Regional Development' in M. Chisholm and G. Manners, eds, *Spatial Policy Problems of the British Economy*, Cambridge University Press.

M. Chisholm and P. O'Sullivan, 1973, *Freight Flows and Spatial Aspects of the British Economy*, Cambridge University Press.

E. J. Cleary and R. E. Thomas, 1972, *The Consequences of the Severn Bridge and its Associated Motorways*, University of Bath Press.

Cmnd 3998, 1969, *The Intermediate Areas — Report of a Committee under the Chairmanship of Sir Joseph Hunt*, HMSO, April.

W. R. Cook, 1967, 'Transport Decisions of Certain Firms in the Black Country', *Journal of Transport Economics and Policy*, 1, 344—56.

J. P. Crecine, 1965, 'A Time Oriented Metropolitan Model for Spatial Location', mimeo. Dept of City Planning, Pittsburgh, Pennsylvania.

J. P. Crecine, 1969, *Spatial Location Decisions and Urban Structure: A Time Oriented Model*, Discussion Paper 4, Institute of Public Policy Studies, University of Michigan. Ann Arbor, Michigan.

CREUE, 1968, *Jobs, People and Land: Bay Area Simulation Study*, Special Report No 6, Centre for Real Estate and Urban Economics, Institute of Urban and Regional Development, University of California, Berkeley.

R. M. Cyert and J. G. March, 1963, *Behavioural Theory of the Firm*, Prentice-Hall, Eaglewood Cliffs.

M. Delaygue, 1971, *Les effets d'entrainement de l'infrastructure de transport*, Report of the 4th Round Table of ECMT, Paris.

Department of Trade and Industry, 1973, 'Inquiry into Location Attitudes and Experiences', in *Regional Development Incentives*, House of Commons Expenditure Committee, Session 1972—73, pp 525—668.

J. W. Dickey and R. Sharpe, 1974, 'Transportation and Urban and Regional Development Impacts', *High Speed Ground Transportation Journal*, 3.

J. S. Dodgson, 1974, 'Motorway Investment, Industrial Transport Costs and Sub-Regional Growth. A Case Study of the M62.' *Regional Studies*, 8, 75—9.

ECMT, 1975, 'Impact of Infrastructural Investment on Industrial Development.' *Report of the 25th Round Table in Transport Economics*, European Conference of Ministers of Transport, Paris.

R. S. Edwards and H. Townsend, 1958, *Business Enterprise: Its Growth and Organisation*, Macmillan.

S. L. Edwards, 1970, 'Transport Costs in British Industry', *Journal of Transport Economics and Policy*, 4, 65—83.

S. L. Edwards, 1975, 'Regional Variations in Freight Costs.' *Journal of Transport Economics and Policy*, 9, 115—26.

D. E. S. Eversley, 1965, 'Social and Psychological Factors in the Determination of Industrial Location' in T. Wilson, ed, *Papers on Regional Development*, Blackwell, Oxford.

L. Fischer, 1971, *Die Berucksichtigung Raumordnungs politiser Zielsetviengen in der Verkehrsplanung.*

R. W. Fogel, 1964, *Railroads and American economic growth: essays in econometric history*, John Hopkins Press, Baltimore, Maryland.

J. Frerich, E. Helms and H. Kreuter, 1972, *Die Erfassung und Quantifizierung der Wachstums and Struktureffekte von Autobahnen*, Bonn, 1972.

W. Goldner, 1972, *Projective Land Use Model*, Institute of Transportation and Traffic Engineering, University of California, Berkeley.

K. M. Gwilliam, 1970, 'The Indirect Effects of Highway Investment', *Regional Studies*, 4.

K. M. Gwilliam and E. J. Judge, 1974, 'Transport and Regional Development: Some Preliminary Reports of the M62 Study.' Paper presented to the Regional Studies Association Conference, London, April.

F. Hayden, 1977, 'Factors Affecting the Location of Industry', GLC unpublished study.

F. L. Hitchcock, 1941, 'The Distribution of a Product from Several Sources to Numerous Localities.' *Journal of Mathematics and Physics*, 20, 224—80.

E. M. Hoover, 1948, *The Location of Economic Activity*, McGraw Hill, New York.

H. Hotelling, 1929, 'Stability in Competition', *Economic Journal*, 39, 41—57.

G. Ingram *et al*, 1972, *The NBER Urban Simulation Model*, Columbia University Press, New York.

W. Isard, 1960, *Methods of Regional Analysis: An Introduction to Regional Science*, Wiley, New York.

D. E. Keeble, 1971, 'Employment Mobility in Britain', in M. Chisholm and G. Manners, eds, *Spatial Policy Problems of the British Economy*, Cambridge University Press.

D. E. Keeble, 1976, *Industrial Location and Planning in the United Kingdom*, Methuen.

G. M. Lamb, 1970, 'Introduction to Transport Planning.' *Traffic Engineering and Control.*

W. Launhardt, 1885, *Mathematisch Begrurung der Volkwirtschaftslobe*, Leipzig.

D. Law, 1964, 'Industrial Movement and Locational Advantage', *Manchester School*, 32, 131—54.

D. B. Lee, Jr, 1973, 'Requiem for Large Scale Models', *Journal of the American Institute of Planners*, 19, 163—78.

W. Leontieff and A. Strout, 1963, 'Multi-Regional Input-Output Analysis' in T. Barna, ed, *Structural Interdependence and Economic Development*, Macmillan.

261

B. J. Loasby, 1967, 'Making Location Policy Work' *Lloyds Bank Review*, 83, 34—47.

A. Losch, 1954, *The Economics of Location*, Yale University Press, New Haven, Connecticut.

I. S. Lowry, 1964, *A Model of Metropolis*, Road Corporation, Santa Monica, California.

W. F. Luttrell, 1963, *Factory Location and Industrial Movement: A Study of Recent Experience in Great Britain*, NIESR.

R. L. Mackett, 1977, 'A dynamic activity allocation-transportation model', in P. W. Bonsall, Q. M. Dalvi, P. J. Hills, eds, *Urban Transportation — Current Trends and Future Prospects*, Abacus Press Ltd, Tunbridge Wells.

M. Marchal, 1975, 'Trois acces fluviaux de transport et de developpement: le Rhin, le Rhone, le Danube.' *Transports*, no 201, 155.

H. Mohring and H. F. Williamson, 1969, 'Scale and "Industrial Reorganisation" Economies of Transport Improvements.' *Journal of Transport Economics and Policy*, 3, 251—71.

L. Moses, 1958, 'Location and the theory of Production.' *Quarterly Journal of Economics*, **73**, 259—72.

J. H. Niedercorn and B. V. Behcdolt, jr, 1969, 'An Economic Derivation of the Gravity Law of Spatial Interaction.' *Journal of Regional Science*, 9.

T. Palander, 1935, *Beitrage zur Standortotheoria*, Almquist and Wiksells, Boktrykeri, Uppsala.

A. Plassard, 1977, 'Impact of transport infrastructure movement on regional economic development.' Paper presented to ECMT/CEMAT seminar on the effect of transport on regional planning in Europe. Paris, November.

S. H. Putman *et al*, 1973, *The Interrelationships of Transportation Development and Land Development*, Institute for Environmental Studies, Dept of City and Regional Planning, University of Pennsylvania, Philadelphia.

S. H. Putman, 1975, *An Empirical Model of Regional Growth*, Regional Science Research Institute, Monograph No 6.

H. W. Richardson, 1969, *Regional Economics*, Wiedenfeld and Nicholson.

C. Sharp, 1971, 'The Optimum Allocation of Freight Traffic', *Journal of Transport Economics and Policy*, 5, 344—56.

H. A. Simon, 1959, 'Theories of Decision Making in Economics and Behavioural Science.' *American Economic Review*, 49, 253—83.

P. M. Townroe, 1974, 'Some Behavioural Considerations in the Industrial Location Decision.' *Regional Studies*, 6, 261—74.

UWIST, 1977, *Transport in the Iron and Steel Industry: A Policy Summary*, Commodity Flows Research Unit, Dept of Maritime Studies, University of Wales Institute of Science and Technology, Cardiff.

A. Weber, 1929, *Theory of the Location of Industries*, Chicago University Press.

A. G. Wilson, 1970, *Entropy in Urban and Regional Modelling*. Pion.

A. G. Wilson, 1970, 'Interregional commodity flows — entropy maximising approaches.' *Geographical Analysis*, 2, 255—82.

14

Spatial unemployment and inequality

P. C. CHESHIRE

Policies specifically designed to influence the geographic distribution of resources, income and opportunities are common to most advanced countries. In Britain regional policy, though it has had its ups and downs,[1] has become well established in the last thirty years. More recently, central governments first in the United States, in the 1960s, now in Britain,[2] have turned their attention to another variety of spatial inequality; the problem, as it has become labelled in Britain, of the Inner Cities[3] and inequality within the Metropolitan regions.

While regional economists have provided substantial analysis of the need for, and desirability of, regional policy, analytical justification for policies directed at the relief of inequality between different parts of metropolitan regions has been less apparent. For a long time, until regional accounting data became available, regional unemployment differences were *the* regional problem, or certainly its most clearly visible sign. As an indicator of inequality across urban areas, unemployment has received less concentrated attention, though it is still a feature of the inner area problem to which, for example, the Inner Area Studies[3] paid considerable attention.

Although the economist's ultimate interest is in the distribution of real income or wealth or in welfare differences, the use of unemployment as a proxy for these is understandable. The more satisfactorily is the concept of economic welfare defined, the more difficult it becomes to measure; even if we resign ourselves to making do with the conceptually imperfect measure, real per capita income, there remain substantial problems. Income data, at a regional level, have only become available since the late 1960s and are still considerably less reliable and complete than national data. Regional price deflators are still not available for Britain though they exist in the US where, it is claimed, price variations offset much of the difference in money per capita incomes. At the sub-regional level, data are available only for fleeting and incomplete snapshot comparisons of small areas with the rest of the country or the surrounding region.

Unemployment data, on the other hand, although a third best proxy, are readily available for every labour exchange area; they have been available on a

s   263 broadly comparable basis for at least thirty years, and superficially at least, need no adjusting to a common national standard. Furthermore, unemployment is to an extent correlated with the incidence of poverty and may, as discussed in slightly greater detail below, have some merit in its own right as an indicator of economic welfare.

Although conventionally it is to income or measures of poverty that investigators and policy makers interested in distributional questions have turned, such measures are transparently incomplete as indicators of welfare. Some practical shortcomings of national income data have been pointed out by Samuelson (1950) and Nordhaus and Tobin (1972); more fundamental objections are implicit in many of the works of Sen, for example, Sen (1970).

More recently, practical objections to the unqualified use of per capita income differences even to measure the inequality of incomes have been raised by Paglin (1975). The argument here is simple; perfect equality with respect to per capita income distribution does not entail that every citizen or even every adult or household should have the same income because income needs vary — both between individuals and households and systematically over the life cycle. Income needs for a household are a direct function of the number of dependants in the household and, where there are children, they are a function of the age of those children. Income needs also vary with the household's accumulated stock of consumer durables and other assets such as real property and savings. Almost certainly official measures of poverty make insufficient allowance for these factors. In the US, as Paglin shows, if due allowance is made for these essentially life cycle variations in income needs, the measured inequality indicated by a crude comparison of household income differences is significantly reduced.

Table 1 below derived from Atkinson (1975) gives historical data on the composition of those in poverty. Two very obvious features are apparent.

There has been an increase in the proportion of pensioners amongst the poor since the Second World War and a longer term reduction in the proportion of families, particularly large families, with a man in work. Unemployment at most dates was a comparatively small immediate cause of poverty. The exception is the depression year of 1936. Van Slooten and Coverdale (1977) estimate that in 1975 70 per cent of all households where the man had been continuously out of work for twelve months, were poor. If the same relationship held in the 1930s, the importance of unemployment as a cause of poverty in 1936 is understandable.

Although the figures in Table 1 reflect some adjustments for life cycle needs and family size it is the present writer's view that perhaps, particularly for more

TABLE 1
Immediate causes of Poverty[4] in Britain 1899—1972

	1899	1936	% of poor 1953/54	1960	1972
Old age	} 10	15	49	33	55
Sickness		4	7	10	11
Unemployed	2	29	5	7	11
Family with man in work:					
4 or fewer children	55	37 }	} 38	32 }	} 14
5 or more children	22	5 }		8 }	
Single parent families	11	10		10	N/A

Source: Atkinson (1975)

recent years, the adjustments are insufficient. Although some needs, for example, for fuel, may increase in old age, some, for example, for food, are reduced. In addition pensioner households will on average have larger accumulated stocks of consumer durables which they own outright (including housing) and may receive certain price advantages; there may also be a greater incidence of unrecorded income supplements in cash or kind, chiefly from children.

The unemployed, although a comparatively small proportion of the poor in the low unemployment years up to 1972, may tend to be a slightly under-estimated proportion in terms of income needs. Unemployment may impose income needs of its own in terms of the cost of looking for a job. This may be particularly important for unemployed workers in low demand labour markets who, if they are to find work, may incur substantial travel costs.

Confining ones interest in the distribution of economic welfare to the incidence of poverty is restrictive in at least four ways: it ignores variation in other components of conceptually defined welfare — the hermit with neither income nor possessions may be in a state of bliss; it ignores price variations; it looks only at one extreme of the income distribution not at the whole distribution; and it may take insufficient account of variation in income needs. To go one stage further and look at the incidence of unemployment is not therefore to sacrifice some ideal indicator for a merely convenient one. After adjusting for income needs the unemployed make up a larger proportion of the poor than before.

For medium term comparisons one may regard the size of the largest group of poor — pensioners — as largely determined exogenously[5] by demographic factors, so if one is interested in changes through time or spatial variation in the poor, unemployment is a reasonable indicator. The evidence for this is presented by Atkinson (1975) who for example quotes Solow (1960): 'the main cause of the equalisation (in income) since the Second World War was the approach to full employment from the relatively depressed conditions before the war'. Lydall (1955) argued a similar case for Britain. If we compare the regional prevalence of poverty in the UK reported by Van Slooten and Coverdale (1977) for 1975 with regional unemployment rates in the same year, we find an r^2 of 0.67. Their figures make no allowance for regional price variations. Judging from the partial information given by the authors in a footnote, and from the fact that East Anglia and Yorkshire and Humberside are two of the lowest cost housing regions in Britain, the correlation between low regional real income and unemployment is almost certainly higher than this.

There are thus quite substantial grounds for regarding unemployment statistics as adequate indicators of variations in real poverty. In addition, there are some grounds for believing unemployment has merit in its own right as an independent indicator of low economic welfare if we drop the assumption that welfare is exclusively derived from the consumption of commodities that enter money transactions and which are thus included in the calculation of income measures.

The most common justification for taking income as a welfare indicator is that other components of welfare are exogeneous and can be assumed to be independent of income. Yet we have seen that income varies with whether a person is employed or unemployed and it is reasonable to suppose that other important aspects of social welfare vary in the same way. In summarizing the arguments favouring the relative rather than absolute definition of poverty, Atkinson quotes the Social Science Research Council (1968):

> People are 'poor' because they are deprived of the opportunities, comforts and self respect regarded as normal in the community to which they belong.

It may be argued on these grounds, therefore, that the unemployed suffer twice over. They suffer a loss of money income and an increased incidence of poverty which deprives them of many of the material 'opportunities and comforts' regarded as normal in their community. But in addition they suffer social deprivation and loss of self respect in a society where work is the norm for adults. The unemployed miss not only the social contact and status provided by work in a society where institutions are geared to work; they also suffer a loss of social esteem and self respect because they are unemployed. They feel less valued members of a community from which they are socially isolated by their joblessness.

The exact functional form relating the level of unemployment in a community to these direct, non-income, welfare costs, is an interesting and potentially important question. Changes in unemployment levels are disproportionately brought about by changes in the duration of unemployment rather than by changes in the flow of people coming onto the register. This implies that average duration rises sharply as unemployment rises. To become unemployed knowing there is a good prospect of getting a job quickly is probably much less painful than facing unemployment with no solid expectation of getting another job. This implies that these non-money welfare costs of unemployment may rise very rapidly as the level of unemployment and its duration rise and the associated prospects of getting a job fall. Once some upper level of unemployment in a community has been reached the average non-money welfare costs of unemployment may begin to fall, however, as unemployment becomes so widespread that the personal stigma of being without a job grows less. Where the community concerned is an identifiable sub-group of a wider society, for example, a local area or a minority group, even if the individual non-money welfare costs do fall at high levels of unemployment, the level might be higher than that at which average costs would fall if unemployment were spread evenly over the wider society. This is because any sub-group affected by unemployment remains part of the larger, work orientated, society.

If this argument is accepted, then it follows that a given unemployment rate for a local labour market or a minority group, is likely to have higher average direct welfare costs than the same rate for the whole labour force.[6] There is the further possibility that, particularly for minority groups, unemployment rates of the order of magnitude currently observed, may have significant external welfare costs on the rest of society. High levels of unemployment in a sub-group may be a factor in generating anti-majority feelings and an unemployment sub-culture which has welfare costs for the rest of society.

The non-income welfare costs of unemployment were recognized by Beveridge (1944) when he argued that full employment should be defined in such a way that the labour market was a sellers' market:

> A person who has difficulty buying labour he wants suffers inconvenience or reduction of profits. A person who cannot sell his

labour is in effect told he is of no use. The first difficulty causes *annoyance* or *loss*. The other is a *personal catastrophe*. This difference remains even if adequate income is provided . . . during unemployment; idleness even on an income corrupts; the feeling of not being wanted demoralises.

Although, therefore, unemployment differentials have no doubt been used on an *ad hoc* basis as an indicator of spatial variations in welfare, their use can in some measure be justified. No measure, even variation in regional income distribution, is ideal. Unemployment, whilst only a proxy for the spatial incidence of poverty, does signal other forms of deprivation as well as just low incomes.

It is possible to hold this, however, without necessarily concluding that policies directed towards reducing spatial differences in unemployment are well founded. We may accept the aim of greater welfare equality but still need to know how far spatial variations in unemployment, and perhaps poverty too, are truly spatial rather than social. We also need to know what effect the policies will have on spatial unemployment differences, and what the over-all costs of the policies will be.

This implies that some analysis of why spatial unemployment differences (and differences in the incidence of poverty) arise, is a necessary first step in assessing the significance of the purely spatial dimension of inequality. Variation in regional industrial structures and different industrial growth rates seem the most likely explanations of inter-regional unemployment differences; especially when it is accepted that industries are not homogeneous and growing and/or declining sectors are more or less evenly distributed than the aggregate data on regional industrial employment might suggest. The well-known case of shipbuilding, which includes both small pleasure craft construction and traditional heavy shipbuilding, is a good example. The reason why direct evidence to support this explanation is difficult to find, however, is because of the amount of mobility in the labour market.

Labour is heterogeneous and it is differentiated with respect to several different characteristics or dimensions. A particular worker has a given occupation, industry, degree of skill, effectiveness, motivation, fitness, location, etc. But mobility with respect to all dimensions of the labour market is occurring all the time. One can analyse this mobility as a rational process whereby a worker will tend to acquire a particular set of characteristics so as to maximize his own net advantage subject to the constraints imposed by his own innate qualities, the labour market and social institutions. Thus, other things being equal, a worker with particular needs for current income — such needs being determined partly by his stage in the life cycle — may seek a less pleasant, higher paying job or a job with more overtime, to meet current income needs. The extent to which this occurs however, ie the amount of this particular sort of mobility observed during a particular period, will vary with a number of exogenous factors which can be viewed as constants in the medium term, and in addition with the expected costs and returns from such mobility. These, adopting a Holt (1970) type model, would vary with the level of excess demand for labour in the labour market.

To the individual the expected costs with respect to mobility in any dimension of the labour market will vary inversely, and expected returns vary positively with excess demand. Thus the over-all volume of mobility will vary positively with excess demand. As the level of excess demand rises there will be more job offers per unit time, a fall in search costs, and a greater probability of finding a 'better' job; hence voluntary separations will rise and mean duration of unemployment fall, Holt (1970). We observe for Britain that, although involuntary separations fall as excess demand rises, the over-all volume of labour turn-over increases with demand, implying that rising voluntary quits more than off-set falling involuntary separations. The volume of inter-regional migration, for Canada at least, has been shown to vary inversely with over-all unemployment. Thus while there will be differences in the mean rates of mobility observed for each dimension of the labour market, for each the volume varies positively with the level of excess demand.

Given the differentials that exist, the mean rate of mobility observed with respect to any dimension will vary inversely with the mean costs associated with that sort of mobility. Where costs are low, such as in the case of inter-industry mobility, or change of workplace without change of residence, a large mean flow will be observed. Thus annual job changes are estimated as being in the order of ten million. Only a third of job changers remain within their industry.

For this reason it is difficult to establish a direct association between industrial rates of growth and industrial unemployment rates. Labour is not to any significant extent industry specific, so job losses in an industry in a region are quickly diffused to other local industries. Other things being equal, within a comparatively short space of time — a matter perhaps of not much more than a year — the only observable effect of the local decline of an industry, is an increase in unemployment in the local labour market generally. Some workers are quickly reabsorbed into jobs in other local industries; some of these jobs may be regarded as short-term expedients and when the workers leave them they are recorded as last employed in an industry other than that to which they

269

originally belonged. In addition, since there will be more applicants for any job in the local labour market, all workers becoming unemployed will expect to spend longer on the register, leading to higher rates being recorded in all industries.

Another important and related form of mobility which is comparatively low cost is the change of job location without change of residential location, what has been called elsewhere 'continuous' mobility (Cheshire (1979)). This form of mobility has important implications both for the definition of 'local' labour markets and for the interpretation of the causes of unemployment differences between localities.

As with mobility with respect to other dimensions of the labour market, net flows of continuous mobility will be to secure a net advantage. This implies that if a particular firm lays off workers, the effects will be transmitted along the various dimensions of the labour market. As has already been suggested unemployment rates in other industries in the local labour market will tend to rise. In addition, since the lost employment will have had a particular geographic location and excess demand will have consequently fallen at that point relative to surrounding areas, there will be at the margin a change of commuting patterns of workers. There will be a tendency for workers to look for new jobs within commuting distance of their homes and so, given the alteration in the spatial pattern of demand that has occurred, there will be a net flow of workers into surrounding labour markets thus leading to the diffusion of localized changes in demand to contiguous local labour markets. These surrounding local labour markets will now have changed levels of excess demand relative to those surrounding them; this in turn will lead to changes in relative levels of excess demand and so to unemployment rates in contiguous labour markets, now two stages removed from the original local market.

This chain interdependence between contiguous local labour markets has a number of consequences. Since continuous mobility — job relocation without residential relocation — is low cost, attempts to define local labour markets in terms of observed commuting patterns as in the concept of 'commuter/labour sheds' used by economic geographers[7] are unsatisfactory. Even as modified by Goodman (1970), definitions of local labour markets which rely on observed commuting patterns remain at best a working compromise though perhaps preferable to those which rely on arbitrary and absolute journey limits. It is possible to analyse changes in commuting patterns in comparative static terms but any observed commuting patterns, given the constant growth and decline of firms and the volume of job turn-over, are likely to be no more than cross sections of disequilibrium situations, not permanent labour market features.

A further implication is that localized changes in the level of excess demand for labour will be diffused relatively quickly throughout a set of contiguous local labour markets, such as a large urban area. Perhaps the findings of Metcalf and Richardson (1976) on the relationship between the number of redundancies in a borough over successive periods and the borough's unemployment rate at the end of the period, can best be explained in these terms. In their study of unemployment differences between London boroughs in 1971, they found that although there was the expected positive relationship between redundancies and borough unemployment rate for the year immediately preceding the census, over a longer period of five preceding years, not only was there not a positive association, there was a significant negative association.

The speed of local labour market adjustment via the process of chain interdependence described above will vary positively with the prevailing overall level of excess demand in the labour market, which determines turnover and the mean duration of unemployment. It will also be faster the greater the density of population and jobs, the larger are the intervening labour markets in the chain and the better are the transport and information links between them.

At the other extreme, spatially separated labour markets such as non-contiguous metropolitan areas — perhaps Merseyside and Birmingham — will have a substantial degree of independence from each other. This is because interaction between them is only via chain interdependence through a long series of relatively much smaller and imperfectly connected intermediate local labour markets or alternatively by movement requiring both job and residential relocation — migration; a form of labour market mobility involving considerable costs and uncertainties and thus substantial friction. It can be expected, therefore, that from the supply side at least, significant demand differences can persist over relatively long periods, perhaps for decades, between, say, regional labour markets. Over a single metropolitan area, in contrast, it is to be expected that demand differences will disappear quite rapidly.

The speed and extent of adjustment on the demand side depends on the view of the regional growth process that one takes. The arguments of writers such as Myrdal or Kaldor, suggest that on the demand side, adjustment reinforces initial destabilization. Abstracting from this problem, there is still some evidence that the volume of adjustment, at least as measured by the flow of industrial moves to Development Areas, is like inter-regional supply adjustment, a function of the over-all level of excess demand. Moore and Rhodes' results suggest that, given its range of variation, a low level of national male unemployment has been as influential in sending new jobs to the areas of high relative unemployment as any specifically designed policy instrument. When unemployment is low and workers are more prone to move to other regions, more employers are likely to be moving and are more likely to be seeking employees in the Development Areas.

These arguments suggest that the welfare implications of unemployment differences between contiguous sub-divisions of larger conurbations are not the same as those of differences between separated local labour markets. In the latter case, unemployment differences persist because of genuine differences in terms of prevailing levels of demand; though it should be added that because of the selective nature of migration, which has a strong bias in favour of the younger, better educated, fitter and more skilled members of an area's population, there will be interaction between persistent demand differences and the characteristics of an area's labour force. This in turn will affect its attractiveness to potential new employers. But persistent differences between areas in their levels of demand are only likely to be important as between free standing conurbations or towns or between broader areas such as regions, where spatial adjustment on the supply side of the labour market is costly and difficult and automatic adjustment on the demand side is at best uncertain. In cases such as this it seems reasonable to interpret the unemployment differences as signalling something about spatial variation in welfare.

However, the variation between these separated markets appears to be small compared to the variation in the distribution of personal incomes in society at large. Taking Department of Employment data for June 1978, and excluding dependent sub-labour markets, over-all unemployment rates varied from a low of 2.6 per cent in Cambridge to a high of 14.0 per cent in Hartlepool. But the figures mean that[8] an individual of given characteristics born in say Liverpool or Hartlepool has significantly lower lifetime expected earnings than a similar individual born in say Aylesbury or Cambridge. In addition the person born in the high unemployment town is substantially more likely to experience, and experience for a longer time, any additional non-monetary losses of welfare associated with being unemployed. In general, the evidence suggests that it is not the unemployed who migrate but these conclusions still hold, though somewhat less strongly, if they do. They still experience the substantial costs of movement and those of being unemployed prior to moving.

Most recent interest has been given to spatial welfare variations across conurbations: the Inner City Problem. It is true that Inner City problems are not seen to consist so predominently of spatial welfare variations as was the case with regional problems. This is perhaps partly because it is planners rather than economists who have been mainly involved and the problems have been identified consequently in environmental and planning terms as well as in economic/social terms. It is also true that unemployment variations have been less exclusively used as indicators of Inner City welfare inequality than was the case with regional problems. Nevertheless, unemployment problems and problems of 'Inner City Labour Markets' have been documented and presented as an important aspect of the Inner City Problem. The final reports of the Inner Area Study teams (Department of the Environment (1977c)), for example, all devote considerable attention to the labour markets and unemployment in their study areas. So, too, did the earlier Department of Environment publication (1973).

If the arguments of this paper are accepted, however, it is implausible to argue that high unemployment rates in inner areas result from a lower level of demand in such areas compared, say, to suburbs or satellite urban sub-centres. In as far as spatial demand differences can play a role, it would seem to be only as the outcome of relatively short-term adjustment processes. These, combined with a pattern of spatial change in demand within the conurbation that persists over a longer period, such as suburbanization of employment, might lead to significant but minor differences of demand. But given the arguments so far, one could not expect demand differences across a conurbation to play a more significant role than this and the significance of even these effects would be strictly a function of the size of the conurbation and the number of sub-markets (so the speed of adjustment) through which demand changes had to be transmitted by continuous mobility.

While the view of how local labour markets work proposed here would predict, therefore, that demand differences between spatially separated labour markets would persist over a relatively long period, it strongly suggests that this will not be the case when the labour markets concerned are contiguous. Most work on spatial unemployment differences seems to be consistent with this. Cheshire (1973) found that differences in demand deficiency unemployment were the most important source of regional variation in unemployment rates. Metcalf (1975) found that demand side variables were the most important explanatory variables in his study of unemployment differences between County Boroughs. It may be argued, however, that even so his results underestimated the true role of demand differences in explaining unemployment differences between free standing or separated local labour markets. First his data did not relate to such areas but to County Boroughs, many of which are in fact sub-areas of larger metropolitan labour markets. His two extreme observations, Solihull and Liverpool, reflect this. Solihull has many of the characteristics of a relatively prosperous suburban labour market; Liverpool many of the characteristics of an inner area labour market — the inner area of the Merseyside conurbation.

Metcalf's results may also have underestimated the role of demand differences because of what he called 'simultaneity bias'. Since migration is the main means of adjustment on the supply side to variations in the level of excess demand between free standing labour markets and there is evidence that patterns of relative excess demand between such labour markets have been relatively constant for some sixty years, we must expect to observe relatively stable spatial patterns of migration. Given the selective nature of migration we must expect the relatively stable patterns of demand variation to have produced systematic variation in area labour force characteristics. Thus to label these characteristics as 'supply' side factors is to overstate the role of pure supply variation since these differences may in large part reflect persistent demand differences. One may similarly argue that the proportion of overseas immigrants observed in a County Borough is chiefly a demand side variable.

These studies can be contrasted with those of Metcalf and Richardson (1976) McGregor (1977) or Evans and Russell (1976) of unemployment variation across urban areas, which found demand differences relatively unimportant and the major explanation to be in terms of characteristics of the labour force.

These differences between contiguous local labour markets reflect the determinants of residential location. As several urban economists have shown, economic theories of residential location are consistent with poor people living at high densities in older, less desirable and cheaper housing on expensive land in the inner parts of cities and richer people living at lower densities in newer houses on the periphery of urban areas, in the suburbs. There are exceptions to this of course: richer areas in central cities and fringe housing estates; but the general pattern has been long observed and recently documented. Evans' (1973) work for example, uses data for London in the 1960s.

Poverty is associated with a constellation of other factors; with low skill, less education, a low degree of physical fitness and a higher incidence of mental-illness and social maladjustment. It is associated with single parent families and, as we have seen, with unemployment itself. Many of these same factors, such as lower skill or education level or physical disability, are also directly associated with the incidence of unemployment. If over-all unemployment rises by 1 per cent, for example, the unemployment rate of the unskilled rises by 2.5 per cent. Thus, the most plausible explanation of variations in unemployment rates across urban areas is that unemployment rates are higher (lower) where the people who suffer a higher (lower) incidence of unemployment tend to live and

274

the same people and the areas in which they are concentrated will tend to exhibit a higher (lower) incidence of poverty.

If we want an explanation of the apparent intensification of Inner Areas problems, we should again look at essentially national factors, the change in the national economy. If nationally the level of demand falls as it has since 1966, then unemployment generally increases and the unemployment rates of those most prone to suffer unemployment, increase most. Thus the areas in which such people are disproportionately concentrated, the inner areas of larger cities, suffer an increase in their unemployment rates, both in absolute terms and relative to other areas.

Suburbanization of people and unemployment is a far from new phenomenon. It has been going on since the nineteenth century. Changes in the rate of suburbanization may have had some influence on the level of unemployment in the inner areas of larger cities but, given the mechanisms of adjustment via chain interdependence — continuous mobility — suggested in this paper, the influence would be small. Given the comparatively depressed conditions of the British economy there is no need to invoke suburbanization to explain high unemployment in the inner areas of larger cities in the 1970s. These factors may have been reinforced by policies designed to reinforce decentralization; but the role of such policies can be overstressed. They were in force long before 'inner area problems' became apparent and, the regional policies, at least, diverted development from prosperous areas generally, not from inner urban areas.

It has been argued that differences in unemployment between separated local labour markets, whether free standing towns or regions, do have implications for the spatial distribution of welfare, though any welfare disadvantages attached to being born or living in a particular place are probably relatively small compared to broader social inequality. When it comes to the purely spatial welfare consequences of unemployment differences within conurbations or metropolitan regions, then one may conclude that there is little, if any, problem. Unemployment rates differ across urban areas and so do incomes but there is no true sense in which such differences are problems of places to be relieved by spatially discriminating policies. It would rather seem that they are social problems and problems of people, the outcome of more general social inequality.

Incomes and opportunities are unequally distributed in Britain; so too is the incidence of unemployment which is heavily concentrated on particular groups including the less skilled, the less educated and the unfit. Such people are not scattered at random but are concentrated as has already been stated in certain areas, particularly in the inner areas of larger cities. Such areas necessarily

275

exhibit, therefore, concentrations of unemployment and of poverty but one cannot conclude from this that they are problems specifically of the areas themselves when the unemployment and poverty results from social inequality, at present compounded by low levels of demand for labour in the economy as a whole.

It follows from this that policies which treat the perceived inner area problem have little chance of success. There may, for some sorts of programmes be administrative convenience in isolating geographical concentration of unemployment but attempts to channel employment creation to central areas, quite apart from the possibility of imposing substantial costs on the employers concerned which would have to be offset in some way, can expect to have comparatively little effect on local unemployment. The additional demand is diffused via chain interdependence throughout the local sub-markets of the conurbation. If it were possible to reverse the spatial pattern of labour demand growth, in favour of central areas, over a significant period, the most favourable outcome would be that the lagged adjustment of demand would favour rather than discriminate against the residents of central areas *vis-à-vis* the suburbs. Programmes of assisted out-migration of the unskilled from inner areas can do little to change their employment prospects unless the movement is to a higher demand local market. It may well deprive them of cheaper housing and an environment with which they are familiar and to at least some extent can manipulate.

Except in so far as shortages of particular skills are constraints on output and employment, the only jobs retraining programmes create are for government instructors who are usually in possession of comparatively scarce skills anyway. It is likely therefore that such programmes have only a marginal affect on the amount of unemployment. They should properly be identified as redistributive programmes; the only programmes to have the specific effect of redistributing unemployment rather than income or wealth. We may assume the skills the trainees acquire are scarcer, on average, than those with which they start. Depending on the degree to which their new skill credentials are accepted by employers (and unions) the trainees will have improved probabilities of getting a job. But in so doing they will be competing against existing possessors of their newly acquired skills and so reducing the possibility of the already skilled finding jobs if they are, or they become, unemployed. It is true, of course, that the trainees disappear from the register of unemployment whilst actually being trained but the extent to which this reduces the number who are truly unemployed is open to question. If one follows the displacement effect through to the limit, therefore, the main effect of training schemes will be to redistribute unemployment. Since employers do not regard trainees and workers trained in traditional ways, as equally skilled, the degree to which training schemes achieve even a redistribution of unemployment is less than complete. Again one may argue that it would be more efficient and perhaps more equitable to give higher priority to raising the level of demand in the national economy and so increase incentives for employers to provide their own training of the skilled workers they actually need.

The conclusion therefore is that though unemployment rates may be a tolerable indicator of differences in welfare over time, they do not always indicate differences between places as such. Unemployment rate differences between separated labour markets indicate genuine spatial welfare differences but those between contiguous sub-divisions of larger conurbations reflect social inequality between people rather than places. This, in turn, suggests that whilst regional policies attempt to relieve a specific dimension of inequality there is a danger that inner area policies are directed towards a spatial dimension of social inequality that is illusory. The spatial dimension in this case is little more than a spatial transformation of social inequality.

Notes

[1] See, for example, the discussion in Brown (1972) or Moore and Rhodes (1973), (1976).

[2] Official policy was set out in 'Policy for the Inner Cities' (Department of the Environment (1977a)).

[3] See, for example, the reports of the Inner Area Studies (Department of the Environment (1977b), (1977c)).

[4] The precise definition of poverty changed but Atkinson concludes that the definition changes made little if any significant change to the basic patterns. One of the more important changes was in 1972 when the sick and unemployed excluded those off work for less than three months. In that year also, single parent families were not distinguished separately and there was a further unclassified group.

[5] Even this may not be true. There are considerable problems in conceptually defining 'unemployment' and it has recently been shown by Joshi (1978) that retirement is itself a cyclical variable. Changes in the number of pensioner households are thus a function, like unemployment, of labour market conditions.

[6] Given certain other fairly reasonable assumptions, it also implies that a given number of unemployed evenly distributed throughout a society has lower welfare costs than the same amount of unemployment unevenly distributed.

[7] See for example, Vance (1960).

[8] This assumes wage rates do not vary positively with unemployment; an assumption that would probably seem neutral to a British regional economist though a North American might expect wage rates to be a direct function of the local unemployment rate.

References

A. B. Atkinson, 1975, *The Economics of Inequality.*
Sir W. H. Beveridge, 1944, *Full Employment in a Free Society.*
A. J. Brown, 1972, *The Framework of Regional Economics in the UK.*

P. C. Cheshire, 1973, *Regional Unemployment Differences in Great Britain*, NIESR Regional Papers II.

P. C. Cheshire, 1979, 'Inner Areas as Spatial Labour Markets: a critique of the Inner Area Studies', *Urban Studies*, 16.

P. R. P. Coelho and M. A. Ghali, 1971, 'The End of the North-South Wage Differential', *American Economic Review*, LXI.

Department of the Environment, 1975, *Census Indicators of Urban Deprivation*, Working Note No 6.

Department of the Environment, 1977a, *Policy for the inner cities*, Cmnd 6845.

Department of the Environment, 1977b, Inner Area Studies: Liverpool, Birmingham and Lambeth, *Summaries of Consultants' Final Reports.*

Department of the Environment, 1977c, Inner Areas Studies Final Reports, *Change or Decay?* Hugh Wilson and Lewis Womesley; *Unequal City*, Lewelyn-Davies Weeks Forestier-Walker and Bar; and *Inner London*, Shankland Cox Partnership.

A. W. Evans, 1973, *The Economics of Residential Location.*

A. W. Evans with Lynne Russell, 1976, 'A Portrait of the London Labour Market', paper read at Inner City Employment Conference, September.

J. F. B. Goodman, 1970, 'The Definition of Local Labour Markets; some Empirical Problems', *British Journal of Industrial Relations*, VIII.

C. Holt, 1970, 'Job Search, Phillip's Wage Relation and Union Influence: Theory and Evidence' and 'How can the Phillip's Curve be Moved to Reduce both Inflation and Unemployment?', in E. S. Phelps, ed, *Microeconomic Foundation of Employment and Inflation Theory.*

H. Joshi, 1978, 'Secondary Workers in the Cycle; Married Women and Older Workers in Employment Fluctuations, Great Britain, 1961—74', *Government Economic Service Working Paper*, No 8.

M. L. Ladenson, 1973, 'The End of the North-South Wage Differential: Comment', *American Economic Review*, LXIII.

H. F. Lydall, 1955, 'The long-term trend in the size distribution of income', *Journal of the Royal Statistical Society*, Series A, 122.

A. McGregor, 1977, 'Intra-Urban Variations in Unemployment Duration', *Urban Studies*, 14.

D. Metcalf, 1975, 'Urban Unemployment in England', *Economic Journal*, 85.

D. Metcalf and R. Richardson, 1976, 'Unemployment in London', in G. D. N. Worswick, ed, *The Theory and Measurement of Involuntary Unemployment.*

B. Moore and J. Rhodes, 1973, 'Evaluating the effects of British Regional Economic Policy', *Economic Journal*, 83.

B. Moore and J. Rhodes, 1976, 'Regional Economic Policy and the Movement of Manufacturing Firms to Development Areas', *Economica*, NS 43.

W. Nordhaus and J. Tobin, 1972, 'Is Growth Obsolete?', in *Fiftieth Anniversary Colloquium*, National Bureau of Economic Research, New York.

M. Paglin, 1975, 'The Measurement and Trend of Inequality: A Basic Revision'. *American Economic Review*, LXV.

P. A. Samuelson, 1950, 'Evaluation of Real National Income', *Oxford Economic Papers* NS 2.

A. K. Sen, 1970, *Collective Choice and Social Welfare.*

Social Science Research Council, 1968, *Research on Poverty.*

R. M. Solow, 1960, 'Income inequality since the war', R. D. Freeman, ed, in *Postwar Economic trends in the United States*, New York.

R. Van Slooten and A. G. Coverdale, 1977, The Characteristics of Low Income Households', *Social Trends,* 8.

J. E. Vance, 1960, 'Labour Shed, Employment Fields and Dynamic Analysis in Urban Geography', *Economic Geography.*

15

Interstate disparities in per capita household
income in Australia 1953–54 to 1976–77

C. P. HARRIS and P. J. CROSSMAN

1. *Regional income studies in Australia*

Almost all studies of regional income in Australia have taken one of two basic
forms. Either the analyst has been concerned with one state of the Commonwealth, and in particular has attempted to estimate the gross regional product
of that state[1] or he has again been concerned with one particular state, but in
this instance the objective has been to disaggregate income data for that state on
a sub-state regional basis. In this second case most studies have taken household
income as the measure of economic activity.[2]

To date, however, little work has been done in Australia on the broader issue
of interregional differences in income and product on a nationwide basis.[3] It is
with this broader issue that this paper is concerned, the analysis being related to
features of interstate differences in per capita household income for the 24-year
period 1953–54 to 1976–77. The data used are the official estimates given by
the Australian Bureau of Statistics in its national production accounts.

In this study, therefore, the region is taken as the state, and the analysis
concentrates on interstate differences in the average per capita income of all
households in each state. No study is made of variations in incomes among
households either in individual states or in Australia as a whole.[4]

2. *Per capita household income by state*

Table 1 gives the household income per head of population for each state as
estimated by the Australian Bureau of Statistics in its national production
accounts. The statistics are on a current value basis, and the income of households in the two territories — Australian Capital Territory and Northern
Territory — are included respectively in the states of New South Wales and
South Australia.

Since this study is concerned with interstate income differentials, emphasis is
placed on the deviation between per capita incomes in each state and the average
per capita income for all states together. This deviation is shown in Table 2 by

T

computing the percentage difference in a given year between the per capita income for a state and the mean income for all states. The main features of these deviations are summarized below:

(i) In all years two states, New South Wales and Victoria, had incomes above the national average, per capita income in Victoria being the largest for all states in every year.

(ii) In the other four states per capita household income was below the national average in all years, although the relative position of the individual states was not constant over the period.

(iii) With respect to the relative position of the four states with incomes below the national average, the period can be divided into two equal 12-year sub-periods. In the first sub-period 1953—54 to 1964—65, South Australia had the highest per capita income of these four states, with the lowest income occurring in Tasmania or Western Australia. In the second sub-period 1965—66 to 1976—77 Western Australia had the highest per capita income in most years, while the lowest incomes were experienced equally by Tasmania and Queensland.

(iv) With respect to the two above-average income states, the major change was a tendency for the differentials between them to narrow, especially in the period after 1969—70.

(v) With respect to the four below-average states, the major changes were the substantial improvement in per capita income in Western Australia in the period since 1965—66, and the relative decline in South Australia from 1956—57 to 1972—73, followed by a significant recovery in that state in the next four years.

The second last column of Table 2 gives the coefficient of variation for the per capita incomes of all states in each of the 24 years, the coefficients being calculated from the current values of these incomes. The values of the coefficients fluctuated over the period, but until 1972—73 there was a certain regularity in the fluctuations which gave a steady long-term trend. In this period the values of the coefficient of variation ranged between 6.0 and 8.0, with peak values being 7.3 in 1957—58, 7.5 in 1960—61 and 1964—65, and 7.6 in 1966—67 and 1960—70. However, this tendency for constancy in the longer term was reversed from 1973—74, and over the last four years shown in Table 2 the values of the coefficient of variation fell to their lowest levels in the 24-year period.

This relative constancy of the coefficients of variation over most of the 24-year period occurred within a situation where money values rose substantially. Thus average per capita income for all states was over six times larger in

1976–77 than it was in 1953–54, but while the absolute dispersions of incomes among the states widened (eg, the standard deviation increased from $48 in 1953–54 to $238 in 1976–77), the relative dispersion, except in the last few years, remained comparatively constant. There has therefore been no ratchet effect with regard to relative interstate dispersion associated with the increasing money values of income per head.

Over the period being analysed there has been some tendency for the interstate dispersion of per capita incomes to fall in the downswings of economic activity and to rise in the upswings, with three of the five peak values of the coefficient of variation coinciding with the troughs of movements in economic activity, a correspondence which again occurred in the mid-1970s. However, in two instances in 1964–65 and 1969–70 peak values of the coefficient of variation were associated with peaks in the fluctuations of economic activity.[5]

An hypothesis that has been advanced regarding interregional dispersions of income per head is that as economic growth takes place over long periods the dispersion tends to be reduced, so that the series of regional incomes per head converge.[6] To test this hypothesis in Australia the per capita income estimates for each state have been converted to constant 1966–67 values, using the only available set of individual state price indexes.[7] The coefficients of variation have been again computed for these constant price estimates, and the values shown in the last column of Table 2. It is evident that deflating the per capita income series makes little significant difference to the measurement of relative dispersion, the coefficients of variation in the last two columns of Table 2 being remarkably similar.

For the period from 1953–54 to 1973–74 the Australian economy showed steady growth, with household income per head (in constant price terms) increasing at an average rate of 3.3 per cent per annum. Moreover, in this period the Australian economy experienced relatively full employment and mild inflation. The later years of the 1970s have seen a marked change in the Australian economy, with very high inflation, large and rising unemployment, and little economic growth. Thus in 1975–76 the increase in real income per head in all states was 2.0 per cent and this increase fell to 0.6 per cent in the following year. As noted above, while the Australian economy was growing the interstate dispersion of incomes per head showed a constant long-term trend, but once the economy entered a period of stagnation associated with both high inflation and unemployment the interstate disparities began to narrow. It appears that the convergence hypothesis requires reconsideration in a world economy where growth is no longer a common economic factor, and where inflation and high unemployment are common phenomena.

281

3. Types of household income

The preceding discussion has been concerned with total household income. However, it is possible to disaggregate household income into five types — wages and salaries, farm income, income of other unincorporated business enterprises, government transfers to persons, and all other income.[8] The relative importance of these types of income is shown in Table 3, which gives the minimum and maximum proportions of total household income in each state which each type of income contributed over the 24-year period.

Table 3 indicates that income from wages and salaries constituted from 57 to 70 per cent of total household income in the six states over the 24-year period, and, as Table 4 shows, income per head from wages and salaries was consistently above the average for the six states in New South Wales and Victoria, with Queensland generally having the lowest per capita income from this source. The relative dispersion of per capita wages and salaries among the states remained fairly constant over the period, generally corresponding to the movements in the relative dispersion of total income per head.

The major features of income from unincorporated farm enterprises (which constitute the major part of the farm sector in Australia) were the substantial decline in its relative importance over the period and the high degree of fluctuation of income of this type. In the mid-1950s farm income constituted about 12 per cent of total household income in all states, but by the mid-1970s this proportion had decreased to about 3 per cent. Table 5 shows the very wide interstate variation in per capita farm income over the period, with large and highly fluctuating values of the coefficient of variation. Queensland and South Australia tended to have farm incomes per head above the all-states averages over the period, and New South Wales and Tasmania below average incomes per head.

Income from non-farm business enterprises also declined in relative importance over the period, from a proportion of total income of 12 per cent at the beginning of the period to less than 8 per cent at the end of the period. Table 6 indicates that this kind of income has been relatively high in Victoria, and generally below-average in South Australia, Tasmania and New South Wales. The degree of interstate dispersion has not been particularly large, and except for a brief period at the end of the 1960s it remained generally constant.

Transfers from government have increased in importance over the period, nearly doubling their 1953—54 proportion of total income of 6 per cent.[9] Government transfers are more evenly distributed among the states than any other kind of income, and as Table 7 shows the degree of interstate dispersion has remained fairly constant over the period. Victoria and South Australia had below-average per capita incomes from this source over the period, with Western Australia also having this feature since 1966—67.

The final source of income consists mainly of property income (including dwelling rent), and for all states the proportion of total income from this source doubled over the period from 6 to 12 per cent. As Table 8 indicates there is a wide interstate dispersion of this type of income among the states, with Victoria having a significantly higher per capita income of this kind, and Queensland, Western Australia and Tasmania having relatively low incomes from this source.

4. *Summary*

This paper has been concerned with a preliminary analysis of interstate differences in per capita household income in Australia. This analysis has revealed the following features of the situation in Australia over the period 1953—54 to 1976—77.

(a) The two most populous states, Victoria and New South Wales, had incomes per head above the Australian average for all years, while the other four states had incomes per head below this average. Victoria had the highest income per head in all years, but the lowest income per head occurred in various years in Tasmania, Western Australia and Queensland.

(b) Except for the last four years of the period being studied, interstate disparities in income per head tended to remain fairly constant in relative terms, after allowing for somewhat regular cyclical variations, with disparities tending to widen in the upswings and narrow in the downswings. Thus, in a 20-year period of steady economic growth in Australia to 1972—73, the interstate dispersion of income per head, although increasing in absolute values as incomes rose in money terms, did not show any significant change in relative terms. However, in the last few years of the 1970s, in a period of economic stagnation, high inflation, and high and rising unemployment, incomes per head among the states have tended to converge to a much greater extent than occurred in any other contraction period of the cycle since 1953—54.

(c) When types of household income are considered separately, farm income and property and other income showed the greatest degree of dispersion among the states. However, while farm income declined in significance as a source of household income over the period being analysed, property and other income doubled its share of total household income. Farm income tended to be more important in the lower income states of Queensland, South Australia and Western Australia, while property and other income was relatively highest in Victoria, the state with the highest income per head.

283

(d) Income from salaries and wages was distributed among the states in a way not very different from that of total income, a feature that is not surprising given that wages and salaries comprised about two-thirds of total household income. However, it is noteworthy that New South Wales, the state with the second highest total income per head, had salaries and wages per head of population greater than those in Victoria, the state with the highest per capita income. The pre-eminent position of Victoria was due to its greater income from property, dwelling rent and non-farm unincorporated business enterprises. These relationships illustrate the general situation in Australia where New South Wales is regarded as being the most industrialized state, and Victoria as the centre of finance and the state with the greatest number of wealthy individuals.[10]

(e) Interstate disparities in wages and salaries reflect interstate differences in labour force participation rates, industry composition of the labour force, occupational mixes of the labour force, unemployment rates, and interregional variations in earnings in given industries and occupations. No attempt has been made in this paper to measure the relative importance of these factors in explaining these interstate disparities.

(f) Interstate differences in the amount of government transfers per head reflect disparities in the distribution of the aged, the young (children aged fifteen years and under), and in more recent years the unemployed. In this respect income from government transfers has been more significant over the period in New South Wales, Queensland and Tasmania than elsewhere, although the degree of dispersion of this type of income has not been large among the states.

Perhaps the most important conclusion to emerge from this analysis is that over a 24-year period of general economic expansion, the states of Australia have remained in two groups, the two states with above-average per capita incomes (Victoria and New South Wales) and the other four states with below-average incomes per head. However, among the four states with below-average incomes per head, there has been considerable change in their ordering over the 24-year period. The only significant convergence in incomes per head that occurred over the period took place in the last few years of the 1970s, years when Australia was experiencing economic stagnation, inflation, and high and rising unemployment. The statistics also indicate the significant decline in the importance of the farm sector in Australia over the last two decades, a change which has brought greater stability to the income per head series because of the highly volatile nature of farm income over time.

Notes

1 W. E. G. Salter, 'The Measurement of Factor Incomes Generated by Productive Sectors in Western Australia'. Research Studies in Community Income, (Nedlands, University of Western Australia, 1953); A. Kerr, 'Personal Income of Western Australia', *Department of Economics Publications*, Series A, no 1 (University of Western Australia, 1951); G. D. Snooks, 'Regional Estimates of Gross Domestic Product and Capital Formation: Western Australia 1923—24 to 1938—39', *Economic Record*, 1972, pp 536—53.

2 Colin Clark, 'Regional Production and Wealth', *Economic News*, Brisbane, Queensland Bureau of Industry, May 1949; R. W. Peters, 'The Measurement of Regional Income in Western Australia 1947—48 to 1950—51', Research Studies in Community Income, op cit. C. P. Harris, 'Interregional Variations in Levels and Growth of Per Capita Personal Income in Queensland 1953/54 and 1960/61' (PhD Thesis, School of Economic Studies, University of Leeds, 1967).

3 The most extensive study of this type has been that by M. T. Gordon, 'The Estimation and Analysis of the Household Sector Income of Australian Regions using Official Statistics as the Data Base, 1965 to 1972', (M Comm Thesis, University of Newcastle, 1978). In this study income estimates are given for sixty-four sub-state regions of Australia.

4 See N. Podder, 'Distribution of Household Income in Australia', *Economic Record*, 1962, pp 181—200, Australian Bureau of Statistics. Income Distribution 1973—74.

5 The cycles referred to are those given in E. A. Boehm, 'Recurring Periods of Plateau Slumps and Sluggish Recoveries in the Australian Economy 1950 to 1976'. *The Australian Economic Review*, 1977, pp 53—60. The peaks of economic fluctuations occurred in March 1955, July 1960, January 1965, February 1970, and August 1973. The troughs occurred in September 1956, July 1961, September 1966, February 1972, and (tentatively) November 1975.

6 J. G. Williamson, 'Regional Inquality and the Process of National Development: a Description of the Patterns', *Economic Development and Cultural Change*, Part II, 1965.

7 The current values of income per head for each state have been deflated by the consumer price index series for the capital city of that state.

8 All other income consists mainly of income from dwellings and other property income.

9 This increase in importance of government transfers represents he combined effects of changes in the age composition of the population (more older and younger persons), improved benefits paid to pensioners, and, in later years, a rising number of persons receiving unemployment benefits.

10 For example in 1973—74 nearly 18 per cent of families in Victoria had incomes greater than $13,000, compared with 16 per cent in New South Wales and 13 per cent in Queensland. The average for Australia was 16 per cent (Australian Bureau of Statistics, Income Distribution 1973—74).

TABLE 1

Per Capita Household Income Australia, by States 1953–54 to 1976–77

Year ended 30 June	Income per head of population $						
	New South Wales	Victoria	Queensland	South Australia	Western Australia	Tasmania	All states
1954	831	868	744	803	772	692	817
1955	863	922	793	846	774	752	857
1956	917	978	824	897	828	839	909
1957	970	1007	882	945	812	847	949
1958	947	997	839	877	779	852	923
1959	999	1041	902	945	830	848	974
1960	1097	1142	970	994	919	936	1063
1961	1143	1213	1011	1061	970	963	1118
1962	1173	1205	1015	1047	1000	1008	1129
1963	1222	1263	1088	1089	1033	1034	1182
1964	1321	1367	1198	1212	1117	1102	1284
1965	1424	1475	1249	1290	1171	1194	1374
1966	1436	1525	1286	1312	1339	1243	1414
1967	1577	1648	1345	1384	1419	1368	1525
1968	1623	1690	1392	1394	1543	1397	1571
1969	1795	1832	1531	1579	1722	1520	1731
1970	1938	1997	1618	1713	1769	1646	1863
1971	2144	2166	1784	1833	1989	1789	2053
1972	2352	2374	2051	2080	2162	1995	2261
1973	2647	2673	2364	2334	2333	2294	2546
1974	3201	3217	2821	2980	3098	2776	3106
1975	3891	3929	3475	3697	3634	3460	3786
1976	4489	4557	3947	4205	4263	3970	4363
1977	5120	5222	4565	4857	4765	4697	4995

Notes: 1. Australian Capital Territory is included in New South Wales and Northern Territory in South Australia.
2. Population is mean population at 31 December.
3. Incomes per head are given in current values.

Source: Australian National Accounts: National Income and Expenditure, Canberra, Australian Bureau of Statistics.

TABLE 2
State Per Capita Income Differentials 1953–54 to 1976–77

Year ended 30 June	% deviation of each state's per capita household income from average per capita income for all states (current values)						Coefficients of variation	
	New South Wales	Victoria	Queensland	South Australia	Western Australia	Tasmania	Current values	Constant values
1954	1.7	6.2	−8.9	−1.7	−5.5	−15.3	5.83	5.87
1955	0.7	7.6	−7.5	−1.3	−9.7	−12.3	6.00	6.81
1956	0.9	7.6	−9.4	−1.3	−8.9	−7.7	6.06	5.70
1957	2.2	6.1	−7.1	−0.4	−14.4	−10.7	6.19	5.86
1958	2.6	8.0	−9.1	−5.0	−15.6	−7.7	7.35	7.13
1959	2.6	6.9	−7.4	−3.0	−14.8	−12.9	6.75	6.62
1960	3.2	7.4	−8.7	−6.5	−13.5	−11.9	7.22	6.89
1961	2.2	8.5	−9.6	−5.1	−13.2	−13.9	7.52	6.93
1962	3.9	6.7	−10.1	−7.3	−11.4	−10.7	7.16	6.67
1963	3.4	6.9	−8.0	−7.9	−12.6	−12.5	7.00	6.55
1964	2.9	6.5	−6.7	−5.6	−13.0	−14.2	6.56	6.30
1965	3.6	7.4	−9.1	−6.1	−14.8	−13.1	7.55	7.10
1966	1.6	7.9	−9.1	−7.2	−5.3	−12.1	6.46	6.33
1967	3.4	8.1	−11.8	−9.2	−7.0	−10.3	7.57	7.57
1968	3.3	7.6	−11.4	−11.3	−1.8	−11.1	7.46	7.38
1969	3.7	5.8	−11.6	−8.8	−0.5	−12.2	6.80	6.54
1970	4.0	7.2	−13.2	−8.1	−5.0	−11.6	7.62	7.28
1971	4.4	5.5	−13.1	−10.7	−3.1	−12.9	7.62	7.20
1972	4.0	5.0	−9.3	−8.0	−4.4	−11.8	6.12	5.72
1973	4.0	5.0	−7.1	−8.3	−8.4	−9.9	5.97	5.35
1974	3.1	3.6	−9.2	−4.1	−0.3	−10.6	4.95	4.85
1975	2.8	3.8	−8.2	−2.4	−4.0	−8.6	4.58	4.20
1976	2.9	4.4	−9.5	−3.6	−2.3	−9.0	5.13	4.93
1977	2.5	4.5	−8.6	−2.8	−4.6	−6.0	4.76	4.78

Note: The coefficients of variation in the last column are computed from estimates of per capita incomes in constant (1966–67) dollars. The deflators used were the consumer price indexes for each of the six state capital cities.

Source: as for Table 1.

TABLE 3

Relative Importance of Types of Household Income 1953—54 to 1976—77

State	Type of income Minimum and maximum % of total income for period 1953—54 to 1976—77				
	Wages and salaries	Farm income	Other business income	Government transfers	All other income
New South Wales	63—71	2—12	6—12	6—12	7—12
Victoria	62—67	2—13	8—12	5—10	8—14
Queensland	57—65	6—17	8—12	7—12	5—11
South Australia	61—69	3—15	7—11	6—11	7—12
Western Australia	59—69	3—15	8—13	7—11	7—12
Tasmania	61—70	1—15	7—11	7—12	5—11
All states	62—69	3—13	7—12	6—11	7—12

Note: The first value in a column is the minimum percentage of total income for the 24 years and the second value is the maximum percentage.

Source: as for Table 1.

TABLE 4

State Per Capita Income Differentials: Wages and Salaries 1953–54 to 1976–77

Year ended 30 June	% deviation of each state's per capita wages and salaries from average per capita wages and salaries for all states (current values)						Coefficient of variation
	New South Wales	Victoria	Queensland	South Australia	Western Australia	Tasmania	
1954	3.9	5.4	−12.9	−3.8	−5.6	−10.1	6.71
1955	4.1	5.4	−12.9	−2.7	−6.8	−11.6	6.86
1956	5.3	5.4	−14.5	−2.4	−9.8	−11.2	7.81
1957	6.2	5.1	−14.1	−4.7	−12.4	−9.6	8.17
1958	6.7	5.6	−14.9	−6.6	−12.3	−10.4	8.74
1959	6.2	6.1	−13.7	−6.3	−14.2	−11.5	8.63
1960	6.8	5.7	−14.6	−5.3	−15.4	−12.2	9.03
1961	8.4	4.3	−15.2	−7.6	−14.9	−13.8	9.63
1962	8.8	4.1	−15.6	−8.4	−14.2	−10.7	9.69
1963	8.2	4.8	−15.3	−8.5	−14.4	−12.2	9.63
1964	8.2	4.5	−14.7	−8.4	−14.5	−12.3	9.44
1965	8.6	4.8	−14.5	−7.9	−16.8	−14.1	9.89
1966	7.9	4.7	−14.8	−9.2	−11.5	−12.4	9.16
1967	8.4	6.1	−13.7	−11.4	−11.7	−8.1	9.41
1968	8.2	5.9	−17.9	−10.0	−9.5	−8.8	10.03
1969	9.0	4.9	−18.1	−10.1	−9.1	−10.7	10.24
1970	8.4	4.7	−18.1	−9.0	−7.3	−10.3	9.78
1971	8.7	3.0	−17.5	−10.7	−7.4	−11.4	9.77
1972	8.9	2.5	−15.3	−9.5	−6.1	−11.3	9.02
1973	7.9	3.6	−12.7	−9.0	−11.3	−9.0	8.46
1974	7.8	3.6	−13.3	−7.2	−10.2	−10.5	8.32
1975	6.8	3.0	−13.6	−4.3	−8.0	−7.4	7.50
1976	6.0	4.0	−14.5	−4.2	−4.9	−8.3	7.43
1977	5.3	3.8	−14.3	−2.6	−4.1	−6.0	6.95

Source: as for Table 1.

289

TABLE 5

State Per Capita Income Differentials: Farm Income 1953–54 to 1976–77

Year ended 30 June	New South Wales	Victoria	Queensland	South Australia	Western Australia	Tasmania	Coefficient of variation
	% deviation of each state's per capita farm income from average per capita farm income for all states (current values)						
1954	−7.1	6.2	16.7	10.0	−15.5	−34.6	11.77
1955	−19.9	20.7	30.1	10.6	−44.4	−1.6	23.50
1956	−24.9	16.4	26.7	10.2	−12.3	31.3	21.64
1957	−14.0	3.6	37.4	24.1	−40.3	−10.9	21.36
1958	−24.8	24.9	41.6	0.2	−63.7	26.3	31.11
1959	−15.3	9.2	34.1	16.0	−34.1	−21.9	20.11
1960	−8.2	13.4	31.5	−33.9	−22.1	−12.6	19.19
1961	−25.2	23.3	27.9	11.3	−18.5	−24.1	23.65
1962	−13.1	6.4	27.6	−5.2	−1.0	−7.3	13.83
1963	−13.9	4.6	43.7	−8.6	−14.4	−15.8	19.59
1964	−14.7	2.8	39.5	13.1	−20.5	−24.0	19.33
1965	−12.9	11.2	19.7	11.3	−28.5	−5.7	15.02
1966	−47.2	21.3	38.9	11.5	69.4	−3.4	39.29
1967	−18.5	2.5	35.9	12.8	11.7	−13.3	18.54
1968	−43.1	5.7	84.4	−24.4	65.0	−15.4	46.22
1969	−30.9	−3.2	50.8	19.8	45.5	−19.1	30.80
1970	−30.4	22.2	47.8	16.9	−42.7	−2.0	31.38
1971	−48.7	23.3	48.5	4.2	49.5	−3.9	39.74
1972	−54.8	19.8	70.6	39.3	16.0	−13.4	46.16
1973	−24.5	−4.1	50.4	14.3	19.6	−8.6	25.64
1974	−25.4	−23.5	13.8	43.1	123.4	−21.2	43.13
1975	−41.7	−33.6	88.8	49.9	94.6	−57.9	56.75
1976	−31.3	−44.2	78.5	21.3	134.0	−59.6	58.93
1977	−26.9	−37.6	87.1	15.5	65.1	−8.3	46.69

Source: as for Table 1.

TABLE 6

State Per Capita Income Differentials: Income from Non-Farm Unincorporated Enterprises 1953–54 to 1976–77

% deviation of each state's per capita income from non-farm unincorporated enterprises from average per capita income of this type for all states (current values)

Year ended 30 June	New South Wales	Victoria	Queensland	South Australia	Western Australia	Tasmania	Coefficient of variation
1954	-0.1	8.9	-7.4	-9.2	3.7	-21.5	7.36
1955	-0.7	9.2	-6.0	-7.4	-0.7	-17.6	6.65
1956	-1.2	9.7	-5.1	-6.2	-6.0	-12.2	6.41
1957	-1.8	10.2	-3.8	-5.0	-10.6	-9.1	6.71
1958	-0.6	10.9	-5.0	-6.9	-12.6	-13.2	7.63
1959	-1.0	9.7	-3.8	-5.1	-10.7	-14.0	6.77
1960	-0.7	9.5	-5.5	-5.6	-7.6	-14.1	6.58
1961	-0.8	8.9	-3.7	-9.3	-5.7	-11.7	6.27
1962	-1.0	8.4	-3.2	-10.2	-2.0	-11.5	6.01
1963	-1.5	7.9	-2.4	-9.9	1.4	-13.8	5.88
1964	-2.8	8.0	0.8	-8.9	1.0	-15.5	6.03
1965	-3.8	7.8	1.8	-10.8	6.9	-13.6	6.60
1966	-4.4	9.0	0.6	-8.8	4.6	-12.5	6.63
1967	-5.7	11.4	2.6	-16.1	15.5	-10.5	9.80
1968	-3.5	6.2	-1.5	-20.5	30.2	-12.9	11.48
1969	-3.7	5.6	-4.2	-18.3	35.3	-15.4	12.38
1970	-4.7	8.8	-6.4	-14.2	28.6	-18.3	11.40
1971	-2.3	8.6	-3.6	-17.5	12.2	-21.8	8.99
1972	-3.4	6.8	6.2	-12.9	3.6	-16.0	6.91
1973	-4.9	8.8	12.3	-15.8	-4.3	-16.0	9.27
1974	-6.8	10.4	8.2	-12.0	-0.3	-11.1	8.60
1975	-8.5	12.0	4.6	-8.8	1.7	-3.2	8.74
1976	-8.2	12.2	4.2	-8.4	0.4	-3.6	8.68
1977	-8.1	12.5	4.1	-8.8	-0.6	-3.3	8.74

Source: as for Table 1.

TABLE 7

State Per Capita Income Differentials: Government Transfers 1953–54 to 1976–77

% deviation of each state's per capita transfer income from average per capita transfer income for all states (current values)

Year ended 30 June	New South Wales	Victoria	Queensland	South Australia	Western Australia	Tasmania	Coefficient of variation
1954	4.1	-6.0	-1.8	-2.0	2.8	8.0	4.46
1955	4.7	-7.4	-0.8	-0.9	3.0	6.9	5.09
1956	3.9	-5.4	0.2	-4.1	2.2	7.1	4.16
1957	3.0	-6.0	1.6	-1.6	5.3	2.7	4.03
1958	4.0	-7.5	3.2	-3.0	4.7	7.0	5.20
1959	4.0	-6.7	1.2	-3.4	7.0	1.1	4.80
1960	3.5	-6.6	1.5	-2.7	7.3	2.0	4.68
1961	1.6	-6.8	4.6	-0.9	7.8	3.5	4.66
1962	2.3	-6.4	6.5	-3.4	4.6	-1.2	4.70
1963	2.8	-6.9	6.4	-4.9	3.3	4.3	5.07
1964	0.6	-7.0	13.1	-5.7	5.7	-2.3	6.66
1965	0.8	-5.6	11.6	-7.3	3.0	2.5	5.86
1966	2.6	-5.8	6.8	-5.9	1.3	4.2	4.78
1967	2.1	-3.2	8.0	-5.2	-0.3	4.4	4.10
1968	2.3	-3.3	4.6	-5.3	-2.3	2.5	3.40
1969	2.2	-4.0	5.1	-4.8	-2.6	5.4	3.70
1970	2.5	-3.9	5.2	-4.4	-5.0	5.4	3.91
1971	1.9	-5.8	4.8	-1.9	-2.9	4.3	3.94
1972	1.9	-4.2	4.0	-1.7	-2.9	8.8	3.41
1973	2.8	-3.8	1.4	-3.9	-1.5	8.4	3.30
1974	2.0	-4.0	4.2	-2.0	-4.0	7.3	3.42
1975	3.7	-3.4	0.0	-2.2	-6.0	8.4	3.73
1976	6.1	-3.1	-0.9	-5.3	-10.3	3.6	5.34
1977	6.1	-4.5	1.0	-5.5	-9.0	4.1	5.42

Source: as for Table 1.

TABLE 8

State Per Capita Income Differentials:
All Other Household Income 1953–54 to 1976–77

% deviation of each state's per capita all other income from average per capita income of this type for all states (current values)

Year ended 30 June	New South Wales	Victoria	Queensland	South Australia	Western Australia	Tasmania	Coefficient of variation
1954	0.2	21.1	−32.1	7.8	−8.6	−35.9	18.10
1955	1.3	17.0	−24.7	2.7	−7.5	−40.9	15.19
1956	0.3	21.8	−29.9	1.8	−10.4	−37.4	17.82
1957	−0.8	22.5	−28.7	5.1	−14.0	−32.9	17.68
1958	−0.8	20.7	−25.7	3.6	−18.3	−22.5	16.04
1959	−1.0	18.4	−19.3	3.6	−22.3	−24.3	14.33
1960	−4.7	24.4	−15.9	9.2	−13.4	−15.7	15.49
1961	−11.7	35.1	−21.4	−1.5	−20.9	−20.2	22.49
1962	−7.8	30.8	−22.1	−1.7	−22.3	−19.2	20.12
1963	−7.1	29.2	−18.3	−3.8	−24.3	−22.1	19.10
1964	−5.8	28.0	−20.4	−2.5	−23.2	−23.1	18.65
1965	−4.5	27.5	−22.0	−3.8	−23.2	−22.4	18.54
1966	−4.4	27.1	−20.2	−5.5	−22.7	−25.3	18.19
1967	−2.6	27.3	−21.4	−8.4	−14.6	−30.3	17.97
1968	−1.6	25.3	−26.2	−10.2	−6.8	−28.9	17.83
1969	−1.8	21.9	−22.3	−10.9	−2.8	−25.0	15.40
1970	−0.1	20.8	−24.7	−9.6	−3.0	−27.7	15.52
1971	2.3	18.4	−23.9	−16.0	−5.5	−27.4	15.12
1972	2.5	18.1	−20.4	−15.6	−7.5	−23.1	14.02
1973	1.4	19.1	−19.8	−12.2	−11.2	−22.7	14.06
1974	0.2	19.5	−19.6	−9.4	−12.3	−17.2	13.79
1975	−0.4	20.3	−22.1	−3.7	−14.1	−16.3	14.50
1976	−1.9	22.0	−20.7	−2.0	−17.5	−14.6	15.15
1977	−2.0	21.7	−17.0	−1.6	−22.3	−16.0	14.89

Source: as for Table 1.

Arthur Joseph Brown: a professional biography and a bibliography

Compiled by M. W. BERESFORD

1914	Born 8 August, Alderley Edge, Cheshire.
1936	1st class Honours, PPE, Oxford University.
1937—40	Lecturer in Economics, Hertford College, Oxford.
1937—46	Fellowship, All Souls College, Oxford.
1940—43	Foreign Research and Press Service.
1943—45	Foreign Office, Research Department.
1945—47	Economic Section, Offices of the Cabinet.
1947—65	Head of the Department of Economics, University of Leeds.
1947—79	Professor of Economics, University of Leeds.
1950	Visiting Professor, Columbia University, City of New York.
1950—68 (and 1974)	Council, Royal Economic Society.
1958	President, Section F, British Association for the Advancement of Science.
1960	Member, East African Economic and Fiscal Commission.
1961—62	United Nations Consultative Group on Economic and Social Consequences of Disarmament.
1962	First Secretary of State's Advisory Group on Central Africa.
1963	Visiting Professor, Australian National University.
1966—72	Director, Regional Economics Project, National Institute of Economic and Social Research.
1967—69	Hunt Committee on Intermediate Areas.
1969—78	University Grants Committee.
1972	FBA.
1974	CBE.
1975	Hon DLitt, University of Bradford.
1975—77	Pro-Vice-Chancellor, University of Leeds.
1976—78	President, Royal Economic Society.
1978	Hon LlD, University of Aberdeen.
1979	Hon DLitt, University of Sheffield.
1979	Hon DLitt, University of Kent at Canterbury.

PUBLICATIONS*

The articles in the *Bulletin of International News* together with a number of the reviews in *International Affairs* appeared over the initials *A.J.B.*

1938

'The Liquidity Preference Schedules of the London Clearing Banks', *Oxford Economic Papers*, NS no 1, 49–82.

1939

'Interest, Prices and the Demand Schedule for Idle Money, ibid, no 2, 46–9; reprinted in T. Wilson and P. W. S. Andrews, eds, *Oxford Studies in the Price Mechanism*, Oxford University Press, 1951, ch I (iv).

'Germany's Mineral Supplies, II — Oil', *Bulletin of International News*, **xvi**, 1307–11.

'Germany's Mineral Supplies, III — Iron, Nickel and Copper', ibid, 1366–70.

'Finance and Man Power in the War', ibid, 1437–9.

1940

'The Use of Advisory Bodies by the Treasury', in R. V. Vernon and N. Mansergh, eds, *Advisory Bodies*, Allen and Unwin, 86–126.

[with M.B.] 'Sweden and the Russo-Finnish War', *Bulletin of International News*, **xvii**, 3–12.

'Empire Trade in the War', ibid, 12–15.

'Finance and Man Power in the War, II — Germany', ibid, 63–5.

[with M.B.] 'The Middle East, II — The Economic Position', ibid, 214–20.

'Finance and Man Power in the War, III — France', ibid, 275–80.

'Notes on the Map (of Finland)', ibid, 346–8.

'Finance and Man Power in the War, IV — Germany and the Allies', ibid, 403–9.

'Franco-British Economic and Political Collaboration, II', ibid, 529–33.

'World Sources of Petroleum', ibid, 769–76.

'The Military Strength of the United States', ibid, 1004–10.

'The Economic Prospects of Latin America', ibid, 1148–52 and 1211–15.

'Europe's Liquid Fuel Supplies', ibid, 1267–74.

[with M.B.] 'The Invasion of Greece', ibid, 1407–14.

[with D.P.E.] 'The Delhi Conference, II — British Resources East of Suez', ibid, 1475–8.

*Place of publication of books is London unless otherwise stated.

'German Exploitation of Occupied Countries', ibid, 1607–13 and 1671–8.

Review of L. Baudin, *Free Trade and Peace* and H. J. Tasca, *World Trading Systems: International Affairs Review Supplement*, **xix**, 33.

Of J. M. Keynes, *How to Pay for the War* and *Round Table Pamphlets: 1:* ibid, 34–6.

Of C. P. Mayhew, *Planned Investment:* ibid, 38.

1941

The Arsenal of Democracy, Oxford University Press, pp 32.

'Europe under Hitler, in Prospect and Perspective', *Bulletin of International News*, **xviii**, 1–32.

'The German New Order in Europe', ibid, 67–73.

'The War Finance of the Dominions', ibid, 127–31.

'Financing of the United States Defence Programme', ibid, 197–201.

'Japan's Strength and Weakness', ibid, 255–9.

'American Aid to Britain', ibid, 319–24.

'Latin America, I — Economic Problems and Western Hemisphere Defence', ibid, 399–408.

'Degrees of Regional and National Self-sufficiency', ibid, 475–9.

'The French Occupation Costs', ibid, 622–4.

'Canada's War Effort', ibid, 679–84.

'A Comparison of War Efforts, I — Great Britain 1914–18 and To-day', ibid, 743–8.

'A Comparison of War Efforts, II — Germany's War Expenditure', ibid, 807–13.

'A Comparison of War Efforts, III — Germany and Britain', ibid, 943–7.

'Russian Income and Defence Expenditure', ibid, 1067–70.

'The Shipping Problem and American Aid', ibid, 1123–7.

'Economic Factors Connected with the Collapse of France', ibid, 1270–5.

'American Aircraft Production', ibid, 1735–8.

'Italy's Economic Weakness, ibid, 1802–6.

'Prices in Some German-occupied Countries', ibid, 1870–2.

'The German ''New Order'' Re-appears', ibid, 1912–14.

'The War Industries of the Belligerents', ibid, 1955–8.

Review of A. Reithinger, *Why France Lost the War: International Affairs Review Supplement*, **xix**, 189.

Of P. Einzig, *Europe in Chains:* ibid, 191.

Of A. W. Zelomek, *This Peculiar War* and J. K. Horsefield, *The Real Cost of the War:* ibid, 192–3.

Of *Studies in American Foreign Relations:* ibid, 257—8.
Of *Europe's Trade* and P. Einzig, *Hitler's 'New Order' in Europe:* ibid, 266.

1942

'Trade Balances and Exchange Stability', *Oxford Economic Papers*, NS no 6, 57—75; reprinted in T. Wilson and P. W. S. Andrews, op cit, ch II(i).
'The Location of German War Industry', *Bulletin of International News*, **xix**, 5—9.
'The United States War Economy', ibid, 43—7 and 83—7.
'The Co-ordination of British and U.S. Supplies', ibid, 131—5.
'Vital Statistics for Enemy-occupied Europe', ibid, 179—82.
'British Post-war Economic Problems', ibid, 227—30, 276—83 and 372—6.
'British Imports before and after the War', ibid, 421—5.
'Industrialisation Overseas', ibid, 473—5, 509—12, 561—4, and 606—10.
'Industrialization and Overseas Trade', ibid, 692—5.
'Industrialization and International Trade', ibid, 692—5, 773—8 and 831—5.
'Pre-war Armament Expenditure', ibid, 925—9.
'Unemployment and National Specialisation', ibid, 969—72.
'The Prospects of International Migration', ibid, 1018—20 and 1121—3.
Review of *World Economic Survey, 1939—41: Economic Journal*, **lii**, 234—7.
Of J. B. Condliffe, *The Reconstruction of World Trade:* ibid, 238—9.
Of M. S. Gordon, *Barriers to World Trade:* ibid, 239—40.

1943

Industrialization and Trade. The Changing World Pattern and the Problem of Britain, Royal Institute of International Affairs, pp 71.
'The Prospects of International Migration', *Bulletin of International News*, **xx**, 8—13.
'Some Implications of Synthetic Rubber', ibid, 194—200.
'Some Reflections on Plastics', ibid, 567—70 and 651—4.
'The Background of the Currency Proposals', ibid, 647—51, 731—7 and 767—73.
'Some Aspects of the Pattern of World Trade', ibid, 855—60.
'Further Aspects of the Pattern of World Trade', ibid, 906—10.
'Some Reflections on Industrial Efficiency', ibid, 983—89.
'Economic War Efforts, I — The U.K. and U.S.A.', ibid, 1113—8.

1944

'Economic War Efforts', ibid, **xxi**, 101—8, 144—7, 181—4, 298—302, and 387—91.

'The Significance of Full Employment Policy', ibid, 461—5, 549—53 and 666—71.

'A Note on South African Income and War Expenditure', ibid, 625—6.

'A Sketch of the European Economy', ibid, 757—61, 805—10, 850—5, and 950—4.

'A Sketch of the Sterling Area', ibid, 1000—5.

Review of *World Trade, Report to the British National Committee of the International Chamber of Commerce: International Affairs*, **xx**, 563.

1945

'War-time Inflation', *Bulletin of International News*, **xxii**, 11—15 and 102—9.

'The Great Industrial Exporters', ibid, 209—18 and 305—10.

'Some Trends in World Population', ibid, 392—9.

'Coal and Cotton', ibid, 474—81.

'Population Trends and Power', *International Affairs*, **xxi**, 79—86.

Review of E. R. Stettinus, *Lend-Lease:* ibid, 269—70.

Of J. E. Meade and R. Stone, *National Income and Expenditure:* ibid, 401.

1947

Applied Economics. Aspects of the World Economy in War and Peace, Allen and Unwin, pp 252; New York, Rinehart, 1948.

Reviews, of A. O. Hirschmann, *National Power and the Structure of Foreign Trade: International Affairs*, **xxiii**, 91—2.

Of F. Hilgerdt, *Industrialization and Foreign Trade:* ibid, 92—3.

Of A. G. B. Fisher, *International Implications of Full Employment in Great Britain: Economic Journal*, **lvii**, 116—17.

1948

'Economic Problems of a Tropical Dependency', in P. A. Bower, A. J. Brown *et al, Mining, Commerce and Finance in Nigeria*, 349—57.

'Economics, Scientific and Otherwise', *Nature*, **clxiv**, 404—5.

'Some Trends in World Trade', *Journal of the Textile Institute*, **xxxix**, 438—48.

Review of J. J. Jewkes, *Ordeal by Planning: International Affairs*, **xxiv**, 580—1.

Of A. E. Kahn, *Great Britain in the World Economy: Economic Journal*, **lviii**, 256—8.

1949

The American Economy and World Trade, Institute of Bankers, pp 18.

'International Equilibrium and National Sovereignty under Full Employment', *International Affairs*, **xxv**, 434—42.

'Introductory Survey', *British Institute of Management Conference Series*, **i**, 3—8.
Review of S. E. Harris, *The New Economics: International Affairs*, **xxv**, 200.
Of N. S. Buchanan and F. A. Lutz, *Rebuilding the World Economy:* ibid, 207.
Of M. A. Heilperin, *The Trade of Nations:* ibid, 201—2.
Of M. A. Heilperin, *The Trade of Nations: Economic Journal*, **lix**, 98—100.
Of L. S. Amery, *The Awakening:* ibid, 101—2.

1950

'Official Papers. Problems of Under-developed Countries', *Economic Journal*, **lx**, 631—3.
Reviews of F. D. Graham, *The Theory of International Values* and S. B. Rangnekar, ed, *Imperfect Competition in International Trade: International Affairs*, **xxvi**, 101—2.
Of W. A. Lewis, *Economic Survey, 1919—39* and A. L. Meyers *Modern Economic Problems:* ibid, 103.
Of W. A. Lewis, *The Principles of Economic Planning* and E. F. M. Durbin, *Problems of Economic Planning:* ibid, **xxvi**, 245—6.

1951

'The Fundamental Elasticities in International Trade' in T. Wilson and P. W. S. Andrews, eds, *Oxford Studies in the Price Mechanism*, Oxford University Press, ch II(ii).
'Some Aspects of International Trade Changes since Devaluation', *Yorkshire Bulletin of Economic and Social Research*, **iii**, 151—63.
Reviews of R. G. Hawtrey, *The Balance of Payments and the Standard of Living: International Affairs*, **xxvii**, 353—4.
Of W. Euchen, *The Foundations of Economics:* ibid, 488—9.

1952

'Some Reflections on the Cost of Economic Energy', *Transactions of the Manchester Statistical Society, 1952*, 1—19; reprinted, Manchester.
Review of T. Wilson, *Modern Capitalism and Economic Progress: Economica*, NS, **xix**, 87—9.
Of C. Clark, *Conditions of Economic Progress: International Affairs*, **xxviii**, 79—80.
Of K. E. Boulding, *A Reconstruction of Economics:* ibid, 215.
Of F. W. Paish, *The Post-War Financial Problem:* ibid, 215—16.
Of J. E. Meade, *The Theory of International Economic Policy, vol. 1:* ibid, 369—70.

1953

'Should Commodity Prices be Stabilised?', *District Bank Review*, December 1953, 3—17.

Review of W. Isard and V. Whitney, *Atomic Power: Manchester Guardian*, 6 January 1953.

1955

The Great Inflation, 1939—1951, Oxford University Press, pp xii + 321.

Review of B. Hansen, *A Study in the Theory of Inflation: Economica*, **xxii**, 80—2.

Of A. H. Hansen and R. V. Clerence, eds, *Readings in Business Cycles and National Income:* ibid, 180—1.

Of R. Harrod, *The Dollar:* ibid, 181—2.

Of W. Diebold, *Trade and Payments: International Affairs*, **xxxi**, 87.

Of United Nations, *Government Policies Concerning Unemployment:* ibid, 88.

1956

'Putting the Brake on Inflation', ibid, 5 January 1956.

'How to Cure Inflation', *The Listener*, 14 June 1956.

1957

'Professor Leontief on the Pattern of World Trade', *Yorkshire Bulletin of Economic & Social Research*, **ix**, 63—75.

Review of J. E. Meade, *The Theory of International Economic Policy, vol. 2: International Affairs*, **xxxiii**, 220—1.

Of L. Robbins, *The Economist at War:* ibid, 222.

1958

'Inflation and the British Economy', *Economic Journal*, **lxviii**, 449—63.

Review of J. Gabillard, *La Fin de l'inflation* and J. Le Bourua, *L'Inflation Française d'Après-guerre, 1945—49:* ibid, 192—4.

1959

Introduction to the World Economy, Allen and Unwin, pp 212.

'Factor Supplies and Comparative Costs in Underdeveloped Countries', *Pakistani Economic Journal*, **ix**, 89—94.

'L. G. Johnson', *University of Leeds Review*, **vi**, 346—7.

Review of M. Friedman, ed, *Studies in the Quantity Theory of Money: Economic Journal*, **lxix**, 773—5.

1960

'Dollars and Crises', *Economic History Review*, 2nd ser, **xii**, 283–91.

Impact of Fluctuations in Economic Activity in Industrial Countries on International Commodity Trade, United Nations, New York, pp 90.

Committee [Radcliffe] on the Working of the Monetary System, *Principal Memoranda of Evidence*, **iii**, 48–50, HMSO.

ibid, *Minutes of Evidence*, **iii**, 591–5.

Review of J. T. Dunlop, ed, *The Theory of Wage Determination: Economica*, NS, **xxvii**, 78–80.

1961

[with others] *East Africa, Report of the Economic and Fiscal Commission* [Raisman Commission]. Cmnd 1279 (PP 1960–1, **xi**, 733–836), HMSO.

'Arnold Nixon Shimmin, 1889–1961', *University of Leeds Review*, **vii**, 276–8.

'Economic Separatism versus a Common Market', *Yorkshire Bulletin of Economic and Social Research*, **xiii**, 33–40 and 88–96.

'The Present Pattern of World Trade and Payments', *Fourth International Banking Summer School*, 24–41.

Review of J. R. Hicks, *Essays in World Economics: Economic History Review*, 2nd ser, **xiii**, 303.

Of R. C. O. Matthews, *The Trade Cycle: Economic Journal*, **lxxi**, 613–15.

Of P. L. Yates, *Forty Years of Foreign Trade: Economica*, NS, **xxviii**, 445–7.

1962

The Economics of Disarmament, United Nations Association, pp 16.

[with others] *Economic and Social Consequences of Disarmament*, United Nations, Department of Economic & Social Affairs, *Report of the Secretary General Transmitting the study of his consultative group*, New York City, pp ix + 66.

1963

Review of H. G. Johnson, *International Trade and Economic Growth: Economic Journal*, **lxxiii**, 492–5.

1964

'Australian Interstate Trade and Payments', *The Economic Record*, **xl**, 363–74.

Economic Consequences of Disarmament, David Davies Memorial Institute of International Studies, pp 20.

1965

'Britain and the World Economy', *Yorkshire Bulletin*, **xvii**, 46–60.

Introduction to the World Economy, 2nd ed, Allen and Unwin, pp 214.

1966

Review of J. Pedersen and K. Laursen, *The German Inflation, 1918–23: Economica*, NS, **xxxiii**, 362–4.

1967

[with J. K. Bowers and H. Lind] 'The "Green Paper" on the Development Areas', *National Institute Economic Review*, no 40, 26–33.

'What is the Leeds Region', in M. W. Beresford and G. R. J. Jones, eds, *Leeds and Its Region*, British Association for the Advancement of Science, Leeds, 200–14.

1968

[with J. K. Bowers, P. C. Cheshire, H. G. Lind, and V. H. Woodward] 'Regional Policy', *National Institute Economic Review*, no 46, 42–51.

1969

[with J. A. Hunt and others] *The Intermediate Areas. Report of a Committee under the Chairmanship of Sir Joseph Hunt.* Cmnd 3998, PP 256, HMSO (and *Note of Dissent by Prof. A. J. Brown*, 155–65; 'Impact of Investment Grants on Capital Intensive Industry', Appendix J, 237–8).

[with V. H. Woodward] 'Regional social accounts for the United Kingdom', *Review of Income and Wealth*, ser 15, 335–47.

'Some English thoughts on the Scottish economy', *Scottish Journal of Political Economy*, **xvi**, 233–47.

'Surveys in Applied Economics: regional economics', *Economic Journal*, **lxviii**, 761–96, reprinted as: 'Regional Economics, with special reference to the United Kingdom', Royal Economic Society and Social Science Research Council, *Surveys of Applied Economics*, Macmillan, 1–44.

1970

'Criteria of Regional Economic Policy', *Yorkshire Bulletin*, **xxii**, 45–53.

'Leonard George Johnson', *University of Leeds Review*, **xiii**, 93–4.

Review of E. A. G. Robinson, ed, *Backward Areas in Advanced Countries: Economic Journal*, **lxxx**, 953–5.

1971

'J. Henry Richardson, 1890–1970', *University of Leeds Review*, **xiv**, 157–8.

1972

The Framework of Regional Economics in the United Kingdom, Cambridge University Press, pp xvii + 352.

1973

'Is there a money crisis', *Yorkshire Post*, 20 July 1973.

1975

'P. M. Sheard', *University of Leeds Review*, **xvii**, 324–5.

'Comment [on W. Elkan and R. Morley's papers]', in A. Whiting, ed, *The Economics of Industrial Subsidies*, HMSO, 189–90.

1976

'UV Analysis', in G. D. N. Worswick, ed, *The Concept and Measurement of Involuntary Unemployment*, Allen and Unwin, 134–45.

'H. C. Hillmann', *University of Leeds Review*, **xix**, 178–80.

Review of N. M. Hansen, *Public Policy and Regional Economic Development*: *Economic Journal*, **lxxxvi**, 145–7.

1977

[with E. M. Burrows] *Regional economic problems: comparative experiences of some market economies*, Allen and Unwin, pp 209.

'The United Kingdom' in [D. MacDougall *et al*] Commission of the European Communities, *Report of the Study Group on the Role of Public Finance in European Integration*, Brussels, **ii**, ch 1.

Review of G. Maynard and W. van Ryckeghem, *A World of Inflation: Economic Journal*, **lxxxvii**, 146–8.

1978

Review of W. M. Corden, *Inflation, Exchange Rates and The World Economy*: *Economic Journal*, **lxxxviii**, 163–4.

'Walter Tessier Newlyn', *University of Leeds Review*, **xxi**, 206–7.

'Harold Speight', ibid, 210–11.

1979

'Inflation and the British Sickness', *Economic Journal*, **lxxxix**, 1–12.